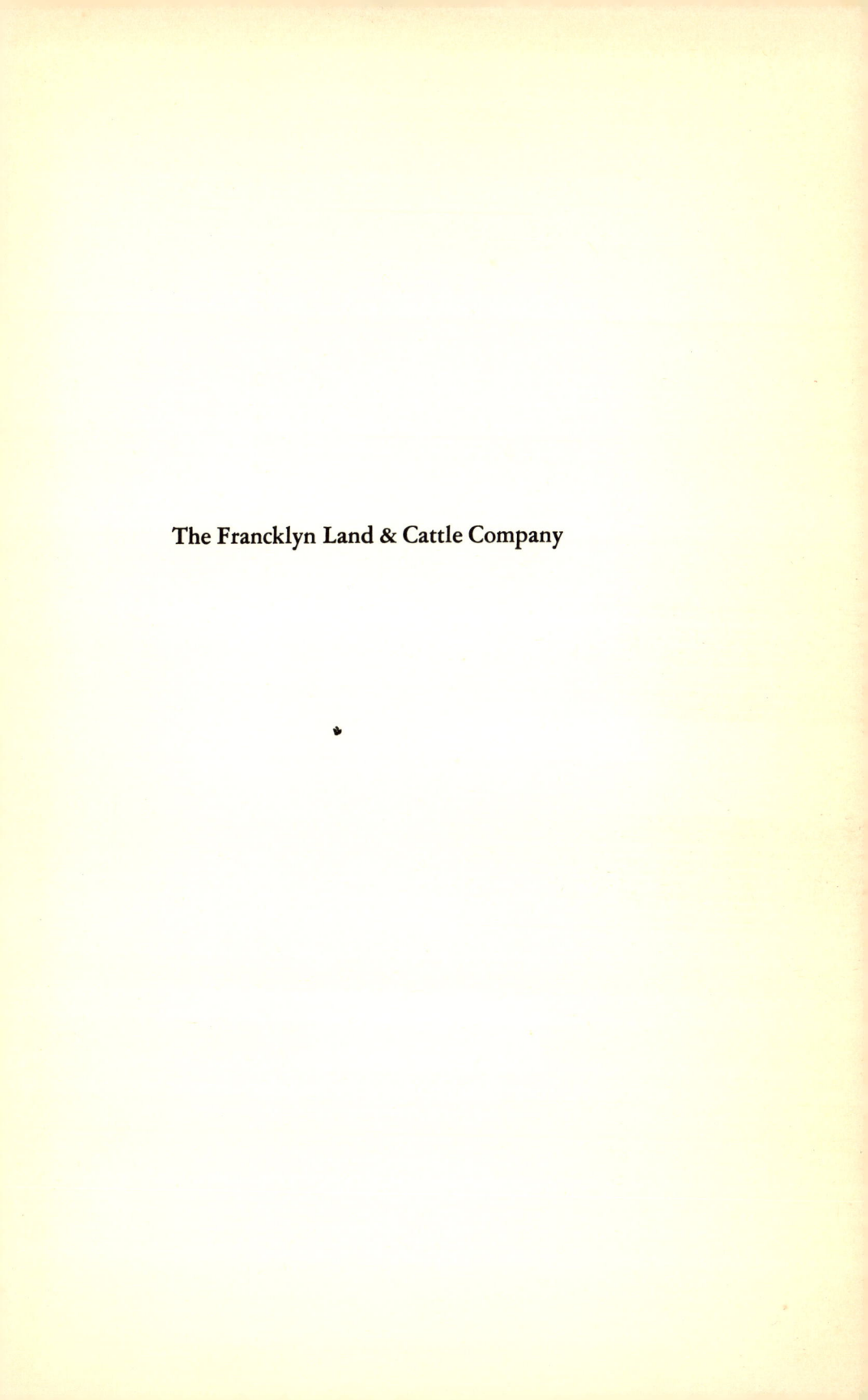

The Francklyn Land & Cattle Company

NUMBER 3 *The M. K. Brown Range Life Series*

THE FRANCKLYN

UNIVERSITY OF TEXAS PRESS • AUSTIN

LAND & CATTLE COMPANY
A Panhandle Enterprise, 1882–1957

By Lester Fields Sheffy

Library of Congress Catalog Card No. 63–7438
Copyright © 1963 by L. F. Sheffy
All Rights Reserved

Printed in the United States of America
by the Printing Division of
the University of Texas

Bound by Universal Bookbindery, Inc.,
San Antonio

This book is dedicated to the pioneer cattlemen and settlers of the Texas Panhandle, who, by their hard work and patient efforts, added much value to the lands on the Texas Plains. It is dedicated also to the farmers on White Deer Lands, who, by their energy and excellent techniques, advanced the remaining unsold farming lands to much greater prices: Perry LeFors, J. S. Wynne, Henry Thut, Siler Faulkner, J. R. Henry, J. B. Baird, the Henrys, Davises, Barretts, Harrahs, Archers, Keaheys, Bentons, Ellers, Sloans, McConnells, Barnards, Noels, Sailors, Arnolds, and many others in the Gray County and Roberts County areas. And it is dedicated finally to a substantial Polish colony in the vicinity of White Deer, in Carson County—excellent farmers whose names are Urbanczyk, Kotara, Haiduk, Gordzelik, Czner, Bednorz, Warminski, Kalka, Rapstine, and others.

PREFACE

No authentic history has ever been written by any historian singlehanded. This account, too, required the services of others than the author. I am indebted to numerous people for their help in the writing of this book. Mr. M. K. Brown and Mr. C. P. Buckler, of Pampa, who have long been closely identified with White Deer Lands in various capacities, have given me full and free access to the immense volumes of records which recount the activities of the Francklyn Land & Cattle Company and the White Deer Lands during the entire period of their operation. Mr. Buckler has shown much interest in this work and has given me invaluable assistance in the preparation of this volume. Mr. Brown has read and reread every chapter of the manuscript, and has made many corrections of factual error, thus contributing substantially to the authenticity of this work. In addition to this service he has made the publication of the book possible through the foundation which he has set up for the publication of books dealing with the early history of the Texas Panhandle and the Southwest. Not only has he helped me in carefully checking the entire manuscript, but he has also been most generous in providing financial aid for the writing of this book. Without his help it would have been impossible for me to have written it. For this help I am most grateful to him.

Much credit is due Dr. Joe Frantz, chairman of the History Department of the University of Texas, who gave invaluable aid in reading and evaluating the entire manuscript.

A number of years ago, in 1918, fate and fortune turned my life work into teaching and placed me at the head of the History Department at the

West Texas State College in Canyon, Texas, where I introduced a course in Texas history and also a course in the history of the Great Plains. Over a period of more than twenty years hundreds of students came into my classes from the plains of Northwest Texas, and we studied together the historical background of our own native section, about which practically nothing was then known and even less written. These young people taught me much about the history of this region, which they had secured from their parents, grandparents, and neighbors who were among the first settlers in Northwest Texas.

Dr. Ima C. Barlow, my former associate in the Department of History at the West Texas State College, has also read the entire manuscript critically and has given me most valuable aid in this work, particularly in the matter of form and sentence structure.

The typists, Mrs. R. D. Oldham and Mrs. Karen Sheffy, have shown much interest in this work, and have been very careful and patient in making all necessary corrections.

Last, but by no means least, I am deeply indebted to my wife, Carrie V. Sheffy, for providing me with every physical comfort possible, and for encouraging me when the going got tough. To all these people I am deeply grateful.

It seems fitting to record here also that this book is a story of men who worked hard at manual labor, with meager wages, yet fully devoted to the tasks at hand, regardless of the dangers and uncertainties involved in the performance of their work. These men labored from the rising to the setting of the sun, and longer if a crisis demanded it. Strikes, labor unions, and government aid were not a part of their vocabulary. They laid well the basic foundations for the institutional life of the Texas Panhandle. Their traditions of self-help have been maintained to this day by their successors, and the cattlemen are perhaps the most independent group of people in our highly organized society today. It is significant to me that this is a story of free enterprise at its best.

I present it with the hope that it may create a more general and widespread interest in the history of the last American frontier.

LESTER FIELDS SHEFFY

CONTENTS

Preface ix

Bibliographical Note xv

Introduction: The Big Bonanza 3

1. A Kentuckian Visits Texas 10
2. Survey Difficulties in Northwest Texas 18
3. Fencing the Francklyn Range 31
4. Foundation Work on Francklyn Pasture 44
5. The Big Cattle Deal of 1883 59
6. The Francklyn Company Assumes Full Control . . . 72
7. Colonel Groom Experiments with Cattle on the Texas Plains . 88
8. One Hundred Miles of Indian Border 101
9. The Big Forgery of 1884 126
10. A Desperate Struggle for Cattle Markets 136
11. Headed for the Last Roundup 155
12. British Bondholders Take Over White Deer Properties . . 172
13. White Deer Lands Emerge from the Francklyn Wreckage . 192
14. A New York Yankee Takes a Look at Texans and Texas . 213

15. The Francklyn Foreclosure Suit 224

16. Cattle Controversies Ended by Foreclosure Sale . . . 233

17. Ancient Grasslands and Modern Beef Production . . . 247

18. Tyng Proves Agricultural Value of White Deer Lands . . 268

19. Boom Towns Boost Northwest Texas Lands 287

20. A Decade of Leasing White Deer Lands 306

21. More Water for White Deer Lands 323

22. Tyng Bids Farewell to White Deer Lands and the Panhandle . 335

23. The White Deer Lands, 1903–1957: A Summation . . 355

Appendix: White Deer Lands Management
(Tables of Organization) 369

Index 373

ILLUSTRATIONS

Title page   A chuck wagon with women visitors on the Rito Blanco Division of the XIT Ranch.

Following page 176:

No. 1 Camp at White Deer, Francklyn Land & Cattle Company

Lord Rosebery

Andrew Kingsmill

A Windmill Scene on White Deer Lands

A Buffalo Herd Grazing on the Goodnight Range

An Estimated 40,000 Buffalo Hides at Dodge City, 1878

A Fencing Crew Hauling Posts and Poles for Fencing the LS Range

Russell Benedict

Frederic de P. Foster

The First Meeting of the Panhandle Stockmens Association

A Chuck-Wagon Scene on the Lee Bivins Ranch

Quanah Parker

Prairie Indians on the Warpath

Plains Indians Moving Camp

Branding Calves on the Open Range

Branding Calves at a Roundup on a Texas Panhandle Range

Colonel Sir Robert Williams, M.P.

Sir Gordon Cunard

Cross L Headquarters

A Trail Herd Headed for Montana Pastures

Cattle Come to Water on LS Range
George Tyng
Timothy Dwight Hobart
LS Ranch Rock-House Headquarters in the Canadian River Valley
Gerlach Bros. General Merchandise Store
A String of Five Ox Teams Hauling Cotton to Market
Settlers Moving into the Texas Panhandle in Covered Wagons
Demonstration of a Model Farm in the Texas Panhandle
R. M. Irick's Freighting Outfit Moves a Two-Story Home
Charley Durham's Panhandle Freighter
White Deer Lands Office at Pampa, Texas
A July 4 Celebration and Picnic in the Texas Panhandle in 1907
Kaffir Cornfield on White Deer Lands near Pampa, Texas
A Harvest Scene in the Texas Panhandle on Francklyn Company Lands
Oldest School Building in the Panhandle
Steam Plow at Work on White Deer Lands
Picnic Scene on White Deer Creek
Santa Fe Railroad Station, Pampa, Texas, 1910
Street Scene, Pampa, Texas, 1912
The Schneider Band

MAPS

The Panhandle in 1875	11
The Panhandle and White Deer Lands	22
White Deer Lands (Showing Location in Hutchinson, Carson, Gray, and Roberts Counties) . . .	23
Proposed Fence Line, July 10, 1884	40
Rivers and Creeks of the Panhandle	53
Indian Reservation Lands Used by Cattlemen	106
Pampa in 1902	304

BIBLIOGRAPHICAL NOTE

Every statement made and every quotation given (unless otherwise stated) in the preparation of this volume may be found and verified by referring to the Francklyn Company files in the Panhandle-Plains Museum at Canyon, Texas. These records, consisting of ledger books, ranch records, and range reports (both general and individual) contain also the original documents of every legal transfer of the Francklyn Company's property from the beginning of its organization in 1882 until the Company defaulted in 1886. These records, which had been stored in New York City until recent months, also include legal transfers of all the properties in Texas, New York, and London.

The principal records used in the preparation of this volume consist of:

Letters and reports, both personal and official, of Colonel B. B. Groom from the inception of the Francklyn Company in 1882 to its default in 1886; the letters and reports of H. T. (Harry) Groom, both personal and official, from 1883 to 1886; the Charles G. Francklyn-Frank G. Brown letters and reports to both of the Grooms in Texas, and to and from the British bondholders in London during the same period.

Hundreds of letters and reports, both personal and official, to Frederic de P. Foster and Russell Benedict, trustees at New York City, and to British bondholders and other officials, written by George Tyng, Texas manager of White Deer Lands, 1886 to 1902, which were used as extensively as space would permit.

The letters and reports of Timothy Dwight Hobart, 1902 to 1924, which furnished much valuable information for this work.

Fourteen or fifteen copies of drawings made by B. B. and Harry Groom in 1884 showing section lines, fence lines, surveys, feeding pens, and other matters related to the Francklyn Company lands; and a number of maps of White Deer Lands showing the various stages of development of the property.

A number of newspaper clippings, properly dated and identified, which give many interesting bits of news from various parts of the Texas Panhandle.

ADDITIONAL REFERENCES

The Panhandle-Plains Historical Review, Vol. 33, (1960). Courtesy, Ernest Archambeau, Amarillo, Texas.

J. E. (Jim) Williams, *Fifty-Eight Years in the Panhandle of Texas,* Firm Foundation Publishing House, Austin, Texas, 1944.

C. C. Clift, "Kentucky Marriages and Obituaries" (courtesy of the author).

Report compiled from official records at Winchester and Lexington, Kentucky, for J. Lindsay Nunn (Lexington) by Kathryn Owen, June, 1962 (copy in files of author).

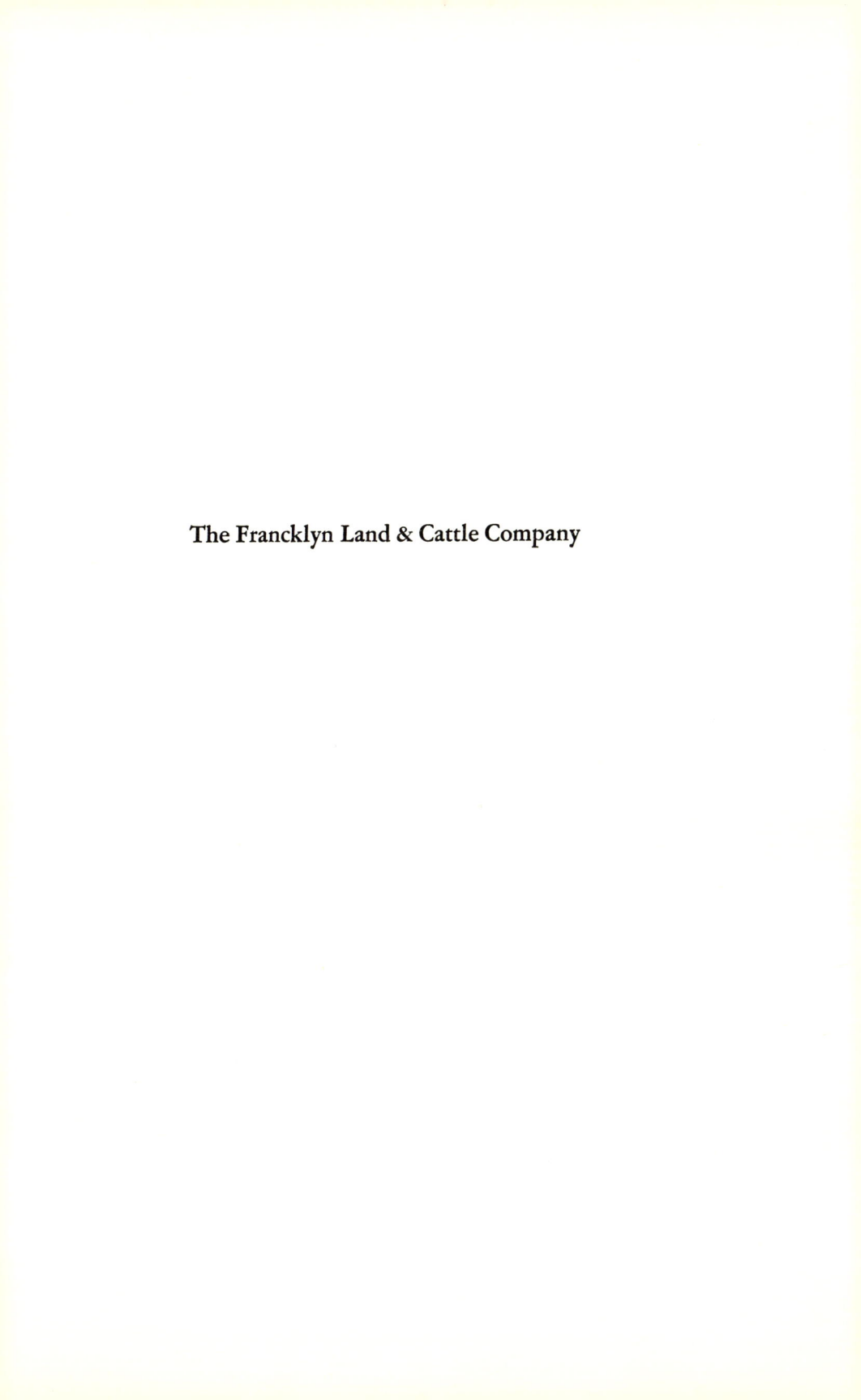

The Francklyn Land & Cattle Company

Introduction: The Big Bonanza

THE STORY OF THE Francklyn Land & Cattle Company abounds in drama, intrigue, and adventure. In that respect it is a typical story of the land where its history was unfolded; for no section of the country has ever produced more adventure, more drama, or more romance than have the Western Plains of the United States. This region, which belongs to the last frontier in Western America, has produced a culture of its own that is separate and distinctive in American life. Strangely enough, no land has ever given less reward in return for hard labor and constant effort than this so-called "Great American Desert." Yet, whether in success or in failure, it has attracted and held by its mystic charm, its first white settlers, and has created within them an insatiable desire to overcome and conquer its physical and environmental obstacles. This romance of the Plains is of itself distinctive: it is a romance of adventure in a world of hard reality where men have had

almost unlimited opportunity to exercise their own God-given talents to overcome and achieve in spite of immense physical deterrents. Herein lies the significance of the Westward Movement in the Great Plains region.

For almost two centuries Europeans in America trudged westward over rugged mountain ranges and followed down river courses finally to reach the Mississippi Valley in the latter part of the eighteenth century. In the nineteenth century, on the contrary, adventurers and explorers, spurred on by the desire for gold and other quick riches, struggled over the forbidding plains and reached the Pacific Coast in a short period of fifty years. Within another half century they backtracked and settled themselves on these same plains, ever striving and ever confident that this region held immense wealth and great latent possibilities.

Before the Adams-Onis, or Florida, Treaty of 1819 had delimited the Spanish lands, Anglo-Americans had pushed into the region. Many of these frontiersmen supported Henry Clay's doctrine of "Manifest Destiny"—the idea that this "Great Southwest" was destined for a free people, the Anglo-American people. A Texas Revolution and a War with Mexico resulted in the addition of the area to the United States. The entire region seemed open to settlement, especially after the Compromise of 1850 adjusted the immediate problems: admitted California as a free state; divided the remaining territory along the 37th parallel, between the North and South; and defined the boundary of Texas, leaving control over its lands to the state. Given adequate transportation, the Anglo-American felt confident that he would soon conquer this new domain.

The Texas Land Company

The human surge to the West inevitably gave impetus to railroad building. As early as 1819 New York capitalists were actively engaged in developing land and water transportation along the Texas Gulf Coast. As a means of actively encouraging railroad companies in Texas, the Texas Legislature passed in 1854 an act giving sixteen sections of land out of its public domain in West Texas for every mile of railroad built and put into operation in the state. This gave much incentive to railroad development. Many companies were formed under this act merely for the purpose of speculating in Texas lands. In the scramble for land, strong competition among various large land and railroad companies finally forced them to consolidate in order to survive. For example, in 1872 the Houston & Great Northern Railroad merged with the International Railroad. The capital stock of the two companies as indicated in the abstract of title was:

> ... placed under the direction of any new board of directors to be chosen by the directors of the consolidated company, so that the franchise, powers and privileges of both companies be represented, controlled, and managed under one name and the joint property be held and all rights of both companies be owned, exercised, and used by the new consolidated company.

In a special meeting held at Palestine, Texas, in 1875, the consolidated company transferred its lands to the Texas Land Company together with 215 miles of railroad already built in Texas. This action was approved by the Texas Legislature in 1875. In 1880 the Texas Company conveyed these lands to the New York & Texas Land Company, Ltd.

The New York & Texas Land Company, Ltd.

At this time, 1880, the New York & Texas Land Company, Ltd., was organized "for the purchase, improving, leasing and sale of lands in the states of Texas and New York, the purchase, holding and sale of stock in other land companies, and the locality of its business to be in the states of Texas and New York" (abstract of title). The headquarters of the Company were located at Palestine, Texas, in 1883, but were removed to Austin in 1885 for easier accessibility to official documents related to the large number of land transactions in the state.

Major Ira H. Evans, a Vermont Yankee, was made president of the New York & Texas Land Company, and Samuel Thorne of New York, vice president. Major Evans came to Texas from New York with the Carpetbaggers immediately after the Civil War, soon becoming prominent in business and political affairs of the state. He was elected speaker of the House of Representatives in 1870, but was deposed in 1871 because of his opposition to the extension of the Carpetbag rule in the face of a duly elected Democratic Legislature. Evans remained president of the New York & Texas Land Company until it was liquidated in 1918. "He was honest, efficient, able and was faithful to every trust that was imposed upon him. Millions of dollars passed through his hands and no account of his was ever questioned," declared W. L. Stark of Austin, one of his contemporaries (interview, August 5, 1942).

In its operations the New York & Texas Land Company, Ltd., acquired some 6,000,000 acres of land, extending from the Texas Panhandle to the Gulf of Mexico, lying mostly in West Texas. This company made its first large land sale to the Francklyn Land & Cattle Company of New York City.

The Francklyn Land & Cattle Company

The Francklyn Land & Cattle Company also had its beginning in the early 1880's. On February 10, 1882, Colonel B. B. Groom, a Kentucky cattleman, leased from the New York & Texas Company 529,920 acres of land situated in Carson, Gray, Hutchinson, and Roberts counties in the Texas Panhandle. The lease agreement provided that Colonel Groom was to have the right to purchase the entire tract at any time before February 10, 1883, at the rate of $1.32 per acre. One-sixth of the purchase money ($116,582.40) was to be paid in cash, and the remaining five-sixths was to be paid in five notes, each payable respectively one, two, three, four, and five years after date, bearing interest at the rate of 5 per cent per annum from date until paid. On June 6, 1882, Colonel Groom, "for and in consideration of the sum of $1.00 to me in hand" conveyed all of his "rights, titles and interest," to Charles G. Francklyn, a capitalist from New York and London.

As a result of this transaction the Francklyn Land & Cattle Company was organized in 1882 with a capital stock of $3,000,000, divided into 150,000 shares, with par value at $20 per share. The Company was chartered under the laws of the state of New Jersey with office headquarters at 44 Wall Street, New York City. Charles G. Francklyn was made president of the Company; Frank G. Brown, a New York attorney who hailed from the state of Kentucky, was chosen secretary and New York manager; William F. Van Pelt became treasurer.

Charles G. Francklyn was a man of considerable means. He had mining investments in Utah and Colorado, and also in San Domingo

The Big Bonanza

in the West Indies. He owned stock in railroads in the United States, including the St. Louis & Pacific, which later came to be known as the Atchison, Topeka, and Santa Fe. In addition to these investments he represented large British investors in this country, especially his good friend and neighbor, Lord Rosebery, reputed to be England's wealthiest subject. Lord Rosebery's marriage into the Rothschild family made him, perhaps, one of the wealthiest men in the Western World at this time.[1]

On November 8, 1882, Samuel Thorne, vice president of the New York & Texas Company, and Charles G. Francklyn, president of the Francklyn Land & Cattle Company, signed a contract in New York City by which the New York & Texas Land Company sold to the Francklyn Company 637,440 acres of land in the Texas Panhandle for the sum of $887,654.40. The payments were to be made as follows: $45,654.40 on signing the agreement; $245,000 on May 1, 1884; the balance in four notes of $146,750 each, payable on February 1 of each of the years 1885, 1886, 1887, and 1888, with interest at the rate of 5 per cent per annum, payable semiannually August 1 and February 1 of each year until paid. These notes were secured by a first-mortgage deed of trust to be executed by the Francklyn Company in accordance with the laws of Texas. The Francklyn Company was to assume the payment of taxes after November, 1884.

In case of default in payment of principal, interest, and taxes on any of the notes in accordance with the agreement, then at the option of the New York & Texas Land Company:

> They may proceed to foreclose, or at their option enter upon the land forthwith and take possession thereof, and sell the same or any portion thereof from time to time at public or private sales, or at their option enforce such other remedies as by the said mortgage or deed of trust, or otherwise may be lawful, and the Francklyn Company agrees to give the purchasers of such lands proper and sufficient deeds to the lands thus sold. Payments to be made in whole or in part, but not in instalments of less than $50,000 at any time before they become due respectively.

[1] It is said that Lord Rosebery had three ambitions: he wanted to become Prime Minister of England, to marry the wealthiest woman in Britain, and to win the English Derby—all three of which he accomplished (M. K. Brown, at Pampa, Texas, to L. F. Sheffy, August 29, 1961).

As the notes were paid, the New York Company was to release the lien from the mortgage or deed of trust on one acre for each $2.50 paid. The Francklyn Company agreed to expend $100,000 during the first year for improving and stocking the land with cattle. The deed was to be given subject to two leases; one, made to Gunter & Munson for a lease on Blocks 4 and 5 in Carson County, commenced July 1, 1881, and extended for ten years; the other lease was made to Colonel B. B. Groom, as noted above, and was merged into the Francklyn Company.

In order to secure funds for this enterprise, the Francklyn Company issued 1,500 First Mortgage Gold Bonds in denominations of $1,000 each. Half of these bonds were set aside for the purchase of cattle and for making improvements, and the other half were reserved to secure the notes mentioned above. These latter bonds carried six-per-cent-interest coupons paying semiannual dividends. As soon as this agreement was signed, and even before the bonds were printed, Francklyn sailed for London, where, after much difficulty, he sold most of the cattle bonds. The largest purchasers were Lord Rosebery and Williams, Deacon & Company of the Bank of London. Francklyn's exit to England left all further details to Frank G. Brown and Colonel Groom, who went immediately to Texas to inspect and evaluate the recently purchased property.

Colonel Groom was an experienced cattleman. He had spent some forty years in breeding and fattening blooded stock in the bluegrass region in Kentucky. His wife was Elizabeth Thomson, the daughter of a prominent cattleman and breeder of fine stock. From their marriage there was only one child, Harrison (Harry) Thomson Groom, who became associated with his father in the cattle business in later years. Colonel Groom imported many Hereford and Polled Angus cattle from England. He introduced into the United States the famous Bates breed of England. His herd attracted breeders from all over the United States. In the heyday of his prosperity in the cattle business Groom was the owner of a fine estate at Winchester, Kentucky, known as the Vinewood Estate. It is said that he patterned his mansion after his ancestral home in England. However, like many other cattlemen, he was caught in the Panic of 1873, which destroyed his fortune. In 1875, when he was forced to hold a two days' sale of his cattle on his Vinewood Estate, 225 head of Shorthorns sold for an average price of

The Big Bonanza

$1,500 each. The highest price paid was $17,500 for a six-months-old heifer, "Duchess of Ardrie."

The local legal and official records at Lexington, Kentucky, where Groom lived for a number of years, and also the records at Winchester, give little information about the ancestry and early life of Groom. Such records as exist, however, indicate that his forbears came to the United States from England in the eighteenth century and settled in Virginia. Groom's name is listed among a number of prominent cattle breeders, among whom is his father-in-law.[2] It has been recorded by one of his contemporaries that Colonel Groom was "a man of great ability and tireless energy, and although he was seventy years of age, he went to Texas and formed a ranch partnership with Chas. G. Francklyn of the Cunard Steamship Company."[3] "After this long experience," Colonel Groom declared, "I think I can safely claim that I am capable of judiciously selecting lands and a location for the purpose."

[2] Report compiled from official records in Winchester and Lexington, Kentucky, by Kathryn Owen, Winchester, for J. Lindsay Nunn, Lexington, June 14, 1962 (copy in hands of author).
[3] C. C. Clift, "Kentucky Marriages and Obituaries" (courtesy of the author).

CHAPTER 1

A Kentuckian Visits Texas

COLONEL GROOM WAS SOON GIVEN an opportunity to test his ability to select suitable lands for a cattle ranch in Texas. After working out plans with Brown in New York City, he left immediately for Texas to inspect and evaluate the Company's recently purchased lands, and to determine their potential value as a cattle ranch. He began his journey with high hopes and much enthusiasm, and before he reached Texas he was actually elated over the possibilities inherent in the Texas property. In Kansas City, about the middle of July, 1882, he wrote Brown: "On reaching Kansas and this place I have been greatly congratulated on securing our ranch. All agree we have a world of the choicest grass. . . . I have seen several men just off of it who speak in the strongest terms of its value." On July 20, 1882, Groom wrote Brown, this time from Mobeetie, Texas: "The reputation of our property

THE PANHANDLE IN 1875

would do you good to hear. Owing to the increased demand for such property, ranches are all the talk, and the merits of ours have been much discussed. . . . All agree in saying that we have richer and less waste land than any in the Country." These glowing reports greatly increased Groom's enthusiasm and more and more convinced him of the value of the Company's lands on the Western plains.

He came into a new and strange land in 1882—a land where rapid political changes were being made, and where climate and topography played an important role in the affairs of its occupants. When Texas was annexed to the Union in 1845 the state retained its public lands. The vast domain lying east of the Rio Grande River contained millions of acres of land deficient in rainfall and otherwise scarce of water, but with an abundance of the most nutritious grasses. Texas, in the Compromise of 1850, ceded approximately half of these lands to the United States government, thereby cancelling the state's $10,000,000 debt. This compromise also defined the boundaries of the great expanse of territory left within the boundaries of Texas. The 36:30 parallel, north latitude, fixed the northern boundary and the 32:00 parallel, north latitude, fixed the southern boundary. The Rio Grande, extending from the 32nd parallel to the Gulf Coast, remained the southwestern boundary, as provided in the 1850 Compromise. The 103rd meridian, west longitude, defined the remaining western boundary of the state, while the eastern boundary was formed by the 100th meridian. The 32nd parallel, as fixed by the Compromise of 1850, cut the vast public domain of Texas nearly in half.

The southern portion of this territory was inhabited almost exclusively by Mexican citizens who had been annexed by the agreement between Mexico and the Republic of Texas in 1836. The northern portion was yet occupied by wild Indian tribes and was little known to the white man. This region later came to be known as "Northwest Texas." Although the rolling plains of this region were carpeted with an abundance of the finest grasses, it was thought to be a part of the so-called "Great American Desert." Its climate was characterized by extreme and sudden changes in temperature, high winds, periodic drouths, violent sandstorms, and occasional severe and destructive blizzards. Such conditions stood in direct contrast to the more evenly

A Kentuckian Visits Texas

adjusted temperatures of the bluegrass region of Kentucky. This, however, Groom had to learn later in the hard school of experience.

During the decade of the 1870's, when buffalo hunting in Northwest Texas became a profitable business, the Indians, realizing that their commissary was being destroyed, dropped back reluctantly onto the reservations in the Indian Territory in Oklahoma and the New Mexico Territory. Vast expanses of free grasslands were thus left open to the cattlemen. Texas and Western cattlemen rushed in to select suitable sites for ranch headquarters and to spread millions of cattle over all the ranges in Northwest Texas. Neither the state nor the national arm of the law had yet been extended to these free grasslands. Therefore, the cattlemen of necessity set up their own customary laws, commonly known as the "laws of the range," and fattened their herds for the market on lands that belonged to the state. As a result an anomalous situation developed. Cattlemen who at first moved their herds onto these grasslands for only temporary use, gradually became more attached to the land as they improved their ranches and the cattle business became more profitable. Moreover, by this time a number of these ranchers had been in the Texas Panhandle for several years and were well established. Colonel Charles Goodnight moved his first herd into the Palo Duro Canyon at the head of the Red River in 1876. Colonel Thomas Bugbee located his Quarter Circle Hearts on the South Canadian in the same year. The Capitol Syndicate was also moving thousands of South Texas cattle onto its 3,000,000-acre spread lying along the western Panhandle. A number of other large cattle concerns followed suit. As a result Texas ranching became a vital part of the state and national economy. In fact, when Colonel Groom arrived in Texas some twenty-five or thirty cattle outfits had already set up well-established semipermanent cattle ranches in Northwest Texas. Among these establishments were the Spurs, the Matadors, Gunter & Munson, the Clarendon Land & Cattle Company, Niedringhaus, and many others. It is significant that all of these ranches had been established in the early 1880's before Groom became interested in Texas. It is also significant that when Groom arrived at Mobeetie there were but three organized counties in the Texas Panhandle: Wheeler (1879), Oldham (1880), and Donley (1882).

Colonel Groom was much impressed by what he saw and learned during his first few weeks on the Texas Plains. He talked with a number of cattlemen about land and cattle prospects. One of his first acquaintances was Colonel Charles Goodnight, who became his chief adviser on land and cattle affairs. He met also J. M. Coburn, of the Turkey Tracks, and Henry Creswell, of the Prairie Cattle Company, both of whom were close neighboring ranchers with whom he was to have much dealing later.

When Groom began his examination of Panhandle lands he was amazed at the vast distances one could see with the naked eye, stretches sometimes extended and elevated by the mirages of the plains. He was enthralled by the sight of thousands of cattle grazing everywhere on the unfenced ranges. After viewing the land, and after talking with scores of people about ranch conditions in the Panhandle, Groom was more convinced than ever of the great bargain his company had made in the purchase of White Deer Pastures.

During the month of August, 1882, Groom, in company with E. B. Spiller, whom the New York & Texas Land Company had employed to survey the lands, traveled over much of the Company's land with horse and buggy. The inspection trip reassured him in his fondest hopes and expectations as to the value of the Texas property. On August 8, 1882, he made a lengthy report on his Texas trip to Brown from Winchester, Kentucky. It reads, in part, as follows:

Leach on the North Fork of Red River . . . has a fine garden containing . . . Indian corn, popcorn, watermelons, cantaloupes, cucumbers, beets, tomatoes, beans, onions, Hubbard squash, all in the most growing condition. A field of German millet as fine as can be found anywhere . . . A rich rolling country covered with a luxuriant growth of grasses, buffalo, some musquite, Sage and Blue Stem grass. Crossing over the river several times we enter the plain on the regularly traveled road from Mobeetie to Tascosa. There I think one of the most beautiful and picturesque sights I have ever seen. Looking off for miles at the meandering line of the river [White Deer Creek] as pointed out by the cottonwood trees which border its course, the valley below with its hills and vales, furnishing ample protection for stock in case of cold or storm, and the plains off in the other direction as far as you could see making by its level and even surface a beautiful contrast with what we had for the last eight miles been coming over . . . White Deer

A Kentuckian Visits Texas

Creek near our western line running north to the Canadian River . . . is valuable, having eighteen miles of lasting water on our land . . . The stream, White Deer . . . has a bottom of splendid land fully one-half mile wide, very rich and a good deal of beautiful cottonwood timber. . . . On this bottom and near the northwest corner is over 2,000 acres of meadow, the best grass and suitable for making all the hay we shall ever want for our blooded animals and work stock. We have a great estate. . . . I had not formed a correct opinion before I traveled over it. They speak of its value in unmeasured terms. . . . Every day some one is telling me of the wonderful value and capacity of our property. . . . Mr. Hudson, who is largely in cattle adjoining us, said today that it is a bonanza and I believe it. We find more water than I anticipated, but will have to improve water facilities in many places so the cattle do not have to travel too far for water. . . . Block 5 of our tract is one of the finest and most desirable bodies [107,520 acres] of land in Texas. It is a very rich body of finely watered land. After spending ten days on and around the property, I am more than convinced of its value. . . . Although indifferently cultivated, the corn is estimated at forty bushels to the acre. We can and should produce everything we need to support ourselves and sell enough to pay the whole of our current expenses. I learn there have been parties looking over the property secretly supposed to be in the interest of the Prairie Cattle Company who are reputed to pay $900,000 for 100,000 acres of land and 20,000 cattle. We ought not to think of taking less than $3,000,000 for our property. I feel it will pay a profit at that figure.

Groom in this report to Brown called attention to the gregarious bird life and numerous wild animals on the property. "Antelope in large numbers," he said, "are found all over the property . . . where by means of the field glass, they can be seen grazing for miles away." He commented further:

Bands of wild horses, numbering from sixteen to twenty in each band watched over and directed by a masterly stallion, who studiously guards his harem, not allowing any others to come in or any of his band to escape. On the approach of danger he drives his family before him always bringing up the rear himself[1] . . . Flag Tail Deer, wild turkeys, thousands of wild ducks and geese, coyotes, grey wolves, wild cats, raccoons and beaver are found in

[1] For some interesting stories about these famous stallions see J. Frank Dobie, *The Mustangs* (Boston: Little, Brown & Company, 1952), particularly Chapters VIII and IX.

the region . . . I have never seen such a variety of fine shooting. It would not be an uneasy matter to kill a wagon load of wild turkeys on our property any night, and kill ducks, geese and quail until tired of doing so.

Since the White Deer Pastures had been ideal grazing grounds for thousands of buffalo only a few years previous to this time, Groom found "thousands of sharpened pegs" which buffalo hunters had used for stretching buffalo hides upon the ground to dry and animals "slaughtered for their skins alone . . . the carcasses being left on the ground, numbering from seven to ten per acre, weighing upon the average about sixty pounds."

Colonel Groom not only talked with cattlemen about the prospects of White Deer Pastures, but he also made inquiry from a number of prominent businessmen and citizens of Mobeetie and its environs about the property. He reported to Brown further that in talking with District Judge Frank Willis, Groom and "about a dozen others in the circle" heard the Judge predict that "If the St. Louis & Pacific and the Fort Worth & Denver City railroads come, as now contemplated, the mesquite lands in this locality will be selling within the next five years at $30 to $50 per acre."

Groom also added this information:

I had an interview this day with the President of the Atlantic Railroad. He stated that they would build 200 miles of railroad next year [1883]. The terminus is now at Tulsa on the Arkansas River, Indian Territory. An extension of 200 miles from the Arkansas would bring the road close to the Texas line and about fifty miles from our lands, thus insuring early communication by rail from our ranch to St. Louis and all points in the United States.

Colonel Groom, in his final evaluation of the Texas property (report of August 8, 1882) after completing his tour of inspection, declared:

Four or five years ago I formed the determination to learn from personal examination what portion of the United States united in the highest degree all the conditions of climate, water, etc. required for the successful prosecution of the business of breeding cattle on a large scale. With this purpose in view, I have within the period named, traveled on horseback and in wagon over the entire scope of country from the Gulf of Mexico to the Yellowstone River, and it is my firm belief and judgment that we have the finest and most desirable cattle ranch in the United States, possessing as it does the happy medium between hot and cold, and being covered with the most nutritious grasses, and with thousands of acres of the best meadow lands.

After his inspection of the property Groom was ready to enter upon the major part of his work in Texas: laying out and establishing a successful cattle ranch in the Texas Panhandle. His daring exploits, his dogged determination, and his supreme confidence in meeting almost superhuman obstacles make interesting chapters in the history of the Francklyn Land & Cattle Company.

CHAPTER 2

Survey Difficulties in Northwest Texas

DESPITE COLONEL GROOM's optimistic report as to the potentialities of the Francklyn lands, he was aware of the many difficulties which confronted him in establishing a ranch on the Company's lands. Groom was amazed at the immense area the land covered, at its far distant reaches. He realized that the property was isolated—travel and communication almost nil, transportation slow and difficult. Although it was late in the season, supplies were yet to be purchased and transported by freight wagons from Dodge City to Mobeetie, two hundred miles distant, and then distributed to various points on the property where they were most needed. Cattle were to be purchased and located on the home range. Most of all in this land without banks, funds must be supplied and a system of business and financial operations worked out. One of the first jobs was to survey the property and establish correct boundary lines.

The history of land surveys in Texas is filled with conflict and litigation, both as to title and as to boundary lines. This situation prevailed especially in Northwest Texas, originally a part of the Old Bexar, or San Antonio Department. When settlement was begun in Northwest Texas the region was detached from the Bexar Department to become a separate political unit. The first land records set up in this area began with the organization of Jack County in 1857, with Jacksboro as the county seat. During the Civil War, when Jack County became disorganized, its records were moved to Henrietta, the county seat of Clay County. In 1873 the twenty-six counties in the Texas Panhandle were attached to Clay for judicial purposes. However, when Wheeler County was organized in 1879 these Panhandle counties were attached to Wheeler, thus becoming independent of Clay. As settlement moved westward the Clay County surveyor made a number of surveys in Jack County. The survey question remained dormant until the 1880's, when land speculators and settlers disputed the title to certain Panhandle lands on the grounds that the Clay County surveyor had no jurisdiction in the Jack County surveys.

When surveys were made by the New York & Texas Land Company, its lands were divided into blocks designated as Blocks 2, 3, 4, 5, 7, and B-2. Most of these lands were in solid blocks; that is, there were no alternate sections, except in Block B-2, where the even-numbered sections were set aside as school lands, and all odd-numbered sections were patented lands. This checkered system in Block B-2 resulted in much competition and continuous litigation, not only among cattlemen, but also between cattlemen and settlers in their efforts to prove title and establish correct boundary lines.

In 1883 the Texas Legislature took the first step toward opening the school lands to settlement by creating a Land Board to administer them. This Board proved to be somewhat partisan and inefficient. As a result strong opposition developed against the Board's policy of leasing the school lands. Block B-2 created unpleasant conflict in the struggle between the cattlemen, who were accustomed to free grass, on the one hand, and the Land Board and the settlers on the other: the Land Board demanding four cents per acre per annum for the state's grass, and the settlers claiming the right to file and settle on the school lands. This land conflict was one of the several factors that finally broke up large units of pasture lands in West Texas. Moreover, the issue got into state politics, both sides bringing strong pressure on the Texas Legislature. It also became an issue in the election of both county and district surveyors. For example, in the election in Wheeler County in 1882 J. O. B. Street, who represented the settlers, defeated E. B. Spiller, who made the survey of the Francklyn Company's lands.

In making the sale to the Francklyn Company, the New York & Texas Land Company was required to make a *correct and satisfactory survey* of the lands to be conveyed. Adjustment of errors in the original surveys and of conflicts in the later surveys were necessary before legal title could be given to the land. Continued delays hampered all efforts to clear the title. This greatly annoyed Colonel Groom, who was eager to close the land deal in order to get the range stocked with cattle before winter set in. In his anxiety to get the range ready for stock, he suspected that Major Evans was delaying the survey in order to break up the sale and retain the land for his own company. In August, 1882, he wrote Brown:

The delays in this matter have been a very serious setback. We have been greatly annoyed by the tardiness of the surveyor. As to the alternate [lands in Block B-2] we have filed the necessary papers, but at this time they amount to nothing, as the Commissioner of the Land Office withdraws school sections from sale until the meeting of the legislature. We are watching these points closely.

Colonel Groom was extremely anxious to establish correct boundary lines as quickly as possible in order to hasten the fencing of the property. Therefore, in July, 1882, he went to Palestine, which at that time was headquarters of the New York & Texas Land Company, to see about getting the Company's lands surveyed. He found that the survey must be delayed because, he said, "There is such a demand the surveyors are constantly engaged." On September 9, 1882, he advised Brown from Mobeetie:

The survey is progressing. . . . We have had much delay owing to the surveyor appointed by the New York & Texas Land Company being detained by his wife's beside who was so very low he could not leave her. We tried to get surveyors from other points but they all have so much work it was impossible to get them.

On November 6, 1882, Samuel Thorne, vice president of the New

York Company, wrote Francklyn, calling his attention to the fact that both the notes and the interest were due semiannually, on February 1 and August 1, but that "Owing to some error in the survey the deed cannot be given until this is satisfied. The deed to be one of the regular deeds and payment to be secured by mortgage and deed of trust."

Colonel Groom was very much interested also in getting title to the Company's land completed as soon as possible. Therefore, in July, 1882, he went from Palestine to Austin and appealed to the land commissioner for help. He was encouraged by the commissioner, but found that his work "greatly exceeded the capacity of his clerical force."

Groom went from Austin to San Antonio to see the surveyor of the Bexar District, who was to appraise the Gray County lands north of the Red River. From San Antonio he journeyed to Jacksboro, county seat of Jack County, to which some of the alternate school lands were attached for surveying purposes. He was unable to see Mr. West of the law firm of Robinson & West, who represented the Francklyn Company in the Jacksboro survey.

On November 29, 1882, Alexander & Green of New York City, who were the counsel for the Francklyn Company, advised Francklyn in London that "Title papers presented of Texas presumably good," but added, "We do not give certificates without personal inspection of records. Have sent competent lawyer to verify data."

On December 2, 1882, Alfred B. Thatcher, a member of the law firm of Alexander & Green, arrived at Palestine, Texas, where he informed Mr. Ward of New York, also a member of the firm, that:

I find that there is a contest over the location of the lands in question. . . . It affects so much of the parcels marked "3" and "B-2" as lies within Gray County . . . and amounting to 293 square miles. The first locations were made from the railroads from which we are deriving title. The lands have subsequently been re-located by other parties who claim that the locations of the railroads were made through district surveyors who had no jurisdiction in the districts in which the locations were made. The parties who have made the locations have filed a protest in the Land Office against the patenting of the lands under the first locations. The New York & Texas Land Company are about to institute proceedings in the US Circuit Court to restrain, as I understand, the parties making the locations from proceeding under them. The counsel of the Land Company who have the matter in

THE PANHANDLE AND WHITE DEER LANDS

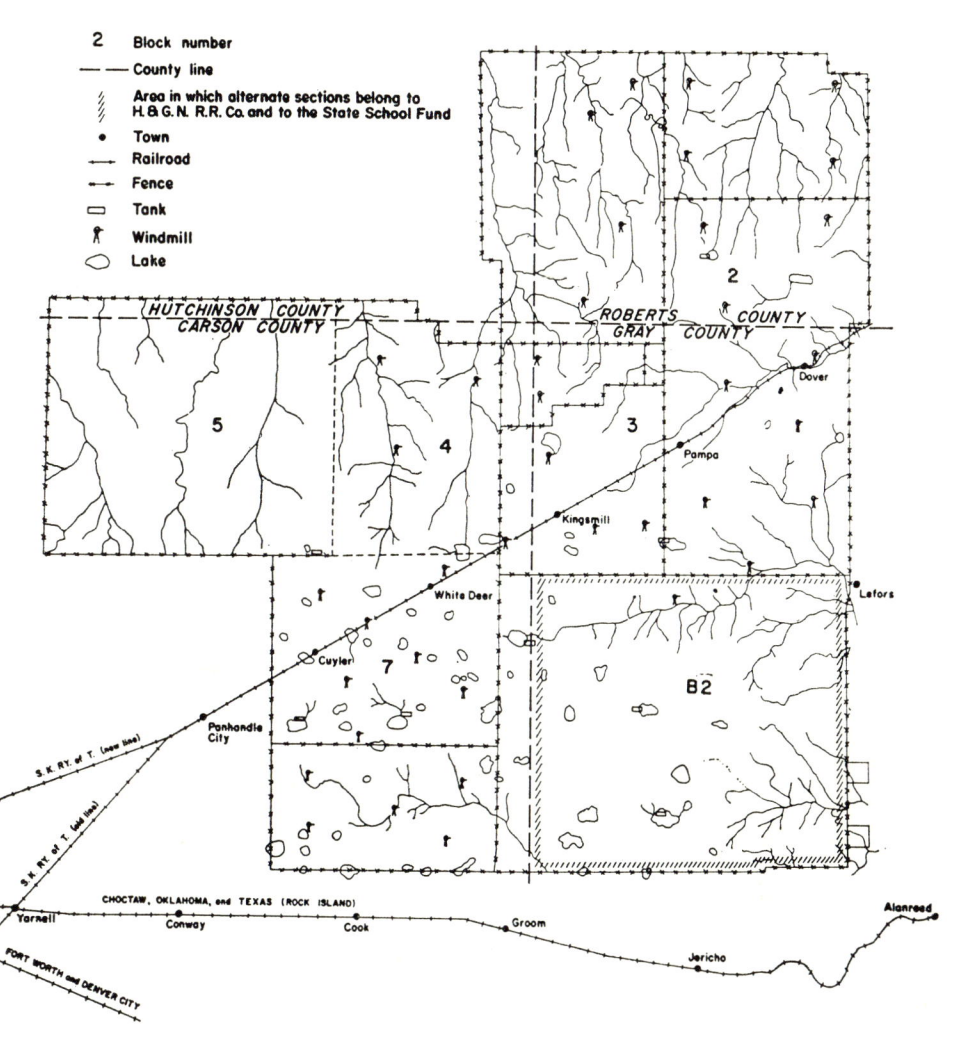

WHITE DEER LANDS
(Showing Location in Hutchinson, Carson, Gray, and Roberts Counties)

charge are in Dallas. . . . As they have the statutes and Digest at the Land Company's office, I shall be able to clear up a little of the law work before leaving here.

On December 4, 1882, Thatcher further advised Ward from Palestine:

I have got nothing into shape as yet to be able to make any report which shall give any definite information as to title. The matter is by no means a simple one. There are a number of instruments of which you had no copy. It was necessary for me before doing anything to advantage to get the run of the practice in the matter of land grants and the law applicable. The people in the Land Company are very accommodating, fairly well up in the practical details, and it seems to me unusually square. I think that I can get an idea more quickly here of the land system than by pushing on to Austin, and I am anxious to make sure of getting everything that I want here before leaving.

Thatcher continued his report to Ward December 6, 1882, saying:

I leave in the morning for Houston where I shall see Baker and Botts attorneys for the International Railroad. I shall go on tomorrow night to Austin. I shall probably have to come here again before finally completing my work. Probably I shall be able to send you a preliminary statement soon after reaching Austin. . . . It is of course possible that I shall be through in a few days, except for searches of official certificates, but if I am not, I wish to know what time is necessary for me to send on the first imperfect report possible. The surveyors' and county clerks' offices where the record of the lands in question are kept, are in Wheeler County in the Pan Handle, a distance from any railroad. It requires a week or more to reach there. If I have to have any searches or certificates from there, I shall probably, therefore, have them sent to you.

On December 11, 1882, Thatcher explained to Ward from Austin:

Before I reached Texas Evans had written to some of the parties who are interested in the purchase, informing them of the claim which I referred to in a former letter . . . written immediately or nearly so upon learning of the claims which was made only a month or so ago. A brief statement of the nature of the claim will perhaps give you an idea of the questions which are liable to come up in connection with land grants such as these with which we are dealing.

The state is divided into land districts each of which has a surveyor. When a land certificate is located, it is done by having a survey of the land made by the surveyor of the district. When, however, a land district is created it is not allowed to act as such until it is organized and obtains the records of the lands covered by it from the district from which it is made. A part of the lands with which we are concerned lay in the Young District which was organized in 1856. During the Civil War the Young District became practically disorganized and its records were taken to Jacksboro and went into the custody of the Jack District. He thereupon assumed to be authorized to survey in the Young District, made surveys there, and was recognized by the General Land Office.

The surveys under which our land was located were made through the Jack County surveyor, that is some of them were. These locations were made in the summer of 1875. On some of the lands so located a new location was recently made by some other parties who contest the validity of the former locations as made through the Jack County surveyor and have filed a protest against the issuance of patents to the New York & Texas Land Company. The principal one among the men who have done this is the former Chief Clerk of the Land Office. He and a number of his assistants have filed a number of such locations and protests affecting large quantities of land. One or two other clerks in the Land Office have left it and gone into the same business. It seems to be generally regarded as a blackmailing scheme. They have made offers to sell out to some parties against whom they have filed protests. I hear that with regard to the land in question they thought they would pay them something for their claims. At the same time any protest will prevent the Land Office from issuing patents until a reasonable time has been allowed to the protesting party to establish its claim and has failed to do so. . . .

There are a number of points in the claims which I have not stated above, and the claim is not the same as to all lands on which it is filed. . . . I do not see why claims might not be filed on all of the lands in question as well as upon some of these lands upon which it is filed. The questions involved in the land location cases are new and undecided by the courts. They are now coming up in considerable numbers. The land which was open to location has become exhausted within the last year. Consequently, the located lands have risen in importance and many men are engaged in looking for chances to disturb them. My feeling at present is that the New York & Texas Land Company will be able to sustain its title. . . . They have immediately put the matter in the hands of the best lawyers in the state at Dallas whom I intend to see the latter part of this week. They are preparing their papers to obtain in the US Court an injunction against the claimants restraining them from taking any steps under the claims. Evans seems much in earnest in pushing the suit. I think he would be willing to allow the consummation of the purchase to stand over until the conclusion of the suit.

It is hard to get information here. The records are not kept as they should be. They are not indexed and arranged so as to put a man on the track of things whose existence he does not know of. It is difficult to find some things he knows are there. I have spent a large share of today hunting through the different departments of the state, which are scattered about the city, for a set of certificates on which issuance of the land certificates were based.

Thatcher reported to Ward from Austin December 14, 1882:

I am engaged in writing a report on the title and as soon as I can complete it will send it to you. I shall go over today with Hancock & West the points that I think it necessary to ask them about. I am disappointed at the length of time that this matter has taken me, but I do not know how I could have shortened it. There was no use in my trying to do anything intelligently without looking over a large body of law relating to these matters which has taken considerable time. The report that I send you will not be complete. There will be several things to look up. Monday at least [will] be required to finish up what I have to do here. I intend to go to Dallas and from there to Palestine. From there I expect to return here and shall wait until hearing from you after receipt of my report. Please let me know by telegram upon receipt of that whether you wish me to wait here longer for further instructions or any other object.

Thatcher concluded by saying that it would take an additional week to go to San Antonio, Jacksboro, and Henrietta—all of which could be reached by rail. He said that "The records for last year or two are in Wheeler County. I should not think of going there. It is reached from here [Austin] via Kansas City and requires four days staging. I could get there as quickly from New York as from here."

Alexander and Green sent Brown a copy of a letter from Thatcher December 18, 1882, suggesting that he "send a copy to Mr. Francklyn by first mail," since he had requested it. Two days later Brown sent a second letter from Thatcher and likewise advised that a copy be sent to Francklyn, "who will thus get the history of the search that is being made."

On January 5, 1883, Major Evans wrote Vice President Thorne from Palestine:

I have your favor of 20th ult in which you desire to know what progress is being made in our fight with the land thieves. As I wrote you before, our counsel at Dallas were greatly delayed in the preparation of our case by the fact that the federal and state courts were in session so that there was a lack of time for the consideration of our case which its preparation required. However, suppose the case is now ready and if the papers have not been filed they will be at once. The District Surveyor in the Panhandle who resurveyed the Francklyn lands has been here on his way to Austin and I have had a full consultation upon all points in connection with this resurvey. . . . The surveyor has returned to his home in the Panhandle and it will take sometime before he can get his papers in proper shape for filing in the State Land Office so as to have the necessary corrections made there. It is extremely doubtful if we can be ready to make the deed by the first of next month, but I shall have the papers ready by that time if possible. I do not think Francklyn's agent over estimated the amount of land filed upon by these land thieves which you say he puts at 200,000 acres.

The more this matter is looked into and investigated the more thoroughly I am satisfied that those parties cannot deprive us of an acre of our land. It will cost us some money to defeat them and I should not hesitate to expend whatever sum I see may become necessary to that end. I will send you a copy of our attorney's brief as soon as I receive it. Thatcher has been here twice and I have had full consultation with him. He has been to Austin and had ransacked the Land Office from top to bottom and has even gone to the extent of finding out if the engineer's certificate of the road had been filed as required by law. No details or incidents however unimportant it might appear to Texas land lawyers has escaped his rigorous search and scrutiny. At my suggestion he has visited Dallas and has conferred with Wellborn, Leake and Henry, attorneys, relative to the case against the land thieves and has requested them to give him all the information they possessed on the subject. I have treated him with entire frankness and have told him if there were any defects in the title we should be glad to know in what they consisted, and that we had no concealments nor reservations to make on the subject. He is certainly one of the most industrious and indefatigable investigators it has been my fortune to meet with and you may rest assured that when he returns to New York he will have found out all that can be found on the subject.

Brown cabled Francklyn January 6, 1883: "Think we can arrange with Thorne as to part in question not to cause delay. Alexander & Green approve now as to 500,000 acres."

On January 8, 1883, Brown informed Alexander & Green:

Francklyn cables me he will remain in London until he has closed the Bond business. Please take with you all necessary copies of papers relating to our business. Also short statement from Ward explaining question of title. In view of our contract with the Texas Land Company we may require here the originals or copies of such papers as you have relating to title, as I do not know what stand the Land Company will take February 1st giving title to us.

Colonel Groom wrote J. K. Donnan, an attorney at Austin, January 10, 1883, and informed him that:

In conjunction with other gentlemen we have made purchase from the New York & Texas Land Company the railroad sections in Block B-2 in the counties of Gray and Carson, and we desire to obtain the school sections in that block. Have enclosed to surveyors of Wheeler and Jack a list of 22 names who desire to file on these lands. As we are not sure which of those counties is the proper place to file and have requested the papers enclosed to you as soon as completed so that you may file them in the Land Office at Austin. We are informed that the Land Commissioner is not disposed to receive files but the law is with us if we use our opportunity we think. Our idea is to protect ourselves by filing now before there is any change of the law. Please ascertain which district the lands alluded to are in and on receipt of this write us anything you have to suggest on the subject.

Colonel Groom on the same day wrote Robinson & West and instructed them to distribute the alternates in Gray and Carson counties "to the parties whose names I sent you, and appraised by the surveyors at once without reference to Walsh [land commissioner] decision, and papers sent to John K. Donnan, Austin, to file in the Land Office." Donnan replied to Groom's request on January 15, 1883, saying that he "had made inquiry at the General Land Office and found that the school lands were not on the market for the reason that there is trouble about the land district to which these counties were attached for surveying purposes."

Major Evans notified Thorne, January 24, 1883, that:

The survey of the land has been made so that it only remains to have the connecting lines and corrected field notes properly signed and recorded and returned to the G.L.O. [General Land Office] where they will have to be examined and passed. Panhandle surveyor, Mr. Spiller, came here with his field book and Mr. Langermann, my chief clerk, took it and from it made up the proper connecting lines and is now at Austin at work in the G.L.O. on the records to see how best to make the corrected field notes. Langermann was one of the principal draughtsmen in G.L.O. for years so that he has special knowledge for this class of work and is the best man who could be had to put this matter into proper shape. Our boundaries are clearly defined, but the question is as to the division of a lot of surveys reduced in size or the entire abolition of some of them. I am trying to get the matter into such shape that it will pass the authorities of the G.L.O. when presented. All is being done that can be done and as rapidly as possible. When completed to the satisfaction of ourselves and G.L.O. I will have certified copy of map made in G.L.O. and send you same. By last mail I sent you forms proposed by our counsel for notes, deeds, and Deed of Trust which I hope may reach you safely.

Sam Warren, vice president of the New York Company, sent these forms to Brown for his approval and suggested that:

The time is so short that we should come to some definite understanding with regard to an extension of time as soon as possible. I send enclosed for your perusal that you may see no time is lost and also what Mr. Evans thinks with regard to where the question regarding title lies.

Major Evans informed Thorne by letter, February 1, 1883, after his return from Dallas and Houston:

At Dallas I witnessed the proceedings in our injunction case. The attorneys for the defendants came in the day before the case was set for hearing and looked over the papers filed by our attorneys. When the case was called the next day the defendants did not put in an appearance, either in person or by counsel. Consequently, the Judge granted our prayer for a preliminary injunction against all the parties to the suit and fixed our bond at $10,000.

... I think the perusal of it sickened the attorneys for the opposite side and left them unprepared for fight.... Colonel John L. Henry, our counsel in this case, is a very able, prudent and cautious lawyer who would not express an opinion upon such a case were there any room for doubt in his mind. Upon leaving him day before yesterday I asked him very pointedly if there was any room for doubt about our case being made out entirely and safe. He replied that he could not see any chance whatever for the opposition to make a case against us.

I have ordered a certified copy of the petition and will send you a copy as soon as practical. The moral effect of our vigorous fight against these thieves is already seen to be excellent, and I take care to see that due publicity is given to our victories over these scoundrels. My chief Clerk and draughtsman has been in the G.L.O., and after conference with the proper authorities there, has found in what shape the corrections will be accepted by the G.L.O. and that those made by us will be received as correct.

With the survey out of the way, Colonel Groom could turn his attention to the problems of fencing and of providing for a more equal distribution of water on the Company's property. His first objective was to save the nutritious grass for the stock he was preparing to bring to the Francklyn range. Until the land was fenced, thousands of cattle bearing other brands grazed on the Francklyn lands.

CHAPTER 3

Fencing the Francklyn Range

THE FRANCKLYN LAND & Cattle Company entered the cattle business at a critical time in the history of the industry. The year 1883 saw the beginning of a transition from the old haphazard methods of handling cattle to more efficient and businesslike methods. Free grass and the open range were being replaced by fenced ranges and leased grass. The Texas Longhorns were on the way out, and pure-bred stock from the North and the East were being introduced rapidly into the Southwest. Hand labor and horse-and-wagon transportation were quickened by rail transportation and telegraphic communication. Close at hand, and adding to the change and uncertainty of things, was a presidential election which was to determine whether a Republican rule of twenty years would be replaced by a more liberal Democratic administration. A new order of things was developing in the cattle business. Moreover, the years 1882–1884 were years of unusual extremes in climatic conditions: years that witnessed some of the severest winters, hottest summers, most extensive drouths, and most destructive prairie fires in the entire recorded history of the Texas Panhandle. Excessive heat and continued cold, plus wet weather, caused much delay in the Francklyn Company's operations, and added to its expense in both time and money.

At this time land speculators and homeseekers were pressing heavily against the Southern Kansas and Northern Indian Territory boundaries, and were rapidly spilling over into the Texas Panhandle. To accelerate this movement two railroads destined to converge, first at Panhandle and Washburn and later at Amarillo, were edging their way along the western and southern borders of the White Deer Lands. Nature had indeed placed these lands in a favorable topographical spot for railroad development. The White Deer stream, with its headwaters flowing off the shelf of the level plains into the fertile valley below and emptying into the Canadian River, made its valley the only feasible route for building a railroad toward the Southwest.

It was on these lands that Colonel B. B. Groom, who was in charge of the Francklyn Company's Texas properties, believed that he could establish one of the best cattle ranches in Texas—one that would quickly yield large profits in cattle and would at the same time bring about a rapid rise in land value. Groom's long years of experience with cattle made him the key man in establishing a ranch on the recently purchased property. When he began his work Kentucky, Missouri, and Kansas were the areas of supply for the White Deer Ranch for both cattle and equipment. While Groom was well versed in cattle matters in Kentucky, he was soon to find that he had much to learn about establishing a successful cattle ranch on the Texas plains. Moreover, he was working directly under the supervision of Frank G. Brown, who gave him considerable advice from his New York office. Brown and Groom, in turn, were subordinate to Charles G. Francklyn, who was the final arbiter when important decisions had to be made. Groom was eager to begin his work and was soon on his way to Texas. At Kansas City he stopped to make partial preparation for his work at White Deer, and from there on July 15, 1882 he wrote Brown:

Distances in this country are so great and means of travel so poor it is very laborious. I start tonight on the "Jerkie" and will travel two days and nights without resting day or night. I expect to travel 600 miles before I get back here through a country almost without supplies or comforts of any kind. I dread the trip.

The Isolated White Deer Lands

When Groom reached Texas to begin his work he found much activity among the cattlemen. High prices for cattle stimulated buying and the introduction of barbed wire encouraged fencing and improved breeding. Groom reported to Brown from White Deer on September 30:

The cattle trade in the Panhandle has been very brisk for a few days past. H. Creswell sold 30,000 to the Prairie Cattle Company for $850,000. J. Bugby [Bugbee] 30,000 to Muscatine Company for $650,000, Wood and Snyder 60,000 for $300,000. F. Moody has given an option of ten days 10,000 head at $30,000. . . . The prices of cattle have been so high and the profits so large that there is great activity in everything connected with the business. There are about 50,000 cattle for sale here, the same class of yearlings that sold here three years ago for $7 each are now stiffly held at $14. . . . There will be hundreds of miles of fence built in the Panhandle this Fall. . . . I am advised on all sides to fence the lands as soon as possible. . . . The country is filling up so fast that the demand will be so great in the Fall that it will be difficult to buy wire at any price. . . . I am sure the wise thing to do is to get our fence built as soon as possible. I am anxious to get the fence done with so we will not be losing our grass. Every pound of fat others make on our grass is lost to us. . . . I feel anxious about the task before me. We have many difficulties to overcome, but when done we will have the most desirable and one of the most paying propositions in this country. . . . I will not rest day or night until I get it under way.

While Groom was in Texas on his tour of inspection he contracted for 25,000 posts to be placed on the top shelf of the Palo Duro Canyon. "I had one or two old friends here," he wrote to Brown from Mobeetie on July 25, 1882, "who assisted me in looking into the question of posts for the fence," and:

. . . soon found the supply of cedar is small and the demand very great and the main part suitable for posts owned by only a few men, principally Goodnight & Adair on the south and H. Creswell on the north, with Rowe &

Co., Towers, and Cudgell all wanting to fence their lands, and with a long string to build from the Indian Territory to New Mexico to stop the drift of cattle from Kansas and Colorado.[1] ... To have lost a day longer would have placed it out of our power to have fenced this Fall, and to have waited until Spring would have ruined our work next year.

On his second trip to Texas, Groom stopped at St. Louis, where he purchased 230,000 pounds of wire and nine one-hundred-pound kegs of staples. He ordered this wire to be shipped to Dodge City, where it was to be hauled over the two-hundred mile freight trail to Mobeetie in the Texas Panhandle. On September 2, 1882, Groom informed Brown from Dodge City that:

After more worry than I ever had with a Rail Road I have been able to start our trains. I have now all the tools and implements and teams needed for hastily improving our property. I will reach White Deer in four days. The teams will take ten to twelve owing to the condition of the roads. The road is very difficult owing to the canyons on Crooked Creek, Cimarron, Beaver and Canadian, all of which have heavy sand and some places dangerous quicksands.

Groom's immediate problem was to move his supplies over this long and dangerous trail, and then distribute them over the isolated White Deer Lands, whose exterior lines, forty-five miles distant, were yet unmarked. In some places the terrain made travel almost impossible. Groom in a long letter from Mobeetie on July 20, 1882, tried to explain his predicament to Brown. He said:

I tried at Dodge City to engage the halling [hauling] of our wire and failed to find anyone willing to do it. I came on to Fort Supply and failed there also. I find one firm here willing to undertake about half of it only. . . . There are teams enough that I can engage to hall half the wire between now and the middle of October. To make it later than that we could not get mechanics to work on the fence. I think I can arrange for the halling in some way but it will be difficult to do. It will not be wise to let an opportunity pass. . . . We want to work like beavers until we get our range enclosed so

[1] This refers to the well-known drift fence that was built across the Texas Panhandle in 1883, just north of the Canadian River, extending from the eastern line of the Territory of New Mexico to the Indian Territory in Oklahoma. This fence was built to prevent the drifting of cattle from Kansas and Colorado into the Canadian Valley during severe blizzards and snow storms.

Fencing the Francklyn Range

as to keep off thousands of head now consuming our food. . . . It represents more money than ever before. There are at least 10,000 head now grazing on us. . . . Immigration has increased but owing to the prospects of railroads, the freighting capacity has not increased with it. Since the Government Post at Fort Elliott, instead of buying teams and doing its own halling, lets out its halling of wood, hay and all kinds of supplies which occupies the time of the two leading firms halling from the Rail Roads to the Panhandle, the fencing will be a much greater undertaking than we at first supposed, especially with the increased demands for halling and no more teams to do it. . . . I have been trying to buy some ox teams but they are very hard to secure. I find a great scarcity of hands owing to the immense quantities of wire being halled. There is more work going on in the Panhandle than ever before and the demand for help makes it hard to command. As I have repeatedly written, it has been extremely difficult to get business forward owing to the great pressure for teams, labor and everything else. . . . I have remained at White Deer trying to put an additional corps on the fence, but have been able to get only half enough. This country is thinly settled and the men are not in it. I am doing all I can to get the posts in as rapidly as possible.

To meet the problem of transportation Brown suggested from Kansas City on August 25, 1882, that the Francklyn Company buy an outfit and do its own hauling. "You could control your own work then," he said. "Would it not be economy in time and money? I fear you will not be able to get your work done by outside parties." Groom replied on August 27, 1882:

Your suggestion in reference to purchasing a freighting outfit in one aspect of the case is first rate, but upon reflection you will see that unless we bought a great many teams we would be a long time in getting our freighting done, and after done we would have no use for the teams without grain which is $1.85 a bushel. We could not get them in good selling condition in view of the fact that we are anxious to get our fencing and building completed. I think it is best to get the greater part of our halling done by regular freighting teams suited to the purpose. We need a number of waggons, one for each post, not so heavy as those used for halling on a large scale. The wagons would be saleable at reduced rates. To the extent we have bought horses and mules we will use them permanently.

As the winter months of 1882–1883 passed, the fencing progressed very slowly, largely because of the bitter cold weather. Harry Groom, B. B. Groom's son, whose first employment with the Francklyn Company was for the purchase of Shorthorns at Lexington, Kentucky, and vicinity, took charge of the survey and fencing in February, 1883. He wrote Brown February 20 that he kept "two outfits of twelve men each on the fence; one distributing stays along the fence line and hauling posts from the north side of the Canadian River, another setting the posts, stretching the wire and putting on the stays." Harry Groom complained in the same letter that:

The Texas men are all getting restless and it is hard to get any work out of them. They are chronic grumblers and discontents. I would rather do anything again than attempt to put up a small lot of wire and use them. The men from Kentucky and one or two from other states are good hands and will work. It now takes four days to go to the cañon, load and get back to the line, scatter the posts and get back to the cañon. The distance for the round trip is about 60 miles, much of it over very rough ground. At the Canadian loads are thrown off, half of them taken across and return for the other half. Thus causing much delay. . . . We often have to haul the water on the fence line . . . six or eight miles for both men and teams.

Harry Groom was not able to hire a sufficient number of men or teams to do the work that needed to be done immediately. Brown, always apprehensive as to what was being done at White Deer under Harry Groom's management, wrote him from Mobeetie on November 13, 1882, saying:

I can make no suggestions regarding the fencing, but I fear some trouble ahead regarding it. I do not see how you can complete it before winter sets in, and you will hardly get started before you will have to stop which may delay in the Spring, besides the risk of losing posts scattered along the line by theft for fuel or other purposes. Of course you will take such measures as you may deem best for such protection as may be necessary.

With the opening of spring, Brown, anxious to finish up the fence as soon as possible, cabled Francklyn (February 26, 1883) in London: "We could not rely upon anybody in the Panhandle to do the post hauling and labor, and I sent out twenty men and bought thirty mules, more wagons, camping outfits, supplies, etc. which have all arrived

O.K. and now affairs are progressing as rapidly as the weather will allow."

The Grooms knew nothing about barbed wire, a complete novelty to them. They therefore sought advice from others more experienced in the wire business. Goodnight and Gunter & Munson advised them to place the posts forty feet apart. "They both say that with posts at that distance, if the fence is struck in any way by force, the rebound saves the wire from breaking." Colonel Groom adopted the suggestion and added three stays between the posts to hold the wire firmly apart.

Of the various types of wire that were being introduced, Brown preferred a flat wire with barbs cut at intervals a few inches apart. Colonel Groom, however, purchased the round wire, "the 4-point galvanized Ross patent," because, he said to Brown in a letter in September, 1882:

I learn from those who use it most largely that it is generally liked best. What you suggest about the flat wire is true; that it is plainer to the eye, but it is my impression that it is not too fierce and sharp pointed. I think the keen points constitute the value of the wire. It is rarely touched by animals I am told after they become acquainted with it.

Colonel Groom was having so much trouble in getting wire delivery started from Dodge City that he made a trip there in October, 1882, where he found "great pressure for all kinds of hauling." In order to relieve the pressure brought on Groom by Brown, Wright & Beverly, of Dodge, wrote Brown on October 11, 1882, explaining the delay:

It seems to us that justice demands in behalf of all concerned that we endeavor to account for the delay in moving the wire for Groom. In the first place this matter of fencing in this country has been of such magnitude as to absorb all transportation which has hitherto almost gone begging, and of course as with every other commodity, increased demand has increased the price. Knowing from experience how closely wire is handled, regarded as it is by cowmen as a dead expense and not felt justified in a too ready compliance with the demands of freighters for increased rates. Another thing the wire has been transported over a comparatively new road and to a seemingly indefinite point. Freighters, like other classes, have their idiosyncracies, and will not easily be brought to consider relations between rates and distance where old familiar routes and new ones are compared. Groom has been indefatigable in his efforts and can corroborate us. As to ourselves we have suffered directly in loss of sales on account of impossibility of getting quick transportation which we think will preclude any charge of inattention. Your wire is moving now and we hope there will be no further serious delay and that all required will be done in reasonable time.

Friends and Enemies

With the transportation problem eased for a time, fencing problems developed into boundary disputes. Colonel Groom met with little opposition in fencing on the north and east lines of the property, but on the west and south lines the story was different. These disputes arose over insufficient title to lands which Groom enclosed, and also over the question of legal title to the school lands in Block B-2, where the state owned the alternate sections. Groom built the fence along the northwest corner of the property, along the west line of Block 2 and the north line of Block 5. He wrote Brown, November 9, 1882, "You observe two sections outside of our boundary which we will enclose, hoping to secure them when we can." He then located additional sections on a map by listing the block and number of each section, "about 38 sections," he said, "with a saving of at least thirteen miles of fencing and the use of 24,300 acres of land. A part of this fence we are liable to lose, but feeling that the use of the land would be worth so much, we determined to risk it."

With reference to the school lands in Block B-2 Groom wrote Robinson & West, of Jacksboro, Texas, January 10, 1883, "I want the alternates in Block B-2 in Gray and Carson counties distributed to the parties whose names I sent you, and appraised by the surveyor at once, without reference to Walsh [land commissioner] decision, and papers sent to John K. Donnan, Austin, to file in the Land Office."

This was the beginning of a long series of quarrels and conflicts between the Francklyn Company and speculators and settlers over the control and ownership of these lands. It should be recalled here that, according to the lease law of 1883, all school lands in Block B-2 were subject to file or lease. The situation is made clear in a letter which Groom wrote Brown, June 20, 1883:

Barton is buying horses and putting them in on Block B-2. J. F. Houston is putting up the money for him. One or two bunches of cattle are moving in on school lands, one lot to the springs on Red River and another on

Red Deer. I will put them out, but they will either lease or buy to force us to buy them out. . . . Houston stopped the boys from fencing the sections on which they have a lease and dugout. . . . As I wrote you, I am of the opinion Block B-2 is as good land as we have, very broken and fine grass. . . . I have had a long talk with Street, County Surveyor. He says there is fraud in this shortage of our lands, and says that if patents have not been issued, we could get it corrected at once. Now if we can do this I will show you how important it is to us. Barton & Williams . . . hold two locations about six miles inside our pasture which have *lasting water* which is worth a great deal to us. If this fraud, in making our block short, is stopped, we will get water on one of our railroad sections and leave them without water. . . . Street and Leach got together and had a talk and Street says there is certainly fraud, and from his knowledge I am inclined to take up this matter now again and try to push the south line where it ought to be. Thus giving us the watered section. . . . If we can get them, will put a quietus on Houston's trying to get a foothold in Block B-2. He is the only party I fear will give us trouble. He would like to own enough land in alternates to force us to give him a tier of sections from the south side of the block to get him out.

Another formidable competitor whom Groom wanted out of his area because of fence problems was the Carhart Company. Carhart, an extensive land owner, leased to the Munson T. Case Company, of Wisconsin, in 1882 a large tract of land lying on both sides of the Francklyn Company's south line. The Case Brothers later became interested in building a railroad from Winona to Green Bay, Wisconsin, and offered to sell their lease to B. B. Groom for $25,000—$10,000 down and $15,000 on time. Groom was anxious to buy the Carhart lease in order to get him out of the way, and acquire at the same time some valuable watered land. He therefore secured an option on the lease until he could hear from Brown. Groom had just recently been urging Brown to buy the Barton & Williams property, which he was unable to secure. On June 21, 1883, Harry Groom wrote Brown a rather apologetic and explanatory letter saying:

Your decision in the Barton matter is satisfactory. I only mentioned it to you that you might use it as you desire. As it was offered to me I thought it best to lay it before you and add what I thought of it, hoping to give you a better idea of the property that you might have the whole data before you.

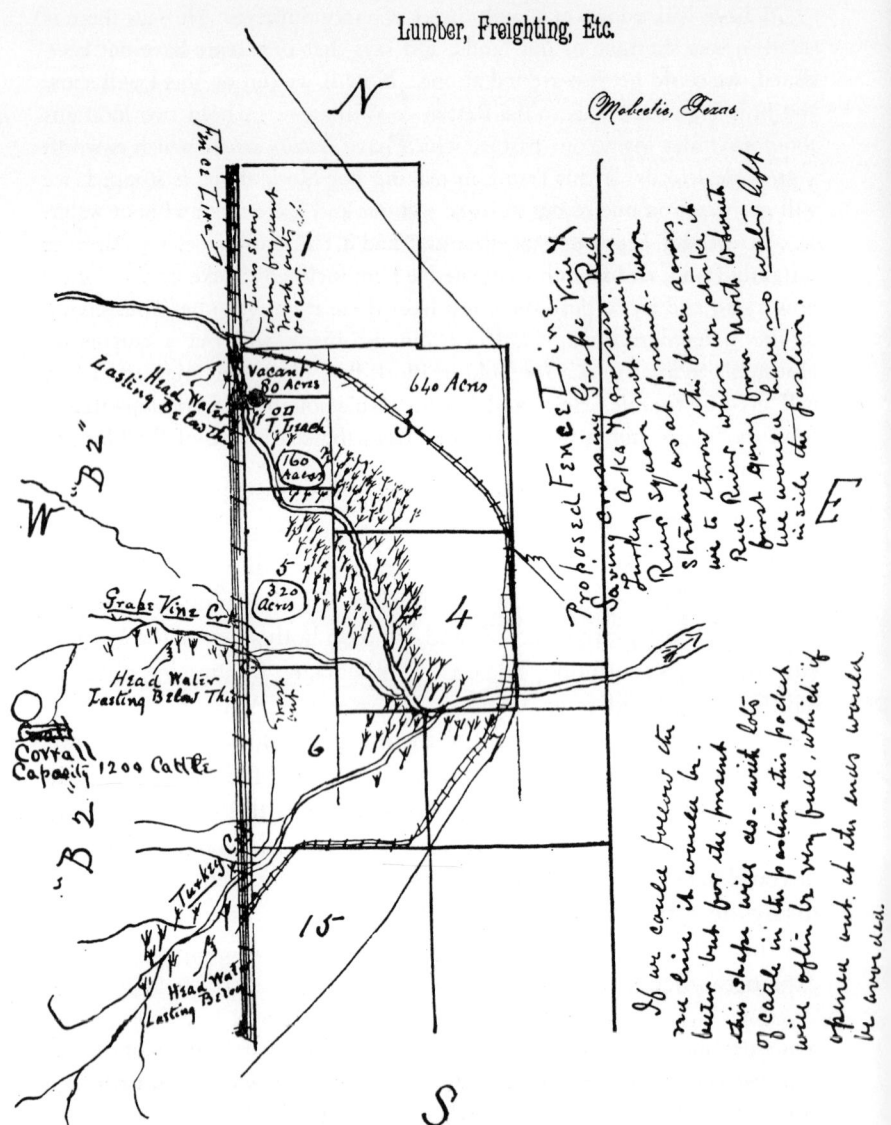

PROPOSED FENCE LINE, July 10, 1884

Fencing the Francklyn Range

I am at a loss to know whether or not to mention another property that has today and last night been laid before me. I hope, however, that you will not think my motives are other than for the best interests of the Company. I mention these matters to you that you may know all the movements being made here. The Munson T. Case Company have just in this mail received a letter from Carhart accepting the property at $27.50 for cattle and makes the payment to suit them. I hold them under their offer to us that I may lay it before you. Owing to Carhart's offer they are now in quite a hurry for an answer. If you are inclined to take hold of it all is well. If not I will, with your permission, lay it before some of my friends who are inquiring of us often about a place to put in some money. Here a small or large amount can be invested after the first payment is made. I enclose a letter from Case and from Carhart. We can pay for only half the fence, as the law will make us divide the fence with Carhart whenever we use it.

In his letter of July 2, 1883, from Green Bay, Wisconsin, to Harry Groom, Case, after explaining his sudden exit from the Panhandle, continued:

My last letter received at Mobeetie from L. N. Carhart who is disposed to be disagreeable in some small matters if we sell our herd to some one else other than himself, determines me to throw aside all sentiment and turn over to you all rights in the lease to the M. J. Cattle Company, even if you have to retain the name of our cattle company. This latter can be done by giving me a nominal interest with you, one cow is sufficient, and circulating that you have bought out all the other interests. We find that our *Manager, J. W. Carhart,* never had this lease recorded as we supposed had been done, but it is binding nevertheless, and L. N. Carhart will not venture to give another lease corresponding to this one. Mr. White, the County Clerk, L. N.'s brother-in-law, objected to recording it because it was not executed before a notary public. This is simply a technical objection and I advise you, if you conclude to use it, to have it recorded.

Case made further comment in the same letter:

When in Panhandle we discovered a great jealousy and tendency to discriminate against parties not on the ground, and against large corporations like the one you represent, and, as a consequence, I feel interested to see you succeed despite the number of old soreheads who would block your way at every turn. If I could have seen you personally I would have given you a few pointers. I hope you acquire Rockwell's interest on the North Fork of McClelland Creek. Persons are doing everything to get ahead of you there. In addition to the $10,000 we would want a note of security of some kind for the balance, $15,000 until the purchase is concluded. As you see we have agreed to everything and you to nothing as to the mode of payment except the cash down. Will make out a bill of sale on hearing from you, after getting the Manager's account of this season's branding.

Brown wired Harry Groom on July 9:

Do not want to make the purchase and prefer that all parties in interest attend strictly to our immediate business in hand until we know the end. We have all the lands and rights we want . . . and prefer to stand where we are for the present and attend to such cattle as we have and do what we can towards making a permanent water supply where it is required on our own tract.

Groom had many other cattle and financial troubles along the south line before the fencing was completed. Harry Groom on March 2, 1883, complained to Brown of "floating outfits which have been south driving back the drift. These outfits," he said, "threw about 12,000 head on the head of White Deer a few days ago. With these I presume there is not less 20,000 to 22,000 head now grazing on White Deer with plenty of grass to take them through till Spring." Groom was also harassed by:

. . . the liberality of the men who now work on the ranch with our supplies. They feed their [drifters'] horses corn. Sometimes they feed as many as twenty at one time. This has grown to be a bore of the first water, and as soon as we get all the cattle inside the fence, I think I will put a man and family near the road and let them run an eating house. I would not be worried another year with this class of impostors for a great deal. I am closing up White Deer entirely and leaving a gate west of the house on Spring Creek road. I hope by this means to get rid of passing. . . . All the wire for the south line has gone out and part of the stays. It will require eight loads of 1500 stays each to finish the south line. Since I last wrote you I have put one outfit at White Deer and put them to enclosing the fields, and will have them put up the gap nine and one-half miles to the corner of Gunter & Munson. In one more week or ten days we will have finished all but twenty-seven miles, and will make quick work of that as soon as I can take the mules out of the crop.

By joining fences with Gunter & Munson, Eaton, Carhart, and Creswell, Groom was able to save some sixty miles of fence, an economy both in money and time. With the range enclosed Groom could turn now to other improvements. Out of necessity some of the first improvements were in process while the fences were being built. The most pressing need was water, for approximately two-thirds of the lands under fence lay on the semi-arid plains.

CHAPTER 4

Foundation Work on Francklyn Pasture

IN 1883 THE FRANCKLYN LANDS were sprawled across the eastern Panhandle for some sixty miles with an average width from forty to fifty miles. The entire area sloped toward the south and east. Wheeler and Roberts counties along the eastern border of the property have an average altitude of 2,600 feet, while Carson County on the western side rises 600 feet higher, that is, to an average altitude of 3,400 feet. The eastern third of these lands, in which the White Deer Valley is situated, was broken land with considerable timber, plenty of fine grass, and adequate water in spots along White Deer Creek. The remaining two-thirds of the property formed a bald, level prairie carpeted with a heavy mat of nutritious grasses, deficient in moisture, but rich in soil structure.

These lands were drained on the north and east by the tributaries of the South Fork of the Canadian River. The main tributaries, from west to east, were Dixon Creek, Spring Creek, Timber Creek, Tallahone

Foundation Work on Francklyn Pasture

Creek, Indian Creek, and Red Deer Creek. On the south and east, White Deer Creek and McClellan Creek emptied their waters into the South Fork of Red River. The head waters of these tributaries, in draining flood waters off the plains region from century to century, had cut deep, narrow gorges.

All of these lands had been occupied for centuries by the primitive tribes of the Comanche, Cheyenne, and Arapahoe Indians until the 1870's and the 1880's. When these people were driven onto the reservations they left behind many remains and artifacts. The cattlemen followed immediately as the Indians emigrated.

Upon land of this character on the Texas Plains Colonel B. B. Groom attempted to establish for the Francklyn Land & Cattle Company a ranch built upon the same pattern and by the same method and techniques which he had used successfully for more than thirty years in the cattle business in Kentucky. A momentous task lay ahead of him in his new work.

Preparations for Cattle and Men

When Groom started his work in the fall of 1882 he first attempted to assemble teams and equipment with which to begin improvements on the property, but he soon ran into difficulties. In a letter to Brown, August, 1882, from Kansas City, he recounted some of these problems:

It is impossible to get men out there [in the Panhandle] we can trust to take care of our stock, not being acquainted there, and the best men are usually employed. I employed three colored men who understand the care of teams, mowing and stacking hay, and are experts in pertaining to such: men I have known for years. I could not do without them. . . . I will have to buy twelve mules in St. Louis. . . . will buy waggons and supplies in Kansas City. We will want three or four good horses, making in all fifteen or sixteen head. Will cost about $150 each. The ballance of what we will need will be cheap mustangs for the use of ordinary men, but for myself and son, we will want something better. My weight is too great to ride so small horses.[1] Then we need a pair to drive from place to place.

[1] These so-called "mustangs" were originally the Arabian horses introduced into the New World by Coronado and other explorers in the sixteenth century. They were lost and abandoned on the Southwestern Plains, where they ran wild for two or three

Our work will be so scattered that we are compelled to get from one place to another as rapidly as possible.

The first improvements on the Francklyn Company's spread had to be made quickly in order to get the lands ready for cattle. In a letter to Brown, August 22, 1882, Colonel Groom laid out this work as follows:

The building of ponds and pools is a large undertaking. The preparation for such work must precede the work itself. . . . I wish you could be with me. There is so much work to do to get started. . . . We will cut from 100 to 150 acres of heavy hay which will require two mowers and four waggons to lay it away. As soon as this is done I want to start eight two-horse scrapers and ploughs to building stock water which is entirely wanting on part of the land. We must also build some stables and houses. Add to this the halling of posts, stays and wire and you see there is much to do.

Cimarron, Beaver, and Crooked creeks, and the dangerous quicksands of the Canadian ran directly across the Dodge freight trail, making it, at times, almost impassable in hauling materials and supplies to the ranch, especially during the flood seasons. Harry Groom wrote Brown on August 20, 1882, that "The Canadian has been on a tare for over three weeks and it is impossible to get goods across."

Despite these handicaps, the work had to go on, and much preparatory work was done on the property during the severe winter of 1882–1883. This work consisted of cutting and stacking prairie hay, building fences and cross fences, plowing fireguards, erecting tanks and dams, boring wells, riding fences, building stables and corrals, setting up a headquarters camp, locating line camps,[2] and experimenting with

---

centuries. In later centuries horses lost by other explorers bred with these wild mustangs. As a result of this mixture an improved stock of mustangs was produced. These strong and hardy horses weighed an average of about eight hundred pounds. They could carry a two-hundred-pound man and a fifty- or sixty-pound saddle and equipment all day if necessary. The old-time cowboys of the open range called them "the best cow horses in the world." These cowboys often named their horses by the characteristic traits of the animal, such as "Old Seventy-five Mile," "Apache Kid," and "Churn Head," "Snake Eye," etc. See L. F. Sheffy, "The Spanish Horse on the Great Plains," *Panhandle-Plains Historical Review,* VI (Panhandle-Plains Museum, Canyon, Texas, 1933).

[2] Line camps were substations of the main ranch headquarters situated on the border of the range where two men camped at night, usually in a dugout, and "rode line" each day to keep the cattle from drifting from the home range. After the ranches were fenced these line riders became fence riders and windmill fixers.

Foundation Work on Francklyn Pasture

farm operations. Moreover, these various tasks must be done simultaneously, with a shortage of labor, with the work widely scattered over the vast isolated range, and with no means of communication except by horseback messengers. Furthermore, all this work must be done hastily and with very limited funds. In addition, Brown and Francklyn were continually urging economy in expenditures for all phases of the work. The Grooms were well aware of the need for economy in expenditures; yet, in their enthusiastic mood as to the potentialities of Panhandle lands, they were ever urging Brown and Francklyn to buy "bargains," both in land and in cattle, on which they could easily figure quick potential paper profits. In response Brown and Francklyn repeatedly demanded economy in all expenditures. Brown advised Harry Groom by letter, September 11, 1882:

I must call your attention to expenses. You have drawn on us since May 1st for $26,000 and it is hard to find anything to show for it. You must get everything down as closely as possible and get down in the strict cattle business as soon as you can. I feel all the work done on the dams will be lost to us. This business must be made to pay somehow or other and every effort must be toward that end.

Francklyn also cabled Brown from London on February 22, 1883, to "Urge Groom to be conservative. We don't want to buy all Texas." On the same day Colonel Groom notified Brown that he was drawing on the Company for $5,500 to buy horses. He assured Brown that he had tried in every way he could to use economy and "am well pleased with my plans.... I have ever since leaving the East devoted every hour to the Company's interest and have made some of the roughest trips of my life."

Colonel Groom, on September 16, 1882, made a lengthy report to Brown concerning improvements. It reads, in part, as follows:

The teams reached the ranch on September 12th [from Dodge City] with our tools and supplies, very tired but looking well for so hard a trip.... Having no place for our work stock and ourselves we have had to put up some cheap improvements for them. We will not build expensive houses, and only such as we are compelled to have. We must have some lots for our horses. The range is too large to have them run over it. We will also fence our corn fields, and ground for millet, hay, etc. Harrison [Harry

Groom] has had a plain strong log stable built for our work horses and mules 25 x 100 feet, and built two log rooms which gives us seven log rooms, a cook room and a sitting room where we all sit together around the same table. Also room for prominent stock men who stop on their way to their ranches, one for my cook and his wife, one for myself, and one for storage. The other is a large room for employees of the ranch.[3] We prefer to use these buildings until the railroads are located and building material is reduced in price. The commonest pine lumber now costs $25 per thousand and other materials in proportion. . . . I have now moved 1,500 corral poles all of which I have used up on the corral for branding. I got the material halled by contract. It will hold 1,500 head of grown cattle, and is the best one in the Panhandle, as all the material is number one with no fancy work, only good work. Everyone speaks well of it. It is about eight feet high, all the poles are peeled cedar posts and wired at the top with wire saved from the bales of barbed wire. I have also built a corral at the house three miles below the ranch and will shed it. This is for the Short Horn cattle.[4]

Conservation of Grass and Water

The whole economy of the Francklyn Company was based on grass, water, and credit. As the fencing progressed—cutting graziers off the Francklyn range—shysters, nesters, and homesteaders pushed in and filed on the school lands in Block B-2. This influx increased the demand for both land and water, and, at the same time, limited the Francklyn Company's expansion, crowded the markets with surplus cattle, at greatly reduced prices, and impaired the Company's credit. Therefore, it was imperative that the Company not only protect and preserve what grass and water it had, but also take steps to conserve water and provide forage to supplement the native grass. Colonel Groom mowed and stacked hundreds of tons of the native grasses, at an average cost of $5.00 per ton, for winter feeding until he could get his farms into production. He explained this point as he continued his report of September 16:

We have unbounded hay grasses of the first order in the beds of dry lakes.

---

[3] Bunk houses were where the cowboys slept.
[4] At this time the cattle were being purchased in Kentucky.

Some of them over 2,000 acres in size of as rich soil as can exist. I think with sufficient moisture will produce wheat every year. I started out one haying outfit from the ranch to put up 50 tons at the ranch, and they will put up 10 to 15 tons at each line camp. I think I will keep this outfit at work as long as hay is good. At this time I am working all hands in hay in addition to Carter's outfit,[5] because I had to use the waggons halling the oats to the stack to get them under cover quickly and in a few days will have 100 acres of millet to cut which will use all hands again, and as soon as this is cut the ballance of nearly 260 acres will be ready to cut. Now in the interim I use the men and teams on wild hay hoping to put up a large lot of it and not have to use any baled hay and thus save pay for baling. I have succeeded in raising 5,000 to 7,500 bushels of oats. I will cut off a lot of men as soon as haying is over, retaining about five besides four teamsters. At this time I have fourteen men besides Arnold[6] haying. Le Fors with ten driving from Greer County [to the Francklyn Pasture, referred to again later], seven inside the fence line, and one at headquarters making a total of thirty-five men on the ranch. As soon as driving is over I can turn loose Le Fors and five or six others, reducing the outfit to about twenty men all told.

I want to sow Fall oats which will require some plowing and some men to do it. I would also like to sow 25 or 50 acres of rye for weak horses and cattle in the early spring, and 10 acres of wheat to see what it would do.

I am trying to reduce the force as much as possible. I have Alexander at work on Indian Creek putting in a pasture to hold horses not at work and building house and putting up stables. He has with him four men. At the same place Robinson has three men running a hay outfit and will put up 30 to 40 tons of hay. Bright has with him at the farm [Highland Farm] seven men; five are now haying, others saving the crops and working such as need work. Selden is at the ranch with three men saving the oat crop and will begin haying as soon as I go back with our old machine. He will also cut on Spring Creek about 2,000 corral poles and a set of house logs to put up a house at Bear Lake on the Gunter and Munson line....

I have given Wakefield a contract for putting up 300 tons of lake hay at $5.00 per ton. This is the very best feed in the country and will winter stock nicely. Much of the lake hay is on Block B-2, and at this time McClelland and de Forest of Clarendon are on it with five machines and as many men required putting it up. They had the cheek to try and cut the

---

[5] Carter and his men had been contracted to build dams and tanks.
[6] Arnold was bookkeeper at the ranch.

hay in the same lake Wakefield was working in. I can stop them from working on our land, but they will continue to cut on the school sections over which we cannot assert any power as we have no lease of them.

Since you were here I have made a lot of works that I would like for you to see, such as small corrals, etc. We have had rain upon rain and it has played smash with us in a dozen places and has caused some loss of hay, but I do not complain as it makes us plenty of grass. At this time I still have a heavy force working, but will cut down as soon as haying is over.... I never saw finer wild hay. Some of it yields two tons per acre of fine grass, free from woody matter. The hay on White Deer and tributaries is poor. Red Deer and Reynolds creeks will have a quarter million tons of fine hay.

Although the White Deer range afforded a great abundance of grass, water also was essential to the success of Colonel Groom's program. Approximately two-thirds of the Company's land was on the upland plain, and therefore entirely dependent upon rainfall. As a temporary measure Colonel Groom constructed tanks and dams for impounding water. These, however, were too uncertain to be depended upon for permanent water. High winds, which characterize the climate of the plains, greatly increased the rate of evaporation, soon drying all basins into empty lake beds or bog holes. Moreover, when blizzards struck they froze these ponds, making even this limited water supply unavailable. Colonel Groom, therefore, had to devise some means of procuring permanent water if his program at White Deer was to succeed. Fortunately, with horse-drawn drills at hand, he could begin to experiment with this crude machinery and make water available on the plains portion of the property.

Water Procurement, Storage, and Distribution

The need for water forced upon the Grooms an extremely difficult and expensive project, first in locating water on the land and then in distributing it over the vast expanse of the Francklyn range. Since the work had to be done quickly, dirt tanks and dams had to be built immediately in order to catch and hold all possible rainfall. At the same time the Grooms had to experiment with bored wells and windmills, which at that time were first being introduced on the Plains, to supply the greatly increasing needs for more water on the range. Brown urged Harry Groom, on June 11, 1882, to:

... push the water at once on the Diamond F range and get that tract in shape as quickly as possible for cattle. It is the most important thing now to be done there. See that the work goes ahead without delay so as to secure all rainwater as soon as we can. We have now a great deal on our hands and must look carefully ahead and be fully prepared for any emergency.

Lack of transportation, severe cold, fencing operations, farming, and other more pressing tasks delayed tank and dam construction during the winter of 1882–1883. Nevertheless, Harry Groom continued the work of tank building as fast as conditions would permit. In August, 1882, he reported to Brown that "I have in my charge one outfit building a tank on survey 19, Block 7, where water is greatly needed. We are discovering springs not before known to anyone that we find."

In June, 1883, Harry wrote Brown that he had sent to Mobeetie for a heavy wagon to be used in hauling water to the fence line, "six or eight miles for men and teams." In the same letter he complained that his mules were afflicted with pink eye and added:

I cannot work them. I give our mules the best care and attention, but it baffles all our medical skill. Two have died, others are sick. The disease seems to be epidemic. The Hansford . . . Company, Rowe, Rocking Chair and Sacra & Richards are heavy losers from it. The Hansford Company have sent to Kansas City for mules to clean out some of the lakes on the range and make water on the plains. I wish our mules were well so we could go to work on ours. There is no doubt but that they can be made. We have one now that 3000 head of cattle could be held at all summer about fifteen miles south of the ranch.

Despite these, and other difficulties, Harry Groom reported to Brown on September 11, 1883:

I am getting dirt moved at 20 cents per cubic yard and would like to have surveyor engineer here at once as in twenty days from now I will have 60 or 70 mules ready to go to work. I have made contracts with good men who will put it through. Clark has gone to work on Tallahone just north of where the road crosses it. This is one of the best places to commence on as it has a fine bottom and holds water in shallow holes for a long time. Rath will begin in about two weeks on some lakes. I will try and get water in reach of every place.

On July 15, 1883, Colonel W. S. Kuper, a civil engineer from West

Virginia, wrote Brown accepting the work as surveyor and supervisor of tank construction, "As it will be employment in the Panhandle of Texas on the Canadian River where I suppose I will be near my old friends, B. B. Groom and his son, in a healthy portion of that state." Colonel Kuper was to receive $500 per month during his employment, with expenses paid to and from Virginia. The Francklyn Company was to purchase all necessary instruments for the work and ship them to Mobeetie. Brown notified Groom on July 30, 1883, that Kuper was enroute to Mobeetie and the ranch. "The first work he must take in hand must be the tanks and water question," said Brown.

Colonel Kuper arrived at the ranch on August 5. When Harry Groom, on August 4, 1883, notified Brown of his arrival he said:

Colonel Kuper took a look at the tanks and likes the soil very much. He is of the opinion both will hold water—both have water in them as a result of the recent heavy rains. Clark will finish two dams then I will put him on tanks in the lake beds. Kuper is attending to the tank business. I will locate other work for the tank builders at once. It requires close examination to get a soil that will pack and hold. The one on Tallahone, I think, will hold like a jug. Van Zandt[7] left this morning for the East. He made a close examination into grass and water while here. I had his assistance in looking out for additional sites for dams and water, all of which he will explain to you fully when he returns to New York. He will also talk with you about a well augur and boring for water.

Colonel B. B. Groom had already begun to experiment in boring wells. On November 9, 1882, he wrote Brown:

I commenced sinking a well in the center of one of broadest dry plains intending to go down 75 feet at a cost of $1 per foot, but the cold stopped the job, so the men said. I think it was the hard rock, called in this country the "Rim Rock" which underlies the top of the plains generally about fifteen feet below the surface. After passing that, it is my opinion that there will be no difficulty. We will be compelled to sink a few wells, for to depend on drinking water from the standing water where so many cattle stand around is almost too rough for our people to drink and cook with at

---

[7] Ferdinand Van Zandt was an Englishman who had become an American citizen. At this time it seems that he was looking after Francklyn's mining interests in Colorado and Wyoming. Later he became the representative and guardian of Lord Rosebery's American holdings.

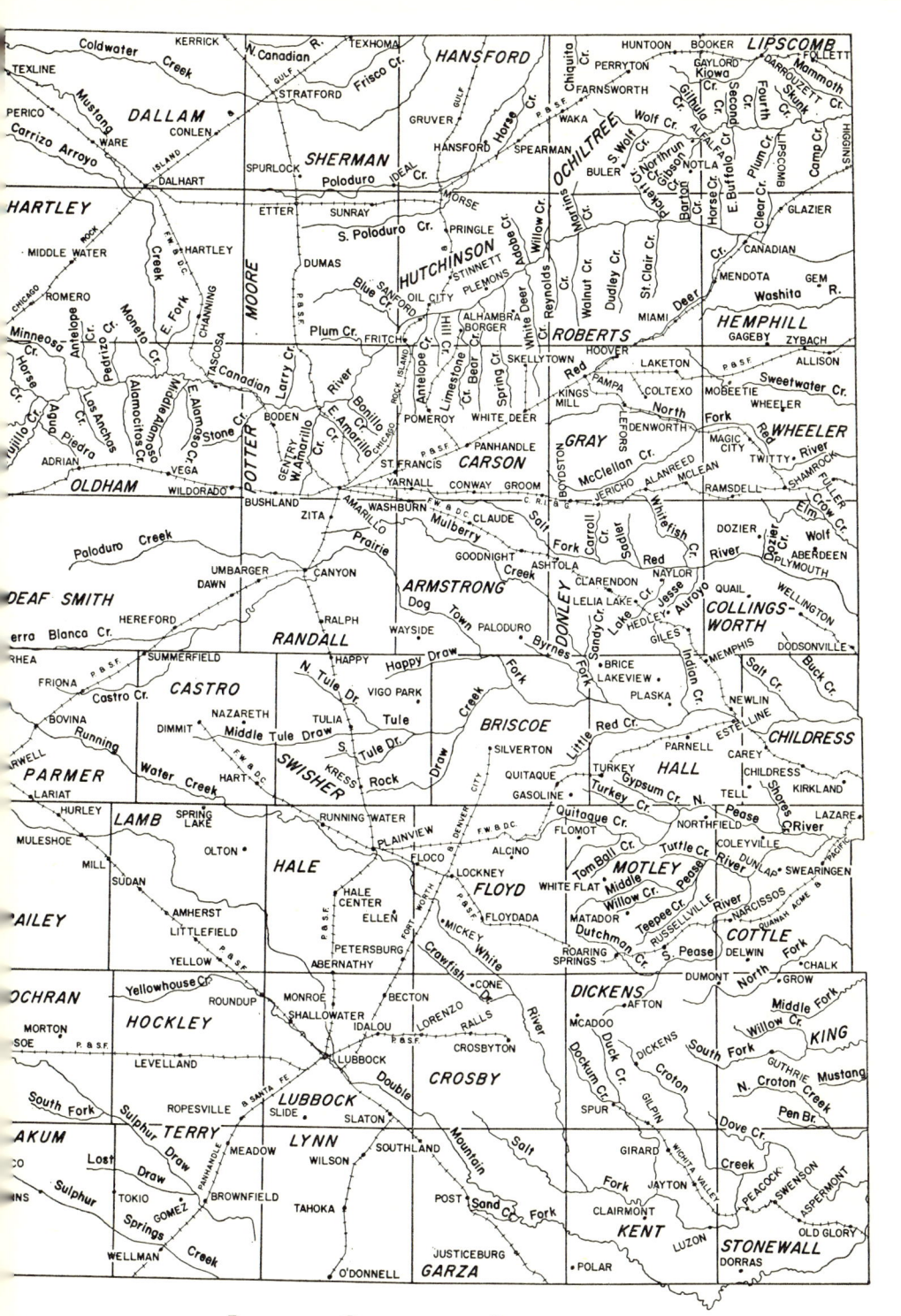

RIVERS AND CREEKS OF THE PANHANDLE

the camps that we are compelled to have at remote parts of the country. I have much more to write but must defer it for the present.

As this was the first well-drilling machine brought into the Texas Panhandle, Groom's neighbors were watching the results of his work with much interest. Colonel Goodnight asked Groom to drill an experimental well on the Palo Duro. When Colonel Groom wrote Brown about the matter Brown, instead of answering Groom's inquiry, complained of too much expense. Groom replied on July 28, 1883:

Now it is true that we have expended a large sum on the Carhart matter and I dislike to expend a cent more, but looking at the danger we are in by Evans getting J. O. B. Street, the County Surveyor's aid to hold B-2 where it is, we may be defeated and certainly delayed very much in the adjustment of this matter. You remember Goodnight is the appraiser agreed upon by Sully and yourself to evaluate the land between Carhart and ourselves. Now Goodnight wants a well bored very much at one of his line camps and had written and asked me about it. I am sorry I have no reply from you upon this subject, and in our last conversation I saw that Goodnight was a little worried with me not able to reply positively one way or the other. So I took the liberty of saying we would bore the well for him, by his paying all expenses and something for the use of the tools. In case of break or damage he is to make it good. I hope you will see how I look at this matter and appreciate the motives that moved me to this action. We could easily make this well back to us with a few cents per acre. On the other hand he could make us pay more than the value. So I thought it best to have him certainly for than likely against us in the matter. . . . I am casing at Chicken Creek now and it is so costly to take up the machinery, take it away and then back, that I will finish the well and let the drill go to Goodnight's. Then suspend until you come or write me what to do.

At the end of December, 1883, A. Ripley, acting temporarily for Harry Groom, reported to Brown that they had seven tanks completed:

. . . one four miles south of the Tascosa road; one straight south from White Deer; one southwest of that about six miles; one north of that about the same distance; one at Bear Lake; one at Tallahone; one three miles north on Mobeetie road just six miles of White Deer. Three of these tanks are brim full. These are Bear Lake, and the one just south of White Deer, and the other north of the Mobeetie road.

Groom's water experiment proved that more water was available on the plains, but later increased demands made necessary the improvement of Colonel Groom's crude machinery and the techniques used with it.

Fires and Fireguards

The greatest hazard to grass was fire. High winds in the fall and winter seasons frequently swept prairie fires across the plains, destroying thousands of acres of grass within a matter of a few hours. Such fires were deadly enemies of the ranchers. Hundreds of cattle, and even wild animals, were sometimes burned to death by these fires. When they broke out all hands on ranches for miles around had to stop work and rush hurriedly to them, day or night, in order to protect their own grass. These conflagrations were often started by traveling campers who failed to put out their fires on leaving camp. At other times they were started by cowboys dropping self-rolled Bull Durham cigarettes on the prairie. Occasionally, after the railroads built into the Panhandle, fires were caused by sparks of coal fire puffed out of the tall smokestack of the engine, caught up by the high wind, and blown out onto the prairie. Sometimes they were started by lightning. Harry Groom in a letter to Brown, April 19, 1883, gave a vivid description of one of these fires:

Our whole outfit has been upset for three days trying to keep from being burned up. At first I did not fear the fire, but the wind turned toward White Deer and it blew so hard that it could not be stopped in the day, but at night the wind would lay and twice it was about put out when the wind would send it along at a fearful rate. Last night I had every available man at work on it and just at dawn we succeeded in surrounding it. It has not got into the Valley of White Deer, but from the rim rock three miles east of White Deer to the east line extending south to Red River all the grass is gone. The new grass is coming rapidly. However, I do not think it will seriously affect us. Had Red Deer caught on fire I cannot tell where it would have stopped.

The quickest and most effective way of fighting these fires was to kill a large cow, split the carcass under the belly, tie one end of a long rope to each foreleg and the other end to a man on horseback. The two riders, one on each side of the blaze, would then drag the bleeding carcass rapidly over the fire. These men were followed by horsemen in organized groups, who worked with wet saddle blankets or wet gunny sacks to extinguish any blaze that might be left by the leaders.

Once fires were started, the ranchmen made their greatest efforts to prevent the spread of the blaze. This was done by plowing fireguards, which were both extensive and expensive. Fires usually burned up to these fireguards, where they were stopped, but occasionally when the winds were high, sparks of fire were blown across them. Then only the subsiding of the winds or barriers of lakes and creeks would stop them. On August 20, 1883, Harry Groom wrote Brown, explaining the location and extent of fireguards, as well as the method of plowing them. The letter is quoted here verbatim in order to show the immense job Groom had in plowing two or three hundred miles of fireguards on the Company's property:

I am starting the fireguards to have them in the right place. I have to lay the fireguards off and have Leach doing this work right now. I have to run a guard around the whole first and then run the guards as follows: First one east and west through the middle of Block B-2; second one east and west along the block line of 2 and 3; one east and west along the middle of the block line of Blocks 4 and 3; one east and west along the block line of 4 and 7 and 3 and B-2; one through the center of 3 and 2 north and south; one north and south commencing at section 110, Block 4 and 195, Block 3 and run south along the block line, and another north and south commencing at sections 160 and 161, Block 7 to the Tascosa road. (See map of White Deer Lands, p. 23.)

In a letter of June 20, 1883, Harry Groom informed Brown: "I have also let the fire guarding [contracts]. It costs $2.50 per mile to run four furrows, two on each side, 65 to 75 feet apart to be turned with a 20 in. plow if I can get it. If not with an 18 in. plow."

In addition to this heavy cost, these fireguards had to be burned off. A. Ripley said in a letter to Harry Groom on December 26, 1883, that this:

... is a very tedious job [on the broken ground]. An outfit can only burn about two miles a day in the long grass, but on the plains they can burn as

Foundation Work on Francklyn Pasture 57

fast as an ordinary team can walk. The bunch grass has to be set very often as it won't catch from one bunch to another without the wind is very high and this is very dangerous and will often get out. The flames on the west line got out of their hands today but we got all hands together and soon subdued them. We will have the worst part of it burned soon.

An added expense in maintaining fireguards was the annual repetition of burning in order to kill out the grass and weeds that grew in the plowed furrows between seasons.

Fireguards, in combination with favorable winds, saved the White Deer property from destruction in 1883, when the wind changed to sweep the fire away from the Francklyn range, thus demonstrating that although fireguards were expensive, in both time and money, to plow and to maintain, they were a big factor in conserving the grass.

In concluding his report to Brown on the subject of improvements on the Francklyn ranch in 1882–1883, Harry Groom made a plea for better mail facilities saying:

I trust you will give our mail route some attention. We are sadly in need of mail facilities. All my mail is by special messenger, now and then I get it out by a passer by. The present route is from Mobeetie to Leaches on Red River where our east line crosses it, thence across the plains to Wheeler on the north side of the Canadian, passing only two ranches between Mobeetie and Wheeler. To come by our place thence across the Canadian it would pass four times as many ranches and 20 times as many people, making the route only 10 or 15 miles longer. We are entitled to a daily mail which would give us our mail from Dodge in 3 days. This would change things with us very much.[8]

[8] This post office is in no way connected with the post office at Wheeler County, Texas. It refers to a post office which was operated on the cattle ranges in the Panhandle from 1897 to 1901. The National Archives at Washington, D.C. comments as follows about this, and other, early Panhandle post offices: "The seven offices established in 1878 indicate the routes of the first mail-hacks. Mail came by way of Camp Supply I.T., to Fort Elliott, with an extension to Clarendon. Another line from Fort Elliott to Las Vegas, N.M., by way of Fort Bascom, served *Tascosa, Hayes,* and *Trujillo. Wheeler,* at the LX headquarters in Potter County, was added to the western line August 18, 1879. Erskine Clements, bookkeeper at the ranch, was the first postmaster. Wm. C. Moore, foreman of the LX, became postmaster October 27, 1879. The office was discontinued March 22, 1883, due perhaps to the sudden departure of the postmaster from the ranch. The new foreman, John Hollicott, re-established the office

With the range enclosed and the foundations of the ranch established, the Grooms and Brown were now ready to begin stocking the range with their own cattle.

June 24, 1884, and continued for several years as postmaster. When *Wheeler* was finally closed January 31, 1901, the mail was sent thereafter to *Tascosa* for the patrons of this office, most of whom no doubt lived north of the Canadian River" (Ernest Archambeau, "Postal History of the Texas Panhandle," *Panhandle-Plains Historical Review*, XXXIII (1960), 123–124. Compiled from reports in National Archives, Washington, D.C.).

CHAPTER 5

The Big Cattle Deal of 1883

A FULL UNDERSTANDING OF the history of the Francklyn Land & Cattle Company can be had only through a knowledge of its regional and national setting. During the decade from 1876 to 1886, following the Reconstruction Period after the Civil War, a rather rapid uptrend in the nation's economic affairs developed, particularly in the devastated Southland. Cotton reached prewar production by 1876; railroads were extended into the South and the West, and the Carpetbaggers turned over state affairs to the Democratic South.

The economic uptrend, however, was most evident in the West, where the land and cattle corporations led the way. Rumors of immense profits in both land and cattle were heralded extensively. These rumors reached England; and, as a result, British capital that had been seeking investments in the unstable Latin American states since the early part of the nineteenth century was shifted to the Western Plains in the United States, which came to be considered a safer and more profitable place for investments. Consequently, millions of pounds of British money were poured into this region to be invested in land and cattle. Moreover, scores of cattlemen in the United States succeeded in borrowing in England large sums of money with which to finance their cattle operations. In this way vast sums of British capital were drawn into the reckless spending and speculation of a decade.

The Francklyn Company became a part of the general pattern. This company was one of the first and one of the largest corporations to enter into the land-and-cattle business during this booming decade. It was natural, therefore, that the Francklyn Company would look to England to secure funds with which to stabilize its credit and to ease the tensions brought about by its rapidly increasing debts, in part caused by the purchase of cattle.

Purchase of Keno Cattle and Shorthorns

As a preliminary to stocking the White Deer Pasture, Colonel B. B. Groom, in September, 1882, purchased the D. C. Cantwell herd of well-blooded cattle then grazing on the range. It consisted of an estimated 1,300 head and included sixteen imported Shorthorns, all carrying the Keno brand, which the Company continued to use as long as it remained in operation. The purchase also included "all the corn, millet, hay, plows, mowing machines, rake and harrow, ranch and house fixtures." The sum paid was $26,500. "I like his cattle," Colonel Groom wrote Brown, "and it is my opinion we should buy them. They are exactly where we want them at home on our range ready to become the nucleus around which to build our herd."

Colonel Groom went to Lexington, Kentucky, in the spring of 1883, where he made arrangements with an old friend and cattle buyer, Captain R. B. Edmunson, to take over Harry Groom's work and finish the purchasing of young Shorthorn and Durham bulls to be placed on the Francklyn range. These bulls had to be bought in a highly competitive market where bulls were scarce and in great demand. Captain Edmunson wrote Brown from Lexington on April 14, 1883:

B. B. Groom has authorized me to buy and superintend the purchase of a

The Big Cattle Deal of 1883

large number of high grade bulls. It is a big thing and I feel quite complimented and will certainly do my very best to have them right in every respect, but he has limited me in such a way that I fear I cannot get such bulls as I want to buy worth the money I am to pay, as farmers feel they ought to have extra to keep them as bulls ought to be kept. He has limited me to an average cost of not over $25. I am now organizing the buying with some first class assistance and will soon know what can be done. There is now, and has been, quite a demand for bulls. Some of the ranchmen have had their agents here buying.

Edmunson was given free access to the Company's funds and was authorized to draw drafts to pay for the bulls as they were purchased. The only requirement was that he should report in detail when the purchase was concluded. The bulls were hand-picked from ten Kentucky counties in the vicinity of Lexington and assembled at a farm near the city to be branded and held for shipment to White Deer at a later date. In his final detailed report to Brown, June 20, 1883, Edmunson concluded his report by saying that he had purchased "between 1,000 and 1,100 head, and I think a very superior lot."

Further Search for Herds

Because Francklyn was in England during the winter and spring of 1883 engaged in the sale of "Gold Bonds," it fell to the lot of Brown and Groom to find desirable cattle in sufficient number to bring the ranch to its full capacity for operation. Since Colonel Groom was in Texas learning land and cattle conditions firsthand, it became his duty to select the stock to be purchased. "I find Colonel Groom understands cattle and everybody I meet in Kentucky speaks of him in the very highest terms," wrote Brown.

Colonel Groom informed Francklyn on January 2, 1883:

Your idea of breeding in the South and finishing in the North is correct, and it is now being practiced by Major Driskill, Mabry, and others who handle cattle on a large scale. In our case I think this is unnecessary, as we are located in that happy medium between heat and cold. From the use of improved blood there are now many herds of cattle in the Panhandle that equal in value any herds to be found anywhere in any part of the West. There are many herds around us from which the yearlings could be sold for $20 per head, almost equaling Kentucky prices, the beeves from which would bring easily $60 per head. The cattle on our range this winter are very fat and many thousands are now grazing on it. We are of the opinion that we will find it to be to our interest to buy heifers from the improved Panhandle stock as cheaply as we can and use upon them Kentucky bulls, and in that way increase their size, quality, and value. Brown and I looked at our Kentucky cattle a few days ago and were very much pleased with them. They will go home as soon as fencing is completed.

Colonel Groom was eager to make further cattle purchases as quickly as possible, since he realized that the time was short and continued delays were hindering his work. Moreover, he feared a rise in prices of cattle would come soon. He wrote Brown from Lexington, Kentucky, on January 26, 1883:

I wish Francklyn was ready to buy cattle. It is painful to see cheap common yearlings selling over the country for $7 and $8 when we so much need them on our range. The disposition to invest in cattle is rapidly increasing. There are so many large companies buying that prices are quite exciting. There is no concealing the fact that cattle are scarce and high. Goodnight sold all his steers to Bugbee just across the Canadian from us at prices rangnig from $20 to $30. I have had two or three opportunities to buy some cheap cattle. I was offered a herd at Texarcana [Texarkana] for $11 per head which could easily bring $30 here. East Texas is now the place to buy cattle beyond a doubt.

Colonel Groom made extensive inquiry in 1882–1883 about available herds for the Francklyn Pasture. He was offered several cattle ranches ranging from 10,000 to 100,000 acres in West Texas. Among these was a ranch which Colonel Groom considered to be ideal for the selection of cattle for the Francklyn range. On January 8, 1883, J. W. Porter, a commission agent from Kansas City, acting as agent for Harrold Brothers & Ikard, of Wichita Falls, Texas, signed an agreement with E. B. Harrold in which he agreed to buy the Harrold & Ikard herds located in Greer County, Texas, and further agreed to "use all diligence in presenting the property to capitalists." The property consisted of an estimated 75,000 head of cattle, "of all ages and descriptions and brands, about 500 saddle horses, all wagons, harness, and branding equipment, together with lease and range rights, extending to

The Big Cattle Deal of 1883 63

1885, on a 50 x 75 mile spread of fine grass lands in Greer County, Texas."

With this deal also went the lease on railroad lands and a lien on school lands of some 200,000 acres in Wheeler County, in the Texas Panhandle, "for what it has cost us," said Groom. The whole of the properties were to be sold for the sum of $1,500,000; or, by excluding horses and ranch equipment, Harrold agreed to deliver the cattle at the branding pens on the Greer range for $22.50 to be counted, branded, and paid for, "upon such terms and in such manner as may be agreed upon by the parties concerned."

Porter was given fifteen days in which to accept or reject either of these propositions. If he accepted either proposal he was to deposit $50,000 in the Chase National Bank in New York City to the order of E. B. Harrold. If upon inspection of the property by an examiner it was found to be as represented in the written description attached to the proposed sale and signed by Harrold, and was so reported by a "good reliable, experienced stock man appointed by Porter," then the trade was to be closed. The purchaser was given the right to remove all cattle from the range at the market price, and any excess above $22.50 was to be placed as a credit of the purchase money. All payments on cattle sales were to be made at the First National Bank in Fort Worth.

Negotiations for Harrold & Ikard Herds

Porter immediately submitted these proposals to Brown and urged him to buy the property. Brown cabled the propositions to Francklyn in London. As a result of this offer a series of triangular negotiations and proposals began between the New York & Texas Land Company, the Francklyn companies and Brown and Francklyn. These negotiations extended through February and March, 1883, and reached an impasse by the first of April. The land surveys, sale of bonds, and purchase of cattle became closely intertwined, since the land survey was still hanging fire, and could not be completed by February 1, 1883. Thorne, vice president of the New York & Texas Company, extended the land payments sixty days without prejudice to either side, and so notified Evans. In his reply of January 24, 1883, Evans approved the extension, saying that "The extension of the payments until

April 1st will suffice to put the matter into proper shape for the trade with the Francklyn Land & Cattle Company," and added:

It should be stipulated, however, that all notes and deeds should bear the date of last month, as in accordance with the agreement as heretofore executed. The survey of the land has been made so that it only remains to have the connecting lines and the corrected field notes properly signed and recorded and returned to the Land Office.

Therefore, title to the lands could not be conveyed before April 1. Moreover, with the sale of bonds not yet completed, land payments could not be made until the money was in hand, and until the Francklyn Company received title to the property.

On February 6, 1883, Brown cabled Francklyn inquiring if there was any chance of effecting sales. "Time is short. Answer. Will make no further purchases until we hear from you." On February 9 Brown again cabled Francklyn and advised that "We must decide on cattle. Otherwise we lose the use of grass."

Brown, in an effort to expedite the cattle purchase, began negotiations with Harrold to take Gold Bonds as part payment on the cattle. As a result he cabled Francklyn that Harrold:

. . . will take half cash and the 750 Bonds as collateral for the Company notes without land lien giving clear title. Cannot take bonds for purchase money. Think they would take notes 1889 or later. Low has details of contract. We cannot do better than purchase if we can arrange finances. Henry R. Rose sailed on the Alaska February 9th. His address, Glen Currie & Company, London. See him. Important cattle matters. Porter, his principal, authorizes this.

While waiting for an answer from Francklyn, Brown wrote Colonel Groom, February 17, 1883, as follows:

Your friend Judge Henry Low has gone to England and Porter has given him copies of all his papers on this with a view of placing it in England. It has occurred to me it may be the best thing to do to buy these cattle if we can arrange finances. In any event I thought it best to let Francklyn look into it. You may know all about these cattle and men. If you do not please quietly inquire about the cattle in case you think it worth while to entertain purchase. It is not necessary that anybody should know about this, or that we

The Big Cattle Deal of 1883

are entertaining purchase. I extended the Thorne contract till April 1st. Our interest on purchase does not begin until they give title.

On February 22, 1883, Brown received a lengthy letter of instructions from Francklyn saying:

My Dear Frank: I was delighted to get your telegram last night about the strike in Horn [Mine]. It did me more good than anything I have heard in many a day. I have sold $750,000 worth of cattle ranch bonds, half payable first of March and half first of July. I cabled you yesterday to buy cattle. The Greer scheme is too big and too risky for us to touch. There is no title to the land and it is departing from our plan of building up a herd of cattle. The profit of the business is in the breeding or increase of cattle and everyone who has bred a herd now seems inclined to sell and realize profits. Low called on me on arrival and I told him he would find it difficult to do anything with his scheme. He has gone to Paris and hopes I may be able to help him place his cattle. He called again yesterday and left all his papers with me, having found, I fancy, that it was impossible to do anything.

From a private letter from Porter which he showed me, they could afford to take $22.50 per head, but my impression is that several companies here have failed to raise the money they required. There are lots of cattle to be had at much lower figures than have been talked about. The Union Company got us money. The Door Nail did not succeed. Creswell's cattle therefore not sold, and in fact the ranch business in this country does not go down, owing chiefly to the fact that the market has been flooded with them.

If we purchase judiciously now I think we will make a good thing of it. Do not make arrangements beyond our receipts, that is $300,000 now, the balance by July 1st. I have agreed to hold the other $750,000 bonds to meet the mortgage notes. So we need not make any other proposition to them. Merely carry out the original agreement. I hope he will be ready with his titles by April 1st. Telegraph me upon receipt of this if he will be ready. We want to close it. Alexander and I have signed the mortgage as trustees before the U.S. Consul and I will send it to you to be recorded. But I suppose it should not be recorded until the Francklyn Land & Cattle Company receives the title papers. Please impress upon Groom the importance of being conservative and judicious in the purchase of cattle. We shall do quite well enough if we start moderately with 20,000 to 30,000 head of good well selected cattle. We cannot expect to own all Texas, but we may make a comfortable thing out of what we have got by careful management and close attention. . . .

My present intention is to take a yacht and go out early next month to the West Indies and have a look at the Gold diggings. I have a notion that we have been robbed down there. If Van Zandt [Ferdinand] can possibly get off, I will take him to look at the property. We should arrive home then about May 1st, but I will telegraph you if this is to come off.

I will write you in a day or two about stock of cattle etc. You should have a resolution passed authorizing me to sell the bonds. If Porter can sell his cattle at $22.50 he must pay Harrold Bros. up. We don't want to pay any middle man a profit.

Brown, upon receiving this letter, was faced with a critical situation. He wrote Groom, on February 24, saying:

Francklyn has just cabled me he has sold $750,000 worth of Bonds, payable half on March 15th and half July 15th, and tells me to purchase 20,000 to 25,000 head of cattle if we can do so making payments fit in with the sale of bonds. I do not feel like going ahead, however, on that basis, as we may not get title from the Land Company until April or May and we cannot execute or deliver Bonds until we get title. Hence, I do not feel like telling you to purchase cattle until we have all this business closed and have the money in hand. I am in favor of bringing Harrold & Ikard herds in with us if we can make some kind of a deal with Harrold and I think we can. Harrold is now at his home in Wapella, Illinois. J. W. Porter who holds contract for sale is here and I have all his papers here in my safe. By the terms of the contract we have until November to count the cattle, brand them and pay for them. An intimate friend of Harrold will be here next Monday to remain here for a few days only. It seems to me if we could get Harrold to take half in cattle and half in our Bonds it would be a good deal for us. We could then retain what cattle we desired and sell off the balance in small lots of from 3000 to 5000 head as we found purchasers. If I can get Francklyn to work with me on this I will have Harrold to come here, and it may be best for you to come on here at once. Do not, however, make any purchase of cattle until I say go ahead, or until I hear from Francklyn in answer to the questions I have raised.

On February 26, 1883, Brown countercabled Francklyn the following suggestions:

Our best chance is to secure Harrold herd. $50,000 March 5th does it. Have until November to count the cattle, paying instalments. Think we can arrange deferred payment half million until Spring of 1884. Terms unusual.

7000 steers, 2000 dry cows for market this Spring. Proceeds credited on purchase. He turns over to purchaser Greer range, one of the best in the country, and leases and filings on 200,000 acres in Wheeler and Collingsworth counties in Texas Panhandle. Groom and others say price quarter million below value. We could take the cattle we desired, balance could be sold in smaller lots this year or organize separate company. Harrold retiring from business. Started 1875 with 3,000 head. Think it over carefully and you will see many advantages.

As if to boost Francklyn's courage Brown added: "Horn [Mine] improving daily. Bassick January profits $90,000. Expenses $17,000. Expect same February."

Brown followed up his cablegram with a letter by way of further explanation:

I cabled you today and now enclose you Porter's contract and Groom's letter. You have of course seen Low's papers with description. The time to make $50,000 payment has been extended to March 5th. I am dealing direct with Porter. The $50,000 is merely put up as earnest money and not to be taken by Harrold. It remains until purchase completed. It strikes me we have a better chance to get what we want than if we buy outright a herd of 20,000 to 35,000 head which would cost from $500,000 to $600,000 and we would have to pay all cash besides. . . .

If Thorne delays title can you get any money? Are we safe in buying 20,000 for cash? This deal gives us all the time we want and secures what we want. I am satisfied I can get in considerable capital from Western cattlemen on this herd and ranch if we had to put it in a separate company. Suppose the Francklyn Land & Cattle Company furnished $750,000 toward the purchasing of the herd which would give them about 36,000 head to remove to their lands. We could then form a separate company putting them entirely in the dark. My cables have given you from time to time bare facts and results of everything of interest here.

On February 27, 1883, Brown explained the Harrold deal by cable to Francklyn, saying:

$50,000 May 5th. $950,000 between May and November as cattle are counted. $500,000 July 4, 1884. Low mistaken about cattle contract. Calls for $1,500,000 for cattle range, horses, outfits, leases, filings or $22.50 per head of all ages to be counted. Both propositions flat prices. If time payments not satisfactory make proposition.

On February 28, 1883, T. J. Allen, who was financing the deal, informed Harrold by letter that:

I have an offer from the best of parties of $1,500,000: $50,000 March 5th. $950,000 between May and November in instalments, July 1, 1884, provided you can guarantee 60,000 head exclusive of calves this Spring. Is there any way you can satisfy the count? Please answer fully at once.

Brown's cables to Francklyn seem to have halfway convinced him that the Harrold & Ikard property was a good deal. At least he gave his consent to the purchase, but advised Brown in a letter of March 3, 1883, that:

Numerous cablegrams have passed between us on the cattle question. I regard the Greer cattle at $22.50 per head for yearlings and all above about right, but if it is to include this year's calves, it is an enormous price. The range may be good but it is in dispute. I remember hearing of the trouble there before now. It has no market value. All very well to have but not to pay for. Anyone buying Greer cattle to sell here would be stuck badly. There must be any number of herds for sale and I don't see why we would have to pay any large commission to get one. The difficulty I am laboring under is this: Low had instructions to sell at $22.50 per head for Porter. Also had information the $22.50 was the price of the cattle to Porter. Now I don't see why we having money etc. should have to pay $3 per head commission, nearly $200,000. I am writing this in a hurry to catch the mail and am expecting every minute to have a cable from you on the subject. I shall sail on March 17th for the Barbados, thence by yacht to San Domingo arriving there about April 8th. I shall take Van Zandt [Ferdinand] for the benefit of his advice on San Domingo property. Don't do anything about cattle which will make us have to skin for money this summer. . . . I hope the title will be all right by April 1st. Telegraph me on receipt of this if there will be any hitch.

After several cablegrams were passed between them Brown, on November 5, notified Francklyn by cable:

We assumed present herd 60,000, increased to 75,000 by November. A total of 39,000 cattle to be sold immediately for $860,000 to be applied on purchase, leaving 34,000 females desirable ages and 2,000 bulls at an average cost of $18 on basis of buying by count 75,000 at $22.50. Moreover, by vigorous count many calves will be dropped after counting. Wheeler lands worth $150,000.

The Big Cattle Deal of 1883

Again to brace Francklyn for the deal, Brown added: "February output of mines 1,200 tons of lead, 93,000 silver."

On March 5, 1883, the $50,000 was deposited in the Chase National Bank as per agreement, and was paid over to Harrold on March 23. By closing this deal the Francklyn Company added a vast cattle domain to its already extensive holdings, which now extended from the Greer-Wichita country to the Canadian River in the Texas Panhandle, a distance of some three hundred miles.

The final step in the deal was the inspection and evaluation of the cattle, to determine whether they measured up to the written description signed by Harrold and attached to the original proposal of the sale. Brown wired Colonel Groom, March 9, to arrange for the examination: "Taking with you reliable business cattlemen. Allen left here Wednesday morning to join you in Fort Worth. Think him a good man to take with you also. The important point is to decide whether they are the cattle we want and worth the price." Colonel Groom left immediately for Fort Worth, where he arrived just as the Cattlemens' Convention was closing a three-day session, and where he reported to Brown on March 10, 1883:

> I found the crowd generally leaving on the morning trains. I have used all the energy in my power in learning all I could about the Harrold and Ikard cattle. Col. J. Peter Smith, Mayor of Fort Worth, and Mathews & Reynolds refer me to W. L. Cotlin of Waco, Suggs Bros. of Indian Territory, Hearn of Baird, W. E. Hughes of St. Louis, A. B. Combs, F. Houston and at least a dozen others. Without exception these men describe these cattle similarly to Allen and Porter. Harrold left on an excursion to El Paso with Chicago and St. Louis cattlemen. Will be back Monday night. Col Smith, the Mayor, is an old friend of mine from Kentucky and Tidball and Van Zandt[1] the bankers are assisting me. I am determined to have a good man and one they recommend to go along with me. Ikard's cattle are all Northwestern.[2] So many have described them as good. I expect it is true.

---

[1] Van Zandt was not related to Ferdinand and Henry Van Zandt.

[2] The territory commonly known as "The Great Southwest" lying between the boundaries of southern Kansas and Colorado and the parallel of 36° 30' north latitude, as fixed by the Compromise of 1850, came to be a meeting ground for the Texas Coast cattle and the thoroughbreds of Kansas, Missouri, and Illinois, throughout the trail-driving days of the 1870's and 1880's. During this period many Texas ranchers had greatly improved their herds by crossing the Texas Coast cattle with thoroughbred

Moreover, I will go as soon as possible and see for myself, and write you at once. I have made considerable inquiry about what we can do with the over plus of cattle without letting it be known what numbers we want to sell. The largest operators in steers I have seen are Simpson & Hughes who said they would take the entire steer cattle at fair value. If we could sell the steer cattle and some of the cows for half the money and retain the females representing the other half, I would consider we have done well, leaving the land out of account which I believe to be worth $150,000. I learn they have had an offer of more money, but I don't know how much. The cattle can now all be considered Northwest, as none from the South have been introduced since 1876. Simpson & Hughes have said to me it is the best purchase that has been made in six months. Leon W. Moore of the Texas Investment Company, raised in Frankfort, Kentucky, says his cattle for several years ran with and adjoining Harrold & Ikard's and that they are the best cattle in the region. Sam Holmes has cattle adjoining and says the same. Robert Strahorn, cattle commission merchant, who was at one time interested in Harrold's cattle, says that the cattle and land at the price are the best bargain made this season. Harrold in his description of the cattle says, "For six years I have been improving the herd by using blooded bulls so that there are now on the range only a few cattle of the original Texas stock and these are cows. The bulls used for the past six years in improving the herd have been one-fourth blood one-half blood thorough Durham and Hereford bulls. The beef cattle for 1882 averaged 965 in the market and the average price was $40 per head net. The horses are good cow horses and worth about $50 per head." To learn more about the general reputation of the cattle would be useless. I will go and see for myself.

On March 14, 1883, Colonel Groom, in company with Captain James Reed, "the oldest and best experienced and by far the wealthiest man about Fort Worth," Thomas Allen, E. B. Harrold, and E. F. Ikard left Fort Worth by train and:

> entered the range occupied by Harrold & Ikard about one mile from Doan's Store in Wilbarger County. We traveled in all by horse and buggy about 200 miles and remained until satisfied that the cattle are equal to the written description given of them. There is a smaller per cent of inferior old cattle than I have seen before in a large herd, but for straight Texans amongst them, the greater part of them showing more or less improved blood, and are

---

Hereford and Durham bulls from the North and the East. The cattle were known as "Northwest cattle," and were sometimes called "Natives."

in a healthy, thrifty condition. Doubtless by searching for them we would have found more, but I saw but one dead one. The bulls are generally good looking animals, good color, many of them very good. The counties which we passed through have several ranches that have a wide reputation, but none of these compares with Harrold & Ikard's.[3] In fact taking water and grass and protection into consideration, I have never seen a better place for cattle. As to its capacity I believe the range to be amply sufficient to keep the year round over 100,000 cattle. As to the number included in the two herds I could not form an opinion. The prevailing grass is mesquite, some parts gramma. Blue Joint and Sage are abundant.

On March 26, 1883, Brown notified H. T. Groom that the examination of the herd had proved satisfactory and "The Francklyn Company have contracted for their purchase. We expect to receive title to the Texas Company very soon now." On March 27, 1883, Harrold & Ikard in consideration of the payment of $150,000, signed and agreed to a contract by which they transferred control of the Greer properties to the Francklyn Land & Cattle Company. By this arrangement the Greer range came under new management.

With the close of this deal the sum total of the Francklyn Company's cattle holdings was almost 80,000 head of mixed cattle—1,100 at Lexington, Kentucky, 1,600 on the White Deer Pasture, and an estimated 75,000 on the 50 x 75-mile spread on the Greer range.

[3] The counties the party passed through were Tarrant, Wise, Clay, Wichita, and Wilbarger, a distance of about 175 miles.

CHAPTER 6

The Francklyn Company Assumes Full Control

IN THE SPRING OF 1883 hundreds of thousands of cattle were grazing on the Greer and White Deer ranges. The severe winter blizzards had drifted thousands of cattle out of Kansas and Colorado into the valley of the South Canadian, and had swept them entirely across the Texas Panhandle ranges. The cattle on the ranges in the Indian Territory were mixed into a confused mass of herds bearing scores of different brands. Cattle were scattered everywhere.

Out of this mingling mass of herds both the Keno and the Harrold and Ikard cattle had to be gathered, counted, branded, and segregated on their home ranges. To add further to the confusion the Harrold and Ikard cattle carried fifteen different brands. Moreover, many of these cattle "had five or six large letters" burned on the left side and "there was no room for others." This roundup was a vast undertaking in which scores of stock men and cowboys, much horse flesh, and thousands of cattle were involved.

Branding 35,000 Cattle on the Open Range

Colonel Groom and Harrold and Ikard were forced to set May 1 as the day on which to begin branding on the Greer and White Deer ranges in order that it might coincide with the general roundup in the Texas Panhandle in the spring of 1883. Groom had much hasty preparation to make for readiness to commence work on the appointed day. Horses had to be purchased, more men had to be hired, branding equipment had to be secured and assembled at the branding pens on the Greer range, and corrals had to be built. Therefore, as soon as the Harrold and Ikard trade was completed Colonel Groom went to Texas to purchase horses for use in the Greer and White Deer work. After a fruitless search in the Fort Worth, Waco, and Austin areas, he went to San Antonio, where he bought 150 horses and 50 Spanish mules, which he shipped immediately to Wichita Falls. On May 1 he arrived at the Elm Fork in Greer County with his recently purchased stock. At the same time J. F. Pierce, an experienced cowman whom Groom had employed to superintend the branding, appeared at the branding pens with fifteen men ready for work. Here they met Harrold and Ikard and the branding was started as scheduled.

In making further preparations for the branding and handling of cattle Colonel Groom made Perry LeFors, who was well known on Panhandle ranges, foreman of the White Deer range. Charley Bright, who, Colonel Groom said, "was one of the most useful and one of the best men first and last I ever had about me," became general handy man. LeFors and Pierce had ten outfits under their supervision.[1]

A bookkeeping system was set up to keep count of the cattle as they were branded and counted, and also to record all financial transactions on both ranges. Harry Groom's brother-in-law, R. H. Arnold, was made bookkeeper at White Deer, where all permanent records were kept. Colonel Groom reported all expense accounts on the Greer range to Arnold, who in turn made copies of expenditures on both ranges

---

[1] An outfit usually consisted of five to seven men, fifty to seventy-five horses, a cook, a horse wrangler, and a chuck wagon.

and sent monthly reports to William F. Van Pelt, treasurer, at the New York office. Large ranching operations require much cash and a larger amount of credit. In the absence of banks in the Texas Panhandle, the Francklyn Company had to finance its ranching business through merchant and business firms located along its lines of operation. The principal firms used were Rath & Hamburg and later Dickerson Bros., in Mobeetie, Robinson Bros. & Co., in Wichita Falls, Wright & Beverly, Dodge City, Greeley Burnham & Co. and J. W. Gates & Co. in St. Louis, Gregory Cooley & Co. and R. Strahorn & Co., Commission Agents, and Armour & Co. all of Chicago.

THE ADOPTION OF BRANDS

The Harrold & Ikard cattle had so many different brands that it became necessary for the Francklyn Company, in order to distinguish its cattle from other brands, to select a brand of its own. The question of a brand came up soon after the cattle purchase was made. When Brown asked Colonel Groom to select a brand, Groom replied on July 15, 1882: "One thing I regret in regard to the brand is that one of the largest herds in this neighborhood is branded with exactly the same as ours (the Arrow brand of Wood & Snyder). Only in their case the point is upward ↑ [the Turkey Track]. We propose to set it thus ← and add the circle." Since the brands were so similar and the ranges so close together, Colonel Groom thought it best to work out a new brand.

To retain the original brand with the circle or square would make their brand subject to our power if our employees were ever disposed to do wrong, which we would avoid hiring if we knew it. But I would rather avoid all such dangers. I decidedly prefer, if Mr. Francklyn will allow it, thus ◇F, or it might be made sharper ◊F . This brand would be known and called and read "Diamond F." If liked better call and read it Circle Ⓕ or Box 🄵 . These would be decidedly my choice if Mr. Francklyn will permit it. Next to that I prefer your own initial. Either Diamond ◈ or Circle Ⓑ. I have no objection to what we had when we first met Diamond ◈ or Circle Ⓖ. But really left to me I would adopt one of the others. I rather like the reading of the Diamond. We could take anything Diamond. Diamond 4, Diamond 7, Diamond 3, or Diamond ◈ or Circle Ⓗ . This is a nice letter to make any straight lines with and is easiest to make as a rule. I have branded our horses and mules on the neck for the present with a small circle

MARKS AND BRANDS

—— OF ——

Francklyn Land and Cattle Company.

MARKS.	BRANDS.	MARKS.	BRANDS.
	X̄ on left side & hip and X on jaw.	Various	E B on left side.
	F A R on left side.	Various	L O L on left side.
	J F on left side and hip.	Various	J W C on left side.
	— F on left side and hip	Various	L O O on left side.
	F on right side, hip & shoulder.	Various	♡ on left side and D on left hip.
Various	O⌒O on left side.	Various	H 2 on left side.
	V on left side and 73 on jaw.		5 O 5 on left side.
	⊓ on left side and 73 on jaw	Various	⊓ on left side.
	W I L on left side and 73 on jaw.		◊ I H on left side.
	W L on left side and 73 on jaw and L left hip		H E S on left side & ∞ on left hip.
	H C H on right side.		R O on left side and ᴙ on left hip.
	H T H on right side.		D ◊ ◊ on left side D on left hip.
	✠ on left side and hip.	Various	H S F on left side F on left hip.
	Z on left side, hip and shoulder.	Various	J G on left side.
Various	OXM on left side, O on left jaw XM on sh'ld'r.	Various	X L on left side.
	B O L on left side.		O L O on left side G on neck.
	F̄ on left side and hip.	Various	D Y R on left side.
	W I T on left side.		◊ F on either side.
Various	OA on left side O on left jaw A on shoulder.		O⊥ₙₒ on left side.
	S U E on left side.	Various	⟨F⟩ on left side.
	B U D on left side.		
	C L E O on left side.		**AMERICAN HERD.**
	M I L T on left side.		Mark: ∞ Brand: ◊ F
Various	M O W on left side.		**ROAD BRANDS.**
Various	T O X on left side.		⊓ 7 H R 4 ⵙP
Various	X on left shoulder, side and hip.		**HORSE AND MULE BRAND.**
Various	H O L on left side.		◊ F on left hip.
Various	A L L on left side.		O⊥ₙₒ on left hip.
Various	C A L on left side.		

so as to have something in case of straying to describe them by. I do not think I have any immediate use for the brand if you have no hurry about it.

On September 8, 1882, Colonel Groom wrote Brown that he had decided to use the Diamond F brand:

I first thought of using it thus ⟨F⟩ but in this case the diamond would have to be very large to admit of an *F* that could be inside of it without blurring in branding. In addition to my own opinion I have had the opportunity to consult Goodnight, Moody, Payne, and Miller all of whom think best of putting them side by side.

The Diamond F was filed as the Company's brand in October, 1882.

Harry Groom also inquired of Brown about the brand on the White Deer range saying:

I have not branded any of our calves yet. What do you think of running this brand ⟊ and ear mark? We own it and I like it as it is so easily seen and already well known. In fact I hate very much to give up this brand as it cannot be improved. We own it as fully as we do the Diamond F. Please let me know your views as soon as possible so I can get to branding.

In reply Brown wrote Groom on July 27: "I have decided to use the Keno brand for all the Keno cattle. So brand accordingly. Also change the Diamond F brand in the paper at Panhandle to the right side. I think the horse brand ⟨F⟩ should be noted also."

When Groom arrived at the Greer range he wrote Brown on May 6, 1883:

After looking at the cattle further and seeing the large amount of branding on the left side, many of them five or six large letters and no room for others, I determined to brand on the right side which is clear except for a few small lots. When the hair grows out long it is difficult to tell one brand from another, but there being but a few cattle branded on the right side, we look at once to any brand on that side. To look at the hair grown out amongst a dozen and a half other brands, all differing from each other, would be a job of so much difficulty, misunderstanding and delay, I preferred to avoid it as far as possible by having it put as near on one point on the animals as could be, then our men will soon learn it.

Before leaving for the isolated Greer range Colonel Groom advised Brown by letter from Doan's Store, "If you should desire to make speedy communication the quickest would be to telegraph Robinson Bros. at Wichita Falls to send from there by well mounted special messenger 110 miles to us. Can easily be done on a good horse in two days, or less if very urgent by changing at Doan's."

OTHER BRANDING TROUBLES

As the branding proceeded it proved to be unsatisfactory both to the Grooms and to Harrold and Ikard. The work had scarcely begun when differences and misunderstandings arose and both parties became suspicious of each other. On May 6, 1883, Colonel Groom wrote Brown that they were:

. . . cutting out the cows that had not calved to hold them back until they do. They claim they inserted the clause which says that they are to count the calves of 1883 for that exact purpose. In this I am disappointed and have been laying out my plans to run a heavy force branding so as to escape screw worms which are troublesome all over the West during the very hot weather, especially if the season is a very wet one. I have been advised by Col. Driskill and others of long experience not to brand during the months of July and August if it can possibly be avoided owing to the worms and milling the cattle around during the very dry weather. The injury in a dry hot season could hardly be estimated.

The Spring in Greer has been dry and late. For that reason beeves will not be shipped as early as usual . . . Capt. Ikard sprung another point that I telegraphed you about. He claims the contract requires the cattle to be paid for as they are branded. Eph Harrold now claims the same. The contract says they are to be paid for at such times as the parties agree upon. The whole party has been jeered on every side about the folly of their trade until they are sensitive and nervous. They are not business but by accident came into a good thing. The cattle have more blood than I first thought and are worth more than I estimated them at, but need improved bulls throughout. The beeves are thin but well boned and thriving rapidly. The delay in shipping the beeves will be more than compensated in the growth they will make. Harry will return to White Deer as soon as I go back from Washita Indian Agency at Anadarko, I.T. and close up there as early as he can to a small force and then come down and help me out.

Groom and Harrold became more discontented with the branding with each passing day. Yet the branding had to be continued as per agreement until some new arrangement could be made. When Groom found out that his company was having to pay $22.50 for every young calf that was branded he was anxious for the work to stop. Harrold and Ikard on the other hand, profiting from the branding, pushed cattle into the branding pens as fast as possible. Groom's suggestion that branding stop on July 1 annoyed and vexed Harrold. Groom detailed the affair for Brown on June 24, 1883:

On receipt of your telegram of the day before yesterday I went at once to see Harrold about letting part of the purchase money remain unpaid which he declined very promptly and said he had already made arrangements to use the whole of it as fast as the cattle were branded . . . When I mentioned to him for the first time about stopping July 1st he showed a good deal of excitement and said he would not think of it for a moment. I told him he had suggested to you we ought to quit July 1st. He said it was true, but at the same time he says we must run two pens branding to do that. I told him I never heard running two pens mentioned until we had been branding at Salt Fork sometime. He then said firmly to make a short story, if you quit branding before July 1st you will have the biggest law suit you ever had anything to do with and under no circumstances will we consent to stop before July 15th and not then unless we are ready and would agree to nothing definitely.

On receiving your letter of June 11th directing me to stop branding July 1st, I thought it over through the night and determined, if possible, to get a permanent day fixed when we would quit branding, as the screw worms are now beginning to make some show . . . When I first mentioned the subject this morning he said he would not think of it; that they intended to go right on until the cattle were rounded up again throughout the range and they could not tell how long it would take to finish their program. I said it was Brown's understanding that we would quit July 1st as well as my own and he had told others so. He said he told no one. I asked Charley Bright and Van Zandt about it. Bright remembered distinctly he told him, but Van Zandt could not remember what he said . . .

I then said you have required us to build our own chutes, gates and fixtures to brand crippled calves and delicate ones . . . I will not receive cattle from you any longer than July 5th, five days longer than we first agreed on. He said I will not do it. Then he said give us a draft for what are not settled for, then you can quit taking if you like. We will bring the cattle whether you take them or not. I said no . . . All I wanted was what had heretofore been agreed upon and understood carried out and that my instructions were to quit July 1st and with his notice already given that he would have a law suit. I shall give no draft further, but refer you to Brown and Francklyn to adjust the matter. They have rights as well as yourself and in their absence I shall protect their interests to the best of my ability, and you know to hammer these cattle and calves around through the hot sun the loss will be terrific. He said he knew there would be many lost but that could not be helped. I said very well you can take your course. I shall never consent to messing up a business after what has occurred stopping or not as you like I will do what I said and no more . . . Then he quieted down and said, I prefer to get along without difficulty. I will go and see the others, meaning his brothers. He returned shortly and consented to quit July 5th, which I consider better than having the matter at loose ends.

Money—and Other—Problems

Several things occurred during the branding season of 1883 to cause delay and the addition of extra expense to the already rapidly increasing debt of the Company. Money was getting tighter and harder to get, and interest rates were climbing higher. With insufficient funds to make payments on cattle notes and with interest coming due, Brown and Groom made an effort to extend part of the payments. Brown sent these instructions to Colonel B. B. Groom on June 11:

I want you to do your best with Harrold to consent to leave a portion of the purchase on time as much as he will, or at least until we can place our securities. We started out you will remember upon basis of 25,000 head and had so arranged our financial matters when the purchase was made. Nothing further was done as Francklyn sailed for this country at once. Upon his arrival I went to Texas and now of course we must know where we stand and make our plans accordingly.

As money matters tightened both parties watched the movements of the other closely. Francklyn's Horn and Bassick mines were facing a financial crisis at this time. In order to keep the mines in operation, Francklyn directed Gregory & Cooley to forward payments on cattle sales to New York instead of sending the proceeds, as per agreement, to R. Strahorn & Company. Harrold made a strong protest against this practice and demanded that the proceeds be sent direct to R. Strahorn as provided for in the agreement. Added to this was Harrold and Ikard's growing discontent with the cattle deal, based on actual count rather than on the customary range delivery, and their irritation at

Colonel Groom's close supervision. Colonel Groom, in commenting on the dissatisfaction of Harrold Bros. in a letter of June 24, 1883, to F. G. Brown, said:

I have watched every movement very closely and turned every branded one [back], watched their roundups, which have been absolutely necessary, and I know they feel they rather have some one else who did not watch as closely as I have. I have been compelled to bring them to the scratch about which I will tell you when I see you, as it would take a volume to write all that has entered into this transaction.

Under these circumstances harmonious relations between Colonel Groom and Harrold were impossible. If the branding was to be continued some other arrangement was inevitable. The new agreement, ending partnership branding, was really a compromise in that Francklyn purchased the remaining remnant of cattle on the Greer range at an estimated 22,000 head, range delivery, rather than by actual count, the method used up to this time. Harrold & Ikard on the other hand actually extended credit to the Francklyn Company by postponing payments on the cattle.

A rather unusual situation had developed as a result of this transaction. Both parties were seeking the same thing—financial security. To Harrold and Ikard financial security meant continued and immediate sale of cattle on a large scale, while to the Francklyn Company it meant extended credit and time to find enough cattle on the Greer range to satisfy the estimated 22,000 head, and at the same time to establish a ranch that would feed thousands of cattle into the markets and finally pay off all notes.

After the branding was stopped in July Harry and Colonel Groom spent the following two or three months in making hasty preparation for the fall work. Harry Groom, having completed the exterior fence lines at White Deer, was busily engaged in gathering the Keno cattle, branding the calves and driving them into the White Deer Pasture, building cross fences, and selecting cows for the market. He was also putting up hay for the winter supply, gathering feed crops, further developing water facilities on the range, and doing much other work that would give permanence and stability to the White Deer Ranch.

The Francklyn Company Assumes Full Control

In Greer Colonel Groom was searching for horses and men preparatory to sending more cattle to market, selecting cows to be sent to White Deer, looking after screwworms, branding calves, and correlating the drives from both ranches. Heavy intermittent rains, beginning to fall in July, continued until October, when they reached flood proportions. At times these downpours stopped all work on the range and greatly hampered and delayed Groom's program. In letters to Brown dated October 18 and October 24, 1883, he gave an excellent weather report for the month of October, explaining its effects on his work on the range. On October 18 he said:

It has been raining every day for more than a week but night before last capped all. It rained all night and yesterday morning the Elm was out of its banks the valley almost three feet under water. The night before I went to Haystack to round up the next day, where we could take but little baggage, the country being so rough. During the night the weather changed from seeming fair to a sudden hard rain which ran under our beds and completely saturated every stitch of clothing and we had to travel wet as we were fifteen miles from camp. I have been wet almost every day for a week. It looks this evening as though it may be fair for a few days, I hope for many. The ground where level is covered with water and out on the level plain many places a horse cannot carry a man out as the ground is so boggy. The last ten days have been fearful on our horses and teams, the ground being so soft. We are afraid to stop for the weather is liable to turn so cold that we cannot work on the open plains and then it would be intensely hard on the cattle . . . Owing to the rain we are more backward than I had hoped to be.

On October 24, 1883, he again reported to Brown:

We have had terrific rains. Had as hard rain last night as I ever saw fall and the ground is everywhere so full of water as to make it impossible for men or teams to move. Horses actually often mire down on the open prairie and our pens seem bottomless. We will be compelled to brand on the open range hereafter altogether . . . There is great danger with the wet weather and lateness of the season. We may have to suspend at almost any time. The men have been almost constantly wet for two weeks. Then the extreme wet has been such as to make pens, plains, and everywhere boggy. Our waggons have been gone to Doan's for over two weeks. Can't get back over the river [Pease] on account of quicksand. I am sorry Doan has suspended. I have not been able to hear whether permanently or not. We are now in an intense cold norther. After it has passed I hope for better weather. Men will hardly leave the fire at all.

Land Bargains—with Water

While the Francklyn Company was trying desperately to meet its financial obligations, Harry Groom was encountering much difficulty in completing the fence on the south line of the White Deer range in Block B-2. This block contained 81,920 acres of alternate school sections which had been set aside for actual settlers by legislative act in 1883. In attempts to evade the law much fraud and chicanery was practiced in making files on this land. As a result the Land Board refused to accept further applications for filing until after the Legislature met in special session in January, 1884. Groom's greatest problem was to place exterior fence lines on the correct land boundary without enclosing lands already filed on. Therefore, the only way left for him to make boundary adjustments was to purchase the claims of others. This Groom was anxious to do in order to acquire some very desirable watered grass lands. Despite the financial crisis the Company was in, he determined to secure these lands if possible. Therefore, he submitted several bargains in land and cattle located mainly along the Company's south boundary line, which he urged Francklyn to buy. On June 11, 1884, he reminded Brown of having met Mr. Barton, and added:

He has an offer for his lands etc which consists of the following: One patented section of land fine timber and fine water laying adjoining our land at the Southeast corner. There is $2500 worth of wood on this tract, 253 acres of land adjoining this to which he holds bond for title. On these is five and one-half miles of 3-strand wire fence on cedar posts, a good house with one store room and one frame room, a large corral put up with cedar posts, a fine well at the house probably thirty feet deep. Two sections of land on which they have improvements laying six miles inside of our fence in Block B-2, one on the South McClelland Creek on which there is living water in quantities sufficient to take all grass in reach. These two sections they propose to secure to us by remaining on them until they make the first payment and turn them over to us. We are to pay the amount of the first payment to them. On these two sections they have about $600 or $700 worth of improvements. They will take up as much more of the school land as they can, by our paying the money out. They have 256 head of horses, not counting 80 colts, pair of large mules, wagon and harness, three plows, harrow, 8 x 10 wall tent, lot of small tools, grindstone, three spades, five axes, saws, chisels, pick, camp outfit, etc. About 75 cords of wood worth $3.00 per cord on the ground now cut and corded. They are to turn over the horses so they can be branded in our brand.

For this property they ask $15,750, and if we do not buy it, Houston has made them this offer and he gets the property in ten days. I have only till the 21st to answer them. The two watering places are valuable to us. The horses are located. This is something. The crop of colts is an extra item. If we see fit to do so, we could cut $2500 worth of wood on the land. I lay all this before you. The water is what I am most anxious about, and in this deal we could get fine water at two points six miles apart and could keep it from falling into Houston's hands, who will if he gets this water try very hard to hold a heavy foothold on Block B-2. If you are inclined to buy this property let me hear from you by wire at once, as on the 21st they must know and will hold it no longer. You said something about having a small bunch of horses when you were here. This would make a good start for us to get mares sufficient to raise all our own horses.

Brown wired Groom on June 16: "We do not desire to purchase Barton section and horses now. We cannot buy anything at once." Undaunted in his zeal for land and cattle bargains Groom wrote Brown on June 20:

Do you think we had best acquire the school lands in Block B-2? If we do not buy them we may be forced to pay the lease of four cents per acre as we have them fenced. Should you be inclined to buy them, I can get several powers of attorney from our men here to take up seven sections for each of them. If we had these lands we could keep every jumper[2] out of them. As it is, any of the small men can go in and brand some of our cattle along with theirs. What will you do with the leased land east of Mobeetie that was acquired with the Harrold & Ikard cattle together with the files they have? If we could get these through and hold our lease for six or eight years it would make us, as Eaton and Goodnight both say, the finest beef range in the country for fattening cattle rapidly in early summer.

I saw Goodnight [at Mobeetie] just before I went out to the ranch. He

---

[2] One who settled on land filed on by others and claimed the owner was not complying with the law as to residence requirements.

gave me the price of the Quiti Qua Ranch and cattle. I sent it to you knowing you would like to have it. There is a total under fence of 300,000 acres. Of this they have leased 70,000 and they own 100,000. They have in cattle 18,000 and in horses and mules 76 with about 55 miles of 4-wire fence of Glidden wire. The horses he will retain at $75 each. Will take $950,000 to buy it. This is a first pass. I think they would mark down quite a lot if business was talked. He was very cordial and asked me to come to see him; that it had cost him years and thousands of dollars to learn some very simple little things which he would present me free. I will visit him as soon as I have some leisure . . .

Since writing the above Munson T Case of the Case Cattle Company came in and desired me to take a note of his cattle he was desiring to sell. . . . If you do not want to go into it I can place it, as this in my opinion is a great bargain. The cattle he offers are *good* and all his young cattle and this spring's calves by good bulls and now located. The best feature is the lease which he holds, paying Carhart $1 per head for pasturage per year, and controlling the range as it were. To pay school lease allowing ten acres per head, makes the grazing cost 40 cents per head. Add to this the fencing and keeping up the fence which Carhart has to do and you will see it is very cheap. We could put in ten or ten thousand just as we want. They have between 700 and 800 in the pasture now, and if we do not pasture 925 they are deducted. They claim we will gather over 1000 head of cattle and have 24 horses . . . worth a total at present of $24,325, with 75 cattle running on the range we will more than likely gather at $25, $1875 or a total of $26,200. In addition to the range which is *well* watered and adjoining our pasture on the south. I want you to look closely into this. I want no interest outside our company, but if I was wanting a good range for cattle and had this chance I would go right if I were not in the Company, as I consider this a big thing. If you do not want it for the Company let me take it and graze what cattle the men who are working want to let them have some place to put a few cattle to get them satisfied to stay and save their money. Our Company needs this chance on account of water provided you and Mr. Francklyn can see it from the same standpoint I do, but what you say about it is law and gospel to me.

Eaton and several men who know of Carharts both say he is out of luck making such a trade. I send you a sketch of about the location. It may not be *just correct* but very nearly so. You might correspond with Munson T. Case at Green Bay, Wisconsin. He allows me only time to hear from you about it. He is anxious to sell and were you here you would say it is a great bargain. Carhart offers him $27.50 for his cattle, range delivery, with no guarantee,

The Francklyn Company Assumes Full Control

but Carhart wants long time which does not suit Case. They are New Yorkers and interested in a railroad from Green Bay to Winona and St. Paul. I believe their father is General Manager or something of the kind. . . . Since the above Messrs. Case have been to see me again. They tryed to get the turning over of the lease made by Carhart with them left out of the trade or consideration in other words. I told them no. They have put it in once and it must so remain this after they have given me the documents I enclose you. They seem to think Carhart will not like it in them disposing of the lease. The truth of the matter is Carhart leased the land too low and would like to get out of the trade. The sketch I enclose you is not correct in one point. It should have Houston's block right up to ours taking in all the land as shown on Evan's map and lying between the Rockwall County School lands, or Houston's, on the east and Sacra & Richards on the west. All the creeks as laid down have water where they are shown to exist and dry creek beds are not drawn.

It requires no stretch of the imagination to know that Francklyn and Brown would have been glad to have any one or all of these so-called bargains, but they were in financial straits and were compelled to attend to matters more immediately pressing.

Since Harrold had refused to extend payments soon coming due, and since debts were rapidly rising, it behooved Francklyn and Brown to seek credit elsewhere. Therefore they attempted to attract Eastern and British capital to the enterprise. Brown had been in touch with George F. Damon of New York since June 11, 1883, when he wrote B. B. Groom:

We are figuring with Damon on the Wheeler County lands upon basis of his taking some of the Greer cattle from us. He seems inclined to do something and wants 9000 head of mixed cattle ages one to three. Put your prices on these cattle and let me hear from you about it as soon as possible. Damon will go to Texas soon and said he would go to Mobeetie. If we cannot settle this with Harrold we shall have to sell some cattle and reduce our holdings . . . We have decided to put the balance of Harrold & Ikard Cattle and Greer range into a separate Company, and when we are ready, move the Diamond F cattle already branded to the fenced range and concentrate the Francklyn Land & Cattle there with 25,000 or 30,000 cattle when you are ready to take them. We do this for various reasons.

On June 16, 1883, Brown notified H. T. Groom at White Deer:

"Damon goes out to look at the Greer range and cattle with a view of joining us. He knows your father. Show him as much attention as you can." Harry assured Brown that he would "meet Damon and go with him to Greer and carry him through as comfortable as possible and show him all that is to be seen in Greer County." Brown wired Damon at Chicago: "Have secured lower berth stateroom no. 33 upper deck on service July 10th. Your letter 16th received and satisfactory."

Brown himself made a trip to Texas in May, 1883, to examine the Texas properties. "I was pleased with the country I saw," he wrote to R. B. Edmunson on June 14, 1883, after returning to New York, "and think it offers inducements for cattle raising." In June, Ferdinand Van Zandt, representing Lord Rosebery, visited both the Greer and White Deer ranges, "to examine cattle and lands for English money." On July 12 Van Zandt wrote Brown from Huselby House in Mobeetie:

> I rode up through Greer after visiting Elm and Salt Fork camps. I have crisscrossed throughout the range and seen the whole thing pretty thoroughly. It is a magnificent tract, well watered and grassed. I saw nearly all the cattle that have been branded and there are very few scrubs among them. Damon no doubt told you of my having met him at Salt Fork and told you as requested what my movements would be.

J. A. Balfour, representing the Balfour family that had invested heavily in cattle bonds, also visited White Deer in July, 1883. In the following September Francklyn came to Texas, "To see the range and cattle and decide whether the balance of cattle by count or range delivery." When the branding season ended in July, 1883, 35,333 head of cattle displayed the Diamond F brand. The 1883 spring branding ended also the partner relationship between Harrold and Ikard and the Francklyn Company. Francklyn informed Groom from Fort Worth, October 4, 1883:

> I have this day settled up matters with Harrold & Ikard by receiving from them a bill of sale of all their cattle, brands, ranch rights etc for the sum of $1,289,992.50. I have given them notes as follows: To Harrold & Ikard next October 9th (1884) secured by deed of trust on cattle, M. B. Loyd Trustee, $295,000. I have also given notes at 6 per cent Harrold Bros., $150,000 with an agreement to deposit with R. Strahorn & Co. the proceeds of sale

The Francklyn Company Assumes Full Control

of beeves sufficient to meet these notes. I have drawn on the Francklyn Company for $781.34 for supplies as turned over to us as per enclosed receipts. Our shipments of cattle are divided between R. Strahorn & Co. and Gregory Cooley & Co. I shall send the bill of sale to Mobeetie to be recorded and returned to New York. Copies of the others I will bring with me. The Wheeler County land I have simply taken an order from Harrold & Ikard requesting Lindsay to exercise his power of attorney and transfer three-fourths interest in land and lease to the Francklyn Land & Cattle Company.[3]

The remaining cattle on the Greer range were put at 22,000 head. In October, 1883, the Farmers Loan and Trust of New York endorsed the New York Company's land notes without recourse, and the Francklyn Company took over complete control of its Texas properties.

[3] Lindsay refused to make this transfer on the ground that Harrold had not kept up payment of his part of the taxes on the school lands and, therefore, had no claim to this property. After requesting Lindsay two or three times to make this transfer, Van Pelt wrote Harrold: "In view of the fact that Lindsay declines to make the transfer of your interest in the Wheeler lease and school lands, we would request that you would return to us the amount of $11,638.13 already paid you in advance on account of said lands and we will cancel whatever rights we may have to said lands under our contract with you, the more particularly as we are not desirous of holding any lands jointly with Lindsay." Harrold repaid the money and the Francklyn Company gave up its claim to the Wheeler lands.

CHAPTER 7

Colonel Groom Experiments with Cattle on the Texas Plains

STOCKING THE WHITE DEER RANGE proved to be a long-drawn-out process and a difficult problem. On September 15, 1883, branding operations, which had been stopped on July 5, were resumed. An inventory of the assets and liabilities of the Francklyn Company made in September showed that it had on White Deer and adjoining ranges about 1,600 head of Keno 0̶ℕ̶O̶¹ cattle with most of the calves yet unbranded, and about 100 young Shorthorns that had been brought from Kentucky in December, 1882, including sixteen head of Polled Angus cattle imported from England. At Lexington, Kentucky, the Company had about 1,200 head of Shorthorn bulls waiting to be shipped to White Deer. Because of the lateness of the season when the cattle were started to White Deer, they were left at Wichita, Kansas, during the winter of 1883 under the care of W. B. Kidd, an experienced cattle buyer and feeder. On the Greer range and on the road to market were 35,000 Diamond F cattle,

Colonel Groom Experiments with Cattle 89

plus an additional 22,000 head yet to be branded and counted on the Greer County range. On the White Deer and the Greer ranges together were about 600 horses and mules. The Company had employed, all together, some eighty-five men.

As to liabilities, the Francklyn Company owed Harrold & Ikard $295,000, due October 5, 1884, and an additional $150,000, due on the cattle, both bearing 6-per-cent interest per annum until paid. The Company also held $750,000 worth of the New York & Texas Land Company's land notes carrying 6-per-cent-interest coupons payable semiannually, all these liabilities making a total debt of more than a million dollars. The Company had its cattle scattered from Kansas to the Greer County range and had not yet decided upon a plan of operation. Brown reminded Colonel Groom, September 20, 1882:

> You remember we have never decided on a plan of operation regarding the cattle part of the business before you left here. As we understand it you were to go ahead with the fence, house etc and buy some Short Horns. The cattle part was left until you had fully decided upon proper basis to go ahead after thoroughly overhauling everything upon your arrival there. You have made your arrangements and bought some Short Horns. The question now comes up what is to be done regarding cattle? You had several plans in view before you left. You talked about buying Southern Texas cattle as one plan; of buying cattle in the Southern States as another, and buying cattle in the Panhandle and North as another. Which have you decided on as the proper one to start in on? Also to what extent is it to our interest to stock this Fall? Are not cattle higher now than they are likely to be later on? Is it going to pay us to stock at present high prices? How are prices now for various ages in the Panhandle compared to last Fall? We must have full information on these points before you can expect Francklyn to pay out hundreds of thousands of dollars. Have you decided upon a brand yet? How have you bought your wire, posts, cattle, horses etc? In whose name?

Moreover, with the acquisition of the New York & Texas Company's land notes, the Francklyn Company was for the first time on its own. This made necessary a reorganization of the ranch administration. As a first step in reorganization the Panhandle Cattle Company was organized in June, 1883. This company was formed for the purpose of siphoning off cattle from under the control of Harrold &

Ikard in order to form an independent company from which to stock the White Deer range, and, at the same time, to supply sufficient beef to pay off all the Harrold & Ikard notes.

Brown also began to check closely on the number of cattle on both the Greer and the White Deer ranges. On July 9, 1883, he questioned Harry Groom about the number of cattle and about his handling of matters on the White Deer range:

> I do not understand why the general roundups this Spring did not bring in the cattle as usual. Judging from your letter I infer you have branded but few Keno calves and have found but few Keno Cattle to put inside the fence. Please give me information on this. We desire to send off the Keno beeves this Fall, or when the proper time comes, so make your plans accordingly. We shall require all the money we can get this year and may conclude to send off 3-year-old steers, although my preference is to ship only 4's and upwards.
>
> I do not feel entirely safe regarding our Greer cattle. I sometimes think they will get away from us by reason of our not being around and guarding them: also that Harrold is holding back his steers and two's which he could easily do. If we have not a sufficiently regular range cowboy at Diamond F and Greer, see to it that we get one at once. We must not start out with all new hands else we will get left. I enclose you a list of Greer cattle as branded which comprises all the Francklyn Land & Cattle Company will take.

As a result of the 1883 spring branding it became evident that some changes in the personnel among the top hands were necessary on both the Greer and the White Deer ranges. During this time many rumors of cattle theft, illegal branding, and other irregularities were reported from the various ranges. At Clarendon Colonel Goodnight, as foreman of a jury made up largely of cattlemen, indicted six or eight men for stealing cattle. Henry Creswell, of the Prairie Cattle Company, "raised old Ned" with J. M. Coburn of the Hansford Land & Cattle Company for allowing his men to put his brand on fifty head of Creswell's cattle. At this time there was also much dissension and suspicion among the top hands on both the Greer and the White Deer ranges. J. F. Pierce, whom Francklyn employed as boss on the Greer range, clashed with Colonel Groom on range procedure, and Groom asked Brown to fire him, because "he was not a systematic business man." However, on June 15, 1883, Colonel Groom notified Brown that:

> Pierce and his particular party quit this morning for reasons that I will explain in my next. . . . He understands many matters with cattle very well but was a very cross, restless, sensitive man and could not be told to change anything. He is bitter toward the Indians and I fear would not get along with them. We will have no trouble to get along nicely. His having raised the price of labor, the coming month will cost us $40 per month. Hot as it is we cannot do better now. Since he left we have the work well done and with about five hands less do more work daily much more pleasantly. There has been some crookedness around this neighborhood in cattle branding but not on a large scale. Some of our best friends advise me to obtain new men out and out.

With reorganization, the Francklyn Company stressed economy, efficiency, and honesty. In line with this policy, Brown wrote Harry Groom, July 30, 1883:

> We now have a great deal of money in cattle and they must be looked after closely. To do this takes experienced and reliable men. You must see that you do not employ too many men strangers to this cattle business and Texas ways. Please investigate Willingham fully whom you suggest as Superintendent at Greer and let me know about him as to whether he has outside interests that would conflict with us. I want an A-1 man on Greer and a Texas man or an Indian Territory man. For cattle business you must have men around you experienced in this line. In the future employ only good, reliable men.

Harry Groom was having considerable difficulties also on the White Deer range—gathering, branding, and counting Keno cattle—as well as making much needed improvements at White Deer. As a result of Brown's complaints about the reported shortage of cattle in the White Deer Pasture, Harry Groom, on August 4, 1883, wrote Brown a lengthy letter giving him a detailed description of conditions in the White Deer Pasture, as well as range conditions in general. Harry's report was rather optimistic. He estimated that from 950 to 1,100 Keno cattle had already been thrown back into the White Deer Pasture, and that others were being gathered on widely scattered ranges as fast as conditions would permit. At the same time he attempted to explain the reasons for the shortage of Keno cattle.

With reference to the cattle program in general at White Deer he inquired of Brown:

What disposition will Mr. Francklyn make of the Polled Angus cattle? Will he allow me to secure from Kentucky or Missouri enough high grade heifers to start a small Polled Angus herd with? The Short Horns here will soon come to the front and make profitable investment for us. I am not discouraged by any means with the past bad luck with them since I have them here now about acclimated and fattening rapidly with thirty head of beautiful red calves about half and half as to sex and the best thirty calves in the State of Texas.

Harry Groom, however, was having trouble with his top hands on the White Deer range. In the same letter to Brown of August 4 he complained that:

I do not like the boss I have (Lovell). He is not a man of capacity to handle any number of men. I am on the eve of making some changes among them from the fact that some have been doing crooked work. I will secure a man who has been working for Bugbee and Nelson. He is a No. 1 man and knows how to handle both men and cattle, having served fourteen years at the business.

On August 20, 1883, Harry Groom again wrote Brown:

In cattle matters I caused quite a racket among our men by making a change from Lovell to LeFors. Lovell came down and asked me who would drive the beeves if we cut them out. I replied Mr. LeFors. He said nothing but he was mad and did not put the cattle together hoping to throw the gathering on LeFors. This is why I had only half the cattle in the roundup. As soon as LeFors gets the fence done will round up the cattle and brand the calves and throw them all south on the flats.

Lovell this Spring had about $800 and asked me if I would allow him to hold some cattle, I told him yes. He bought thirty-five head and the pasture understanding was to brand only the produce of the cows. I found he was buying what is called "Sleepers," that is he would put any brand not used on a maverick [a calf with a different brand from that of its mother], and when the roundup came if no one claimed it he got it. If it was claimed he lost nothing. I told Lovell he must quit work or sell his

Colonel Groom Experiments with Cattle

cattle. He sold his cattle. LeFors has about 250 cattle he wants us to buy all counted out to us at $25 per head. They are well graded cattle, as good as Goodnight's or Creswell's. Let me hear from you.

In reply to Brown's request to investigate Cape Willingham, Harry Groom wrote him on July 21, 1883,

I have had opportunity to secure Mr. Willingham whom Messrs Goodnight and Creswell say is the best man in the Panhandle. He was sheriff of Oldham County last year and prior to that he was one of Goodnight's leading men. He is quick and is not afraid of anything, a settled man with a wife and four children whom he wants to take to Greer with him if he goes.

On August 21, 1883, Brown wrote Harry Groom at Mobeetie:

I'm in receipt of your favors of 6th and 14th. I wired you today to engage Willingham if he was not the kind of man to get us in trouble with the Indians—also stating that we could not allow him to run a herd with ours. We shall start branding again about September 15th. . . . Have Willingham report to B. B. Groom on Greer range at that time unless he sends for him to meet him at San Antonio to help him get some horses. You remember we discussed the question of allowing the men and horses to run their own herds with us and I was absolutely opposed to it and we so decided that point.

Willingham, however, went with Creswell under the same offer that Groom had made him, and Colonel Groom hired George Cranmer, Harrold's former boss. Harry Groom was also in need of a good man to supervise the driving of the cattle from the Greer range to the White Deer Pasture and to select cattle for the northern markets. On August 22, 1883, he informed Brown:

I have a very fine man in LeFors. He just puts things right through and he waltzes the boys around to lively music. There has been a lot of dirty work in branding the cattle this season and I have had to contend with some of it, but now I have a very different atmosphere around me.

In making further changes in the personnel of the Francklyn Company, Colonel Groom employed Captain John Knight, an experienced cattleman, to superintend the shipping of beeves selected from the September branding on the Greer range. Knight hired and paid his own men. His job was to deliver the cattle off the Greer range to Wichita

Falls as they were selected for the market. Half of each drove so delivered was received by L. B. Collins, agent for R. Strahorn & Co.; the other half by S. S. Maddox, agent for Gregory & Cooley. The cattle were then sent forward to the Chicago markets by the respective company's regular shippers. H. T. Garnett was sent to Greer in September to take charge of the store and supplies, and to assist in the counting. "I do not desire Van Zandt to do that work again, as I am not satisfied with his movements while there on the first branding," Brown wrote Groom on August 21, 1883.

With Colonel B. B. Groom as general manager of both ranges, and with George Cranmer as boss of the Greer range, assisted by Charley Bright, the reorganization of the ranch personnel was completed.

After the Panhandle Cattle Company was organized it became necessary also to revise the Francklyn Company's plan of operation. The success of the Company, as well as that of the whole enterprise, depended largely on finding enough cattle on the Greer range to satisfy the estimated 22,000 head. Cattle were now the only collateral the Francklyn Company had with which to secure its credit and pay off its notes. Therefore Brown advised Harry Groom, who was still interested in more land and cattle bargains for the Company, that:

> You have all the work you can do now before you and unless this business is thoroughly attended to at your end of the line we cannot make a success of it. We prefer that you have nothing else before you but the affairs of the Francklyn Land and Cattle Company until we have placed it upon a successfully lasting basis.

By way of explanation to Brown about the failure to get more cattle for the White Deer Pasture, Harry said, in his letter of August 4, that he had tried to keep his men at work on the outside as much as possible while the surrounding ranches were gathering their cattle:

> Most of them have now knocked off for the purpose of resting up horses and in this time we will brand up and tally out and drive the beef. I am reducing the force as rapidly as possible. . . . Lovell is now rounding up the cattle and will have all in the pasture thrown together in a few days. Then I can send you an accurate tally of the Keno cattle in a few days. We have now about 1100 in the pasture. I will cut out all the beef suitable for market and send them to Dodge.

The Francklyn Company's cattle were separated into three widely separated herds in 1883. The Shorthorns were in Wichita, Kansas, where they remained during the severe winter of 1882–1883 under the care of W. B. Kidd; the Keno cattle were scattered from the Canadian River to the Wichita Falls country; and the remainder were still grazing on the Greer range and vicinity. The Company decided to consolidate the herds as closely as possible and to concentrate on the White Deer range.

As a first step in this direction the Shorthorns were removed to White Deer in June, 1883. With this removal Colonel Groom began a new experiment in cattle raising on the Texas plains by crossing Shorthorns and Polled Angus bulls with the so-called "Northwest," or "native," cattle.[1] At the very beginning the experiment was endangered by the problem of Texas fever, which resulted from drives of Gulf Coast cattle along the Texas trail passing through the Texas Panhandle and Northwest Texas on their way to the northern markets. It was generally believed that the fever was transmitted by the grazing of Coast cattle on the ranges of the Texas plains. For several years, however, this was a moot question upon which cattlemen all over the country were divided. As a result the state Legislature of Kansas passed in 1884 a quarantine law which forbade Texas cattle from entering Kansas. The Colorado Legislature soon passed a similar law.

Colonel Groom, who was anxious to begin driving cattle to the northern markets, did not believe that the quarantine law was the solution of the problem of Texas fever. He maintained that the fever was the result of climatic conditions. In a letter to Francklyn written January 3, 1883, he analyzed the situation as follows:

As to Texas fever we are entirely exempt from it except as it is brought

[1] During the period from 1876 to 1883 many cattlemen in the Southwest had greatly improved their South Texas herds by crossing them with blooded stock largely from Kentucky and Missouri. The spread of the Texas fever during the trail days in the 1880's resulted in the passage of a quarantine law by the legislature of the state of Kansas which fixed the dividing line between Southern or Texas Coast cattle and the Northern herds at the parallel of 36° 30' north latitude. As a result all cattle between the parallel of 36° 30' and the southern Kansas line were called "Northwest," or "Natives," in order to distinguish them from the lower grades of South Texas cattle. This law, soon followed by a similar one passed by the Colorado legislature, greatly hindered the shipping of Texas Coast cattle to the northern markets.

to us from other countries bordering on the Gulf Coast, by cattle from that locality. It is not because they are Texas cattle that this disease is imported by them, but entirely owing to the section of country from which they come. Acclimated Short Horns driven from the Gulf would as fully inoculate northern cattle as would the Long Horn Spanish in Texas, and it is a singular fact that those that carry the malady are in perfect condition themselves and they must come in contact to communicate the disease. It is not because they are Short Horns or any other breed that cattle die from this disease. It would be just as fatal among pure acclimated Texans taken from the North to the South as it is to Short Horns. Cattle in all the countries in the world lose their health and vigor by going south. Cattle driven from the South increase in health and vigor in every country as they go north. I know from costly experience that cattle driven from Kentucky into Tennessee have a fever—into Mississippi they begin to die, and at New Orleans half die; at Vera Cruz they nearly all die.

After one year's experience with Texas cattle Colonel Groom became convinced of their value as range stock. He suggested to Brown in October, 1883: "We ought to stop our bull purchase and if these do well go in that direction another year. . . . I have selected quite a sprinkle of good calves from the Greer herd and have a plan which I will lay before you by which we can produce all we want in the future out of the Greer herd."

Colonel Groom was not only interested in the source of cattle, but also concerned about the quality of stock he secured for White Deer, and a cheaper price for such cattle. He was much impressed with the so-called "Northwest" cattle in the Texas Panhandle. On October 18, 1883, he presented his plan to Brown in a letter written from Greer:

I wish almost the Polled Angus bulls were in cash. I am convinced more and more every day the Hereford is the one for the plains. They seem to completely remodel the Texas type. Even one-sixteenth shows plainly. I believe our true plan to be to select about 500 of the best cows we have and put them with thirty pure Hereford bulls. In that way eighty per cent to have calves we would have 200 half breed Herefords out of excellent cows which ought to produce, if we get 5,000 cows for White Deer out of the Greer herd, 2,000 bull calves and 2,000 heifers. These bulls would suit to put in the herd down here. With this plan we ought to sell our yearlings to feeders and put in their places breeding cattle. The bulls bought in Kentucky will be sufficient until this can be done. The Kentucky bulls will pay a good profit on their cost for beef if they do well and at the same time greatly improve the herd. I know of no cheaper way to raise our values than the above. Our steers will then bring as easily $60 per head at three years as they do now $30.

Since the fall roundup of 1883 was near at hand, it became necessary to make some definite plans as to what should be done with the cattle gathered on the Greer range: whether or not some should be sent to White Deer; and what kinds of cattle, if any, should be sent to market. On August 13, 1883, E. B. Harrold inquired of Brown if they were going to "cut out any beef this Fall. If you are they are going to commence the general roundup September 10th and this would be a good time to cut out a herd or two. If you are going to take out any let me know so I can make my plans accordingly." Brown sent this letter to Colonel Groom, who returned it with the advice that "You had better reply as you know better what you want done," and adding: "I hope you will not fail to let me hear from you fully how I had best proceed. I will have the men ready to begin branding September 15th and find out about the beeves. All the rest I must learn from you."

Harry Groom also requested Brown on August 20 to "please let me know where we will stock up from as soon as you know," and expressed the hope of hearing "fully in a few days about future movements concerning cattle and land." Brown replied by wire on September 6: "Have wired Francklyn. The understanding is to ship the beeves and continue Diamond F brand at White Deer."

In preparation for the roundups on the Greer and White Deer ranges both Grooms called for more horses. Colonel Groom wrote Brown, August 24, 1883, that in the interest of economy:

I think we will buy only half the horses Harrold says are actually necessary. He used last year near 600. I think we will go through with 250. I expect to feed grain. He used little grain. The advantage will be in having less invested in horses, fewer to watch from straying, which they are liable to do where we are now located. The price of grain cannot be high next year. . . .

The horse question is one of great difficulty in this country. The distance the grain has to be halled, and the cost of it altogether makes it a difficult problem. The experience of those who have handled cattle here is that the common Texas horses do the work cheapest. I have looked at horses at Wichita Falls and Fort Worth and know that Merrill's were cheaper and better than Harrold's or Ikard's. It must be remembered also that as we are now working it takes not only a host of horses but of men also. For instance when this lot starts tomorrow there will be three beef outfits on the road, ten men to each, and a boss and team to hall supplies. This is the least any drive beeves with. They not only have to drive during the day, but must guard them during the night. While they are gone another outfit must hold the beeves as they are gathered for the next drive. The cows for White Deer must have an outfit ready to start now, another must be ready to recruit the next lot of them. To gather the cattle on the range requires two outfits and one to bring them to the pens. So you see this is a big force equal to ten outfits. I cannot see how to do it with less and get the work done. It takes sixteen days to go down to Greer and back if not detained by high water.

Harry Groom, in a letter to F. G. Brown from Mobeetie, August 4, 1883, estimated that it would require about forty head of horses to move the beeves and to keep the fence riders mounted on White Deer. "For this I will use some of the small mules and the tail end of the cow ponies, keeping the rest for cattle."

On September 16, 1883, Colonel Groom drew on the Company for $5,500 to "buy horses for the ranch, wages and supplies, and outfits for three sets of beef men. I do hate to draw for money and expenses, but fifty men must have supplies."

Under the new setup things moved along much better. On July 31, 1883, Colonel Groom wired Francklyn that 40,000 had been remitted to Harrold and added, "More in a few days. Cattle moving to points of delivery." He reported to Brown from Salt Fork, September 20, 1883:

Under the new arrangement we have sent to market 882 beeves, three train loads which will be in Wichita Falls about today. 1744 calves have been branded and 400 cows cut out for White Deer. . . . It is my purpose to send up there 5,000 of the very best cows from which we can hereafter draw all the bulls we need and the cows will soon increase sufficiently to become the foundation of the entire herd. Of course it will take awhile to get the new arrangement under way.

By the twelfth of October, 1,446 cows and heifers had been sent to

White Deer and 4,969 calves had been branded; Groom estimated that they would be able to brand from 1,000 to 1,500 more, which he claimed, "will be almost conclusive proof that we get over 22,000 head by the late trade."

In his last report for the year, made November 3, 1883, Colonel Groom stated:

Up to this date 6782 beeves have been started, 6777 calves have been branded, and now ready 1,000 more blooded cattle, making 1,330 in all for White Deer. Cannot send any more this winter owing to the immense rainfall. The number of cattle will exceed our purchase at least 1,000 head. We will be compelled to go into winter quarters very soon. I have closed up our bills for wages up to November 20th, and for supplies up to about March 1st, and have drawn on the office to Robinson Bros. for $4,500. The more I see of Herefords the more I believe they will most speedily bring our cattle up. There is a difference of one-half between the best bred three-year olds and the lowest class.

Francklyn, in acknowledging Groom's October report, commented:

I note your change of view about Herefords as against Short Horns. I do not think we can afford at present to put more cattle on the range, but when you come in we can talk it over. Before you come away if you hear of 4,000 or 5,000 good heifers for sale *on time* you might bring in the offer.

At the end of the year 1883 the Francklyn Company had marketed sufficient cattle to make the following payments on its financial obligations:

$150,000 paid on cattle note
$20,725 to the New York Company for interest to November 1, 1884, on land note of $829,000
$6,000 to Park National Bank, Kansas City, to Harry Groom to pay for Shorthorns
$616 to Captain Knight for labor and expenses
$32,000 for Kentucky bulls
£3,750 to Williams, Deacon & Co., London, in payment of coupons due January 1, 1884
Making a total of $227,529.50.

Francklyn was pleased with the report, and on November 22, 1883, he wrote Colonel Groom: "I congratulate you on the success of your Autumn work. You have shipped more beeves than I supposed you had, and branded more cattle than I thought were there. Cattle are reported doing well on the range and I think we are on the road to success."

With this optimistic note the Francklyn officials looked forward with much promise to the year 1884.

CHAPTER 8

One Hundred Miles of Indian Border

DURING THE FIRST HALF of the 1880's hundreds of thousands of cattle were grazing on the ranges of the Southwest. This decade was a period of recovery from the Panic of 1875.

With this recovery a rapid rise in the cattle business reached boom proportions in 1883. The great increase in cattle multiplied the demand for grass, soon overstocked the ranges, and caused the grass to become short and scarce. Across the boundary in the Indian Territory were millions of acres of succulent grass, untouched and unused, that tempted Texas and Kansas cattlemen to drift their herds into the Territory. Soon thousands of the white men's cattle were growing fat on the Indian's grass under the guise of leasing that was usually paid for in high-priced beef unsuited for the markets, if paid for at all.

As a result H. M. Teller, Secretary of the Interior, received scores of applications for leases in the Territory. These applications were made through the various local agencies, who sent them to H. Price, Commissioner of Indian Affairs, who in turn referred them to the Secretary for his approval or rejection. Teller was steadfastly opposed to all such leases because, he said, they were in violation of the treaties made between the United States government and the Indians in 1866 and 1867. He believed strongly that the United States government was morally obligated to protect the Indians in their treaty rights.

Texas Cattlemen Invade Indian Territory

Stock men from Texas and Kansas, however, paid little or no attention to the Secretary's views and moved their herds into all parts of the Indian Territory with or without the consent of either the government or the Indians. When the cattle were once in, it was difficult to remove them. Where leases were made with the Indians they were made, in most cases, with a few of the most powerful Indian chiefs. This practice brought about great dissatisfaction among the less influential chiefs and all other Indians who were not allowed to participate in the leases. This fight for grass centered largely in Greer County and also in the Neutral Strip in the Indian Territory lying between the 98th and 103rd meridian. The boundary of Greer County, as it came to be known later, was originally determined by the Florida Treaty of 1819 between Spain and the United States, which left the area in Spanish territory.

During the entire period from 1819 to 1883 there were many disputes and much discussion as to whether it was the North Fork or the South Fork of the Red River that was referred to in the Florida Treaty. The question was simple: Did Greer County lie in Texas or in Indian Territory? During this period a number of commissions were appointed by both Texas and the United States government to study and adjust this matter, but no decision could ever be reached. Finally the whole argument centered around Captain R. B. Marcy's discovery, in 1852, of the headwaters of the Red River in the present Randall County in the Texas Panhandle.

Governor O. M. Roberts addressed a joint session of the Texas Legislature on the subject, January 10, 1885, giving a detailed account of all the attempts that had been made to settle the dispute and presenting much evidence to show that it was the North Fork of the river that was referred to in the Treaty of 1819. He then declared:

> The true question is which one of the two equal branches corresponds most nearly with the "Rio Roxo of the Nachitoches, or Red River," as it was known in 1819, when the treaty was made, "as laid down in Melish's map, of the United States, published at Philadelphia, improved the first of January, 1818." It is not the South Fork, for it is not laid down in Melish's map, and was not then known to exist by white men, either Americans or Mexicans, who gave any public notice or made any known record of it. Nor was such a fork known to exist before Capt. Marcy was informed of it by his Indian guide. . . . The Indian called it (not Red River but) "Ke-che-a-qua-ho-no," or, "Prairie Dog Town River."

This river Capt. Marcy afterwards found and traversed in his exploration of 1852. In the introduction to his report he explains the extent of all previous explorations and shows that he and his party were the first to reach and traverse that river. Capt. Marcy in this exploration was instructed to make "examination of the Red River and the country bordering upon it from the mouth of Cache Creek to its sources." In going up from that point, he speaks of the two branches being about the same size at their junction, and went up the fork now known as the North Fork, and followed it near its source. In the route there is no surprise expressed in finding it where he did or at its course. He had Indian guides and hunters with him, and they gave it no Indian name. It was known and called by no other name than that of Red River. He traced it to near its source a little north of $35\frac{1}{2}$ degrees north latitude which he found to be about twenty-five miles south of the Canadian River. And here he discovered the only thing about Red River that did not seem to be known before to some other explorers, which was, that the upper waters of the Canadian did not run into and constitute a part of Red River of Natchitoches, as they were supposed to do.

Melish made his second map in the short period of five years afterwards (in 1823), in which Red River is laid down with its one main stream pointing still toward Santa Fe, and with its source in latitude 35 degrees north. It shows no south fork such as found by Capt. Marcy. In that map he laid down "The Great Spanish Road," one fork of which crossed the Canadian and ran down north of Red River to the mouth of the Washita, in the direction of Natchitoches. This great Spanish road (which at that day, meant a well known and much traveled mule trail), may explain why the North Fork was known as the Red River. And no road being laid down as running south of the Red River. . . . may explain why the south fork was entirely unknown, except to the Indians, perhaps, who called it by a different name. Desternell's map of Mexico used in the Treaty of 1848 between the United States and Mexico, does not lay down the South Fork as now known to exist, but at a point about one-half a degree west of the 100th degree of longitude he makes a stream run into the Red River, coming in its whole course from the southwest called, Ensenado. "The north fork above the junction is called R Colorado," which is the Spanish name for Red River.

In concluding his address Governor Roberts said:

If the history of this matter, including the former efforts to establish this line, be examined into, in addition to what Texas has lately done in regard to the settlement of this disputed line, it will be found that Texas and her authorities have acted with a becoming fairness, which, I undertake to say, has not been met in the same spirit by the authorities of the United States. Having thus submitted this explanation of the merits of our claim, and of what has been done concerning it during my administration, it is now left to the wisdom of my successor and of the legislature to take such further action as may be deemed necessary, right, and just in protecting the interest of the State.

After Governor Robert's administration no further steps were taken by either Texas or the United States to determine the question of ownership of this part of the Indian Territory. Although Commissioner H. Price, commissioner of Indian Affairs, did not believe that Texas had any legal claim to the territory in question, he advised Colonel P. B. Hunt, Indian agent at Anadarko, that he deemed it best not to interfere there until Congress decided to whom it belonged. This opened up a temporary haven for Texas cowmen, who were desperately in need of grass. As a result thousands of Texas cattle flocked into this region and soon Greer was overcrowded.[1]

In the 1880's the so-called Neutral Strip, situated between the southern Kansas and the northern Texas Panhandle boundaries, was in the direct path of the cattle trails. Since this region was not settled, it be-

---

[1] See Address of Governor O. M. Roberts, Francklyn Files, Panhandle-Plains Museum, Canyon, Texas.

For an excellent brief survey of Greer County during this period see *Handbook of Texas,* I, 70–71.

came a No-Man's land where all sorts of lawless, as well as law-abiding, men gathered. It also furnished grass and pasturage for thousands of cattle during the trail driving period. Moreover, it was a convenient avenue through which Kansas stockmen pushed their cattle down into the Indian Territory, where they found an abundance of cheap, nutritious grass. The Cheyennes and Arapahoes not only claimed a portion of this strip, but their ranges also extended far over into the Indian Territory. General John Pope, in command at Fort Leavenworth, estimated in March, 1883, that not fewer than 150,000 cattle were supposed to be herded on the neutral Cherokee strip under arrangements with the Indians; but, he said, "The trouble is they spread themselves far beyond the limits of the Cherokee strip and trespass upon the lands of the Cheyennes and Arapahoes." General Tufts, who was ordered to make a firsthand survey of the cattle situation in Greer, reported to Commissioner Price, March 6, 1883, that about 100,000 cattle on these lands belonged to citizens of Kansas, "Who turn their cattle loose on these lands and pay no tax."

Greer County was also located on the cattle trails to the north and served as a corridor through which South Texas cattlemen attempted to channel their herds to northern markets and thereby escape the restrictions imposed upon them by the Kansas quarantine line of 1884. Colonel Groom's problem was to ward these cattle off the Greer range and protect his grass.

Indian Troubles and Finance

The Francklyn Company, with one hundred miles of Indian border, was in a precarious condition in 1884–1885. The Company's lease was to expire in 1885, and many of its cattle were scattered over the Kiowa and Comanche reserves in the Indian Territory. Major Guy Henry, in command at Fort Sill, declared, February 27, 1882, that "No less than 50,000 cattle are grazing between Fort Sill and Red River without authority." The Francklyn Company was faced with the problem of keeping invading herds off its range or abandoning the lease. Good judgment dictated the latter course, but the lease of 200,-000 acres of well-watered lands capable of producing $100,000 annually was too much of a temptation for Colonel Groom to resist. This was especially true since he had seen his Company forced to pass up

INDIAN RESERVATION LANDS USED BY CATTLEMEN

what he considered to be good land and cattle bargains because of inability to handle them financially. Therefore, he determined to hold on to the lease at any cost, in the hope that times would be better.

The Francklyn Company was in desperate financial straits in 1884. Pressure from creditors on all sides made it impossible for Groom to fight his battles alone. In order to strengthen forces he joined with other large cattle companies who, in their efforts to get complete control of the Greer ranges, held the favor of the leading Indian chiefs.

One of the first of the numerous applications for leases in Greer was made by Harrold and Ikard, of Wapella, Illinois, in 1883. Secretary Teller refused to grant the lease. However, these men joined with a combination of other large cattle concerns and moved their herds into Greer without permission from the Secretary. When they learned of Secretary Teller's orders to the Secretary of War to remove all such intruders who were there in violation of the law, E. B. Harrold wrote Teller, July 13, 1884, and explained his Company's presence there:

> I have heard that the Cheyennes and Arapahoes and Kiowa Indians of the Indian Nation are petitioning you to lease their territory to stockmen for grazing purposes, but have seen nothing in regard to it. We wanted to lease Greer last winter, but you declined to lease to us on what we thought were very just reasons, but we are now occupying Greer County with 60,000 head of cattle, and have been for about 18 months. We got consent of those nations before we went in there. We gave them 200 cattle last June, and once in awhile we gave them some beef, probably 100 since we have been there, and have four bucks working for us. We are getting along with them without any trouble, and they appear to be well satisfied, and bring in all our cattle and horses that stray amongst them, and if you can lease that country would like to have a show to get it, as we are already there and am satisfied we can get along with the Indians peaceably. Can give you all the reference that is necessary I think.

As a result of the purchase of the Harrold and Ikard cattle in 1883, the Francklyn Company inherited a complicated and difficult Indian problem, which, because of deep involvements in state and national politics, forced the Company to seek relief in Washington. A presidential election added to the confusion and uncertainty.

While pursuing his complicated program in Greer, Colonel Groom, in a letter from Wichita Falls, dated February 11, 1884, informed

Brown that he arrived there on February 9 and found only a few Indians, but that "Those that came are prominent ones." He found the Indians much divided on the question of leasing and wrote Brown immediately as follows:

> Knowing the agent, P. B. Hunt, of the Anadarko Agency would not be allowed to lease any considerable part to any one concern, and that he had several promises out before ours, I determined to effect a compromise, which I think is done about as follows: It is agreed that all the land lying along the south side of the Territory shall be divided into three parts and to run a line 25 miles deep, or rather to a point three miles north of Otter Creek where it empties into the North Fork of Red River, and from that point to run a line due east through the Territory. The other three parties are to stay south of it as far as Fort Sill. We are to be permitted to occupy the land north of that line including the country along Elk Creek, and up North Fork as far as the Agent will allow us. It is my impression that the Agent intends Hunter & Evans of St. Louis to have a large slice in there, but I don't know just where. I know he intends us, if we get consent of the Indians, to have the country along Elk Creek back of Ikard's Peak. It is, I think, the very best of the Territory. I think the council will leave here tomorrow to meet again in the Indian country about this day one week.

Colonel Groom attended the council meeting and reported to Brown from Fort Worth, February 14, 1884:

> The Indian Council closed yesterday with the following results: After asking us what part of their country those of us present desired to lease, the first speech was made by Quana, who is admitted to be the most influential and brave man in the three tribes. He began by pointing at me saying, "Col. Groom was the first man that talked to me about getting money for our grass and the more he thought and talked about it the more he believed it that I was right." At first he nor anyone else liked it but now almost all want to sell grass. He said there were four men present whom he believed to be their friends, namely, Burnett, Waggoner, Fox (Sloan & Fox) and Groom, but in addition to these they had four other friends that had talked to them about grass, Harrold, Cap Ikard, Huntley and a Mr. Cleveland; that these must have a part. Next to him A-sa-ha-be addressed the council and said that he agreed with all that had been said by Quana, but added that our friends must come with big hearts. He said they must not think they would give their grass away as their neighbors the Cheyennes had done; that that trade had not a thing to do with theirs which was a fine country and was

worth heap money, and that we must watch and see that our horses ran faster than the strangers' horses . . . if we got any part of the grass . . .

The first day they talked of adjourning to meet on Deep Red Run before meeting at the Agency, but others kept coming until the number reached about 100, of which at least 25 were chiefs. Before adjourning they concluded to meet at the Agency at Anadarko the next new moon which will be February 26th, and then with the Agent they will determine what lands and to whom they shall be leased, but repeatedly expressed their preference for the four then present and those above named. I know the Agent will want Col. Suggs to have a big slice for he has at all times from the start been Col. Hunt's bondsman and Agent in the sum of $75,000. . . . The whole country occupied by these three tribes, Kiowas, Apaches, and Comanches, contain but little if any over 3,000,000 acres, at least one-third of which will be withheld for leasing to white men who have married Indians, and for farming purposes for which they are now getting quite a taste. If the Agent should feel inclined to, or is directed by the Interior Department at Washington to divide the country equally amongst his and the various friends of the Indians the amount to each must be small. Of course I shall use everything in my power to convince both that we ought to have a large boundary, but how far we may succeed is a different story. I have already told Quana I would give him 500 cattle if we got 600,000 acres. You know of another promise I have made, so that means we will have to bleed if we succeed.

Colonel Groom went to Anadarko a few days in advance of the meeting to make some definite plans in carrying out his program at the meeting. He went by way of Fort Sill to see the agent there, who, he said, "has some sort of control in the matter." C. F. Doan of Doan's Store, who understood the Indians' language, promised to meet him at Anadarko on February 20. "I know the lands will lease high," he warned Brown, "and you must give me your idea about what should be our limit as to price." But it was all to no avail. After several days of wrangling Groom informed Brown that "We give up for the present."

Abundant evidence shows that the intrusion of the white men onto the Indian ranges had created a strong undercurrent of discontent among the redmen. Under the leadership of their respective chiefs several bands made strong protests to their local agents, either because they had been fenced in, or because their lands had been confiscated altogether. Major Henry, in his report in 1882, declared that "The Kiowas, Comanches, and Apaches are apparently well satisfied, but are in a nervous state of *tensive,* [*sic*] fearing an occupation of their country."

To all appeals for leases in the Kiowa, Comanche, and Apache lands, Secretary Teller informed Commissioner Price, March 19, 1884, that "The Department declines to recognize any such leases." Not to be outdone, Colonel Groom began immediately to make further plans in his efforts to secure an Indian lease. He addressed a letter to the Secretary of the Interior asking for permission to take a vote of the three tribes on the question of a lease, with the understanding that if they voted in favor of it, then the lease could be made. He addressed the letter to Agent Hunt, who endorsed it and sent it to the authorities at Washington. Colonel Groom left Anadarko on March 6, 1884. On his return he visited among the Indians, spending one night at Tepee Creek, the next night with Quanah and his band on Elk Creek, and one night at the Greer headquarters camp at Navajo Mountain. Before leaving Anadarko, however, Colonel Groom made arrangements with Bruner Bros., who, he said, traded all over the Territory, to find out all about the leases of the lands in the various tribes. "I pay them nothing, but promised if they would find a good range at a low price I would help them get the 1,000 cattle they want."

Colonel Groom also went to Olathe, Kansas, to see James Haworth, who was in charge of the Indian schools, only to find that he had gone to Washington to await the outcome of an Indian appropriation bill. Haworth was a former agent at Anadarko, and was purported to be popular with the Kiowas and Comanches, especially with those who were opposed to leasing. He was also thought to be intimate with Agent Hunt. Groom urged Brown to go to Washington to obtain his assistance in obtaining the lease, for "he is believed to exert more influence on these tribes than anyone else. I am sure he is potent with them."

The Francklyn Company was having much trouble with the Indians at this time; this, along with heavy expenses, worried Colonel Groom. In a letter to Brown from Fort Worth, March 7, 1884, he said:

> Cranmer talks of employing new men at $25 per month. I do not know

that it is wise, but expenses have been too great and I have been fussing about it all the time, but it must be remembered that we have Indians for neighbors, and if they are treated badly they will steal cattle to immense numbers, and would burn the whole country up, so it is absolutely necessary to feed them when they require it.

In the meantime George Cranmer, who was looking after matters on the Greer range, reported to Van Pelt from Vernon, Texas, March 25, 1884:

The Indians have been killing our cattle of late. I sent a man to see the Agent at the Wichita Agency yesterday. If I can get one Indian arrested that killed nine head of cattle a few days ago I will put a stop to further depredations as he is a big Meddison [Medicine] man. Some of the men on the ranch would kill the Indians when they catch them if I would agree to it, but that would make matters worse. If the Agent does not give us some protection by prosecuting the ones killing cattle, we shall have to adopt some other course.

On May 2, 1884, Brown notified Colonel Groom, at Doan's, that "Cranmer writes that the Indian delegation is enroute [to Washington]. I shall run over there next week and will see Haworth then. I do not think the Greer bill will go through the Senate this year." On the twelfth Colonel Groom wrote that "There will be no leases made at all in 1884 by the Kiowas and Comanches," and that *"Haworth would not advise anybody making money in the lease business unless nearly all the Indians approved; that if they did not it would lead to trouble very soon."*

Since Congress was in session, Agent Hunt thought it would be a good thing for some of the Indian chiefs to go to Washington and appear before the Committee on Indian Affairs, of each House, and present their side of the lease question. Therefore, he asked permission for the Indians to be heard. According to Colonel Groom's report of May 12, Acting Agent McKisker had written him from Anadarko that the Indians would not claim Greer County, except on the basis that it was theirs as a part of the Indian Territory. "I present this for your consideration. Quana will be here this week to confer with the Agent."

Colonel Groom's Race to Anadarko Agency

On July 7, 1884, President Cleveland ordered the Secretary of War to remove all settlers from the Indian Territory. As a result of this order the commanding officer of the Department of Missouri wired the commanding officer at Fort Sill to send a detachment of troops into the southwest portion of the Indian Territory, "called by the authorities in Texas, Greer County, to warn those going into that portion of the Territory for settlement, that they are there in violation of the law and must leave it." In the execution of this order the President said:

> This officer will be instructed to give those people a reasonable time to move and take their property with them. Should they refuse to leave he is to inform them that it will be better for them to go gently themselves. Should they still refuse they are to be moved by force including their property. Only such force is to be used as may be necessary to secure obedience to his orders. All parties will be treated with as little severity as their conduct will permit. If any settler should assert any license or national claim of a right to remain you will have the case reported to headquarters before proceeding to extremities with him. . . . You are to take all practical measures to see that none others come to settle.[2]

On learning of these orders Groom, anxious to explain and, as he thought, to justify the Francklyn Company's presence in Greer, reported to Brown from Greer, July 17, 1884:

> On my return from Wichita Falls I set out to see the officer directed to issue the order and found him after several days. He said his instructions included all. . . . I told him we were not settlers and laid no claim to the land and would go out any time when practically needed; that we bought the herd where it now runs and are gathering cattle to send off all the time; that we have a place for cattle as soon as we get watering places fixed, etc. He then said I think you ought to write to Gen. C. C. Augur, Commander of the Department of Missouri, at Leavenworth these facts. I told him further that while we stay here we would prevent the growing groves of

---

[2] Colonel Groom had informed Brown as early as March 27, 1884, that there was a colony of some thirty families settling in Greer, and that if the Indian Bureau knew this they would send someone to put a stop to it. "They go in on Texas Veteran scrip under Fisher, Sweet etc. As I have to live among them," he said, "it is best that I should not be known as alluding to it."

One Hundred Miles of Indian Border

timber from being destroyed; that if permitted to remain, we would obligate ourselves to leave as soon as the country is needed for any other occupancy. The purpose of the Government is to prevent it from being taken by settlers until the title is determined. Should they require us to leave, this country would be filled at once by drift cattle from other ranges. *In fact I fear that some cattlemen or others look upon it with a wistful eye and may have got in with the authorities to suggest this movement.* I shall not write Gen. Augur now, hoping the thing will be allowed to drift along until too late to go this year. You never saw a better place for cattle and I hope we will not have to move this year or next. Immediately after the order was issued some of the settlers applied to the Government of Texas for protection, but as yet they have had no reply.

Events moved rapidly now between Texas and Washington. Groom had already suspected Fox of foul play. His suspicions were further aroused when Brown received a telegram from Robinson Bros., at Wichita Falls, saying: "The Indians left Saturday night for Washington. We telegraphed Fox Groom's message as soon as received, but presume he could not detain them." The story is told in detail in Groom's report to Brown from Salt Fork, August 30, 1884:

On my way up here at Fort Worth I met a John Welder and a brother of his and a lawyer named Holliday of Goliad, Texas, on their way up here to look at Swisher's interest in Greer and also at a lease that George Fox (a former interpreter of the Anadarko Agency) professes to have obtained from the Comanches, Kiowas, and Apaches, and is located exactly where we need the land most and where it had been promised to us by the other gentlemen in our combination, including this same man Fox who was to have lands near the center of the reservation. Welder asked me at Fort Worth about the lease Fox proposed to control. I told him I felt sure there had been no leasing done to anyone and supposed that was the end of it.

But in the morning Welder was on the train on his way to look at the two tracts, and left the Falls very soon after his arrival in company with his brother, Holliday and a man named Stimson from Colorado City, who claims to be Fox's partner. Driving fresh hired teams they reached Doan's Store about two hours before me and had talked to Doan and showed him a map of Fox's lease lying on the east side of North Fork beginning at the mouth of Otter Creek to a point a little above the mouth of Elk Creek about twenty miles square and containing 250,000 acres, and went right on to look at it. Doan expressed himself as being surprised that I allowed Fox to get this land. I told him I never heard until the night before that Fox had been trying to lease it. He said Fox claimed to have the signatures of all the leading Indians interested in these lands, and that it was his best opinion that Fox had obtained a lease. Casually Welder had asked me how leases were confirmed, etc. to which I told him I had never made one and could not therefore instruct him.

This being a matter of so much importance, I determined to overtake Welder and try to learn from him the exact status of the matter which I did after driving rapidly about five miles. He said Fox claimed to have the signatures of 52 of the 57 leading chiefs and that his lease would join ours and that we were going to fence (which he had no right to say) so that one division fence would answer. Fox made Welder believe we were willing to his lease. I told him no and I never would consent to it, taking as it did the very land next to us; that I should certainly contend for our rights, to which Welder said he did not want a difficulty and said what I had told him shook his faith in Fox; that he would go on and see the land anyhow and return home.

Fearing that he would go on and see the Agent, Col. Hunt, and maybe get it confirmed, I determined to beat him to the Agency, so I traveled all that night only sleeping two hours and went right on to our outfit [in Greer] and got fresh horses and traveled a part of the next night and on the following night reached the Agency. I hunted up Tom Woodward, one of the best interpreters, and asked him for news and casually told him I heard that Fox had obtained a lease. He said Fox had been very hard at work, but did not believe he had completed it. As early as was decent next morning to go to a private house I went to see Col. Hunt and told him of this matter to which he soon replied he would not permit it, and said further Fox had no cattle and if he let him have any it would be only a small boundary.

Now you cannot imagine the relief this gave me as I was laboring under the most intense anxiety, and had been from the time I reached Doan's. I then asked the Agent what he thought of the probability of them leasing to which he replied he did not believe them any nearer than they were in the Spring. But confidentially told me what I believed before and told you when last with you, that a few leading men amongst the opposition would have to be treated with. No lease will ever be obtained until the opposition Labalanica, White Wolf, and Cheevers of the Comanches, Lone Wolf, Big Tree and Sun Boy of the Kiowas, and the squaw men about two or three enterprises. I have thrown out feelers to see what can be done and Lone Wolf and one or two others are coming to see me. The others I have not been able to get to listen. It is a tedious undertaking presenting many difficulties, most of which I believe I can overcome.

The bitterness on this question has been running so high that it has culminated in a very determined effort to remove the Agent, Col. P. B. Hunt. The Commissioner of Indian Affairs [H. Price] has lately resigned so that the Acting Commissioner is Chief Clerk Stevens, who Col. Hunt says is very unfriendly to him and has given him trouble. The charges against Hunt I saw and know them to be of the most flimsy character. Four of them spring out of one lot of cattle numbering 327 head, a donation Col. Hunt obtained gratuitously in 1882 under the following circumstances: In 1882 Congress failed to pass an appropriation bill before adjourning, so that the Department informed the Indian Agent only to deliver half rations. Under this state of affairs the Indians became very restless and very insubordinate. Some of the herds belonging to the Texas men were grazing over into the Indian Territory. Col. Hunt applied to them for a donation of beef on account of their cattle grazing on the Indians' land which resulted in the giving of the 327 cattle. One charge is that he sold 22 calves which he did and applied to the payment of expenses in bringing the 327 onto the reservation.

Fox Attempts to Oust Colonel P. B. Hunt

As a result of Fox's clandestine scheme the leasing combination in Greer was divided into two bitterly opposing factions. Fox, in order to attain his objective, proposed to oust Hunt from the Anadarko Agency and secure his lease through Acting Secretary Stevens. Colonel Groom and the other members of the combination countered with a strong fight to retain Hunt as agent, and at the same time get the leading Indians who were opposed to the lease to consent to it. In a letter written at Elm Fork on September 3, 1884, Groom reminded Brown that:

In my last letter I told you I was expecting to have an interview with Thos. Woodward, the Indian interpreter, who seems to have the confidence of the anti-leasing Kiowas and Comanches more than any other person engaged in the same way. He sent for me and we had a meeting yesterday on North Fork. Those present were Lone Wolf, Black Bear, and Gan Ganky, Indians, and Thos. Woodward and W. H. Conover, white. The last is a squaw man who perhaps is as much respected as any man in the whole Territory. He has always heretofore opposed leasing for the simple reason no provision was made for him. He is a good business man and smart and anxious to make money. Whilst over at the Agency last time, I made an arrangement with Woodward to go to work and feel of all parties opposed to leasing. Conover agreed to assist in obtaining consent to lease if he was allowed sufficient land in the lease to graze 5,000 cattle, at the same time selecting territory that none of our parties desired, lying northeast of Fort Sill on the west fork of Beaver Creek. Woodward wants about $1,000, 25 or 30 cattle and a small tract of land. To these requests I was authorized by Waggoner, Burnett, Suggs, and Addington to consent to. Woodward and Conover agreed to go to work at once and continue till the matter was accomplished. They advised not saying anything to the chiefs present, but allow them to manage the matter. They are of the opinion they have made a good start with all of the leading Kiowas and Comanches. They agree to follow nothing else for 20 days and will send a messenger in about ten days to report their progress. It now looks more like breaking down the opposition than at any time before. This last meeting was composed of men every one of whom was opposed to Fox and say that he has secured the consent of a number of prominent Indians, but that they and the Agent will never consent.

On September 18, 1884, Woodward notified Colonel Groom from Anadarko that he would be at Groom's camp about the twenty-seventh, and added:

Think I am getting along bully with those Comanche chiefs if we can keep those Quahadas quiet for awhile, I think I can work the Comanches all right in a short time. The Kiowas are very anxious to go to Washington this fall. Will see you about everything when I get to your camp. Lone Wolf is a little afraid of his people, but I think we can work that all right. Any instructions you would like to give will find me at Mr. Brown's store at any time.

Colonel Groom Unites with Large Cattle Concerns in Greer

Encouraged by this report, Burnett, Suggs, Waggoner, and Groom met at Fort Worth two or three days later "to devise some plan to induce the chiefs who object, to consent to the lease. I go to Wichita Falls Friday morning to meet the gentlemen I have before named" (Colonel Groom to Brown from Fort Worth, September 23, 1884).

In a letter dated September 27, 1884, Colonel Groom reported the happenings of the meeting at Wichita Falls and stressed the importance of keeping Colonel Hunt at the Anadarko Agency. Brown had advised Colonel Groom not to get mixed up in the fight against Fox, but Groom felt that it was necessary to join the combination if they were to succeed in obtaining a lease. His letter follows:

We had a meeting this morning composed of Waggoner, Burnett, Suggs, Addington, and Gregory & Cooley represented. I am satisfied we can get a lease as soon as we can get around through the instrumentalities at work. One thing of the very greatest importance is to see that Agent P. B. Hunt is sustained. Those opposed to the lease have been getting all the proof up they can against him and there is very great danger they will succeed unless something is done. He applied to the Interior Department for permission to come and show the charges are unjust and was refused. Confidentially he is our fast fixed friend, and we will eventually succeed if he stays in. I have heard all sides and know you are safe in urging him to be kept in his present position. I am sure if Hunt is put out we will never get the country. I cannot say too much about the importance of retaining Hunt. If allowed to he will show himself to be a very pure good man. Both the Senators from Kentucky will fully endorse him. General Boynton, Secretary Gresham, and I think Teller will also when understood all to be his friends. He must be sustained. It is unfair to send out and secretly take proof and not allow him to meet proof for himself. In reference to Fox he has his parties with him and has had all the time. But while Hunt is Agent he will never confirm any trade Fox will make with the Indians. Last winter it was agreed . . . that we were to have the country lying on North Fork, north of Waggoner and McGibbin north of us. Fox was to have the country east of us and north of Burnett. Now don't you see if we go in with Fox we would have to impose on some of those setting with us in good faith which would be unwise as it seems to me. Harrold & Ikard clashed with Suggs, Addington, and Gregory & Cooley. As Harrold & Ikard are not aiming to get any part it relieves the trouble on that part. In this back country I think it is best to get along with neighbors smoothly.

R. D. Hunter did not think the opposition to him was coming from Secretary Teller, but from some of his deputies. "Confidentially," he said in a letter of September 29, 1884, to Brown:

. . . the worst opposition comes from anti-lease parties who want the land really but know they cannot get it while Hunt is Agent. All the other parties who know the value of these lands are anxious to go into the arrangement mentioned in my last to you. . . . Hunt may be removed at any time. If he is it will be done to defeat us in getting these lands. . . . There is no telling what he is worth to us, what his removal will cost us. I think you ought to study this branch of our business.

Colonel Groom also confided other trouble to Brown in a letter of November 21, 1884:

We have an Indian border considerably over 100 miles, three thieving tribes, who steal cattle and horses and we constantly have good men scouting amongst them. They call on us every day for supplies. Suppose we refuse. They would steal the worse, kill cattle and shoot our men and it is deemed best to try to pacify them by employing some of them as cowboys, but they make none the less to employ for they will not keep the cattle back they want to steal. I have no doubt they check others by holding them in fear. . . . We have five employed who cost us $2,500 per year: Quana $50 and four others $25 per month. We have spent considerable in trying to obtain a lease having traveled several times about 100 miles to see them, then 100 to Fort Sill twice to see the Military about their orders; to Washington, to New York and elsewhere.

Colonel P. B. Hunt Resigns and Appeals to Washington

The opposition to Agent Hunt at Anadarko became so strong that he was forced to resign. He sent his letter of resignation to Secretary Teller effective January 1, 1885, and sent a copy of the letter to Colonel Groom, to which Hunt added:

I am sure this is the best thing to do. Now I had thought if you and Senator Beck would call to see General Boynton and talk the matter over and then go on to see Secretary Teller, he might accept it to take effect as of March 1, 1885, or fail to act upon it at all. In this connection there is another matter to be considered. . . . You know when Quana was at Washington the Acting Secretary [Stevens] first said he would direct the Commissioner to write their agent to let them rent the grass, or advise him to do so. The next day, however, after the Commissioner had been talked to about the matter, Quana was informed that a Special Agent would be sent to attend to the grass business. Well, Special Agent P. H. Folsom reached here just about one month ago and is still here working on the grass. He first told the Indians if they wanted the money they would have to go to

Washington, but I think there is a trick at the bottom of it. He has taken the vote and I understand there was about 50 majority against leasing. When he chooses to tell them the money will not go to Washington, how easy it will be to turn the 50 the other way! It seems he is largely after a majority. The Indians have charged in Council to Folsom's face that he, Haworth, Thos. Woodward and Conover are trying to make the lease for themselves and there does not seem to be any doubt about the first three. Folsom admitted in Council that Haworth wanted grass. Haworth has been in constant communication with Folsom since his arrival here. By some disappointment Haworth did not come to the Agency as he contemplated, but sent a telegram to Orlando Woodward, who is Clerk at the Lawrence school, and was here looking for children for the school saying, "If it will assist in securing children bring two chiefs each from the Kiowas, Comanches, and Apaches and three from the Caddoes and Wichitas, and Thos. Woodward, Interpreter. I will arrange railway transportation to Lawrence." That simply means grass. He wishes to get the chiefs away from here and he will doctor them. Orlando Woodward left Lawrence without the chiefs, but it is believed that Folsom will take them as they have been detected in their scheme here and dare not carry it too far. I understand it is Folsom's intention to leave here and come back here [Anadarko] February 1st and press the matter for all there is in it. . . . Folsom's point is, if possible, to get rid of me and get assigned to this place and be in charge and force his point. . . . It seems to me you ought to see, if possible, that he be ordered away to some other Agency where he may be needed. I think you can do it through Mr. Teller. I hope you will give this matter your attention, and it is unnecessary for me to suggest how to do it for you know better than I do. I will not write Mr. Beck, but will expect you to see him.

Following Hunt's suggestion Colonel Groom and Senator Beck visited Secretary Teller. As a result Groom sent Francklyn a hurried note, December 9, 1884, stating:

I have been in a run all day and have just got an answer from Assistant Secretary of Interior, Joslyn. By the aid of Senator Beck of Kentucky we got him first to say he would not accept the resignation of Colonel Hunt until after Secretary Teller's return, but before leaving, he wrote Senator Beck saying Hunt should not be removed if Beck desired him to remain for which he is as anxious as can well be. I am sure that ends the trouble for the present administration. Senator Beck is determined to have him retained.

With the Hunt question settled Colonel Groom and his combination could turn with more security to the matter of dividing the Greer lands among themselves. Groom reported to Francklyn from Fort Worth, December 15, 1884, that he had been called to Wichita Falls to meet with Suggs, Waggoner, and Burnett. "I will go there in the morning," he said. "Of course, I will not pay out anything, but will watch our interests until we see what Congress will do in the matter of Indian leases." On December 18, 1884, Groom made the following report of the meeting:

I came here on Tuesday and found S. B. Burnett and Daniel Waggoner here. Night before last E. C. Suggs and P. Addington came. The whole day yesterday was spent in counciling together. The Indian chiefs came last night and the conclusion arrived at is this: If we succeed in getting a lease, D. Waggoner, S. B. Burnett, and E. C. Suggs get 200,000 acres each. P. Addington 150,000. Five squaw men get 50,000 each and one or two others small amounts which in all makes 1,475,000 acres. Now it is the opinion that the whole amount they will consent to lease will be about 1,900,000 acres. If so, after allowing Addington 150,000 acres, the overplus is to be divided between the other four of us in the ratio of three to us and two to each of the other three. If I figure it right we would get about 300,000 acres. I remember you suggested not to bind ourselves for it at present, and this I should have done fully, but the time for compromise and allotment has come, and it was either get out entirely, or lay claim to our part. It will take at least two months to mature the trade if it succeeds, which is very doubtful. Then it is six months before the first half of the lease money is due. Now there is so great a demand for these lands I thought it was best to stand in for our share, and if we don't want it we can easily relet it at two cents per acre to others. The price we pay is six cents if we get any, and add to this two cents. This makes the eight the same as the State now charges.

Francklyn evidently approved of Colonel Groom's stand, since he informed Lord Rosebery on December 19, 1884, that "We still occupy Greer and shall continue to do so until the Government decides who it belongs to, which they are not not likely to do yet awhile."

Early in February, 1885, Cal Suggs, accompanied by four Indians and Horace Jones, interpreter, arrived at Washington bringing with them a reported fair majority in favor of leasing, together with an official letter of approval from Agent Hunt. However, Colonel Groom, who was in Washington at the time, reported to Brown, February 2, 1885, that "They have not made any move yet and will not until the opinion of others in favor of the lease has been obtained." On February 4, 1885, he advised Brown :

Nothing new has occurred since I wrote you except Secretary Teller talks very kindly about the Indian lease. Our party was introduced by Senator Coke of Texas, who I may say is the best authority on Indian matters. . . . Senator Coke read the lease carefully and is taking great interest in having the matter accomplished. In the event we have to leave Greer it will be indispensable to us as a gathering point and to spill back into Greer. When we get ready to leave that range we will have something tangible and solid to offer.

On his way from Texas to Washington, Colonel Groom wrote Brown from Louisville, March 11, 1885: "I stopped last Wednesday at Fort Worth to see Burnett about the Indian lease and learned that the papers were signed, and that our lease is safe. I do not think we want to turn over any part of the lease until we see further."

Northern Cattlemen Join with Colonel Groom in Support of Kansas Quarantine Law of 1884

In January and February, 1885, the quarantine law and the trail question were before Congress. This required the closest attention of Colonel Groom, since the Greer properties were directly involved in both questions. On January 30, 1885, he wrote Brown from Washington that the amended Trail bill passed the House, April 8, 1884, and passed the Senate, January 21, 1885, "and now is in the hands of the President for his signature, so there is the only chance to defeat it." He continued:

I intended to leave last night but trail matters are up in the Committee on Commerce and Judge Simpson in whose hands the matter has been placed said to me yesterday if I could testify before the Committee the trail could be thrown on the 100th meridian, so I agree to stay longer on that account. Judge James Miller of Gonzales, Texas, is also here to testify favoring the same line. The effect of this plan would be to rid the Indian Territory along North Fork of the trail and all its annoyances. I intend going to see Mr.

Loring, the Commissioner of Agriculture, with a view of showing him if he recommends a quarantine line that we should be placed north of it. Everything looks well for us here except the Greer question. I have seen all the Texas members of congress but one and all agree and determine that when the next administration appoints an Agent for the Comanches, Kiowas, and Apaches he must be a Texan and should be approved by that part of the state bordering on the Indian Territory. . . . After hearing our views of the matter, Judge Simpson, the Agent appointed at the St. Louis meeting and at the Southwest and State Associations, has agreed to make the bill he will present read as corrected in the copy I herein enclose you. The effect of the bill will be to take both the Southern drive and the New Mexico out of Greer and the Indian Territory. I have had several interviews since reaching here with Governor Click of Kansas whose term expires on the 12th of this month, who says he thinks the Kansas legislature can be prevailed on not to quarantine against the Indian Territory. I have also talked with Hon. S. R. Peters, Congressman from Newton, Kansas, who says that whenever it was made known that so many people from Kansas were grazing in the Indian Territory they would not think of doing so. I cannot give any idea when I will leave here until Suggs and party reach here and see what is to be done.

Colonel Groom sounded his first pessimistic note about Greer in a letter to Brown from Austin, March 30, 1885, in which he stated:

The gloom over the cattle trade all over South Texas is terrible. I have some fear there will be a disposition to crowd in Greer so they can get north next year. Of course, I am expecting to sell all the one's and two's, and as many more as can be sold to good advantage, say about 5,000 cows with calves and all that will be fat enough to go to Chicago. I believe this course is wise for it looks to me as if we may have to leave Greer at no distant day whether the title is settled or not. It looks to me that Oklahoma is going to be cleared and Greer may soon follow the same idea. I am very much inclined to believe we had better concentrate all our business into pasture at no distant day and try to add to the value of the herd by saving all our best animals. By this, risk and expense will be greatly reduced and be found equally profitable.

On April 12, 1885, Colonel Groom inquired of Brown:

Now with all these points of view would it not be best to lease as much as we now occupy? Of course, I leave these matters to you to decide. If we had no cattle to secure range for this is a valuable investment. You must determine quickly as it may have to be surveyed. . . . I think we will get some of the Indians' land but not more than 150,000 or 200,000 acres.

In the spring of 1885 the fear of an invasion of South Texas cattle into Greer became general among stockmen who were grazing there. Consequently, they took immediate steps to prevent any such disaster. On April 14, 1885, they inserted the following resolution in the *Texas Live Stock Journal* under the heading "No Quarantine in Greer":

To All Whom It May Concern: In view of the probability of Southern stock men trying to make Greer and adjacent counties a quarantine ground for cattle enroute to ranges further north, we take this means of, in some manner, explaining to them the disadvantages to both the present occupants and themselves of such a course. 1. The ranges are already stocked to their full capacity. 2. The cattle of this section are just as liable to infection from any contagious disease as cattle farther north. 3. Cattle brought here must be held over for one year before they can be moved north, and owing to the crowded condition of the range cannot possibly be wintered without great loss to all concerned. In the absence of any legislation on the subject, we, the undersigned, *occupants of the above mentioned country*, pledge ourselves to use every means in our power to confine all through cattle strictly to the trails. We mean business, and the ends aimed at must justify any means which we may deem expedient to use. Do not leave home with the idea in view that cattle can be held over here (Signed) by,

> The Francklyn Land & Cattle Company
> The Kimberlin Cattle Company and representatives
>   of Y Cross Y Ranch, Cross S. Ranch, Diamond
>   Tail Ranch, O Bar O Ranch, and W. O. Ranch

This notice was accompanied by an editorial entitled "The Greer County Notice" and evidently inspired by these concerns. It reads as follows:

In this issue appears a notice by stock men of Greer to Southern Texas stock men, written under the supposition that an attempt will be made to use Greer County as a quarantine ground for Coast cattle. As it is important that the matter be understood first and last for the good of all parties interested, this notice should receive the attention it merits. At first sight it might appear to the stock men of the South as being rather premature, but it is not so. There has been a project on foot to do exactly what the ranch men of

Greer oppose, as being injurious to the interests of all parties[. Therefore] on account of the reasons given, the notice should be read in its full sense of opposing scattering herds amongst northern Texas herds together with the guarantee of permanency of the trail. The stock men of Texas north of the dead line [34th parallel] as established by Kansas are in no way responsible for the state of affairs existing, nor do they desire that changes not necessarily injurious to themselves be made by forcing their herds off the accustomed ranges, either by overstocking a country fully stocked or by running the risk of loss of cattle by infectious diseases. The change in the cattle business caused by the Kansas enactment ought to be understood by this time, and it will be readily seen that a cattle movement that is not a through movement can be of no benefit. The trail is open and will be kept open, and the through herds can pass up to the Kansas line, and failing to find sale can be moved west on the neutral strip where a trail cannot be denied, even to the extent of pasturage for the time necessary to satisfy the provisions of the Colorado law. It is not promising truly, but it is the only guarantee of profitable through movements of Southern stock.

On April 18, 1885, Colonel Groom wrote Brown from Fort Worth:

I have great fears we will be overrun in Greer by Southern cattle and I see no remedy for it. The opinion is rapidly being formed that the present administration will clear the Indian reservations of white occupants as the actions in regard to Oklahoma and Winnebago in Dakota. A notice of which I enclose seems to look in that direction, so that it is certainly wise to look ahead and see what we may have to do with our cattle. The quarrel amongst the Indians makes the lease from the Comanches and Kiowas doubtful. In fact, I have informed them that we want none of it unless consented to by all as we will not consent to fight for it and pay for it too. The veto of the Governor puts the lands where they stood before in the hands of the old Land Board at 8 cents per acre and it is too high to think of paying for land in Greer, and then it would be inconsistent in us taking our present position on the tax question.

On April 20, 1885, an article appeared in an Austin paper [name not given] entitled, "A Proposed Lease in Greer County," which reads as follows:

At an informal meeting of the Land Board today a proposition was submitted to lease 600,000 acres in Greer County for five years at $30,000 annually. The Board took no definite action but the bid evidently met with approval and is almost certain to be accepted. Final action, however, will not be taken until Governor Ireland, Comptroller Swain, and Treasurer Lubbock, all of whom are now absent, return.

Colonel Groom's only hope now was to retain control of the Greer range long enough for the Company to gather what cattle were left there and on adjoining ranges. However, the Company was now in serious financial straits and Groom was compelled to turn his entire attention and efforts to making cattle sales sufficient to meet the Company's financial obligations, a large amount of which was already past due. The failure to make further cattle sales forced Groom to join with Francklyn and Brown in a desperate effort to secure a loan sufficient to tide the Company over the crisis and at the same time save the White Deer properties.

CHAPTER 9

The Big Forgery of 1884

THE DESCRIPTIVE PHRASE "Wild West" used to characterize the Plains region in the early 1880's implied a land of reckless and questionable characters. The conflict between the written and the unwritten law during this period produced its share of lawless men. The wide open spaces gave such people almost unlimited opportunity to ply their trades without let or hindrance, and they gave both cattlemen and settlers much trouble and anxiety in their efforts to get settled down to a routine and secure way of life. These men and women consisted of gunmen, bank robbers, prostitutes, daring adventurers, cattle thieves, and just plain, sorry, shrewd, scheming scoundrels who are ever present in the business world. The Francklyn Company, set in such surroundings, could not escape contact with those unscrupulous characters, who gave the Company much trouble and concern in its efforts to establish a cattle ranch on the Texas Plains.

The Big Forgery of 1884 127

One such man was Henry C. Young, who wormed his way into the financial and business affairs of the Francklyn Company at a very critical time in the Company's financial operations. He ran riot over the country with a self-faked business reputation as a cattleman, cashing thousands of dollars worth of worthless paper, and leaving in his trail bank shortages and purchase contracts which were of no value whatever. Lack of communication and slow transportation enabled Young to remain in one place for days and sometimes for weeks before he was suspected of treachery and deceit. He then had to move on to greener pastures in order to escape the clutches of the law.

On July 2, 1884, Charles G. Francklyn, stunned by a draft for $20,000 which he thought Harry Groom had written, wired Brown, who was at that time inspecting the White Deer range, as follows: "Harry Groom has drawn for over $20,000 favor Henry C. Young. I have refused to accept and will never accept drafts in this way. Have not yet decided about Harry." Francklyn requested the telegraph operator at Fort Elliott to send the message by speed messenger to the Francklyn Company headquarters at White Deer. Brown and Harry Groom, out inspecting the range, came in a day after the messenger arrived. They hastily sent word back by the messenger saying:

Your telegram to Brown is quite a surprise. I know nothing absolutely of any Henry C. Young. No such name has ever come to me in any way whatever, business or otherwise. He is trying to beat us out of a lot of money by forging my name. . . . I send you a list of all drafts drawn since February 9th and purpose to which each applied. Please write me fully concerning this matter. As the messenger is waiting I will close promising you full letter by next mail concerning ranch, cattle etc.

The draft referred to above was drawn on June 10, 1884, and read as follows: "After 7 days sight pay to the order of Henry C. Young or *bearer* $7,530 account of Maintenance Department. Value rec'd, No. 72." The draft was signed by H. T. Groom and was endorsed by R. M. Wright & Co. of Dodge City. At the same time Young presented a draft for $12,300 drawn on the Francklyn Company and made payable to Henry C. Young. It too was endorsed by H. T. Groom.

On June 23, 1884, Francklyn wrote to Harry Groom, severely reprimanding him for his extravagant expenditures, to which Harry, stung by this letter, sent the following curt reply:

Your letter of June 23rd came to hand today. I would have answered earlier had opportunity presented itself. I am very much annoyed and troubled over the drafts of Young which are *forgeries*. I have never drawn on you for other than current expenses, except under your instruction or that of Brown. The expenses here I know are high, but there is work to be done to show for itself, and it has been done after consulting with both of you. There is not a ranch in Texas, or elsewhere such as ours—none doing the amount of improvement that we are. Until we began not a tank had been made. Since that the Hansford Land & Cattle Company have built six or seven shallow pools, while Goodnight is now building twenty or more ten to twenty-five feet deep. Take out this item of expense and you will find our cattle are not costing so much. I have tried very hard to manage everything here as you and Brown would like, and I feel that your letter to me is more severe than I should have. I am not to blame because Young or anyone else forges my name, but I am led to think you feel harshly toward me. My accounts are all straight and I have used every dollar I have drawn as scrupulously correct as if my life depended upon it. My honor is all that I have and I protect that above my life. I wish it were so you could be here and see the inside running of our ranch machinery. I try daily to reduce all expenses and not cause the ranch to suffer. I will not draw another draft without mailing you advice on same. I have never realized until now the necessity of doing so, little thinking anyone else would try to use my name in such a base way.

In a letter to Francklyn on July 10, 1884, Harry Groom reported that Brown had returned to New York and that he (Harry) had written to R. M. Wright, who lost $3,000 in cashing the drafts, for particulars and could not understand why he had not heard from him. "I am not positive," he said, but, "if the drafts are on our yellow paper, I know the party who drew them, and am of the opinion he has an accomplice in this place now." He then explained in greater detail:

The party came to Mobeetie only a few weeks ago and I met him in Temple Houston's office where he was doing some work on the Assessor's books and making some maps for Houston and Spiller. Never had but a passing word with him as I was busy. . . . Now if these drafts are on our paper this is the man who did it as he left here about the 9th of June for Dodge, the

The Big Forgery of 1884

day after I went down to Greer County. Spiller and others here seem sure this is the man. In addition to this, R. M. Wright wrote that the man who presented the drafts was a German. While here he passed under the name of Henry Werner. He is about 35 or 40 years old, reddish face, rather sharp features, talks little broken, and was formerly from San Antonio, Texas, where he served his term in the penitentiary, and was connected with a large bank robbery, the First National Bank of Fort Worth some few years ago. I heard from rumor here that he had caught some Kansas City party for the $12,000. He also swindled Israel of Henrietta, Texas, out of $10,000. The operator at Dodge told the one here that they are on track of him. I hope very much they will catch the fellow for he is certainly a bad man.

In presenting his drafts to R. M. Wright for payment, Young handed him the following letter of introduction purported to have been written by Harry Groom, but which he himself had written as a part of his slippery scheme:

Gents: Send letter with drafts enclosed in favor Henry C. Young. Please deliver same to him on call. To avoid any mistake I give you description of Young below. Young is a prominent stock man of Southern Texas. Have bought some horses of him. Please introduce him to the bank should he require that favor. Any courtesy shown Mr. Young will be appreciated by—Yours respectfully, H. T. Groom.
Added note: About 6 feet, light hair, blue eyes, 45 years old—German.

On July 12, 1884, R. M. Wright wrote Harry Groom:

I have just got back from St. Louis and elsewhere where I have been on the hunt for Henry C. Young and will write you full particulars. On the Morning of June 17th, while I was opening and reading the mail, this man Young stepped up to the desk and said his name was Young and wanted to know if you had written to us about him. Not suspecting a forgery or having the least suspicion but what everything was right, I answered yes I have just received a yetter from Mr. Groom about you (as you had frequently written about parties coming to Dodge to us before). Young says, Do I answer the description? I looked him over and said perfectly, what can I do for you Mr. Young? He answered I don't know I have a draft here for $7,530 which I would like to get some money on and leave the draft with you for collection. I asked him how much he wanted on the draft. He said he did not know. I then asked him if $2,000 or $3,000 would be sufficient.

He said it would and he wanted to buy $30,000 worth of wire. I figured with him on it and gave him my figures which he said was lower than what he could lay it down here for and was going to Kansas City to remain five or six days, then go on to St. Louis, Lindell Hotel, where he would remain until Fall and from whence he would write me when and how to ship the wire.

I went down to the telephone office to wire Temple Houston who he said he knew very well, but we met a lawyer from Jacksboro by the name of Thos. F. West and Young went up to West and asked him if he did not recognize him and he and West had a long talk what about I don't know, but think it was about old times and old friends in that part of Texas. Anyhow I heard enough to lead me to believe that Young was all right, and I thought no more about it until five days afterward when we received a telegram from German Bank saying acceptance was refused on Groom draft. I immediately telegraphed Francklyn to give his reasons in full for non acceptance. He answered, Groom has sent us no advice and has no right to draw unless he advises, or words to that effect.

I tried to wire you and Temple Houston but the wires were down and remained so for ten or twelve days, and as soon as I got your telegram I went to Kansas City where I learned he had cashed two of our checks at Armour Bros and had left $1000 with them to be placed to his credit and also left another draft on Francklyn for $12,300 and ordered it sent to New York for collection and placed to his credit also. I got the $1,000 that he left of course. He had one similar to the one we got sent to Underwood Clark & Co, a great deal stronger letter than ours and I firmly believe Wilson would have cashed this $12,300 draft if he had required them to do so, as they were so thoroughly satisfied that he was all right and your signature was genuine both to letter and draft. Young remained in Kansas City nearly a week, but there I lost all trace of him.

I enclose you the letter of advice to us which came through the mail; also drafts he left with us for collection—three notes of yours for 30–60– and 90 days for $5400 each which he said was for land he sold you after you had bought his horses. Please let me know how he got hold of your blank drafts and Temple Houston's letter. Young must have accomplices down in your country who know all about your business and our business relations with you. We think the whole scheme was concocted somewhere in the Panhandle and maybe at Mobeetie.

Wright then added a full description of Young as he appeared at Dodge:

The Big Forgery of 1884

He was about 6 feet, 45 or 50 years old, rather large nose, well proportioned in build, weighed about 180 pounds, full head of light hair, very much bleared in the eyes as if by the sun and weather and looked as if he had been exposed to the weather all his life. No surplus flesh but seemed to have ridden it off. In short he looked a regular cow man and we think he was.

P.S. I have offered a reward of $250 for his capture.

On July 18, 1884, Harry Groom, after he had learned how the drafts were made, explained in detail to Francklyn as follows:

I enclose you the Henry C. Young drafts and letter of introduction that he played on R. M. Wright & Co. Also Wright's letter that you may see the way in which he presented the matter to him. I doubt very much if he will ever be caught. He is a sharp fellow. I wrote you in a recent letter that if the drafts were drawn on our paper I know the forger. Until last night I did not know how they were drawn. I can tell you now the whole thing. When in Mobeetie I make Temple Houston's office my headquarters and write many of my letters there. This man was in Houston's office working on the Assessor's books and doing some drawing for Houston and Spiller. Houston introduced me to Werner saying he, Werner, had known him since boyhood and had come to the Pan Handle to live. It seems Houston's early life was rather a thorny path and this Werner had done him some kindly acts which Houston had not forgotten and consequently was glad to see him.

I talked over the business that was not of a private nature, discussed matters of the day etc. Finally I began to write some letters and Werner took a position very near me. I never thought anything of this matter. I had my coat off laying across my knee. As I wrote and drew my draft book out and wrote a draft for McCord & Nave for $225 and J. M. Keller $125, enclosed them to the parties and went over to the Post Office and mailed them. The day was very warm and I had my coat off. Not thinking of thieves, forgers and such like, I hung my coat on a nail and went to the Post Office. Not having any need during the day I left my coat hanging there all day as I had done before. Here the work was done and the man did it was Werner. I will do all I can to catch him but doubt very much ever doing so.

After Young left Kansas City nothing was heard of him for some time. Early in September, 1884, he appeared at Galveston, where he created something of a sensation as a result of his attempt to cash

Harry Groom's second check, No. 73, for $12,300. *The Globe Democrat* of Galveston had the following to say about Young's arrival:

A Swindler's Operations in Texas. C. A. Grothouse who arrived in this City last Friday a week ago and registered at the Atlanta House as A. A. Yeager, and latterly at Mrs. Klein's boarding house as Mr. Fisher, was arrested by the police authorities on telegrams received from the Francklyn Land & Cattle Company, 44 Wall St., New York. The cause leading to his arrest was as follows: During the latter part of last week C. A. Grothouse, alias Yeager, alias Fisher had attempted to negotiate three drafts drawn in his favor against the Francklyn Land & Cattle Company of New York by B. B. Groome and George Groome for $7500 each making a total of $22,000 [*sic*]. Having failed in his negotiations at the First National Bank, the Texas Banking & Insurance Company, and Ball Hutchings & Co. . . . he drafts from M. W. Shaw, the well-known jeweler by representing to Shaw that he wanted to purchase $1000 in jewelry. This was last Saturday, and by some means Shaw secured possession of the three drafts and informed Grothouse that he would wire the Francklyn Company and, if genuine, he would make the deal with him. Grothouse requested Shaw not to telegraph until after banking hours. In response to his telegram Saturday evening Shaw received the following reply: Have Grothouse arrested. He is a swindler. The drafts are a forgery. He attempted to play the same game on us through the firm of R. M. Wright & Co. of Dodge City, Kansas, a short time ago. Communicate with our attorney, Temple Houston at Fort Elliott. Upon receipt of this Shaw placed the matter in the hands of the Chief of Police, who soon had Grothouse in custody.

The newspaper then gave a graphic description of Grothouse: "Grothouse is about 45 years old, a German by descent, with heavy black chin whiskers cropped close and heavy mustache of same color and with lurking dark gray eyes, bronze features, high cheek bones, 5 feet 11 inches high, and rather poorly dressed, but in the garb of a cattleman."

The newspaper reported that Young did not seem to be excited in any way and took the arrest very nonchalantly. He said he would come out all right in explaining how he received the three notes from the "Groomes," who, he said, were agents of the Francklyn Land & Cattle Company and had charge of the Company's ranch in the Pan-

The Big Forgery of 1884

handle. He declared that he had received the three notes in payment of 1,722 head of cattle, which he had driven from McMullen County to Mobeetie and sold to the Grooms, payable, one on sight, one in seven days, and the third in ten days. According to the newspaper account Young further commented that he had:

... left Mobeetie on the 20th of last month, coming direct to Galveston, where he expected to have no difficulty in negotiating the drafts. When interrogated if he had not tried the same game in Dodge City on the Francklyn Land & Cattle Company through the firm of R. M. Wright & Co. he flushed up indignantly and denied that he had been in Dodge City for the past two years. He claims to be well acquainted in Abeline, Topeka, Kansas City and St. Louis, and says he was under arrest in St. Louis a short time but does not say when or for what. He will not give his nativity and is quite reticent as to his movements and will allow no telegrams to be sent to any stockman who he claims to know. When searched at the police station no papers were found upon his person and 25 cents in money.

Telegrams passed rapidly between the Francklyn Company's New York office and police authorities at Galveston, R. M. Wright & Co., Temple Houston, and Harry Groom. On September 8, 1884, Francklyn wired M. W. Shaw at Galveston:

Despatch just received. Drafts you refer to not good but forgeries. Same party swindled R. M. Wright & Co, Dodge City, Kansas. Hold them if possible and advise us immediately. Consult our attorney Temple Houston Fort Elliott by wire. Both Grooms on range. Cannot get to Galveston inside of five days.

On September 10, 1884, Brown wrote Colonel Groom at Doan's Store:

The forger is again at his work. He has presented to M. W. Shaw, Galveston, three drafts for $7500 each drawn by H. T. Groom and endorsed by B. B. Groom to the order of C. A. Grothouse. I have had the party that presented the drafts arrested. Have wired all along the line and Houston and R. M. Wright & Co. now have the matter in hand. We are in hopes we can hold him. The matter here very hot. Please be careful not to draw any drafts unless you first advise as we do not pay until we first receive advice of the drafts having been drawn.

On September 26, 1884, Harry Groom wrote Brown from Dodge City that:

The forger is here in jail. He is the fellow I was introduced to in Mobeetie by the name of Werner. He looks all broken up and very much changed from what he was when I first saw him. He says he took only two drafts out of my book, but I know he took three and probably four. Only two of them are in our possession. The one he forged for $20,000 is not to be found. He said he did not expect to get the last forgeries through when I told him they were very poorly executed. I asked him where he got my father's signature. He said in a hotel register in Kansas City and that he never saw any draft drawn in Texas by my father for any amount. The men who brought him claim they are offered $1000 for him by the Texas parties; that he victimized Gov. Ireland for $2500 and that there are other things against him.

On October 26, 1884, the following article concerning the Young forgery was carried in the Dodge City paper:

Caught at Last, The man Henry C. Young with many aliases who forged the drafts on the Francklyn Land & Cattle Company here last June, and on one of them obtaining $3000 fraudulently, from R. M. Wright of Dodge City has very properly come to grief. He deposited $1000 of the money obtained from Wright with some papers at a bank in Kansas City, and perhaps from some cause was frightened away, never returned for it, so that it was rightfully recovered by the rightful owner. He went thence to St. Louis, and by playing stockman artfully, and by letters furnish proof of his assertions, ingratiated himself in the good graces of the Livestock Commission there. On the strength of this he obtained credit with Jaccard Jewelry House which he beat in goods to the amount of $9000. After doing the Commission men for various sums he skipped, since which time he has remained in obscurity. On last Monday, 8th inst. at Galveston he offered three forged drafts for large amounts on the Francklyn Land & Cattle Company purporting to be drawn by H. T. Groom in favor of C. A. Grothouse and endorsed by B. B. Groom. M. W. Shaw to whom the drafts were presented for payment had his suspicions aroused in some way and caused Grothouse to be arrested. The party proves to be the same we knew here last June and who did the little transaction for the Francklyn Company under the name of H. C. Young. The country is to be congratulated that so bold an operator has gotten to the end of his tether.

The Big Forgery of 1884

After attending the trial of Young at Dodge City, Harry Groom notified Brown on October 21, 1884, that "Today Young was tried and sent to the penitentiary for ten years. He could be tried on only two counts here and was given five years on each count."

In a letter written by Henry C. Young to Harry Groom from the Leavenworth, Kansas, prison on November 10, 1884, he took one last parting shot at Groom as follows:

> You have succeeded in convicting me of forgery in the District Court at Dodge City, Kansas. I have no cause to complain so far as conviction is concerned, but the amount of punishment (10) years is in my opinion a little too large for the offense, considering that you tried to work me in that same institution in Texas by helping Groom to defraud the State in some lands ostensibly in your favor.[1] Now I know all about your land transactions and know the inwardness, should I say the crookedness of it all, which gives me in my opinion some advantage. Your opinion may differ. You may think I am out of the way and cannot speak. Allow me to inform you that I can and will speak with effect when I see you will not come to my relief. No answer to this will be taken as a hint to crack my whip. Hoping you will thoroughly consider the matter, I am, Yours very respectfully, (Signed) H. C. Young

The case was closed with a letter from Harry Groom to Francklyn from Dodge City on December 14, 1884, in which Harry said:

> I saw R. M. Wright this morning. He was satisfied with the draft for $3000 which I sent to his credit at the German National Bank, Leavenworth, Kansas, but said he would be very glad if you could place the same amount in the same bank by January 1st as he had to make settlement with that bank then and was hard pressed for cash. I hope very much you will have no trouble with this and that you can do it conveniently.

With the Francklyn Company now having plenty of financial problems of its own, Colonel Groom and Mr. Brown were compelled to turn all of their efforts to the sale of cattle sufficient to meet a large note already past due.

---

[1] This passage refers to B. B. Groom's search for "twenty-three friends" to file on school lands in Block B-2 for the Francklyn Company in order to keep settlers and others out of the White Deer Pasture.

CHAPTER 10

A Desperate Struggle for Cattle Markets

THE YEAR 1884 WAS FILLED with failure and disappointments for the Francklyn Company. The weather was cold, wet, and windy during the winter months; it was extremely hot and wet during the summer season. Disease struck both cattle and horses, bringing heavy losses. These extremes in climate hindered and delayed work on the range and added greatly to the expense of cattle operation. Along with many other financial difficulties, the big forgery stripped the Company of several thousand dollars. Debts were piling up rapidly and expenses for feeding and protecting the bulls at Wichita, Kansas, where they spent the winter, were excessively heavy. Harry Groom wrote Brown from Wichita on January 25, 1884:

Since the bulls arrived the weather has been very cold and consequently hard on them. I have been with them almost constantly arranging them so as to have the stronger ones separated from the weaker. Have put up sheds so they all are protected and have good warm places to lay down.... Without shelter I do not know what we would have done day before yesterday with the wind from the north and so very cold.... The natural water here in creeks and River is shallow and at the same time boggy. This cold weather both are very mean to water from.... At night have arranged so as to draw the water out of the troughs so they will not freeze up; the water is run into barrels that are sunk under each trough and takes up all the surplus water in this way avoiding mud.... Mr. Kidd who is a practical man of large experience thinks everything is arranged in the best manner possible.

In a letter to Brown on February 16, 1884, Kidd said, "We had quite a number of very poor ones when we came and have lost 21 head of them. Do not think will lose any more as all except two or three are doing well as they can. Harry used fine judgment in the selection of a place to feed them. Has cost considerable to fix for them but it was money well spent."

Harry Groom reported to Brown on March 18, 1884:

It is raining here and everything disagreeable, as Kansas soil sticks like wax to everything it touches.... I expected we would have a little corn and hay left when I was here a week ago but now I do not think there will be any feed left at the rate it has gone for the week just past. I got strapped or broke rather at Fort Worth and had to draw a small draft at sight. I hope you will look over this draft. I had to go to the bank and get the money and none of these western banks will take a time draft. It would be taken almost as an insult to offer where a man is not personally known.

George Cranmer in a letter to Van Pelt, April 18, 1884, said that the spring roundup had begun and that "We have a large force out getting cattle that drifted from the range last winter. Hope to get them back early." He reported prospects good for a large calf crop, good grass, and fast stock improvement. He continued:

Though I saw a newspaper report that cattle were dying by the hundreds and the losses were verry heavy. There is not a word of truth in it. There was probably 100 died on this ranch last winter from poverty and the severe sleet in the latter part of the winter. There was probably 50 died from being burnt. The grass was set on fire when the wind was blowing hard. It burned so rapid that cattle or even deer could not get out of its way. As I wrote you I had sent a man to the Indian Agent in regard to the killing of our cattle. It amounted to nothing as he from want of power or inclination would not stop them. Since then I have had all of the cattle driven out of the Nation and will hold them in this country for the present. I have at present but one branding outfit at work. Our horses are too poor to start another for some days yet. Was pressed to mount our present force.

On April 21 Colonel Groom sent twenty-five horses to Kansas for Harry's use in bringing down the young bulls, and on the same day the Colonel reached Wichita Falls with one hundred "well broke horses, [and] branded and clipped the left ear of each" in order to distinguish them from other horses and distributed them among the men on the ranges. "A great part of them," he wrote to Brown that day, "have been used and fed grain through the winter and are ready for service at once." By the end of April Colonel Groom had eighty-seven men at work bringing the cattle back onto the range. "Distances are so great," he said, "I do not see how a less number could do the work. In fact all complain that their force is too light for what they are required to do."

Bank Notes and Cattle Sales

Brown wrote Colonel Groom at Doan's on May 2, 1884:

Francklyn sails on the 10th for home. I think he expects to return again before long. Everything on that side as well as here is fearfully quiet and stagnant. It has been useless to attempt to sell the bonds and we must worry along somehow or other till Fall. . . . We have a payment to make this month on account of land and there is the balance due on the cattle. Francklyn just writes me to see if we could sell 10,000 one's and two's if it comes to that point, or which would be best to sell. If we could do that together with our 5-year olds this Fall it would pull us through pretty well. I figured up ten days ago and find that we have made to date a cash outlay of $1,490,000 which includes everything but May 1st interest which added brings it up to $1,510,000. Think this over and if you can dispose of 10,000 head, advise me. I infer you do not calculate to ship any beeves to market this Fall. I do not see that we can. We certainly would get but little for the beeves this Spring as they must be poor in flesh. Therefore, do not see that it is necessary to decide on shipping point. Of course I cannot decide on these points here as they all depend on local questions which you and those around you must judge. . . . I think sometimes we will lose by not having the brand question in better shape and I sometimes think our policy is to put everything into Bar X,[1] Short Horns, Polled Angus and all.

On May 12, 1884, Brown inquired of Colonel Groom whether there was any chance to sell 10,000 one's and two's. "I did not know you intended to ship beeves this Spring and I think it is a mistake to do so, but as we are situated I suppose we must do so." Brown also reminded Groom that "the payment of $295,000 falls due July 1st." Colonel Groom thought it was too late in the season to sell one's and two's, as cattlemen had already supplied themselves. He inquired of Brown whether Francklyn wanted to include heifers in selecting the 10,000 to be sold. He declared that it would be impossible for him to leave the range to hunt buyers. He said:

For me to leave here to hunt buyers would be a very serious drawback to our business. We are now employing near 100 men in the roundups in the various directions going on at the same time as the branding of calves, selection of cows to go above, the current expenses to watch, with any amount of border to watch after, while everybody is gathering the unbranded calves that we missed last season. . . . As to the beeves the early cattle generally bring more per 100 pounds than the late when the market is thronged. I suppose the best way to get money out of this herd is to begin at once sending fat cows, steers, and bulls. We must commence and quit earlier than last year. To continue milling the cattle late we are in danger of losing thousands of head.

In a letter to Colonel Groom, May 29, 1884, Brown gave the following information:

Harrold is thinking of taking a portion of Hunter & Evans' land and if he does he will want 20,000 one's and two's. He is now in Fort Worth, having gone there on business. I told him we would not be able to pay him his money July 1st and he must either renew it, let it run until we could sell our beeves, or he must buy from us 10,000 one's and two's steers. He said if he took the land he would buy from us as he knew the cattle and delivery was close, but he could not tell anything about it until he had arrived at Fort Worth and had a talk with his brothers and Ikard. You know he never commits himself in advance and it is hard to tell what he will do. He will likely

---

[1] Bar X was a road brand used by the Francklyn Company in driving cattle to market, in order to distinguish their cattle from other trail herds.

as not sit down on the whole thing and want his money which we can't pay, until we get it from sales. The May 1st payment of $245,000 we have not yet paid and we can't. The interest we paid May 1st. You know we had a terrible crash here all along the line and the outlook is not pleasant. We did nothing on the other side with disposing of our bonds and we have put in all the money we can spare. None of the cattle schemes taken to England went through this year. For the present, therefore, I see no way out but to sell off and reduce the herd. Of course this is private information and not to be repeated. As we are now running, our interest and expense accounts are very heavy. I do not object so much to the Greer County expenses, but the upper ranch does consume a fearful lot of money and all to no apparent benefit.

Brown complained to the Colonel also about Harry's being off the range. He said: "I regret that Harry did not get back to the upper range before this as it does not seem to be the right time for those in interest to be off the ranges." Brown informed Groom that he planned to "be off to your place next week," and sent the same information to Robinson Bros. at Wichita Falls. Robinson Bros. wired Brown: ". . . better delay starting a few days. All rivers impossible on account of heavy rains and will be a week before traveling will be pleasant and presumed you would rather wait in New York than here." Brown wired back, "Will take chances on full streams. Leave Saturday night. Party will consist of four men and Mrs. Brown. Give me as good and complete outfit as you can—well provisioned."

Harrold also wired Francklyn, on June 6, from Fort Worth:

I saw Brown here a few days ago and he wanted to make some arrangements with us in regard to the money due us July 1st as you are aware by telegram from him as to our proposition. I had a telegram from him Saturday saying he wanted to hear from you before making final decision which I am at a loss to know what that decision is. May hear from him today or tomorrow as the time is getting close at hand and we would like to know what you intend to do by July 1st. Please advise us.

Meanwhile Colonel Groom reported to Brown, on June 7, 1884, that 8,160 calves had been branded despite excessive rains and that "all have been repeatedly drenched moving as we are dependent upon sheets and tents in severe storms, it has been impossible to keep dry."

A Desperate Struggle for Cattle Markets

He reported abundant grass on the range, and fat strong calves, but regretted to report that screwworms had:

... made a very bold start. If they grow much worse we will have to quit branding and go to doctoring. If so we might round up, doctor, and cut out beef at the same time. You would be satisfied to see the fine coat of grass on the range now. A dry Fall insures good grass for the winter and good cattle in the Spring. We are on the road to success.

On June 30, 1884, Colonel Groom in a message to Francklyn changed his tune somewhat, saying, "We have had ten days of intolerably hot weather on Greer. We have kept straight at work but it has been severe on both horses and men." He reported that 10,000 calves had been branded and predicted 10,000 more would be branded during the season. He wistfully hoped "that it will not be necessary to sell our yearlings at $7.50.... It will be a pity to sell them when there is such an abundance of feed to mature them. Cranmer says we have not near 5,000 2-year old steers as that calf crop was short." He further commented:

I do believe we ought to brand every cow beast owned by the Bar X. As it now stands there are so few men who know all the brands that we are too dependent on a few persons who use that fact and our friends can never know our cattle and inform us where they are, but if they were all in one brand we could employ men anywhere to help gather them. As it is with twenty odd brands it is impossible to do the work well. I am sure I do not attach too much importance to this matter of rebranding. Write me fully at once your views on this point as it is a very large undertaking and I wish to act advisedly according to your wishes.

On July 1, 1884, Francklyn wired Harrold, "Have deposited 100,000 Chemical National Bank [New York] in accordance with proposition wired me by Brown. Have written you today. If not your understanding will make it right on hearing from you in answer to my letter." On July 2 Van Pelt cabled through the Bank of New York 4,900 pounds:

... to meet payment of coupon No. 3 due July 1st. Will you kindly send us statement showing amount paid you for interest on above bonds due January 1st? (coupon no. 2) together with coupons which please cancel as there will be no more of that series presented to you. The balance in your hands from coupon no. 2 please retain toward payment of coupon no. 3.

On July 3, 1884, Van Pelt mailed to Harry Groom a statement of drafts drawn since March 19, 1884, those by him amounting to $34,367.16 and those by B. B. Groom totalling $21,368.06. Van Pelt advised Groom:

Check these drafts carefully with your draft account and report at once any differences you may find. You must use as much economy as possible in working the White Deer Ranch. Already this year it has cost us *more than double* what the lower ranch has. I know there are expenses in drives and tanks but still the other expenses are very heavy and must be cut down.

Harry, in a letter to Brown, August 20, 1884, in defense of his lavish spending, said:

My father writes me you are displeased with expenses at White Deer and compare the two ranches. There are not the number of cattle at White Deer but the same outlay will handle almost as many more. Still the two will not compare. In Greer they use no teams that cannot work on grass. At White Deer at this time we are working 30 mules plowing fireguards. These mules consume almost 50 cents worth of corn per day [per mule] which is equal to the pay of 15 men. I think our pay roll will show about 35 men. Carter has about 22 men and 50 mules which is equal to 15 men. This makes the equivalent of 50 men for the ranch and 37 for Carter, or about 87 men in all. The wire we buy, the permanent improvements we are making and all taken will clearly show why the expenses are heavy.

Now we could run this on the old plan, put up no hay for the bulls, build no tanks, not try to separate the bulls from our cows, let the yearlings and 2-year olds suck the cows and kill off the young calves, put up no corrals but kill up horses in roping and lose a big per cent of the calves by running them away from the herds—to leave off all these innovations on the old plan we cut expenses like everything, but when we get these things fixed then compare our profits and our cattle with those of the old plan and the difference will be seen. No man watches closer than I try to do and try to keep everything going in good shape and if I fail it is because no man can do it. I have stayed at headquarters just two nights in three weeks and do not expect to be able to be there more than that in the next three. . . . I hope the cattle will sell well but my father did not say to whom the cattle should go. I am in the dark as to prices. I wrote Gregory & Cooley if they were sell-

A Desperate Struggle for Cattle Markets 143

ing them to send me a note of the number and prices. . . . I have put my shoulder to the wheel and am going to succeed if a man can do it.

On July 12, 1884, Harrold acknowledged receipt of $100,000 from Francklyn credited at the First National Bank of Fort Worth for the use of Harrold & Ikard. The amount was credited as follows:

E. F. Ikard note $29,750, Harrold Bros. $70,270 which we hope will be all satisfactory. Have not read your letter but payment is agreed by us and Brown will send your note for the additional five per cent for you to sign and return to us. I expect you think the interest is exhorbitant but if we had the money we could get 1½ for it. Money is very close here and if we had not made arrangements to use some would have given you time on all of it. Am glad you have made arrangements not to sell your young steers for I think they will beat 25 per cent and then it will pay you to keep them. You have plenty of grass and are liable to stay there for sometime. Cattle are a little dull; that is, cattlemen have to sell and no place, to keep them. Interest payments July 1, 1884:
   Note $295,000 interest paid $22,125
   Payments July 1, 1884, $100,000, leaving $217,125
   Interest for four months on $217,125, $10,856.25
   $3,618.75 cut for four months.
If any errors in figuring will correct same.

Cattle Sales and Herd Depletion

During the summer months of 1884 Colonel Groom had the very difficult job of selecting suitable cows to send to market. "In order to get anything like fat cattle enough," he said, "we will be compelled to go pretty deep into good cows since almost all are going to have calves." He was also troubled with extremely hot weather and scarcity of water on the drives, factors which reduced the flesh rapidly. On July 27, 1884, he wrote Brown:

I feel safe in saying we can send off during the season 12,000 head, but in this number would be many young serviceable cows, regular breeders half of which would raise a calf this year and worth as much to keep as any that are not better bred than they are. The sending of each of these means one less calf to brand next year.

In reply to Francklyn's inquiry as to the number of two's and three's

Groom said it would be impossible to determine accurately. He explained:

There are so many contingencies to change the condition of cattle. Sometimes short feed or water through a whole season cattle that will do to go dry season will [be] this one. Old and young will be in better flesh this year than usual. In reference to the strength and number of the whole herd we can judge more accurately by comparing with last year's sales. Last year when persons would inquire about our number, they would ask us how many calves we branded. They would at once multiply by four and say we had that number. Now you will discover that as Harrold & Ikard branded only 9,000 calves year before last in all, this herd is now mainly composed of cows in their prime as breeders. Add the calves this year to the calves last year and this fact is apparent and it shows in every roundup made—a host of cows and a few steers.

Colonel Groom rushed shipments as rapidly as possible and kept Brown informed as to the number shipped from week to week. In a letter to Brown, September 3, 1884, he said:

If we contemplate selling our young steers next Spring they ought not to be disturbed this Fall. The horses are too poor in flesh to go further than I have already laid out for them as I hope to save them this winter, and with grass short as it is, the cattle must be let alone early or hazard the most dangerous loss. . . . Taking everything together our business looks as well as could be hoped. The cattle look healthy and well. The greater part of all females are either preparing to or have calves at their sides. I cannot tell yet how much beef we will send. What we get from this on will be scattering.

Brown was not satisfied with weights and prices of cattle that were shipped to market. He complained to Colonel Groom, September 10, 1884:

I do not like the way our cattle run this year, nor do I see what has become of our 3-year old steers. As I take it most of our lots so far have been made up of cows and two's. Do you think the three's have been run off or disposed of? Are we feeding them to the Indians? We seem to have so many enemies all around us that I sometimes think that our stock will constantly grow less instead of increasing.

Colonel Groom was called to Chicago early in September, 1884, to

A Desperate Struggle for Cattle Markets

straighten out delays in cattle shipments caused by the alleged appearance of Texas fever among the cattle of one of the shipments. As soon as this matter was cleared he went immediately to Greer, where he reported to Brown, September 14, 1884:

Upon my return I found everything doing well except the horses. In all my life I have never seen the flies so bad. Only during the night will they eat at all. Then throughout the range it is extremely dry and parched which adds to the trouble. The grass being so dry we are kept in constant dread of fire. There have been several but so far have been able to suppress them before extending far, and will work night and day should others occur. . . . The cattle look well although the flies trouble them very much also. . . . Since writing the above I find my horses have cut out and left owing to the flies which they have never done before. One of my horses, a grey light colored, looked yesterday as though he had been bled with knives and was actually red with blood on the upper part of the body. I am having as many as possible covered with sheets, especially the draft stock which are far most valuable. I hardly know what we will do if they continue much longer. Our hard-worked horses have to be worked anyway and this annoying new feature perplexes me. There is not a night some of the horses do not break away.

While the Company was struggling to meet its notes, J. C. Loving, acting as collector for the Northwest Cattlemen's Association, of which the Francklyn Company was a member, assessed the Company one per cent per head per annum, which Groom was compelled to pay in order to maintain the Company's financial standing among other cattle firms belonging to the Association. "I hate to draw a check," Groom said, "and hope to make sales hereafter as rapidly as possible so as to liquidate our liabilities." Groom was also having much trouble in selecting enough suitable cattle to fill the 10,000 quota that Francklyn and Brown had asked for. In closing out the shipments for 1884, he said, "Branding up the small herds has been a big undertaking . . . but the most difficult job I have undertaken is to select cattle out of a herd that is not there." Francklyn's order not to sell any one's and two's made it next to impossible to get a sufficient number of cows without sending producing stock.

Not only were the herds of the Francklyn Company being depleted, but also its financial standing was being questioned by its creditors.

Ferdinand Van Zandt[2] wrote Treasurer Van Pelt from San Francisco October 6, 1884, and requested him as follows:

Kindly forward to me at your earliest convenience a statement of the Francklyn Land & Cattle Company from January 1, 1884, to October 1, 1884, regarding payments on accounts of land notes and cattle and approximately the expenses to said date. Also will you kindly let me know the number of cattle and calves branded in 1884 and the sales of beef cattle etc. Also the total number of first mortgage 6 per cent bonds sold by the Company. I make this request as Lord Rosebery's representative and as the Director who has charge of his interests.

Van Pelt replied to this request, October 15, 1884, saying:

Your two favors 6th inst. received. When statement is made copy will be sent you. Francklyn who has just returned from England explained the condition of the Company to Lord Rosebery just before sailing. The number of calves branded up to September 1st was 15,000 and will probably reach 20,000 by November 1st. The Company has sold $1,000,000 worth of bonds to date. At the annual meeting today you were elected as a member of the Board to serve for the ensuing year.

On January 23, 1885, Van Zandt again called for the report and said:

If my statement has been prepared of the operation of the Francklyn Land & Cattle Company for the year ending December 31, 1884, will you kindly forward me a copy. I hear the loss in Texas has been unusually severe. Will you kindly tell me how our cattle came through the cold spell and if our loss has been greater than usual. I also see by clipping from the New York Times that the remaining $500,000 of the bonds of the Francklyn Land & Cattle Company have been offered for sale and would like to know if same have been sold or any portion of them and to whom. I dislike to bother you as I know how very busy you are in January, but wish to know what the sales of cattle were last year and if the payments on land and cattle were paid when due last summer.

Colonel Groom, in a strong effort to recoup the Company's treasury and improve its credit, sought a loan. On October 8, 1884, Brown received a letter bearing on this move addressed to the Francklyn Company from W. F. Somerville of Fort Worth:

[2] Ferdinand Van Zandt was the American agent of Lord Rosebery, who looked after Rosebery's interest in the United States.

Mr. B. B. Groom has been in communication with me in regard to a loan of $200,000, and as I do not at present know his address, and my clerk failed to give him the proper address, I write to ask you to see W. B. Shattuck, the Managing Director of the British American Company, who has an office in New York, but who dates his letters from Lennox, Massachusetts. Shattuck will consider your proposal and from what the firm of Shattuck and Hoffman write me, I have no doubt that you can arrange your loan with the Company. I would have advised you by wire had I been sure of your address, but hope this will not be too late.

Cattle Sales and Harrold Payments

Francklyn was interested in looking after money matters closer home. He sent Harrold the following explanatory letter dated October 20, 1884:

We have been expecting to see Mr. Loyd here for sometime past as he promised to call and see us before going West, but on inquiry at his hotel we find that he has gone away. We wanted to have a conference with him about our notes which come due next month. We have, as you know, been spending a lot of money in fencing, tanking etc to put the upper place in position to carry a number of cattle in the event of having some day to leave Greer County. It has taken nearly all our money and we have none to apply to your notes. We have lots of cattle, however, and we want you to make some arrangements to carry us along, either by giving us an extension sufficiently long to enable us to turn the cattle, or by joining with us on some fair basis in the Greer County range with say 40,000, forming a separate concern for it under your management. Or we would be willing to sell the Greer County range and the 40,000 head of cattle. You know the Government has exempted us cattlemen from the order turning out settlers or those claiming land in Greer County. Or would you contract to take one and two-year old steers at a price agreed upon deliverable next season? We have nothing but cattle to pay our debts with and trust you will deal fairly with us and help us to carry this matter along in one of the ways indicated above. I have just returned last week from Europe where I had hoped to raise some money for you but was unsuccessful.

Brown confided the following information to Colonel Groom on October 27, 1884:

Your various favors received. I wired you some days ago not to draw any more drafts until you heard from us. The reason is plain. No more money and the drafts were coming in so fast, especially from Harry Groom, that we had to cry halt. We have interest on bonds, interest on land purchase, and Harrold payments to meet and we do not see our way clear to take care of them at present. Times are getting very dull and getting worse from day to day. We do not look for a change for better until Spring, if then. We must make arrangements to sell off a portion of our herd in Greer County, else sell the upper tract of land. If we do not do this, we must sell our one's and two's and concentrate our business on one range. In the present aspect of affairs it may be best not to try to do anything in the way of binding us on the Indian lease unless you first inform us and get consent of Company before acting finally. I should advise you winding up for winter as soon as you can and shut down expenses to the lowest point. Do not overlook the point of selling cattle to be delivered next year. I do not know how and just when these sales are made, but we must be in the market in time with our goods and not get left. I hope you are now well and will get through all right. . . . I may go to St. Louis Convention. Tell Cranmer he must write me once a week or oftener if he can, in your absence, so we may keep run of affairs. Do not know how to meet Harrold payments due November 1st. We are figuring with him on an extension.

Francklyn wired Harrold at Fort Worth, October 28, 1884, that it was "impossible to pay anything November 1st except interest. Renew until July. In meantime will pay up soon as possible." On the same day Francklyn made the following appeal to Harrold:

I have your telegram saying pay $100,000 and renew balance in July. I have tried everywhere to raise the money, but with your claim on the cattle it is impossible. I therefore, telegraphed you today to renew until July and I would pay up as soon as possible. This is simply all I can say. I am very much grieved at having to ask this indulgence, but in these days I have no other alternative. You are quite safe to get your money, and I hope after the efforts I have made to pay you, I hope you will see your way clear. We shall leave no stone unturned to raise the money as soon as possible and I have little doubt we shall be able to pay you. These times men do little. You can have no idea out West how bad things are in New York. Gold dollars are the only ones anyone will take as security. We shall want to sell a block of cattle at the earliest moment and I hope you will help us to do so. You are in the way of hearing of purchasers perhaps more than we are, but we shall do our best. Groom writes me the cattle are all right and doing well. I shall go out and have a talk with him, but I cannot get the money by November 1st to pay you. You know we are acting in perfect good faith and I feel you are too, and the reverses of business may come to any of us.

Colonel Groom was stunned upon receiving a telegram from Brown, October 31, 1884, saying. "Do not draw any more drafts. Letter follows." He immediately wrote Francklyn from Fort Worth that:

Received Brown's telegram and letter. I sent to the office for the next mail after I supposed a sufficient time for the letter to reach there had elapsed but none came. I then determined to meet the next mail at Doan's myself and left the men on Sunday and expected to reach Doan's on Monday night, but the Red River could not be crossed until Tuesday morning. Still no letter came. I then went to Vernon to try to intercept it Tuesday night. Still none came and at Wichita Falls yesterday I got the Post Master to look into the Doan mail and under Brown's suggestion have applied to the office here and they have agreed to keep it for me if it comes this way as only part of the Wichita Falls mail stops here, I telegraphed for it to be sent back from Wichita Falls.

Except Brown's telegram I heard nothing of our business only through Larry Morris who was at the Falls and was told by Elin Harrold that the cattle had not all been paid for and that he expected to come up and seize them. This had made some stir before I heard there was any trouble about Harrold's payments amongst our hands. I traveled night and day to get where I could communicate and try to do anything in my power. I reached here last night to see anyone, but talked with every business man I met as to the aspect for cattle and all say the worst is over. As soon as the banks here were open I went to see Major K. M. Van Zandt, President of the Fort Worth National Bank, who is a gentleman of the first order and is my bosom friend. I talked confidentially with him and I know he gave me the exact condition of things here. He says bankers from the neighboring towns of the highest standing have been here trying to borrow without success; that money is not in this country and it is useless to try. Mr. Britton, President of the Traders National Bank said about the same. W. I. Boaz of the Traders National says there is not a firm in the country that can raise money anything like that amount. Harrold said he regretted he did not know a month ago that it did not suit to pay it, but Cap Ikard had bought cattle and promised his also. I tried to get him to tell me what he would do, but he would not do so. Said he would talk to Doc and Cap and he was expecting a telegram from you. I feel very much troubled about our orders out now for August and September that have not reached Robinson Bros. There is $4,000 still out and it will require about $3,500 to pay out for October. If that was out of the way I would then give notice that we would not pay again before the first of January. I am sure many of the men and some of the best of them will be compelled to quit for the want of clothing. Many of them spend their money as soon as they get it.

Another difficulty presents itself. We have at least thirty men we do not want to keep and don't see very well how we can get rid of them without paying them. They will not have money in many instances to go home on, and then the $4,000 I alluded to is orders on Robinson Bros. in amounts of from $5 to $50 and $60 much scattered among the bankers and merchants all over North Texas and must impair our credit and make it very difficult hereafter for us to get and keep the best men on the ranch. As I came down Robinson Bros. had paid about $200 more than our deposit and by this time he has paid from $1,000 to $1,500 as Dave Yokum's outfit and quite a lot of other orders on Robinson had been placed in his hands to collect and buy clothes etc for them. Robinson will be almost deranged if he pays much ahead. Says he cannot continue his business without his means. I do not allude to these things for but one purpose, that is, for you to understand the exact situation of the matters. I think it will be unfortunate if we cannot pay those small amounts. After paying them we might notify them we would not pay again for three months, but to have orders scattered all over the country on a house where we have no money will be most unfortunate for us. We have a grand property if we can only bridge it over these terrible times. I wish I could do more to help and I shall do all I can.

Harry Groom Piles Up More Debts

These were not all of the unpaid bills. Harry Groom used another faucet to draw out funds from the pool he thought was the Francklyn Company's Midas money barrel. His expenditures had to be reckoned with in some manner. On November 1, 1884, Harry wrote Van Pelt an explanatory and apologetic letter for having drawn drafts without first advising the Company, as he had been instructed to do, in which he stated:

I hope this will be satisfactory to you and Brown from whom I had a message not to draw any more drafts and saying a letter had been mailed. As I have

A Desperate Struggle for Cattle Markets

heard nothing further I presume this instruction to suspend drawing was caused by Brown thinking I had forgotten or was negligent in sending letter of advice. I have refused to give drafts to all the merchants to whom we are indebted asking them to give us a little extension for a few days and have succeeded in every case save in two and these were for labor and had to be given or raise a row with a class of fellows a man cannot explain anything to. One of these drafts I gave to Harrah for $600 for paying his hay cutters who have been working for us all summer and who were about being turned off as the work was finished. The other draft I gave to Chas. Rath for $2000 to cover labor during October for Carter and for the ranch. Rath had paid his money out to the men who were being paid off and he was overdrawn at his bank who were raising a row with him and he had to have this or feel that we proposed to use his money and see him left to hold the consequences at his bank. I am sorry that I had to draw these drafts and would not have done so except I knew they would meet Brown's approval if he knew the urgency of these cases. Now the balance I will leave over till I hear from you or Brown further.

The major part of the bills outstanding had been paid by R. M. Wright & Company for grain, supplies, and freight, which amounted to a considerable sum. "I did not pay Wright for any of these things," said Harry, "but asked them to wait till I got up there again about the 15th of this month. To this lot of stuff will be some additional for freight to the ranch." Colonel Groom became concerned over Harry's complete disregard of instructions about money and expenditures. In a letter of November 10, 1884, he gave the son some straight fatherly advice.

Your favor of November 1st to Van Pelt received. I wrote you on the 27th which I infer you have received ere this. It is not our purpose or design not to pay our bills and labor, but we long ago reached the point where economy must be used. The fact is we have too big a work on our hands and we are doing too much for the capital we have in the Company. If we were running only the lower range we would be all right and we would see our way clear to the end, but with the big purchase of cattle and with the big expenditures on the upper range we are using up a pile of money. To be sure our cattle are increasing rapidly, but we get no benefit of the increase until they become steers and in the meantime cash to a large extent is required to keep them going and the amount of money we are spending is general gossip and ridicule with all the cattlemen. They look for absolute failure which will be the result if we keep on as we are going. We have repeatedly been told before we went into this business fully that any undertaking with B. B. Groom and they had charge would only result in complete failure. We believed different and I think so now notwithstanding we are constantly warned of our danger.

We only ask that you run your part of the business same as others do who make a success and that you dispel from your mind that you have unlimited capital to draw upon; that you are to own the whole state of Texas, and that this Company will back you up in all your movements and doings. We think your policy is to make friends and be rather more quiet and easy in your movements with others rather than combat and fight and curse those you are thrown with. We must protest against your erratic movements all over the country which lead us into new dangers and much expense. Our business is and must be on the range watching and protecting our property. If we cannot make the money there we certainly cannot elsewhere. You must aim to get affairs down to proper system and economical working basis and above all look after the cattle.

Francklyn Creditors Call for Reports on Status of Francklyn Affairs

Colonel Groom was kept busy during November and December closing out the year's work on the ranges and providing for winter work and supplies. Although he had been instructed to remain at Fort Worth during this period, he wrote Brown, on November 6, 1884:

I have thought for a day or two that I ought to go up and stop the work and finish sending our horses to the White Deer place, all that can be spared to winter before they get too much scattered. . . . It will be best I think for me to go there very soon not knowing when I will be needed. Will return soon as possible. Another reason is that when winter begins I want to rule everything down to the very lowest prices. Many of the best men leave if this feature is carried too far. Just at this point Eph Harrold has come to see me and said to tell Francklyn to tell them in New York we must have $50,000 in the Chemical Bank in New York by the 10th and 50,000 more in a few days. I said you will of course wait ten days. He said very quickly no. Our Company fixed the 10th. Then he said he did not want to run us to expense but said they had to have the money; that they had been trying and had not succeeded in getting any. I have said all to him that I thought would have

A Desperate Struggle for Cattle Markets

any tendency to cause him to be content to wait but all to no avail. I believe Eph Harrold would have consented but I have learned in two or three ways that Cap Ikard is pressed for money, having bought a large interest in land and cattle of his brother and a good many cattle besides Elin Harrold was also buying and was receiving at the Falls as I came down. I am sorry they are so stubborn. I have just this minute received Francklyn's telegram telling me to remain in Fort Worth until our matters are arranged which I shall do and remain here until I hear further. Robinson was greatly relieved when I gave him the draft today. The excitement here is intense and the result of the State election not known.

Colonel Groom wrote to Brown on November 9, 1884, "I suppose having arranged to pay Harrold $100,000 tomorrow and 50,000 more in a few days and the balance deferred until July, completes all that is necessary to do about money now." Therefore he went to Dallas:

... to make some inquiry about money and found there parties loaning foreign money: Viz. Jas. B. Simpson who said he could loan 200,000 but would require 35 days to mature matters the arrangement of which I knew would be too long for us. His money would cost us 12 per cent. J. B. Watkins loans only on land. Paul Glucksen said his party had the money they wanted to loan and he would inquire. Wellesly & Co. loan English and Scotch money and said with a little time they could arrange $200,000. Their rate is 10 per cent and 2 per cent commission. . . . Unless there is something of importance to keep me here, I think I ought at once to go to the St. Louis Convention November 17th.

On December 19, 1884, Francklyn made the following report to Lord Rosebery:

Cattle on hand [various classes are listed] 76,629 head.

To carry on this business and pay for cattle I have had to borrow a good deal of money and I want now to pay Williams, Deacon & Co. 30,000 pounds which I borrowed from them on $300,000 of the Cattle Company's bonds.

Our inventory this year shows 720,000 acres of land at $3 an acre, $2,160,000 less amount due next five years $1,376,000.

76,629 head of cattle at $22.50 all around	$1,724,132
600 horses at $50	30,000
A grand total of	$3,130,152

Bonds on hand or pledged	$1,500,000
Bonds taken	$1,000,000
Debt of	$1,630,152
Due next July on cattle	$ 132,000
Williams, Deacon & Co. 300,000 [debt]	$ 150,000 [payment]
Bank note on $200,000 bonds	$ 100,000
Due on my securities	$ 240,000
For a total of	$ 622,000
Deduct the $500,000 bonds it leaves balance	$ 122,000

which is the worth of the capital stock.

I expect to sell a lot of one and two-year old steers this coming Spring and devote ourselves more to breeding than fattening cattle hereafter. The young cattle will bring high prices owing to their high grade and will be taken north to fatten. Please send me a telegram if you can take up the 30,000 pound loan. I think we shall be able to pay if off in six months. Of course sooner if we sell the bonds. I think we shall sell about $450,000 worth of cattle in 1885 which will put us in first rate condition and leave us with as many cattle as we have now, but a larger proportion of females.

With this report the hopes, prospects, and financial difficulties of the Francklyn Company pass over into 1885.

CHAPTER 11

Headed for the Last Roundup

THE YEARS 1885–1886 BROUGHT Colonel Groom the hardest work and the most disappointing experiences in all of his fifty years in the cattle business. He realized in 1885 that the continual drain on producing cows from the Francklyn range, if continued, would soon dry up the financial resources and put his company out of business. At the same time he was working against insuperable odds to protect his grass in both the Francklyn and the Greer ranges. His great courage and indomitable spirit never failed him and his loyalty to Francklyn and his Company never faltered. He used every means within his power to prevent the loss of the range he loved so well. Adding to his problems, controversy over the trails to northern markets, which ran through the Francklyn and the Greer ranges, was a constant source of annoyance. In Austin and vicinity Doc Day, George Breckenridge, John Blocker, and other large drovers were determined to defy the

Kansas quarantine law and continue to deliver their herds to the markets and pasture lands further north over any trail that was convenient for them. This coterie of capitalists kept in close daily touch with the most influential members of the Texas Legislature who were in opposition to the radical elements. These elements were making a strong fight to destroy the large cattle corporations in Texas.

Groom realized that he needed to keep closely in touch with legislative proceedings at Austin, particularly with reference to taxes and land leases. At the same time he had to keep himself as well informed as possible about the proposed changes in the quarantine law at Topeka, since both of his company's ranges were vitally affected by the trails and cattle drives through the territory that lay between the two states.

Brown spent the first part of February at Washington, D.C. watching closely the quarantine law then before Congress. "I have been trying to learn whether Kansas will quarantine against the Territory cattle, but it is not yet fully settled." On February 5, 1885, Groom notified Brown that:

I will not wait here longer on the Indian matters, but will leave here and pursue the course I have already laid out to you. . . . I have been suffering intensely with a carbuncle at my shoulder blade . . . and really ought to be in bed but will not stop while I can go at all. Will keep you posted about what I see and hear.

On February 13 Colonel Groom was at Kansas City, where he wrote Brown:

I reached St. Louis night before last and spent yesterday in that place and gathered all the information in my power in reference to cattle. Was introduced by Col. R. D. Hunter to Mr. Gregory of the City who will want 5000, and Wisner of Emporia, Kansas 2000. Mr. Atwater, Col. Hunter's former clerk and now Secretary of the National Cattle & Horse Association, is going to attend several of the Northwest cattle meetings and has agreed to gather for us all the information in his reach as to the sale of cattle. In fact I proposed to pay him a commission on any sales he may bring about.

I knew this last feature would stimulate Col. Hunter to assist, as Atwater is quite a pet with him. I left St. Louis at 8:30 last evening and arrived here at 8:30 this morning, having made all the inquiries I could think of, and hoped to find three men here I was desirous of talking to about cattle; that is, Andrew Snyder, Major Seth Mabry, and Judge Quinlin of Quinlin & Montgomery. Of the three Judge Quinlin is the most important. . . . I had a full long interview with Judge Quinlin in which it was agreed that any sales he made for us he was to receive 25 cents per head. He knows cattle well and thinks the yearlings ought to bring $16 and the two's $20. I talked up all I could but would be pleased with that figure. I am anxious to learn if Dick Head is wanting any cattle for any of the Companies he represents. If he does I will try to enlist him also.

While Groom was at Kansas City he received a telegram from Captain John T. Lytle saying, "Letter just received. Can meet you at Austin any time." In his letter of February 13 to Brown, Groom said:

As soon as I get away from Topeka I will go to Austin to meet him [Lytle] and J. Henry Stephens. . . . After having seen them I shall feel sure I have brought to our assistance that many of the very best aids in the country. I had intended to go to Greer the last of this month and remain pretty well through March, but in view of wanting to do all I can think of toward selling, I think it will be unwise to do so. . . . From all I can learn Kansas has not concluded whether they will quarantine with south line of the state, or include the Panhandle and Indian Territory down to Red River. Our sales may be affected to an important extent by their decision. I have just met Mr. McCoy, one of the leading men of Kansas, who thinks the matter will be up next week; that Mr. Willard and Mr. Frost all of Dodge City will be in Topeka next week when the matter is expected to come up. As soon as I can learn what I can, I will go to see Stephens and Lytle. I suppose you and Francklyn were pleased to see Lord Rosebery promoted to a Cabinet position.

On February 15 Colonel Groom again wrote Brown from Topeka that he was working with several interested parties and the Legislature to establish the quarantine line at the 34th parallel. On February 26, 1885, Groom informed Brown: "I made arrangements yesterday with Col. J. H. Stephens and Capt. John Lytle to sell cattle for us if the plan suits you, and for the purpose of laying out plans to carry out our purposes. They agreed to meet you and myself . . . at Chicago March 9th."

While waiting for matters to be decided both at Topeka and at Austin, Colonel Groom, eager to start the cattle drives, spent much of his time searching for cattle buyers. He traveled back and forth from Texas to Kansas City, St. Louis, Chicago, and other points in an effort to sell enough cattle to maintain the property and also to secure enough money to meet note payments as they came due. "The necessity of selling is increased by the crowd that will be pressed north of 34 this season so as to get out to market next year," Colonel Groom declared. "No one man could do what we have before us next year. It will be all I can do to see to the gathering and branding, shaping up the herds, branding calves and sending more to the upper place."

After spending several days at Topeka, Colonel Groom went to Austin, where he informed Brown that he had reached an agreement with Stephens and Lytle and urged him to meet with these men at Chicago March 9 to discuss the situation.

Meantime Harry Groom, "About knocked to pieces with a heavy cold, together with rheumatism," was busy providing corn and hay at high prices for the cattle and horses, preparing farms for forage crops on White Deer, gathering cattle outside the range, and looking after ranch affairs in general. On February 26, 1885, he appealed to Brown to "Come as early a date as you can and look over the range if possible before we begin work. There are many things I would like for you to see and decide the best way to accomplish, and I do not think we should put off longer preparing some of them." On March 11 he declared, "I have tried to do the best I could under the circumstances, though we have had a very severe winter. The stock are *all* thin, horses as well as cattle—so very cold long continued spells that it took off all the flesh."

The Groom-Lytle Agreement

Prospective sales greatly encouraged Colonel Groom and, as a result, he made an agreement with Stephens and Lytle. According to the contract Stephens and Lytle were to take charge of the cattle in Greer, select the route, see to all matters on the trail, sell the cattle, and place the money as Brown directed. They were to furnish the best bosses to go with them and attend to the whole matter as though the cattle belonged to them. For these services they were to receive $1.00 per head. In commenting on the agreement Groom advised Brown:

Headed for the Last Roundup

These gentlemen are better acquainted with the trade in cattle than any other two men I know of in the country. Col. Stephens has sold the increase of the King & Kennedy herds for more than ten years numbering over 20,000 per annum. They sold between them 75,000 head last year. . . . They have the advantage of obtaining horses, as they have the buying usually of so many. Their management all the way through is certainly desirable to us.

In preparing for the delivery of cattle to Stephens and Lytle, Colonel Groom was faced with the problem of finding more horses. Harry Groom reported to Brown on February 28:

All the horses in the country are dog poor, a heavy winter and such poor grass the frost killed that it is rotten and will come off right at the ground if you pull it. . . . Some of them are almost naked having lost their hair from itch during the winter and the weather so cold I could not have them washed. They have had one washing but the hair is so long and woolly is hard to get them thoroughly soaked with the wash Chrysillic ointment. All of them need cleaning out and boiling, as all their sheaths are foul and some badly swollen.

Colonel Groom estimated that it would take at least a carload of well-broken corn-fed horses. "The cutting of 25,000 cattle to send off, many of them still sucking, will be a terrible job on horses," he said. "I will aim to be on the ground ten days before we commence cutting or moving any cattle. I will have to draw a little for current expenses. The horses will cost about $12 to $14. I will use all possible economy in every way."

Groom felt that there was no prospect of selling cattle at a reasonable price without driving them. In a letter to Brown, February 26, 1885, he observed that:

All buyers south of Kansas are bound to see that cattle can be obtained at very low prices and that the scope of country between 34 and 37 will be thoroughly crammed with cattle, and if the quarantine line is fixed where now spoken of, which now seems almost certain, Kansas will allow no cattle to pass through except such as are north of 34 the year previous to the first of December to go into Kansas, and other states and territories seem to be fixing about the same regulations.

Groom further explained to Brown, on March 30:

It was fortunate for us that the Kansas quarantine line was located at 34, south of us. I have been told by several that the yearling cattle are selling in some Southern localities as low as $8 per head. Gov. Sayer says he expects to get all he can pay for at $7. . . . I believe in selling all we can for the reason that we are north of the line and could fill again at greatly below what we will be able to sell for. The gloom of the cattle trade all over South Texas is terrible.

Colonel Groom, therefore, urged Stephens and Lytle to sell from 5,000 to 7,000 cows and calves in addition to all the one's and two's. He said in a letter to Brown from Austin, April 1, 1885:

They will try but deem it uncertain about selling any cows. Stephens passed through here [Austin] on his way to Wyoming and Montana to look after buyers. . . . They seem about as sanguine as at first about sales. They say that a greater part of the cattle that are to go to the Northwest this year must be supplied by New Mexico and they have learned that drovers are paying about $17 for one's and $18 for two's from which ours can undersell them when all expenses are added. Just as soon as cattle do move we will begin. From the present appearance of grass we suppose the first can start between April 25th and May 1st.

Harry Groom believed that "A little later on will be the best time to sell as the Northern men will see that Southern cattle cannot get north, I think the price will spring upward. With New Mexico, Colorado, and Kansas making such stringent quarantine laws we should get big prices for our cattle."

Colonel Groom suffered much anxiety about the invasion of Southern cattle into both Greer and White Deer ranges because of the danger from both short grass and Texas fever. In his letter of April 1 he said:

I am doing all in my power to get drovers of Southern cattle to keep away from us as much as possible both by begging and a little threatening sometimes. These times and surroundings are so different from any before we cannot tell. Many men seem to have become desperate. . . . Col. Babcock, the Agent for the new Capitol Syndicate has bought about 20,000 cheap Sea Coast one's and talks of driving them through Greer, then through Mobeetie to that part of their land lying in Dallam County which is the extreme Northwest corner of Texas. They are to come up to the end of the railroad above Wichita Falls at Harrold by the cars and being so fresh from the Coast will endanger all the cattle they strike. I have talked to Col. Babcock and told him we would hold their Syndicate responsible for all we lost by fever. He was very gentlemanly about it and said he would try to avoid us entirely. . . . The opposition in the Indian Territory and the Panhandle to Coast cattle is almost as great as that of Kansas.

There was general opposition to Coast cattle in the Northwest. Western cattlemen were aroused by the appearance of Texas fever on the Western Plains. At a meeting of several Western associations in St. Louis on April 1, 1885, they protested strongly against the forwarding of Southern cattle by railroad and trail into northern ranges. "Such cattle," they said, "impart to ours Texas spenic or Spanish fever which has caused loss of 300,000 in Colorado, 500,000 in Kansas and Indian Territory, and 300,000 in the Texas Panhandle in addition to heavy losses on beef cattle shipped to Eastern markets." They also called attention to the quarantine laws passed by Kansas and Colorado and the territories of New Mexico, Wyoming, and Montana. They declared:

> The same reasons exist for the protection against this class of cattle being driven over or held upon ranges represented by us. Therefore, We the undersigned do solemnly protest the introduction of such cattle into our country from the south and east. . . . The high breed of cattle upon our respective ranges represent the accumulation of years of toil and industry and we can ill afford to suffer them to come in contact with cattle which invariably communicate disease to an extent liable to annihilate our herds. While deprecating the use of force, self preservation is the first law of nature. Therefore we the undersigned associations combined as a unit in the Committee assembled, do hereby pledge our associations to resist by all legal and necessary means the encroachment of such cattle on our ranges, and notice is hereby given that any attempt to hold or graze such cattle on any range along the trail will be met with prompt and united resistance by the associations here represented.
>
> (Signed)   The Panhandle Stock Association
>   Western Kansas Cattle Growers Association
>   Cherokee Strip Livestock Association
>   Cheyenne and Arapahoe Cattle Association
>   Bent County Colorado Stock Association

Meanwhile Colonel Groom was desperately searching for a loan. On April 9, 1885, in reply to an inquiry he made about the Greer cattle, Colonel C. R. Smith of Gainesville, Texas, was informed that a lien of $135,000 was held on the Bar X herd by Harrold and Ikard. Colonel Groom was anxious to get the 25,000 cattle into the hands of Stephens and Lytle in order to remove this lien, and he was almost ready to begin deliveries. On April 22, 1885, Stephens arrived at Wichita Falls with seventy-five men and 475 horses, together with about 130 horses he had purchased for Groom. The town was flooded. In a letter to Brown from Wichita Falls, April 21, 1885, he said:

It is pouring down in torrents of rain and until the streams run down it is useless to try to cross them. . . . Some gentlemen have just come in who had to swim the small streams and with everything soaked in their waggons, barely escaped safely. . . . It will be utterly impossible to do anything with the cattle until the ground settles. As it is now, a horse cannot carry a man two miles. As we have such a heavy work before us, we must save horse flesh all we can. As the force here is large I shall use every possible means to put things forward, but it would be the height of folly to rush men and supplies out in the flood and rain.

On his way to Wichita Falls from Fort Worth, Colonel Stephens stopped at Henrietta to deliver 6,000 King & Kenedy steers, and a Forsyth herd of 2,000 head to J. M. Coburn, Indian beef contractor, to be delivered to the nearby Indian reservation. Groom also hoped to sell to Coburn, since deliveries would be close. However, the railroad was washed out in several places between Fort Worth and Wichita Falls and no trains had passed for three days. This stopped all deliveries. Colonel Groom in his report of April 26, 1885, to Brown said:

These cattle all due and locked up on the road caused great confusion and with Waggoner, Worsham and Burnett all trying to sell to him, it was impossible to get anything definite out of Coburn. . . . He intimated he would give $18 for our dry cows and $25 for our steers we have over three years old delivered on the ranch, but said he would buy no more until after the new contracts for the Indian beef were let May 5th. I feared to press the matter that it would cause too much anxiety. I would prefer to sell on the ranch if we could do anything like as well. Although Stephens & Lytle say cattle expenses wear and tear are only $1 per head, I would sell every time at $1 less and some more.... All these prices are very low. The confusion caused by the new laws in Texas with the tightness of money are making many simply desperate and many will be entirely ruined. I never saw so much difficulty in knowing what is best to do. I am still very clearly in the belief that to dispose of our one's and two's the only thing to do is to drive them.

Groom informed Francklyn from Turkey Creek in Greer, April 28, 1885:

Stephens and Lytle will move out Monday morning with waggons and horses. Their movements contain seven outfits designed to move 3000 cattle to each one. Immediately after reaching Elm [Creek] one will keep right on to White Deer and reach there ready to take a herd to be gathered by May 5th.... Two outfits commenced to gather one's and two's today. We think our horses have done badly but out of 92 Stephens expected to go with our cattle only 22 are alive and not a single one he can take on the drive. It seems to be their purpose to go ahead and make examinations for purchases. Their general direction will be near the southwest corner of Kansas and then point them for Cheyenne. In reference to money I have requested them to raise $100,000 as soon as the cattle get fully into their hands. From direct sales they will hardly be able to send any returns I think short of sixty days, but with very little trouble I believe they could get $100,000 soon.... I have not succeeded in finding a buyer for cows and calves this season owing to the quarantine and change of Texas laws, and some confusion in the Indian lands, and the ordering of removing fences in the Northwest all taken together have caused a great disposition to buy steer cattle. I have urged Stephens & Lytle to use every means to sell cows and calves and I shall keep trying.... It has been my constant purpose to comply with your wishes and, although I have been engaged in the cattle business for over forty years, I constantly seek the advice and experience of the best informed men I can find. All my movements are made under one or the other to comply with your wishes, or by the advice of those who ought to know and my own experience.... I shall look to concentrating everything on the upper place as soon as practicable. We calculate to send off all the one's and two's we have except such two's as are forward with calf.

Stephens returned from the Northwest about April 14, 1885, but no sales were made. "Good demand for cattle," he said, "but everybody seems disposed to wait."

Cattle Invaders and Money Shortage

W. D. Searles, vice president of the New York & Texas Land Company, warned Francklyn on May 4, 1885:

> Referring to your favor of the 1st instant. in which you say that your Company intends to postpone payment of its note for $146,000 which has become due. We would advise you that the failure to pay same at maturity destroys the extension granted on $200,000 which became due November 1, 1882, and makes you personally liable for said $200,000 under your guarantee given at the time of the extension, and we hereby demand payment of same. An early answer will oblige us and avoid delay in calling a meeting of the scrip holders.

In an effort to meet this demand Groom analyzed the cattle situation and pondered the possibility of screening the herds closer and sending off still more cattle from the Company's ranges. He advised Francklyn, May 9, 1885, that "we have before us the sending off of the one's and two's, the old cows and calves, and the sending of five or six herds to White Deer. So you can see we have no time to idle. If you think best we might be able to send over 3000 cows and calves to market, but of course it would lessen our breeding capacity."

Colonel Groom in coming through Greer on his way to Dallas, May 14, met:

> ... five thousand cattle on our road from Doan's to Salt Fork pens ... to be delivered to the Capitol Syndicate in Dallam County. I at once inquired for the boss. A large man presented himself and says, "Have you any guns in that waggon?" I said no. He then came close. I said where are your cattle destined? he said to the Capitol lands. "I am going through Mobeetie and take the mail line to Tascosa." ... This man turned out to be Ab Blocker one of the owners of the cattle. He was accompanied by a young Mr. Babcock, son of the Capitol contractor. They were at first very much excited, but after telling them what we lost last year from fever by cattle driven in ... they said they would not enter our enclosure but would go around. About one mile from them I met 1000 more who said they were going with Blocker's herd. After being told what Blocker and Babcock

Headed for the Last Roundup

agreed to, they said they would pursue the same course. In a few minutes I met John Pierce, Agent of the Panhandle Association, who said he was directed to notify them to stop which they did. . . . On reaching Wichita Falls I found Rayland, Manager for Rachel, with 7000 Coast Cattle of the most infectious kind who said he was instructed to drive through our pasture. Pierce had also stopped Rayland who with Collins appealed to the Governor. . . . It is believed the Governor will support the trail laid out and the trouble will end. If so, our pasture is clear of danger.

I had another purpose in coming here, that is to see Hughes and Simpson who have as bankers negotiated for large sums of money for cattlemen heretofore. I explained to them that in a few days I wanted $100,000 on cattle that were placed in Stephens and Lytle's hands and asked them to assist me which they both consented to do. They have an office in St. Louis and said they would be there about the 23rd or 24th and would like to have me be there. If the money is obtained it will cost at least 12 per cent per annum and require a lien on the cattle placed in Stephens and Lytle's hands for sale to secure the payment. The money to be furnished about the 27th of May and the note to be for 90 or 120 days as we prefer. These men are both my friends and will get the money if they can I am sure. I got a telegram from Capt. Lytle today saying Stephens will return in a few days. He is now at Corpus Christi. I shall go to San Antonio in the morning reaching there tomorrow night and if Stephens will be gone longer will go right down and see him and insist on his raising $100,000. Between the two chances I hope to obtain money. At all events I shall not stop until every means in my power is exhausted until I get it or see I cannot.

Colonel Groom notified Brown from Dallas, on June 19, that he went to San Antonio to fix up the papers for the $100,000:

. . . which are to be sent to New York for Francklyn's signature and returned when the money is to be ready. Lytle and Stephens speak of it as a certainty. They expect to get it through Mr. Chick, President of the City National Bank. I will telegraph you as soon as the thing is positive. . . . I asked Harrold to wait until we got some proceeds from the cattle. He said they made their arrangements to use it, but said he would see me again. He came to me a little while ago and said he would like to buy 7000 steers, 5000 one's and 2000 two's. I replied they were in the hands of Stephens and Lytle and I would see Lytle and let him know. Just then Doc Harrold came up and joined in the chat and said they were for him and he would like to get them as he was partial to the cattle and that he wanted them delivered at the Rosebud Agency near Cheyenne where he owns land. I promised to let him know when I see Lytle.

R. H. Arnold at Mobeetie sent Brown a notice, on May 20, that the herd concerning which Groom had wired him:

... passed here today going north. It belongs to Dawson from the head of Pecos. People here think there is no danger on this trail. There are, however, several through herds from the Coast countries now holding on Bitter Creek twenty miles north of Doan's. A committee of stock men (Doc Day, Alfred Rowe and young Ellis) went down to meet them so as to get their consent to go north on the trail until they get to Creswell's drift fence north of the Canadian River and follow along that trail to Dallam County where they are going. If they do not consent to do this an injunction will at once be made and parties arrested if they attempt trespassing. What stirred us up so was their way bill which directed them to pass just up North Fork until they came into the pasture and right over to White Deer and on to the Canadian north jeopardizing our whole stock. If the law don't stop them before they get to the pasture we will use force of arms.... The cattlemen here are altogether in the matter and will use all means in their power to keep them on the route they have picked for them.

Harry Groom wrote Francklyn, May 27, that "The cattle have turned and are going back so they will give us no more trouble."

During the summer and fall of 1885 the Francklyn Company's creditors began watching the cattle movements closely and periodically checked on the Company's financial status. On May 11 the Farmers Loan & Trust of New York notified the New York & Texas Land Company that:

A meeting of the holders of this Company's land note certificate issued as provided by an agreement dated June 1, 1883 between the New York & Texas Land Company will be held in this office May 13th at 3 p.m. to take action in reference to certain securities held under that agreement. This meeting is called at the request of several parties in interest.

On May 22 E. B. Harrold gave notice to the Francklyn Company that "As the time is drawing near when the money will be due July 1st, hope you will meet it promptly as we have made arrangements to use it then."

On June 2 Ferdinand Van Zandt at Butte, Montana, requested Van Pelt that he:

... kindly send ... as soon as possible a complete statement of the financial condition of The Francklyn Land & Cattle Company as Lord Rosebery has requested me, as his Agent and attorney in this matter, to ascertain and report to him personally regarding same. I must request you to send me a complete memorandum of all outstanding liabilities upon land, cattle, etc., the dates on which they came due and the measures taken to meet same. I wish particularly to know what arrangements have been made with Harrold Bros. in regard to the $132,000 due them on July 1st, 1885. I regret to see the small amount realized on your last year's sales—8147 head selling for $161,888 net, $2.61 less than was originally paid for the range cattle. I would also be obliged if you would send with the statement a list of stockholders with the number of shares owned by each and the number of bonds owned by them. I would also like to have copies of the Directors meetings and some information regarding the Company's plans for this year. I regret very much to trouble you to this extent but circumstances compel me to do so, and in doing so I am acting as Lord Rosebery's authorized Agent, as I represent his interests on the Board of Directors.

The note of $73,000 was paid on May 29, 1885, but the settlement with Harrold and Van Zandt was a far different matter. In order to ease the matter with Harrold, Colonel Groom offered to sell him 7,000 one- and two-year-old steers at $23 and $18, but Harrold wanted ten days in which to answer. Groom stipulated that:

In the event you do not buy the cattle you all must wait until Stephens and Lytle sell some cattle for your money to which he replied there would be no trouble about that.... They will expect the money when Stephens and Lytle get it. I shall do all I can to sell cows and will commence sending beeves to Chicago very soon.... I asked Lytle at Kansas City when he thought other money might be expected. He said $100,000 July 1st, and $200,000 about August 1st, and the ballance [balance] about the middle of September, but said, "I cannot tell of course until the sales are made."

Colonel Groom notified Francklyn, June 14, 1885, that Colonel Stephens started for the Northwest on April 14 and would remain there until all the cattle were sold. Groom also advised that he had withdrawn from the Indian lease in Greer and added:

I shall notify the Indian Agent that we will have nothing more to do with the lease. The Commissioner of Indian Affairs disturbed and made so much stir and fear about the lease that I saw it would be folly to try for any further bonus. . . . I am enclosing a letter from Harrold which he sent me by special messenger so as to let me know what to reply to it. . . . I am trying to get Stephens and Lytle to raise some money for him. If you have any spare money about July 1st, it might be well to pay him some and then I think he will wait for the ballance. . . . Our work has been greatly delayed this Spring by almost constant wet and muddy weather. Red and Pease rivers are now past fording. . . . I do hope to commence sending beef as soon as the last two herds get off north.

E. B. Harrold Demands Cattle Payments

Harrold was not easily appeased on the money question and he kept pressing the matter. Groom wrote Harrold, June 14, that he had telegraphed Stephens and Lytle to "rustle up some money by July 1st" and assured him that:

I have all the time told them that I wanted to hurry up sales enough for this purpose and that the first proceeds must be for you. The cattle we send them should bring in all over $500,000 and the first will be for you. Francklyn expects me to meet this matter out of sales of cattle. They said they could give us $150,000 in July and $200,000 in August. Now I feel that you can arrange this without serious inconvenience to yourself. You feel I know that we have been large customers of yours and we have had dull, slow markets, and I think deserve indulgence as far as possible.

Immediately after receiving Harrold's letter saying that he wanted some money by July 1st, I telegraphed Stephens and Lytle and got the following reply: "Cattle going through via Coolidge [Kansas] all right. Will notify you about money July 1st." . . . I have nothing further than my last contained except the fear of flat beef markets. Be sure and give me your ideas of how low prices we must quit sending out on until they are better. We must rest men and horses latter part of July and August. The work of cutting out 20,000 cattle is no child's play either for men or horses.

Colonel Groom explained to Francklyn, also, on July 1, that:

It has been a hard season on all. It has taken active work to get where we are now. We have branded 6675 calves, but fear to brand any more on account of screw worms which all are expecting to be very bad owing to the great amount of wet weather. You never saw so many flies and mosquitoes in your life. We often build fire to create smoke so the horses can eat.

On August 26, 1885, Stephens and Lytle reported to Francklyn from Ogalalla, Nebraska that they had 10,700 cattle there and said:

> We are unable to find any buyers and we fear the market is over for this season as it is becoming late to move cattle very far north. We will use every effort in our power to find purchasers for the stock, but in case of failure would like one of you here to suggest what disposition to make of them. . . . We feel confident that if we should make any sales we shall have to shave the price considerable as quite a number of cattle are being offered at much lower prices than we sold for. Our sales so far amount to $262,000, part of which has been paid, part due on delivery of cattle, and balance October 1st. Hope you or Groom will come to Nebraska soon, as something must be done within twenty days.

Colonel Groom went to Ogalalla, where he remained until all the Stephens and Lytle herds had been disposed of. He and Lytle simply scoured the country between Chicago and Denver and all intervening points in search of cattle buyers. They finally had to sacrifice the entire stock at "ruinously low prices." He wrote Francklyn the following explanatory letter from Ogalalla on September 3, 1885:

> When I came here I had not the remotest idea that I would ever consent to take the mean price for which the last cattle have been sold. . . . I have tried everybody I could hear of. . . . I tried every possible means I could to cause a sale by personal favor, commission etc. I canvassed the money question with men who supply more money to cattlemen than anything else and they all say they are oversupplied with money in the Spring, but in the Fall and Winter their money is used in moving grain and pork. The crash in the beef market at Chicago last Saturday, followed up the following Wednesday by the heaviest run of cattle ever made to the Union Stock Yards seems to have paralyzed the cattle trade for this season. From my best friends in this place, and from others, the most experienced men here, I learned a peculiar and alarming state of affairs. The losses north of this have always been larger than I had ever supposed, in the past winter it has been simply terrific. W. M. Paxton of the Swan Land & Cattle Company told me that of the Sheedy herd sold to him for 32,000 they had gathered only 12,000 and did not expect to gather over 1000 more. On the same range Stephens and Lytle turned loose 1600 steers and when they quit had less than 500. Shep-

herd, Wood, and a dozen others have talked as alarming. They say none of the Northwest has done any good. Add to this the stringency in money. There are simply no buyers at any price.

Groom Returns to Diamond F and Greer Ranges in Desperate Search of Cattle and Credit

With the Stephens and Lytle cattle out of the way, Colonel Groom was back at Harrold, Texas, on September 24 mulling over the problem of finding more cattle to send to market. He wrote Francklyn that "according to what we agreed when I saw you last, I must pay these men off with cattle. To do so we will have to draw heavily on White Deer." He continued:

> I hope you will write me at Mobeetie on receipt of this and tell me if I run short of cattle fat enough to go, whether to continue to send until the debts are paid.... From what I can see and learn it is going to rub us hard to get cattle enough that ought to go to pay Strahorn and Gregory & Cooley. To send good young cows as we are now doing, and will have to continue to do from this time on, is like killing the goose for the golden egg. From this on they are bound to be light and rather thin.... Now you must telegraph me at Mobeetie what to do.... I know no one can estimate the drawbacks that present themselves when there is so large a scope to look over. I am very anxious to concentrate and hope we can do so next year.

Francklyn began to check closely on affairs at White Deer, and on December 10, 1885, Brown requested Harry Groom to examine the records at Mobeetie to find whether any papers had been filed concerning the Company. The record showed a note in the sum of $139,400, due September 1, 1886, secured by 5,000 cows with 5,000 calves by their side, and also a note of $25,000 due September 1, 1885, secured by 2,000 cattle in the various brands of the Company.

During the latter months of 1885, the bondholders also began to check on the land and cattle situation on the Company's lands. On October 28, 1885, Cranmer informed Colonel Groom:

> As I came down yesterday [from White Deer] I met Van Zandt who used to keep books for you. He told me at first he was to look into the ranch business. He asked me many questions and said he came out to look at the books. I told him the books were correct and open to inspection at any

Headed for the Last Roundup

time, and all questions he had asked me would appear on the books. . . . I told him the books would show everything but the loss and no one could tell that. I found before he left that he was sent out (or claimed to be sent out) by Lord Rosebery and his brother, both of whom he said were largely interested in the ranch. . . . He said just before he left me that he could not get any satisfaction from New York about the business and that was why he was sent out. He asked me many questions about the other ranch [White Deer]. I told him I knew nothing about their business up there as I was only on the ranch one time. He told me he would be at Harrold tonight, but I find he went from Vernon and will not be here.

Creditors were now moving in fast in their efforts to secure payment on loans which they had made to the defunct company. As a result of these pressures, Colonel Groom was flitting about all over the country in one last effort to secure a loan with which to save his company from bankruptcy, but it was all to no avail, since his credit was wiped out. On March 26, 1886, he wrote Brown from Lexington, Kentucky: "I feel that I have exhausted every means within my power to arrange for money and start the drive and the time is right on us."

As if to revive the hopes of Francklyn he sent him a telegram from Denver on April 17, 1886, in which he wistfully reminded him that, "Sen. H. A. W. Tabor, H. B. Gillespie, and eight others in London, have 25 million dollars of available funds. All of them are gentlemen of large means representing fully 100 million dollars." The Francklyn Company, however, had used up its credit facilities and could no longer borrow money. Consequently Francklyn resigned as President of the Company and Charles B. Alexander, alternate trustee, followed suit. On April 17, 1886, Frederic de P. Foster, a New York attorney representing the British bondholders, was appointed trustee, and Russell Benedict, a member of the firm at New York, was named as his assistant in accordance with the deed of trust executed by the Francklyn Company in 1882.

With these documents legally recorded, exit the Francklyn Land & Cattle Company and with it the fondest hopes and dreams of Colonel B. B. Groom to establish at White Deer "The finest cattle ranch in Texas."

CHAPTER 12

British Bondholders Take Over White Deer Properties

THE RESIGNATION of Charles G. Francklyn and other officials of the Francklyn Company left a hiatus in the Company's affairs. Texas law did not permit alien nonresidents to hold land in Texas. Therefore, it became necessary to make some arrangement by which the English subjects could control and manage the Company's lands despite the fact that the Atlantic Ocean and some 3,000 miles of land lay between them and their Texas properties. To meet the situation a trusteeship was set up under the management of Frederic de P. Foster with power of attorney to receive and transfer title to both land and cattle owned by the Company.

Foster headed a large law firm in New York City and actively participated in the City's political and social affairs. Russell Benedict, a prominent young attorney and also a member of Foster's firm, became secretary to the trustee. In taking over the trusteeship Foster and Benedict moved with caution. The Company's affairs were complicated with much uncertainty as to its future prospects. All kinds of rumors were floating about in West Texas about fraud and mismanagement. Colonel Groom's failure to meet his financial obligations sparked these rumors. Such a situation inevitably provoked dissatisfaction among employees of the Company.

S. W. Morrow Makes Secret Inspection Trip to Texas

The elusive Grooms, not yet aware of Francklyn's resignation, gave out as little information as possible about the financial affairs of the Company. Consequently, Foster and Benedict resorted to an indirect method of investigating the Company's affairs. Oddly enough Foster was a close friend of one Mr. Swenson of New York City, who operated a ranch in Jones County, Texas, some two hundred miles south of the Francklyn range. Mr. S. W. Morrow, also a resident of New York City, formerly managed the Swenson Company's interests. Foster deemed it wise to send Morrow to Texas, ostensibly for a visit to the Jones County ranch. Morrow was an old friend of Temple Houston's, who at that time was the attorney for the Francklyn Company. Morrow called on Houston and told him what was afoot. Harry Groom learned of Morrow's visit and reported to Francklyn on March 29, 1886, that Houston had received some information of a private character from Morrow. Harry relayed Houston's information to Francklyn and introduced the report with the comment "Today I got him to dictate the following as the sum and substance of his conversation on the subject." The summary of the Houston-Morrow conversation followed:

> It appears that Swenson & Jones of New York as the representatives of certain capitalists, have sent a young man out here to observe the property of the Company and inspect the manner in which it is managed, and see particularly that no cattle are driven away from our range in order to defeat certain liens held by parties whom Swenson & Jones represent. The young man is a practical cowman. He seems to know nothing about the holders of the liens, further than they are represented by Swenson & Jones. The information came to Houston in the strictest confidence and, for obvious reasons, his name must never be used in this connection. He can fathom the purpose of the party and ascertain the matters and contents of his reports. . . . As fast as the information is obtained it will be forwarded to you. . . . From the above you will know how to proceed. I am afraid he will make a report

to cause some one to proceed, as I understood him to say that . . . proceedings to begin by those holding liens. . . . I hope very much Morrow will not give us any trouble. *I dropped to him incidentally today the fact that we had over 45,000 head of cattle on the two ranges and I thought 50,000 when counted out.*

On May 8, 1886, Harry Groom further notified Francklyn that:

There is no longer any doubt as to the origin of the confidential matter of which I wrote you. Gordon Cunard is the party who is pushing the matter, and I learn confidentially that in certain contingencies the cattle sold will be attached at the place of delivery. I do not know, nor does my informant, what those contingencies are. The party here is under orders from a lawyer of Austin to report to him and act under him. You know more about this than I do . . . I only hope that you will be able to get these matters all arranged satisfactory to yourself.

On May 9, 1886, a Mr. Allen of the Standard Cattle Company demanded satisfaction on a contract which he held on the part of the Francklyn Company's cattle before he would permit Colonel Groom to proceed further with the gathering of the Company's cattle on the two ranges. Allen also paid the interest in the amount of $21,300, which the Francklyn Company was unable to pay as holder of the mortgages made by the Francklyn Company July 1, 1882, and November 27, 1883. He advised the Farmers Loan & Trust, which had signed these notes without recourse, that: "This was done to prevent a foreclosure under the mortgage of the above dates. You are hereby notified that I claim that such payment will enable me to be abrogated to all the rights of the mortgage dated May 1, 1883."

The Grooms, still unaware of Francklyn's resignation as president of the Company, were busily engaged in gathering cattle with which to fulfill contracts with Head & Horn and the Home Cattle Company. Colonel Groom on hearing of Francklyn's resignation begged him to remain as president. "I should feel everything is gone without you," he said. "Stay in there. It has a great future if matters can be held together a while."

Harry Groom was having his usual troubles. Without money and with two lawsuits, he appealed to Francklyn for advice and informed him that "The gathering of the cattle designed to be driven to fill the

British Bondholders Take Over

various contracts will proceed rapidly from this time forward." On May 19, 1886, he received notice by wire that:

You are hereby notified as Agent for the Francklyn Land & Cattle Company, that Gordon Cunard, who holds a mortgage of the said Company, will at once file in the United States Court to prevent the removal, sale, or otherwise disposition of said cattle; that a restraining order will be applied for at Dallas on Monday next, and the motion for injunction will be passed on Monday 31st. After receiving this notice you will be held responsible for your action in the matter.

On May 21, 1886, Colonel Groom, bewildered and confused, wired Francklyn about the injunction and inquired: "Labor deranged unless satisfactory arrangements. What provision is made for Harry and myself? What shall I do next? Calves need branding and cattle sent to upper ranch. Waiting answer." To Colonel Groom's inquiry, Francklyn sent the following reply, June 1, 1886, by order of the Board of Directors of the Francklyn Land & Cattle Company:

Col. B. B. and Harry Groom: Messrs Russell Benedict, Secretary of the Company, and George Tyng of Victoria, Texas, are hereby directed to proceed to the Company's ranges and to such other places as they may deem proper and make a thorough investigation of the conditions, affairs, prospects, liabilities and resources of the Company. They are authorized to employ such assistance and to engage such counsel as they think fit and desirable. Messrs. B. B. and H. T. Groom, and all other employees of the Francklyn Company, are hereby directed to give to Messrs. Benedict and Tyng, and to each of them, all the aid and assistance in their power to enable them to accomplish the objects they have in view. Benedict and Tyng are authorized to make a full examination of the books and accounts of the Company, and to make an actual count of the cattle on the ranges if they so desire, and Grooms are directed to see that such count be made without delay.

Lodging for Benedict and Tyng and all expenses were to be charged to the Company's account.

Benedict Leaves for Texas June 2, 1886

On his trip to Texas Benedict carried a letter of introduction and also a letter of credit for $3,000, "which you will kindly honor. Mr. Benedict visits your city in connection with certain business interests," said the letter, "and may desire to become acquainted with an attorney in your place. Any attention you may be pleased to extend Mr. Benedict will be appreciated."

Benedict's original destination was Fort Worth, but on June 8 he arrived at Dallas, where he explained to Foster:

> On the way down it struck me forcibly that it would be very foolish to go to Fort Worth and deal with the same people B. B. Groom touched in all his transactions, and that it would be especially unwise to get an attorney from those people who might, and doubtless would, feel that the present Mr. Groom was of more worth to him than the absent Mr. Benedict. That this view was correct has been demonstrated to me ever since I got here. Dallas is far better as headquarters than Fort Worth in every respect. It is a substantial city which has grown from a village to a town of 25,000 to 30,000 in ten years, and is the commercial center of Northern Texas.

Benedict summoned Ferdinand Van Zandt and George Tyng to assist him in the investigation at White Deer and Greer. On June 5, 1886, Van Zandt wired Benedict from Montana, "Will arrive Thursday morning. Get all the information you can." George Tyng also wired from Victoria, Texas, "Can go immediately. Wire instructions regardless of compensation."

George Tyng was a native of New York. As a young man he wandered out into the California frontier, where he grew to maturity during the middle years of the nineteenth century. His wandering spirit was caught up in the reckless craze of mining and speculation in land and cattle which was in full swing during the 1850's and 1860's. Therefore, he became well versed in land and cattle matters as a result of his work on the frontier of the Southwest. Tyng became intensely interested in White Deer Lands largely through his intimate and trusted friend, Frederic de P. Foster. As a result he spent fifteen of the best years of his life as manager of the Texas property. His years of experience in the West and his prophetic insight challenged his best efforts in his determination to prove to Foster and the British trustees the potential value of White Deer Lands. His honest and efficient administration of this vast estate proved to be of inestimable value in successfully steering the property through a most critical period.

COURTESY A. H. DOUCETTE AND M. K. BROWN, PAMPA, TEXAS

No. 1 Camp at White Deer, Francklyn Land & Cattle Company. This camp was moved about two miles northeast in 1888, on Section 25, Block 7, I. & G. N. Survey in Carson County, Texas. It was built of logs from White Deer Creek, fifteen miles distant to the north. Notice snow on the ground, scales at right-hand corner, and bathtub in lower center to the right of door. Dugout near lake on Section 27 was used for an icehouse where the boys kept cold beer during the summer with ice cut from the lake during the winter (A. H. Doucette to L. F. Sheffy March 17, 1959).

Lord Rosebery *(left)*. British financier, author, sportsman, and statesman, having served as Prime Minister of Great Britain, 1894–1895. He was a close friend of David Lloyd George, who said at the time of Lord Rosebery's passing, May 21, 1929: "Today recalled a striking prophecy made twenty-five years ago. I was staying at Lord Rosebery's home with him, and I remember what he said to me on the day that the Anglo-French entente was announced in the papers—that was before 1905—. I said, 'You are well pleased I suppose as the rest of them with this.' He said, 'Well you are wrong. This will lead straight to war'." Lord Rosebery was the largest holder of the Francklyn Company Bonds.

This picture was secured by Mr. M. K. Brown, through his brother L. H. K. Brown of London. Lady Bisley, wife of the artist, Sir Oswald Bisley, held the copyright of the painting by her late husband. The portrait was presented by the courtesy of F. M. Locke of Francis Peak and Company, Ltd., to the Williams Deacon Bank.

Andrew Kingsmill *(right)*. School teacher and civil-service employee, who in July, 1865, received an appointment for office in the Discount Department of the Bank of England, and later became the first senior-deputy principal of the Privy Drawing Office. Later Lord Rosebery appointed him manager of the British Linen Company Bank in London, a position which he filled most ably for twenty-four years. Kingsmill, an expert horticulturist, specializing in daffodils, traveled constantly and was always an eager student of horticulture in the various countries he visited. He was a member of the City Club of London, and was for years English representative and general financial adviser of Lord Rosebery.

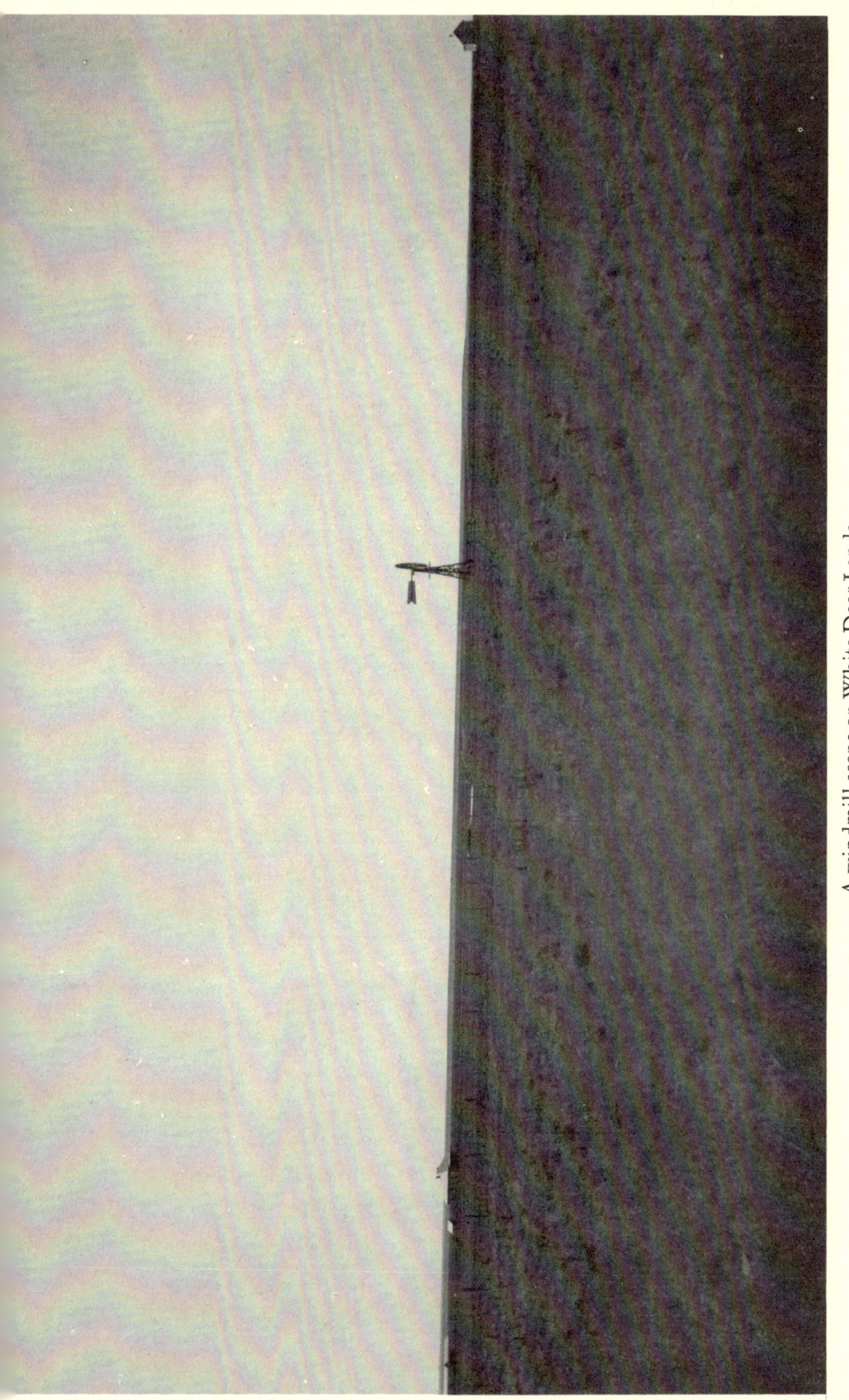

A windmill scene on White Deer Lands.

A buffalo herd grazing on the Goodnight range.

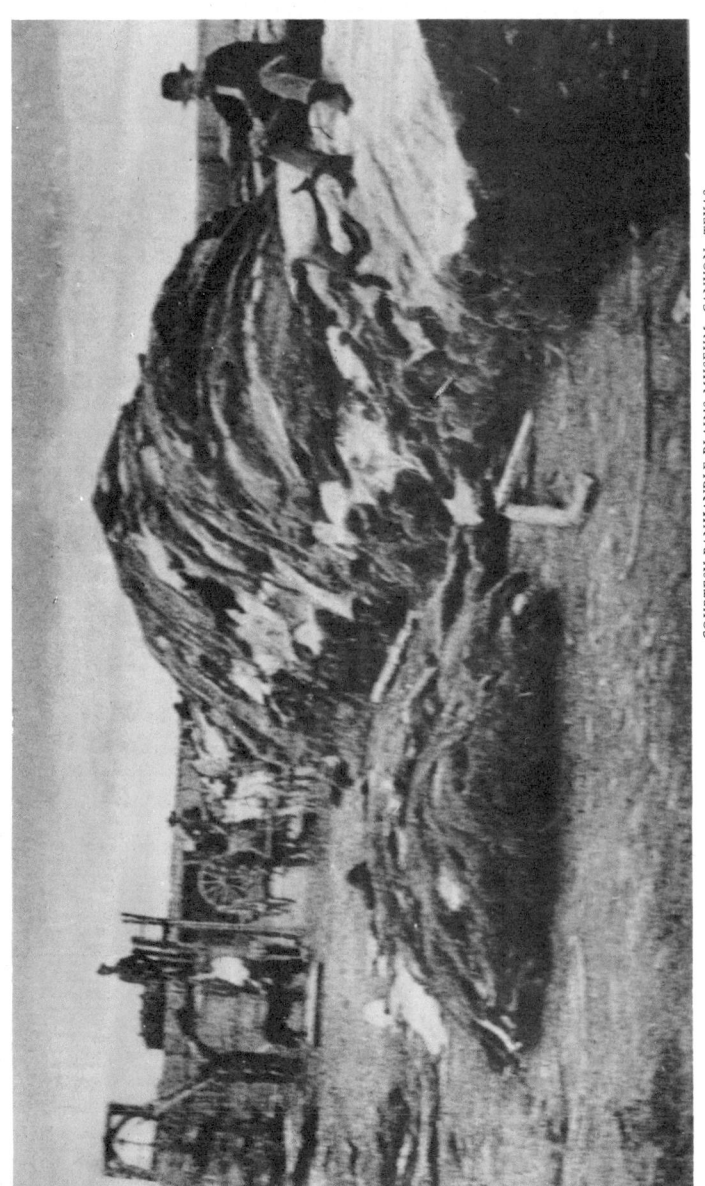

COURTESY PANHANDLE-PLAINS MUSEUM, CANYON, TEXAS

An estimated 40,000 buffalo hides ricked up at Dodge City, Kansas, 1878, for shipment to Eastern tanneries. These hides came from the Texas Panhandle, and were freighted to Dodge via the Dodge City trail from Mobeetie, which was known in 1878 as "Hide Town."

A fencing crew hauling posts and poles from the Canadian River for fencing the LS range in the early 1880's.

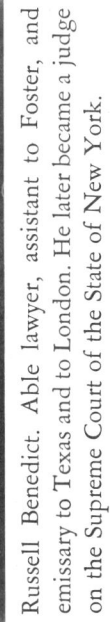

Russell Benedict. Able lawyer, assistant to Foster, and emissary to Texas and to London. He later became a judge on the Supreme Court of the State of New York.

Frederic de P. Foster. Distinguished lawyer and head of one of the leading law firms of New York City. Served as a trustee for White Deer Lands from 1886 to 1929.

The first meeting of the Panhandle Stockmens Association held at Mobeetie, Texas, in 1880. These men formed the association for the purpose of stopping cattle rustling in the Texas Panhandle. Colonel Charles Goodnight (in white shirt, right end of front row) presided.

A chuck-wagon scene on the Lee Bivins ranch along the Canadian River just north of Amarillo. Lee Bivins, in white shirt, is seated on left of chuck wagon.

COURTESY PANHANDLE-PLAINS MUSEUM, CANYON, TEXAS

Quanah Parker. Chief of the Qua-ha-da Band of Comanche Indians; son of Pete Nocona and Cynthia Ann Parker, whose habitat was in the Palo Duro Canyon and its environs.

COURTESY PANHANDLE-PLAINS MUSEUM, CANYON, TEXAS

Prairie Indians on the warpath. A band of Kiowa Indians seeking revenge.

COURTESY PANHANDLE-PLAINS MUSEUM, CANYON, TEXAS

Plains Indians moving camp, having been driven out of their former camp or having abandoned it. Notice squaw and papoose on left front horse and baggage on travois poles on horse in center. This was the only means the prairie Indians had for carrying their tepees and other belongings.

Branding calves on the open range in the Texas Panhandle.

COURTESY PANHANDLE-PLAINS MUSEUM, CANYON, TEXAS

Branding calves at a roundup on a Texas Panhandle range.

COURTESY LADY BISLEY

Colonel Sir Robert Williams, M.P. Banker, investor, and the second largest holder of the Francklyn Company Bonds *(left)*. About 1912 he visited what was then known as "White Deer Lands," thus becoming one of the two English proprietors who visited their property in Texas.

Sir Gordon Cunard *(right)*. Grandson of the founder of the Cunard Steamship Company, who held the chattel mortgage on the Francklyn Company cattle. This copy of the portrait was secured by Mr. L. H. K. Brown, to whom Lady Bisley gave permission to publish the photograph in the history of the Francklyn Company. Sir Gordon and Lady Cunard visited Pampa in 1908, making an inspection tour of all the property owned by the English proprietors.

Cross L Headquarters near the present town of Lubbock. Wagon outfit ready to start for spring roundup. R. A. (Bob) Haley, wagon boss, is seated on white horse in center foreground.

A trail herd headed for Montana pastures to be fattened for market. Trail drivers in background.

Cattle come to water on LS range, then move out for more luscious grass on the range.

George Tyng. Adventurer, cattleman, linguist, and a practical, self-made statesman. Texas agent and administrator of White Deer Lands, 1886–1903.

Timothy Dwight Hobart. Expert land man and Texas agent, New York & Texas Land Company, 1886–1902. Successor to George Tyng in 1903, and independent executor of the Cornelia Adair Estate, 1915–1935.

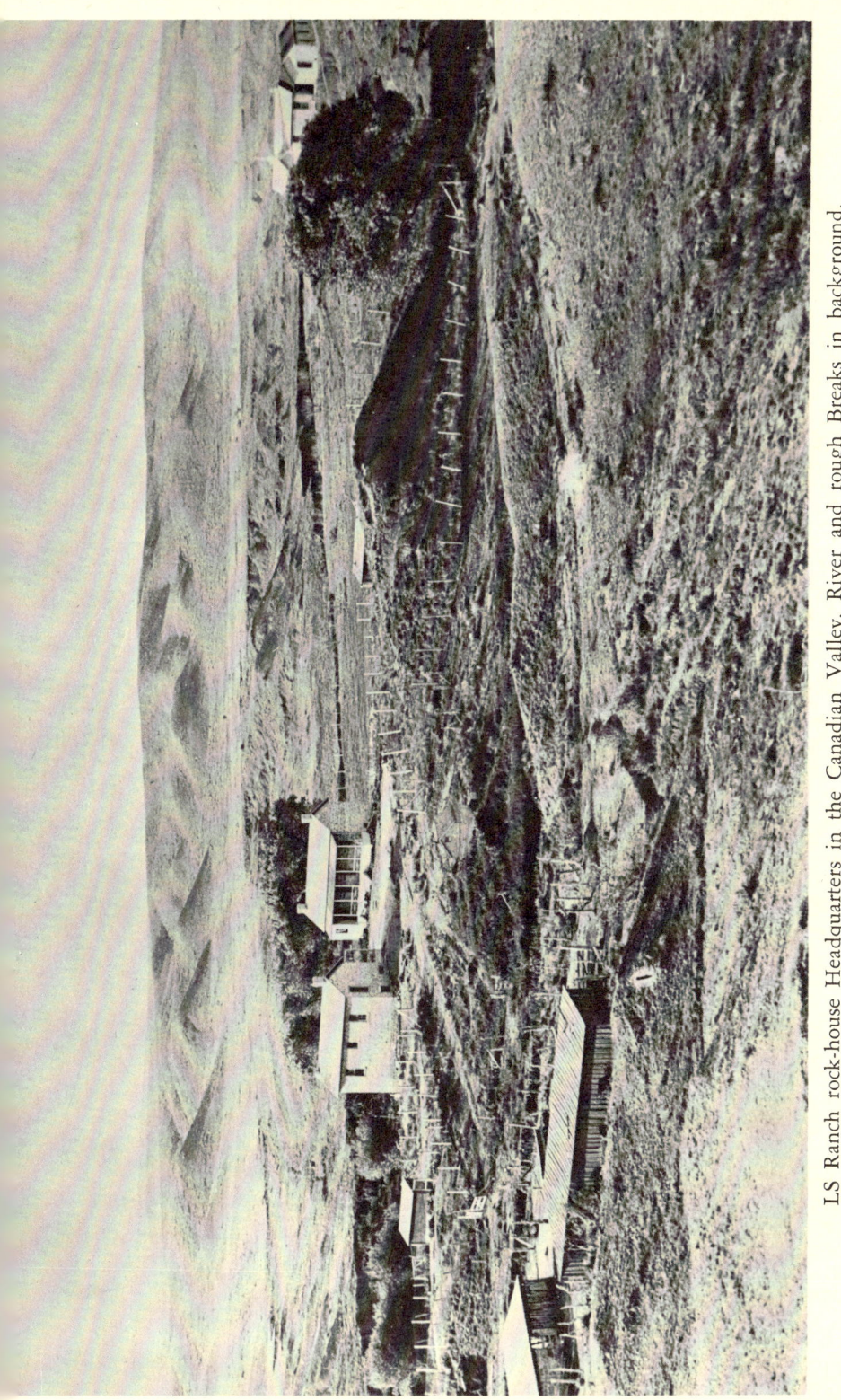

LS Ranch rock-house Headquarters in the Canadian Valley. River and rough Breaks in background.

Gerlach Bros. general merchandise store located at the terminus of the Southern Kansas Railroad on the north side of the Canadian River in Hemphill County, Texas, in 1887. For a brief inventory of supplies, see sign at top of right-hand corner. The present town of Canadian is just across the river on the south side.

A string of five ox teams hauling cotton to market in the Texas Panhandle in the early 1900's. Ox teams were used on a rather large scale in the early days of freighting. It was claimed by many freighters that they were stronger, steadier, and less excitable than horses and mules in pulling stuck wagons out of mud holes. They were driven by the use of long black snake whips only.

Settlers with their families and all of their earthly possessions move into the Texas Panhandle in covered wagons. The pipe through the cover of the front wagon is from a stove used to give some protection to women and children during the extremely cold weather.

Demonstration of a model farm in the Texas Panhandle. With the rapid influx of prospective settlers into the Panhandle, railroads, colonizers, and land agents put forth much effort to demonstrate the farming possibilities of Panhandle lands. These agents were very effective in advertising lands and in attracting immigrants.

R. M. Irick's big freighting outfit moves a two-story home from Dimmitt, in Castro County, to Plainview, in Hale County, some forty miles, without mishap. Notice high fronts on stores for advertising wares. This was the customary type of architecture for business concerns in all frontier towns.

Charley Durham's Panhandle freighter. At the turn of the century Charley Durham's ten-team outfit made regular weekly trips to haul supplies from Amarillo to Plainview. He rode the left-wheel horse, or mule, and drove the outfit with a single "jerk line," which was run through the ring of the bridle bit of the left lead horse. A log chain, fastened to the bit of the left lead horse, was strung between the members of each team, and each doubletree was fastened to the hame of each horse to hold the outfit together. By making a constant slight jerk on the line the driver could swing the outfit around to the right as far as necessary. Then by a constant pull on the line he could swing the teams back into a straight line. At the crack of a long "black-snake" whip all the teams would be pulling together and

COURTESY MRS. C. R. BURROW AND MRS. DOROTHY NEBLETT, CANYON, TEXAS

thus could usually pull the wagons out of the hub-deep ruts in which they were frequently stuck. If flood rains continued wagons were often untrailed and left unattended for several days at a time, until the roads were passable. These outfits hauled from 4,000 pounds on the front wagon to 2,000 pounds on the trailers. The freighters received from 60 to 70 cents per hundred pounds for the 150-mile round trip. Wagon freighting was a big business during the days preceding the coming of the railroads, and these six- to ten-mule freighting outfits which could be seen for several miles going in both directions made quite a novel sight for the spectator. At night, when several such outfits would camp at the same water hole along the way, many tall tales would be told around their glowing campfires.

White Deer Lands Office at Pampa, Texas. This structure, erected in 1906, was the first office building in Pampa. Opposite the entrance stands the first flagpole in the town. The first brick building erected in Pampa (1907), owned by the First National Bank, is visible in the background.

A July 4 celebration and picnic in the Texas Panhandle in 1906.

Kaffir cornfield on White Deer Lands near Pampa, Texas.

A Harvest Scene in the Texas Panhandle on Francklyn Company lands.

Oldest School Building in the Panhandle, Mobeetie, Texas.

Steam plow at work on White Deer Lands.

Picnic Scene on White Deer Creek, 1902.

Santa Fe Railroad Station, Pampa, Texas, 1910.

Street Scene, Pampa, Texas, 1912.

The Schneider Band, Pampa's first band, conducted by Alex Schneider, Sr. The above picture was taken in 1914 in front of the First State Bank of Old Mobeetie. The Band was advertising a Chatauqua to be held in Pampa that year.

Top row, left to right—Tom Eller, Jeff Buckler,* M. K. Brown, a traveling salesman out of Amarillo whose identity is unknown, Alex Schneider, Sr.,* DeLea Vicars, L. C. McMurtry,* Lee Newman, John Cox,* C. P. Buckler.

Bottom row, left to right—Hamp Brown,* John Hamilton, Jack Voyd,* Ed Warminski.*

Deceased

British Bondholders Take Over

In the early 1880's Tyng established a home at Victoria, Texas, near which place he owned a pecan farm. Here he planned to spend his declining years with his cultured wife and three sons. But Fate decreed otherwise. Tyng could never resist wanderlust. He was ever alert and on the go, eager to make a quick fortune out of the rich minerals that lay beneath the arid plains. Though a great lover of family life, his home never became more than a periodic haven of rest and relaxation from stress and overwork in ceaseless activity on the frontier. When settlers began to move onto the White Deer Pasture, Tyng went back to the open, free ranges of the Old West, where he became engaged in the work of his first love—the mining business. While busy with this work he was killed in a snow slide in a silver mine near Ogden, Utah, in 1906.[1] This was the man with whom Benedict was to work on the White Deer range.

While waiting for the arrival of Van Zandt, Benedict wrote Foster on June 8, 1886:

I saw George Tyng Atkins Sunday. He is a nephew of Stephen H. Tyng of New York, whose family name was Atkins. He is a man of great influence here, although a Northerner. . . . His friendship for me has been shown in every way; introducing me to cattlemen, bankers and men of prominence in all departments of life. He has been especially valuable in showing me how to avoid entanglements that might hurt or compromise our interprise. He knows all the lawyers here and thinks most of them would sell out as calmly as they would a cow, with two or three exceptions. He said there was a young lawyer here named Miller who knows titles better than any other attorney in the place; that he was probably incorruptible, as well as industrious and was well educated. . . . In looking over the register, I saw Mr. Tyng's name, and found that he was stopping over here Sunday in order to meet me in Fort Worth on Monday. I am immensely pleased with him. He is everything you say. Very curiously George Tyng and George Tyng Atkins are cousins, but had never met until I introduced them today. I believe that George Tyng would make an excellent manager of the property. He is poor just now and I believe would undertake it.

[1] M. K. Brown to L. F. Sheffy, August 29, 1961. Courtesy Mrs. DeLea Vicars, Pampa, Texas. Mrs. Vicars is a daughter of Mr. Jesse Wynne. Wynne, an intimate friend of Tyng, at Tyng's request lived some two or three years, without charge, at White Deer, where he kept tramps and other intruders off the property. In return Wynne was allowed to graze his horses in the Company's pasture.

Benedict retained Miller, of the Miller & Shepherd law firm, as a consultant in examining titles, giving him a retainer's fee of $750. Benedict commented further in his report of June 8, 1886:

In looking over the papers I brought with me I find that the Francklyn Land & Cattle Company holds a chattel mortgage to secure the notes of Stephens and Lytle for $100,000 due next September, with interest, and I wired you to get the notes. They ought to be good for their face. . . . *This is an important item.* . . . I talked with Tyng until twelve o'clock. I regret very much the delay occasioned here by Van Zandt's non arrival. It seems to be best not to go to the ranch without first seeing him, as it takes two days staging and one day on the railway to get there. . . . This was all the more important because I am in doubt at present whether it is desirable that Van Zandt should accompany us at all. He ought, however, to be here to help us plan.

My present plan is to start from here Friday, if Van Zandt arrives, and take my attorney and go to Mobeetie, fix up the title there, and go with the attorney to Henrietta, county seat of Donley County,[2] leaving Tyng and Van Zandt if he accompanies us, at Mobeetie to inspect the place, count the cattle, etc. Please send me by express to this hotel [Windsor] the statements of alternate sections *anywhere* taken up. I am afraid none of them are in the Company, but all in the hands of Brown and Francklyn. *Cunard must hold off*. He will get his money in time, but must not press matters now. Keep a tight rein on Francklyn. *I am going to carry this matter through* and make billions for our bondholders. . . . The land notes must be kept down. If a default occurs they can forfeit our estate. The bondholders must eventually take up that mortgage or deed. The vendor's lien is the highest security known to the law here. We must get the notes and deed and reorganize the Company. I am afraid the cattle have been sacrificed to Groom's extravagance. His reputation here is good-for nothing but he is too powerful for people to talk openly against him.

Benedict added the following postscript to his letter:

I have pretty reliable confidential advice that the New York & Texas Land Company is worth ten million dollars and does not want to call in our loan unless forced to do so, but would just as soon get the property back—is

---

[2] Clarendon was the county seat of Donley County and Henrietta was the seat of justice in Clay County. Benedict was not familiar with the geography of Texas.

rather different. I can, I am sure, get an extension down here from the Company if it is necessary, especially if the interest is paid promptly.

About June 10, 1886, Benedict, accompanied by Miller, Tyng, and Van Zandt, went by rail to Harrold, Texas. From there they hired a private conveyance, as Colonel Groom had advised. This was a novel experience for Benedict. He described his journey thus:

We had a most tiresome journey, but I think none of the party suffered from it. . . . We drove all day over the prairie, stopping for dinner at Chillicothe. We passed the night in a log hut with cowboys and slept on a blanket on the floor. We started at 6 a.m. Monday and drove about 40 miles until we reached water, and there we made camp on the prairie cooking our supper over a fire of cow dung, and used stagnant water for our coffee. However, the night was fine and it was a pleasant experience.

After the work was completed at Clarendon and Mobeetie, Benedict went back to Austin to make further investigation as to the title, and to search for the deed and patents. Tyng went to White Deer and began his investigation of the Greer and White Deer ranges, while Van Zandt hurried back to New York.

After completing his work at Mobeetie and Austin, Benedict reported to Foster from Austin, June 18, 1886, that the records at Clarendon were clear, and, with the exception of a few technical points, which he said could be easily corrected, that the chain of title at Mobeetie was in order. He declared:

Gordon Cunard's mortgage is *absolutely worthless,* both as to the Company and the bondholders. It does not identify the cattle mortgaged in any way. They are not separated from the common herd, besides our supplemental mortgage was properly recorded and filed. Not only is this the situation here, but I believe that Cunard owes the Company $40,000 to $50,000 paid to him by Francklyn out of the Company's treasury without authority and for a private debt of Francklyn's. . . . I have tried to become acquainted with the Texas law on all the very intricate matters affecting the Company's interests and also to get at the facts of the business that has been done here. This became necessary [when] I found that the attorney whom I have employed would in New York rank very low in capacity for examining titles. So I have done it nearly all myself, after studying the statutes, and this I trust will be of assistance to us in future proceedings.

Inspection of White Deer Lands

On arrival at Mobeetie, Benedict and Miller found Colonel Groom waiting for them. Groom thought Mobeetie was the best starting place for the inspection of the ranges, "As I have with me all that is needed for the trip, and at White Deer we do not as H. T. Groom is away." Tyng, at Colonel Goodnight's suggestion, had already engaged Perry LeFors to accompany him to White Deer. In his report of June 18, 1886, Benedict continued:

I feel that Tyng and Groom did not get along very smoothly from what Tyng said. However, he is very courteous to me and we have got along very well. He [Groom] is, I believe, completely in our hands. I commenced by showing him the former king no longer held the *sceptre* and he made haste to cry, "Long live the king." He complains bitterly of the treatment he has received, and blames Francklyn for keeping him so completely in the dark about the New York end of the circuit. I pumped him yesterday for a long time and have got his fullest confidence, and I must confess that I incline to the belief that he has been the dupe of Francklyn. He tells me Francklyn controlled all of his actions and that he never made a sale without Francklyn's orders. From papers shown me I incline to the same view. I can do nothing better than enclose to you the brief memo of our conversation which I made as we talked. It will no doubt give you much light without further explanation. He says there are 20,000 arces which are capable of irrigation. He told me some wonderful stories of the extreme fertility of the soil, and these are corroborated by many disinterested persons all around here. . . . He believes that $5000 will cover the debts on both ranges; that there are no liens on any of the cattle except ours and Cunards; that the Head & Horn Company and the Home Cattle Company are virtually paid off; that the Head & Horn sale was bona fide and for a high price and the money was actually paid to Francklyn in Groom's presence, and was used to pay the vendor's lien balance on the Harrold & Ikard purchase, and the $40,000 or $50,000 to Cunard. My own opinion, after talking with Goodnight, is to accept these transfers and clear up the business. It will be difficult to do any thing in this peculiar country if you repudiate these sales, especially as the money was paid at the time, $140,000 from Head & Horn, and $50,000 from the Home Cattle Company.

Foster was pleased with Benedict's report. On June 19, 1886, he advised Benedict that he had quoted parts of it in a letter to Williams,

Deacon & Company and to Mr. Andrew Kingsmill of London.[3] He added:

> It seems to me you have done exceedingly well thus far, and I hope for a prosperous issue. I am naturally a little uneasy concerning the $21,300 note, but expect to get a short extension should we not be ready to take it up by July 1st. I have in mind, among other plans, a scheme to take it up by a bondholders' agreement. I would in such case have all the bonds deposited with me, or with a trust company with authority to borrow say $100 a bond on them to tide over the payment and the one in November. Before such an agreement would become expedient it would be necessary to make an arrangement with Francklyn to transfer (his or the) title which may be attended with difficulty. If you should find a superabundance of cattle so that a few could be sold to pay them the $21,300 let me know.

Colonel Groom assured Francklyn on June 16, 1886, from Mobeetie, "I shall do all in my power to facilitate them [Benedict and Tyng]."

The Cunard matter also seemed more possible of solution. M. K. Smith, a member of Foster's law firm, wrote Benedict, at Dallas, on June 16, 1886, that:

> There have been lengthy conversations day after day between the Land Company's people with Foster and has been *rushed* right along. Van Zandt has just come in [from Texas] and seems pleased with the little chat he had with you in Texas. Foster says yours was a splendid letter and he is quite sanguine about Company matters. . . . I think the Cunard matter will be fixed up. His last proposition, through Gutherie, is to take $100,000 in Bonds (at 80%) and the balance to be paid in annual instalments of $14,000 each.

Benedict also appeared to be somewhat optimistic in a letter to Foster from Austin, June 15, 1886, in which he said:

> The title is complicated by many questions which, however, I am unrolling slowly. I think the whole transaction was conceived in iniquity and born in sin, but we shall be able, *provided the title is good*, to bring R[osebery] and the others out in good shape. . . . Capt. Goodnight says he cannot undertake the management of the ranch, but can pick out many good men here. He will

---

[3] Williams, Deacon & Company were bankers in London. They owned the second largest number of shares of the Francklyn Company cattle bonds.

help and advise all that he can. He is very friendly and does not care very much for Groom, nor does anyone else so far as I can find out.

Affairs at White Deer, however, were not progressing as smoothly as the above letters would seem to indicate. With Tyng and the Texas creditors pressing the Grooms for their claims, the former managers began their machinations aimed at evasion of any further responsibility for the Francklyn's business, and at the same time acquirement of as much of the loot as possible from the wreckage. Benedict advised Foster, June 19, 1886:

> I write to impart to you a suspicion which I cannot rid my mind of. It is that Gordon Cunard is preparing to get hold of the vendor's lien on the land. I discovered that the local attorney employed by Peeler in the injunction case has ordered copies from the Clerk of the Court here of all the papers affecting the title as well as the chattel mortgage to be made in great haste. I can conceive no other use to which they can be put, but I may be wrong. Try to discover the symptoms from Gutherie and instruct me at Austin. I shall endeavor to head him off by getting an option to purchase the notes and trust deed from the Company at Austin for thirty days or so, before he can act. . . . I have been told on all sides that the Grooms have been preparing to leave the management for a year. Groom himself indicated as much to me. He will be in New York on July 1st. . . . I think if the title is good the Grooms should be dismissed at once and either Tyng or myself put in charge temporarily, or given power until permanent arrangements can be made. A first class cowman can be got here at about $2000 a year, and Tyng could manage the enterprise as to finances. I think if you can spare me for another thirty days it would be desirable to have me remain on the range or at Dallas until the financial questions are settled in July. If the mortgage is foreclosed it would be exceedingly desirable to have it done as reasonably as possible. This I could attend to better if on the ground than by correspondence with the attorneys in Texas. I have not yet found an attorney with whom I am thoroughly satisfied. They all seem so mercenary and have so little energy for work, that I am disgusted. All these questions, however, I leave entirely in your hands. . . . The air is full of rumors of fraud in the Company, but except what I have written, there is nothing tangible.

George Tyng also found much on the White Deer range to confirm his suspicions as to what was happening to the cattle. He informed

Foster from White Horse Tank in the Francklyn Pasture, June 22, 1886, that:

> Grooms have been lying to me in regard to movements of cattle. Taking advantages of my absence from the stock while examining the land, they have slipped some 3000 head out of the northwest corner of the pasture and have now about 300 head at this tank, camped and under orders to join the others. They went out yesterday. Becoming suspicious I went last night to Mobeetie to look for information by mail or telegraph that might justify Groom's movements. Finding none and reaching this tank tonight my suspicions are confirmed by what I see and learn here. I send you a telegram which I cannot copy for want of light. Perry LeFors, who will envelop and mail this letter was Foreman here for nearly three years and will do very well until you can make definite and permanent arrangements. You will understand that my action now as to the Grooms makes it indelicate and impossible for me to permanently succeed them in your service, but for a few weeks or so until you can straighten out this muddle you can count on me.

On June 23 Tyng informed Benedict:

> Both Grooms now on Canadian at mouth of Spring Creek waiting for 500 head here to add to 3000 there, sixty miles north takes them to the neutral strip outside Mobeetie jurisdiction. I go on tonight alone to delay pending further instructions, or take possession if none received within reasonable time, or ample credentials not exhibited by Groom. I send $50 to retain J. N. Browning at Mobeetie and direct LeFors to send a few good men to help retain cattle within Francklyn Pasture. . . . My suspicions may be unfounded and Grooms may be lawfully removing cattle. If so telegraph me promptly. Otherwise telegraph Grooms officially to turn over to me at once all Company property and records in such case, and pending further arrangements, I propose to place this property in charge of Perry LeFors and proceed to Greer to protect property there.

Benedict wired Foster from Dallas, June 24, 1886:

> Evans says land notes endorsed by Farmers Loan and Trust and he can do nothing about extension. Am confident Cunard intends to forestall us in foreclosure trust mortgage. Trustees suit should be commenced by July 1st. Telegram just received from Tyng. Grooms driving off cattle. Have both Grooms removed at once and appoint Tyng by wire at Mobeetie. Wire me

full authority to do whatever seems best in Texas. Will wire you estimated foreclosure. There is no other course open.

Foster wired removal of the Grooms June 25, 1886, and appointed Tyng as manager:

As soon as examination is finished at Austin, join Tyng. Confer with him. Telegraph your joint advice. Shall pay land notes unless you advise otherwise. Remain in Texas as long as advisable.

The Groom-Tyng Feud and Foreclosure

Although Tyng expressed his appreciation in accepting the appointment as Texas manager of the Francklyn Company, he steadfastly refused to execute any orders of the Company officials as long as the Grooms and Francklyn were connected with the business in any way. He simply referred all such orders to the Grooms to be put into effect by them. In order to explain and clarify his position on this matter he advised Foster:

The interests of all concerned will be best served by leaving enforcement of that resolution to my discretion for a few days yet. Fully appreciate the honor and may soon be seeking employment, but as my reports on some of the Company's affairs may have influenced your proposed change of Managers, I cannot accept the appointment permanently, nor except in emergency until you can do better, and where the services will not conflict with that I am on contract (expiring July 3rd) to render under instructions from Russell Benedict. My compensation is already provided for and covers every emergency until July 3rd.

Tyng in commenting further on the management at White Deer wrote Foster, June 24, 1886:

The Company's resolution changing Managers (while not accepted) makes an excellent weapon to hold against expropriation of Company property—should it be contemplated—until definite and permanent arrangements can be made. H. T. is not a man to attempt it himself on any considerable scale, and B. B. is enroute to New York and will for awhile have his attention directed in other directions. In late deliveries of cattle Grooms appear to be fully covered by the signature of Francklyn. . . . Grooms have been entrusted with immense property scattered over large territory. A great part of that property does not today exist in their custody. They and the Company tell creditors that it *does* exist. A turn over of it in lump without inventory (which is just now practically impossible) might wipe off their slate and relieve them and the Company of the onus of exhibiting or accounting for the property, if made upon demand of creditors. The Company might insist that the property turned over was of value and quantity largely in excess of indebtedness, and ask us what has become of the property just as we now ask Grooms and the Company. Even assuming that a majority of creditors also own majority stock interest, there may be a troublesome dissentient minority.

The readiness of the Company to throw its Managers overboard and to appoint a stranger invites consideration of "eventualities." H. T. Groom claims that one-third or one-fourth interest in the land, when paid for, was reserved by him and his father as a part of the consideration when selling the option (1882) to the Francklyn enterprise. This claim would probably be wiped out if the vendor's lien and land notes were not paid to the New York & Texas Land Company. . . . It is a fatal mistake for a company ever to give its Managers a bill of sale for any of its cattle. The Francklyn Company has made this mistake twice and perhaps oftener. Such a bill of sale is like charity, but with intenser covering capacity. . . . There is in my judgment only two possible courses. 1. Assume land notes and mortgage at once if Evans will resign Trusteeship, in which case don't pay interest. 2. Pay interest before July 1st and instantly foreclose Bondholders's mortgage. No receivership is necessary unless stockholders elect new Directors in October. . . . Wire instructions immediately so as to commence suit July 1st. in advance of Cunard as I am convinced he intends foreclosure of our mortgage. He is gathering certified copies of papers.

Benedict urged all possible haste in preparing for the foreclosure suit July 1. On June 28 he again wrote Foster:

After my letter to you yesterday I thought I would have nothing more to say, but find that there are several matters to be considered. I am confident that the most urgent necessity exists and the wisest policy demands that the Trustees should foreclose the Bondholders' mortgage with the utmost haste possible in order to forestall what I firmly believe Cunard is about to do; Viz: foreclose the mortgage himself. Among the many advantages which this course would secure are the nullification of illegal but de facto stock in the hands of Francklyn, which he will use in the next annual meeting in October to secure repossession of the Board and the destruction of Cunard's lien upon the property of the Company under his chattel mortgage which is subordinate to ours. It will also prevent the appointment of a receiver at the suit of Cunard, or any other bondholders so long as the present Board continues in office.

Gutherie and Benedict disagreed on the question of foreclosure. Foster advised Benedict June 29:

Gutherie says second mortgage to Cunard recorded to cure defects in first. No fear he will do more than foreclose his mortgage. Telegraph whether Texas practice would compel us to give bond in his foreclosure before judgment in order to retain cattle. Shall I pay land note? I think immediate foreclosure undesirable. Telegraph why you think otherwise giving any point not yet communicated. . . . After seeing Tyng at Harrold, as you suggest, telegraph me if you think it wise to come to New York and await answer. I think well of that plan.

During June and July, 1886, Tyng wrote a number of letters to Foster and Benedict giving accounts of duplicity in dealing with the Grooms at White Deer Pasture, making suggestions as to procedures to be followed, and urging them to oust the Grooms from control of the property. After making considerable investigation of the Grooms' activities on the White Deer range, he found much evidence to confirm all of his suspicions of his adversaries. As a result he now spoke more firmly and frankly of their efforts to double-cross him. He reported to Foster:

Arriving at White Deer on the morning of June 23rd to meet B. B. Groom, I was told by H. T. Groom that his father had the previous day crossed the Canadian at the mouth of Bear Creek enroute to Kansas and anxious to reach New York without delay. He thought that with fresh horses I might overtake him about the Zulu range near the neutral strip; the road being good and his father having business there with Capt. Lytle for a day. Lytle was then at Harrold. On my starting across for Spring Creek west instead of north—Groom represented the difficulties of getting across, and sent a man to pilot me despite my assurance that this was unnecessary. The pilot was detained some twenty minutes after he had saddled and was ready to start. He overtook me in the sandhills a couple of miles out and afterwards went ahead with a letter to B. B. Groom who was camped with the herd on Spring Creek, outside the Company's range, and who expressed his expectations of staying with the herd until across the Canadian.

All the foregoing facts are susceptible to explanation, but while not satisfactorily explained, they justify the suspicion implied in my telegram of the 22nd, and give color to rumor and gossip otherwise not deserving of attention. . . . The herd of 500 (more or less) then issuing from the pasture were said by B. B. Groom to be for the purpose of replacing cows to be cut from the larger herd by the receiving parties, as not within the terms of the contract, both cuts to be retained within the pasture. The detention or possession of the herd, or its return to the pasture presented no great difficulty, attending circumstances being exceptionally favorable for either course, but your instructions were explicit not to detain Head & Horn cattle, though you had not mentioned the Home Cattle Company in any way, it was proper to assume that the same instructions would apply, having been served with the notice like Head & Horn.

During this time Tyng and the Grooms exchanged several letters, in which certain charges and countercharges were made as to who was the legal representative of the Francklyn Company. On June 10 Harry Groom notified Arnold that "Mr. Tyng takes entire control of the ranch this morning. . . . Look to him for instructions." Tyng on the other hand declared: "They [the Grooms] are absent without leave, neglecting duty here, and I believe have paid themselves amply in advance, to say nothing of corrections of errors in revision of accounts. The Company letter of attorney of June 1st confers ample power for carrying out your instructions." There were also sharp differences as to the number of cattle left on the range. On June 22 the Grooms estimated that there were about 7,000 head within the pasture, "not counting cattle sent out during the past ten days." Tyng asserted that no regular "cattle accounts" had been kept at White Deer headquarters, and declared that "After careful examination as possible within the time available, I assert that not one-half that number of cattle (not counting calves and fancy stock) were inside the Company's pasture on June 22nd, and I believe an actual count would show up less than 3000."

Tyng, still fearing that Harry Groom might misrepresent him, wrote Groom, July 11:

It occurs to me that you may go to New York, and that you may represent that I have accepted, or that you have transferred to me any part of your responsibility as to the Francklyn Land & Cattle Company. Nothing whatever has yet occurred to justify such representation, not even by implication. Circumstances might have hampered your action at Adobe Walls on the morning of July 9th, or on that morning you may not have understood me when voluntarily telling you that my words having been premeditated, could not be retracted, and that I stood responsible to you for them and ready to give you the satisfaction that an offended man can demand. Since your departure the *Mobeetie News* has published an article reflecting on you, and using my name for authority for its statements. While this was a wrong use of my name, the information published having been given to the editor partly by you and partly by others, I seek no responsibility to you for it, believing the statements to be substantially true. I may not be here on your return. Therefore, please note that I live seven miles east from Victoria which is my Post Office address.

In order to prevent further disorganization on the Greer range, Tyng was instructed to pay all necessary expenses for wages and maintenance from June 1, when Benedict became secretary, to July 1. Tyng commented in making the settlement:

The Greer men appear accustomed to dictate, and B. B. Groom calls them "fierce." They are merely pretty good cowmen, a little spoiled by easy jobs, good wages, and weak concessions. Their familiarity with the range, with the stock, brands etc. made desirable their employment in gathering the cattle together, but the cattle once on the road, these men can be easily replaced by half their number, at lower wages, and without detriment to the Company's interests, and can be dispensed with on arrival of the cattle at the Francklyn Pasture. Meredith is to come here tomorrow or the next day to receive guarantee for the men's pay for June and July, or till discharged. . . . As security for their wages for June and since the men hold B. B. Groom's bill-of-sale to them of the Company's horses and mules, 250 head, they also believe themselves to have a first lien on the cattle for the amount of their wages unless they give up the cattle. Of course we can take the cattle from them easily enough, but the cost will be about the same as payment of the $1034 due them for June, and you are paying now accruing wages in July anyway.

Meanwhile the Grooms were still playing hide-and-seek with Tyng in an effort to avoid sharing any part of the responsibility for what was happening on the White Deer range. In relating the matter to Benedict, July 11, Tyng said:

On the 7th I met B. B. Groom on the road about twenty miles south of here. Our surprise was mutual. He attributed his not having gone on to New York when within 100 miles of the Kansas railroads to complications that had arisen in deliveries of cattle to Head, Taylor & Co. I informed him in detail of all done in Greer County under your instructions. He expressed his approval and declared all to be in strict conformity with his understanding with you while here previous to June 20th, since confirmed by your letter of June 21st. He stated that he should not distrust the program as made out; that he is enroute hurriedly for New York. . . . I advised non payment of Groom's checks for reasons for which I prefer to give verbally because, like other Company liabilities, they should be purchased by parties now advancing the funds for their own protection against non contributing creditors, and not paid for the Company. . . . On the chance that you might want to be in communication with him by the 12th I arranged here for prompt carriage, day or night, to him of any telegram you might send him. . . . The number of cattle in the Francklyn Pasture is a disputed one. It seems that their actual count could be made in the presence of the Company's representative.

It is also desirable that the Company's business here should not, at this time, be left in acephalous condition. . . . Besides a considerable number of strays, there are reported to be along the Canadian some 200 head of Bar X cattle escaped from herds recently delivered from the Francklyn Pasture. By all rules of the range these cattle should not be recovered by the drovers and will be returned to the Pasture if employees of the Company do their duty promptly and firmly. If attendance on this roundup be now interrupted or faint-hearted, the drovers may not only recover the forfeited cattle, but may also (intentionally and unavoidably) sweep in the Company's strays. . . . R. H. Arnold informed me that in view of a possible racket with the drovers on the Canadian and of rumors sometimes current the White Deer men were uneasy as to their wages for July, and wanted some guarantee, H. T. Groom having made no provision for them before leaving. This guarantee I gave. . . . The sheriff says he learns that the Company has no property in Texas not mortgaged for more than it is worth. . . . There has been much that does not yet look quite right. If you think anything of a fight likely to occur at New York I fancy that an intelligent search instituted at this end may strike a crooked trail leading through the labyrinth and into New York, that may enable you to strike the enemy in the flank.

On July 18, 1886, Foster instructed Tyng:

Count Diamond F cattle and inventory all property. Proceed with Greer drive making accurate count of cattle as they pass into the pasture. Make count in presence of Grooms or their representatives. Notify me when Grooms can be properly relieved. . . . Hereafter have no one but yourself draw on me. Purchase claims for wages till cattle transferred then dismiss outfits. Rehire only necessary hands. Plan for meeting claims of Texas creditors will be submitted speedily.

Tyng replied on July 15, saying that he would immediately carry out Foster's instructions as to the counting of the cattle, and added:

Affidavits will also be taken as to Greer cattle and estimates of cattle remaining on the outside. The Grooms can properly be relieved when: 1. The Francklyn Company mortgage and debts beyond possible recall or equivocation. Correctness of inventory now being made. 2. When the Grooms officially admit such correctness in writing, and in the presence of credible witnesses. 3. When the Francklyn Company *as* such voluntarily and honestly appoints their successor, *not* in bad faith nor on demand of mortgages or creditors. 4. When questions now pending between the Company and its creditors shall have been *finally* and fully wiped out by compromise or otherwise. I have no delicacy in supplanting the Grooms, but if accepted an appointment from the Francklyn Company, I should loyally help it defeat its creditors. There is no pressing need of change. The Grooms still carry official responsibility, true it bears lightly as ever, but from the moment they cease to draw money they can do little harm, and I must henceforth be responsible to you for the real management of details here. No allowance of their salaries since June 15th need be contemplated.

In reply to a request from Foster for suggestions as to liquidation, Tyng wrote him, July 20, 1886:

Further liquidation of Texas indebtedness not urgent. If your plans are matured, without foreclosure and require liquidation, compromise for cash, give notes twelve months, giving time for realizing enough personal property without sacrifice. Liquidation and its character of Texas indebtedness are so dependent on the nature of your plans, that it is difficult to make feasible suggestions without knowing what you propose doing with the business. I have assumed a non contested foreclosure suit might be arranged at comparatively light expense; that in any event a foreclosure would be necessary to forestall other bondholders to extinguish the Company (mere control not being enough for protection for fighting against a minority) and to wipe out a possible large New York indebtedness; that any sale of the property would be engineered to either whip-in, or freeze out recalcitrant bondholders; that the holders of the land notes might, if necessary, be indemnified or satisfied for destruction of his collateral of Francklyn stock; that your foreclosure would put your party in position either to buy in cheap or sell out dear, and that small motive now exists for preserving this particular organization, or for ressurrecting its local credit. The Francklyn Company can be so managed as to meet its regular current expenses and to yield something over by this Fall selling a few steers and dry cows . . . but it cannot be managed to produce enough to pay off the land notes as they mature unless extensions be secured—not likely. The land as a real estate investment can within a few years repay all losses and make a very handsome profit. I have thought your party as able as any to force the play.

Tyng recommended that Foster hire a good, experienced cowman as manager on the White Deer range, and that after all matters were straightened out he manage the business from the New York office. He wired Foster, July 23, 1886: "Arnold resigned and went 18th. Wm. Frazer Acting Manager and doing work well. Suffer no Company property whatever to be sold to Groom. . . . Telegraph me whereabouts old Groom."

With inventories now complete and satisfactory, with Groom removed, and with title to both land and cattle in the hands of the Trustees, it became necessary to turn attention to foreclosure proceedings.

CHAPTER 13

White Deer Lands Emerge from the Francklyn Wreckage

AFTER THE GROOMS had been dismissed from the Francklyn Company much restoration work was necessary. The tools and machinery left from the wreckage at White Deer and Greer must be gathered up and evaluated. The livestock, which were widely scattered as a result of Groom's cattle deliveries during the past two or three years, must be gathered, counted, branded, and thrown back into the White Deer Pasture. The deeds and patents to the land must be located, and the title to both land and cattle must be secured. Gordon Cunard's lawsuit must be stayed, and a new administrative order must be set up by which the British bondholders could own and operate their Texas properties. Movements of the Grooms must be watched closely in order to prevent further misrepresentation of the Company's affairs. The Francklyn Company's credit must be restored and its financial obligations must be assured.

Tyng Takes Inventory of the Wreckage

During the summer and fall of 1886 Tyng was busily engaged in clearing the outside ranges of White Deer cattle. These cattle were scattered over such a wide area that their recovery proved to be very expensive. Moreover, White Deer cattle were often exaggeratedly reported as far as two hundred miles from the Company's range. Tyng, however, was determined to protect the bondholders' property by whatever action was necessary, no matter how few the number of cattle reported, or how far distant they might be.

With reference to identifying the cattle, Tyng advised Frederic de P. Foster, trustee, July 23, 1886, that the brand kept up by the Francklyn Company was Bar X on the left jaw, left side, and left hip, and cropped left ear. "But," he said, "Some of the older cattle carry on a war map of old brands, that leaves little room for new ones." He further advised:

The foregoing suggestions may facilitate your determination of the manner in which the desired identity may be satisfactorily maintained. The inventory is being taken by H. Kimball for you, and by R. Luckett for the Company. In the absence of the official Manager [Harry Groom] it seems proper to inventory all the scattered wreck implements etc. that lie around like discarded toys, and upon which no money value can be appraised. The inventory, however, should be complete by the time the stock has been gone through. Have heard of some 200 head outside Greer Bar X cattle which have been cut from the J-Buckle roundup and are to be thrown into the Greer herd enroute.

On August 6, 1886, Tyng gave Benedict the following description of the wreckage at White Deer:

As you have not seen the Diamond F, I despair of ever giving you the faintest idea of the *appalling* wreck and confusion. It is enough to make one sit down and cry on seeing it. Except two riding cultivators, brand new, there is not a wagon, harness, tool, or implement on the whole place in good order or working condition—*literally not one!* It all seems as if a big reckless gang had been hired to buy stuff and throw it away or destroy it. In Greer County remains a lot of broken wagons, harness etc. that would make a pile you couldn't throw a stone over it, that *is* an exaggeration. However, you don't know how *bad* things are so much as how good they can be made. . . .

So much dry rot has permeated the outfit that lots of decay must continue until we can get the excision process applied all over it. Work has dragged, but the heft of it has "done been" performed, and we soon can allow the boys a Sunday or two for washing their clothes etc. I have telegraphed that I had better be interviewed, either here or at New York, before making suggestions for straightening out some of the crooks and future conduct of the business. That is so. A noble ship has been wrecked. Some of the fragments must be left to rot on the beach, others can be used for construction of some kind of a boat or raft on which to yet save part of the valuable cargo, but for making a *good* boat and saving more of the stuff, new material must be supplied. Can you folks supply it? Do they want to? How much of a new boat do they want? And in what direction do they want her navigated? I don't want to "shiver your timbers" with a lot of nautical poetry, but if all that remains is to stretch a royal over a spar, camp under it, and pile up stuff as it comes onto the beach, why then you don't need me for long, and I can within a few weeks gather all that the mourning waves are likely to wash up.

In exasperation, Tyng commented further:

At the beginning of my Diamond F career I recklessly accused the Grooms of lying and—so forth. My life has been checkered by contact with thieves—contact more or less good natured, but I have never before bumped up against men who would burn up a house to steal a pie out of it. Mutual irritation is so fatal to good judgment that I have struggled against its overpowering me. We have had to make this campaign short handed, proving negatives and against men who are defending an inside circle. So far many of the advantages have been theirs, and I sometimes wake up picturing to myself the unctious smile with which a certain old gent sits back and twirls thumbs of hands crossed over well-filled paunches while he thinks of the baffled cuss following up blind trails out here. However, there is some compensation, and I'll bet he sometimes grinds his teeth when he thinks how much more *could* have been scooped up if only he could have had 30 or 60 more days time. The bell has rung and puts an end to garrulity.

Meanwhile Tyng was working as fast as possible gathering up this heap of trash in order to get to the more constructive work of rebuilding White Deer Lands. He believed that by cutting out fencing and farm operations the Diamond F could be conducted for a year with "one Foreman, two fence riders, a cook, two cow men, and a horse wrangler for about $5000." He told Benedict:

Your clients should have an old Western man on whose judgment they can rely out here for a month. That would be enough. An Eastern man would not do. Things would appear crude to him and a long way behind civilized occupation. Not so with a man who has shot buffalo eight or ten years ago in Kansas where now are flourishing towns.

In a letter dated August 6, 1886, Tyng advised Foster:

> Upon closing up and remitting inventory a few days hence matters at Diamond F will be as snug as at present possible. . . . I do not see my way clear to much longer earning wages for you. Questions still pending and future conduct of the business and management of the property can only be well determined on an intimate knowledge of matters here which I may fail to convey to you by mail, and of matters at New York which may or may not become proper for me to thoroughly understand. By August 15th it appears to me that this business *here* will not suffer under W. R. Frazer for a couple of weeks, or before the expiration of which time you can have made satisfactory arrangements. If you can come onto this ground I can wait for you. If you judge well for me to consult you at New York I am willing to come there. If neither course is desired I think best to make you a detailed report and can accommodate what was required of me, as far as possible. The business will not be in good shape, but will have stopped going down hill.

On his departure August 17, 1886, Tyng left Frazer in charge at White Deer, as subordinate to LeFors, who had general management of the Company's affairs. Tyng instructed Frazer to allow no one to have access to the ranch records or to allow anything to be removed from the ranch without a written order. Each week Frazer was to pay all hands and give Foster detailed information of the happenings on the range. Tyng suggested to Frazer that "Courtesies should be extended to your neighbors, even at some trouble or reasonable expense which will be more than compensated by reciprocity. Let them all see that you are making a new and square deal and are desirous to accommodate."

Benedict Returns to Texas

Benedict returned to Texas in September, 1886, to assist Tyng in clearing up all unsettled questions and in getting the trustee's program into operation. Remembering his first experience in camp life on the Texas plains, he fortified himself at Dodge City and Camp Supply with "two slickers and two pairs of blankets, three boxes of crackers, two cans of pears, one can of beef, three boxes of sardines, two cans of ham, three cans of beans, one cheese, two spoons and a can opener."

Tyng also returned to White Deer in September. He wrote Foster from Dallas, September 15, 1886: "I start tomorrow for the Panhandle to carry out the program aranged for that end of the business. No difficulty is anticipated. I shall report frequently and endeavor to keep you minutely informed as to the condition of the property and business there."

Tyng took over the management of the White Deer Lands on September 21, 1886, and two days later he appointed Perry LeFors,

. . . as my true and lawful attorney for me and in my place and stead to recover and take possession of property wherever found of the Francklyn Land & Cattle Co., more particularly of horses, cattle and mules in their brand and to cause their delivery there at the Diamond F Pasture; to protect and care for the same and to employ assistants or agents for the above named purposes hereby ratifying and confirming all that my said attorney shall lawfully do or cause to be done by notice hereof.

He then informed Foster, September 24, 1886, that he had taken possession of the Company's property and that Frazer had resigned.

Every employee is now in my service as Agent for the Trustee and understands that the Trustee now holds the property. . . . I note your reference to Goodnight's advice to hold on to the school lands. Of course, we hold on this winter because it would cause inconvenience not to do so, but you will scarcely put money into them while the title is in the name of Groom and other "such friends."

On the same date, Tyng made Foster a detailed report of the condition of the farms, cattle, grass, fences, supplies, etc. He reported that the last working of the cattle for 1886 in branding calves and throwing out strays would begin at once. He published notices in the *Panhandle* (newspaper), the *Live Stock Journal,* and the *Globe Live Stock Journal of Kansas City* for 10,000 to 15,000 cattle to be pastured at $1.50 per head. He estimated that there was some $30,000 worth of livestock on the property, and that it would require an outlay of

White Deer Lands Emerge from the Wreckage

about $2,000 to carry them through the winter. He declared that should such outlay not be allowable:

> Some trust must be placed in Providence and more on the chance of a mild winter. . . . Many unprofitable savings can be effected if made necessary by want of funds. The cost can be cut according to the cloth. . . . In general it may be said that the property has been looted and gutted: that the present outlay is necessary to the collection and preservation of what is left, for which outlay returns can be looked for in the growth, improvement, and increase of the livestock, and the increase in the value of the land. . . . Several holders of drafts drawn by ex-Manager Groom, and refused by the Company, have been notified by him to forward the dishonored drafts to a bank in Kansas City for redemption. If this is being done in good faith it will materially reduce the amount of outstanding claims against the property.

At this same time Colonel Groom was making every possible effort in defense of his program as manager of the Francklyn Company. On October 5, 1886, he succeeded in getting published in the *Northwest Live Stock Journal,* of Cheyenne, Wyoming, an article which quoted an earlier article in the *Trinidad Advertiser* (September 25, 1886). It reads as follows:

> The *Trinidad Advertiser* reviews the many opinions that have been given by the newspapers of the range country and elsewhere upon the affairs of the Francklyn Land & Cattle Co., and deduces therefrom another version which is unquestionably in harmony with the facts, and which makes a most satisfactory showing for the late management of the Company. We reproduce the article in full.
>
> "The newspapers have recently contained so many references to the Francklyn Land & Cattle Co., many of which have been incorrect, that we have thought a brief statement of the facts in relation to this Company might prove of general interest to our readers.
>
> From prominent cattle men we learn that in the first place the Francklyn Company put $1,289,000 into cattle purchased of Harrold & Ikard, which constituted their herd, except two or three small bands of cattle purchased afterwards. Col. B. B. Groom the noted breeder of Kentucky was selected as Manager of this Company, and under his administration $1,038,000 was realized by the Francklyn Company from sales of cattle within two and one-half years from the receiving of the Harrold & Ikard cattle. It will be seen from this statement of facts that the cattle have been

so well handled that nearly all of the original purchase has been paid back.

The Francklyn Company have delivered this season 17,600 head of cattle that were sold last year and through the winter, and they have on hand in their pasture at White Deer, in the Panhandle, over 6000 head of cattle, including several valuable Short Horns and Galloways, some of which were imported from Great Britain. It has been the aim of the Company to move their cattle from the Greer County range to the Company's Panhandle ranch, and of the numbers so moved it is reasonable to suppose that many have got out of the pastures, owing to fences having been down, and strayed off. The gathering of the cattle this season on the Company's Greer County range, which covers an area 125 x 50 miles, was retarded by the extreme drouth and Pink Eye among the horses, but notwithstanding this fact, over 11,000 were taken from the Greer County range this Spring. The Francklyn Company own 700,000 acres of the choicest land in the Panhandle of Texas, upon which they owe about $1 per acre, leaving an equity, based upon prices at which similar lands are held at $2 an acre, which would amount to $1,400,000.

From this brief statement it would appear the original investors of the Francklyn Company are protected in their investments. When all the facts bearing on this Company are known, it will be seen that under Col. Groom's management, its affairs will compare favorably with other large companies, and the papers that have given prejudiced and distorted statements of the affairs of this Company are doing the entire range industry great harm."

Although this shrewd move on the part of Colonel Groom put Tyng on the defensive, he went on in the even tenor of his way, confident of his ability to match wits with the ever-pressing and the ever-present ex-manager of the White Deer range. In a letter to Benedict at New York, October 16, 1886, he made only a brief comment on the above article, saying:

The enclosed newspaper excerpt reads as if written by B. B. himself. It may amuse you. . . . All is going as well here as could be expected. Everything promises good outcome. It will be sometime before we get this old thing put together and braced up, and the work is not cheering. I think if a big fire (that would spare our grass) could come and burn up all this trash and rattle traps and put us to living in a dugout, we should feel happier for making a new and clean start.

In a letter to Ferdinand Van Zandt, October 17, 1886, Tyng accepted employment at White Deer for one year from September 1, 1886, which, he said, "clinches my loyalty and best efforts." His letter continued:

> I have not seen Goodnight since June 15th. There can be no doubt of his hearty good will toward you, nor of his disposition to give any assistance he can to my employers. He made me feel that I can go to him freely, and in any emergency or doubt I shall not hesitate in doing so. He thought June 15th that the Francklyn Company *might* have 30,000 to 50,000 head but said his own constant occupation debarred him from accurate information on this matter. Messrs Groom gave no unnecessary publicity as to cattle deliveries. Nothing has occurred yet to warrant change in statements reported August 20th and since, further than that the land appears to have been valued fully *low* and the personal property too high. . . . The implements, merchandise and supplies prove to have less value than was given them in the cursory examination possible in August. The number of outside cattle may prove to be 100 or 200 head more than the 500 then estimated. The country is being thoroughly worked for them at our expense and justifiable under other circumstances. Any appearance of abandonment on our part now would open a way for much dirt and loss of cattle.

Tyng, in the same letter, laid out the main provisions of the program that he was to follow as long as he was connected with the White Deer lands:

> Now for the "gist" of your letter. You asked *what would you recommend in case we decide to take up the mortgage.*
> 1. Fence off Block 2 which contains nearly 200,000 acres . . . and make a good stock ranch that will pay profits. . . . Put $10,000 on it in wells and windmills which will water it very well. . . . Put another $1000 into putting it up in proper shape for business. . . . Then run the rest of the land entirely as a real estate operation. Make accurate surveys to locate the land honestly without trying to steal adjoining slices. Move fences to their true places. Rent out the grass until farmers begin to want the land, which will be very soon. Sub-divide and sell to actual cultivators at long time and 6 per cent interest. Pursue a *seemingly* liberal policy toward the first settlers. Do not think of occupying or working any part of the land outside of Block 2, unless this is done in detached and separate enterprises proportionate to capacity of your agents. Anything over 200,000 acres becomes too large for proper supervision and goes to the bow-wows for lack of attention. Block 2 has more than enough good arable land and plenty of good shelter to make

it, by itself, a very good ranch when better watered. The rest of the estate except the southeast corner is fine land and very suitable for small *stock* farms where artificial shelter can be made for small herds with sod walls and other cheap construction not adapted for large herds. Headquarters should be about the center of Block 2.

2. If objection is made to the outlay of money for making Block 2 into a paying stock ranch, then sell off the cattle in the Spring regardless of condition of next year's market, and shape the whole business as above into a Real Estate Operation. Funds will then be derived from sale of cattle for the necessary surveys, moving of fences, etc., and more too. It is idle to hope to profitably manage the present stock of cattle while giving them the run of all this enormous tract, and I certainly cannot advise the purchase of cattle enough to stock so poor a range. . . .

I don't want to say more lest it appear like magnifying difficulties, but you can see that no man could be proud of such a prospective winter work. We have no hay to spare and must use it for carrying through the horses, bulls, and best stock, after getting the outside cattle, go as far as possible this Fall. We must *let the cattle alone* as far as it can be done. All the healthy and proper stock look now as if it is going to winter finely. Horses are fat and in good condition for the winter. The school lands in Block B-2 are in the names of the Grooms and their immediate friends and relations. I do not favor trying to consummate their [the lands'] acquisition, but if that is thought desirable, then the first thing to do is to get deeds from the Grooms and their chums, then pay for them in full to the State and get patents as soon as possible and before grangers[1] get to squatting on them. . . . I suppose the vendor's lien of $700,000 (which bears 6 per cent interest and is splendidly secured) will be bought and the *land* taken under it upon the first default in payment, and that the delays and fight of foreclosure will go over the cattle only, unless the Trustees can just sell them out according to the terms of the mortgage. However, I am not lawyer enough to judge *how* you are going to get the land, though I hope you *will* get it before the prices jump. The Southern Kansas railroad is now running a line along the north bank of the Canadian, thirteen miles from here. Looks like a final location rather than like a preliminary survey. I hope the foregoing is what you want. Command me freely.

While Tyng was scouring the Greer ranges for any cattle left by

[1] The word *granger* is generally used in referring to the earliest farm settlers on land, but with the implication that such settlers were illegal occupants of the land.

the Grooms, he advised Benedict at New York from Vernon, November 4, 1886, that:

> Col. B. B. Groom is working to the northwest of us to secure testimony as to his managing capacity and integrity, and as to his blamelessness for the Company's misfortunes. He has been very active in the country between us and Fort Worth. The latter activity has seemed to me to have taken a direction toward gathering evidence of a large remnant of cattle still existing in the Company's hands, and of lack of due diligence on the part of the Trustee's servants in gathering and protecting the property. He has now gone up to Mobeetie. He has secured (I think) the services of some very good men. I cannot conceive what for, unless it be for his own protection against personal violence. This, true is entirely unnecessary, because he has enough grey hair to protect him against everything but a little cursing.

Tyng assured Benedict that there was no chance of Groom's re-taking the property, and that he had, therefore, decided not to return to Mobeetie "until satisfied that there is no longer *value* in my presence in Greer."

He continued further:

> If he [Groom] should perpetrate such cunning folly, why, we shall simply recapture the works, certainly without expense and probably without anybody's getting hurt. This gathering of scattered cattle has been an insufferably tedious job. Letting it out on contract per head would have been about as effective and considerably cheaper. But it seemed prudent to thoroughly protect the Trustee against any charge of negligence, by having his immediate employees put in an appearance at every roundup we could hear of and get to. The sprinkling of two's and three's we are getting with the cattle shows that we are gathering many Bar X cattle which the Francklyn Company never got upon their range and that there cannot be very many more left on the outside.

Tyng took advantage of a few days' delay in the work on the range to go to Dallas, where he spent one day visiting with Miller and seeing the Fair. He consulted Miller:

> About the taxes sought to be levied on the Bar X cattle in the newly-organized county of Greer and for whose payment the hungry new officials *talk* of holding the cattle we have thrown in there from surrounding country.

We shall probably drive the cattle home when we get ready. Inquiry at the Fair indicated a no market for Short Horn cattle except at ridiculous prices which is to be regretted as our Short Horns, though very good, are not adapted—not at all—to Panhandle range and climate, and *are* a source of very great expense, always have been, and for many years will be. After awhile small farmers in the Panhandle will want them, and later will be able to buy them. I leave here in the morning and should be at Mobeetie about the 10th unless the work in Greer County can be hurried a little.

On reaching Mobeetie, Tyng notified Benedict, November 10, 1886, that:

B. B. Groom was here and finding nothing being done against him before the Grand Jury was truculent, vituperative, and went away via Clarendon. As I came via Greer County, we did not meet. He brought two fighting men with him, but was careful in selection of objects for scolding. He talked very sweetly to LeFors and told him that he had arranged with Foster for an early payment of his account in full. He is a queer old cad. I telegraphed him that I was coming and hurried all I could without neglect of duty, but he seems to prefer written criticism to personal demand for reparation. I fancy that the Francklyn creditors may yet conclude to withdraw the matter of charity and substitute it with striped suits.

In a letter to Foster, dated November 22, 1886, Tyng made a report on the general condition of affairs at White Deer. He declared that he could not get cattle to pasture "this Autumn," since all work must be stopped because of lateness of the season. He deplored the fact that money must be expended for supplies and for work stock, and for extra care of imported stock and Shorthorns—which was required because of their inability to adjust to the Plains climate. He added:

The collection of scattered Bar X cattle has been done very thoroughly and well. Credit is due our Foreman and employees for the energy and fidelity they have displayed in this work. . . . Much has been gained by the moral effect produced upon outside ranges by the presence and activities of the Trustee's employees: thus direct, palpable evidence has been given of no unwillingness to neglect or abandon any kind of property to which the Trustee's trustors can sustain a claim. The cattle from the southwest were gathered into Greer County upon the old Bar X range and driven out without the payment of taxes or giving bond for their later payment. . . . A deal of picking up, storing away, cleaning and repairing is yet to be done,

White Deer Lands Emerge from the Wreckage

less for the money value to be derived (though that is something) than to promote a better morale and more persistent care of minor property, and also to terminate the depressing and disgraceful appearance of things at headquarters and elsewhere on the ranch.

Time has not yet been available for examining documents transmitted by your office October 21st as carefully and dispassionately as demanded by their volume and by Groom's charges to malice. Your suggestion as to any publication is duly heeded. While in your service your permission is a prerequisite to my publication of anything relating to Francklyn matters. The publication of August 19th was very opportune by submitting to *cowmen of the Panhandle* the question as to existence of property. It effectually guarded misrepresentations made for confusing and delaying action of creditors and of their Trustee in a way that never could have been done had the questions remained confined to privacy at New York and subject only to Groom's plausible assertations.

Allow me to take the liberty of remarking that the vituperation of Groom's report of September 30th is not accurately defined by the word "criticism." Of course the absurd exposure irritated him, but his excitement may also be attributed to your Board's resolution of July 30th (I have never seen it) which perhaps called on him to account for money, as his report gives no account of monies rumored to have been received by him early in July. It is possible that your Board had no proof of his having received them.

Francklyn Affairs Shift to London

The British bondholders were following events at White Deer with much interest and concern. In order to secure their investments they took steps to purchase the first lien on the land notes held by the New York & Texas Land Company. They also hastened to get control of all the cattle left on the Company's ranges so as to forestall a foreclosure suit by Gordon Cunard. A trusteeship was set up to work with the American trustee in the operation and management of the Company's Texas properties. Godden Son & Holme, solicitors for the British investors, wrote Foster, November 5, 1886:

We write at the request of Mr. Kingsmill on behalf of Lord Rosebery and Messrs Williams, Deacon & Co., as represented by Mr. Courthorpe as to the details for carrying out their purchase of the land notes of the Francklyn Company effected in accordance with your recent telegrams, and especially your explanatory letter of October 15th to Mr. Kingsmill which arrived before the purchase money was cabled, in connection with the payment of £151,464 6:6[2] rental. On the 28th it was agreed between Lord Rosebery and Mr. Courthorpe that any bondholder in actual possession of his bonds, free from encumbrance, who within six months, contributes his proportion of that sum and executes the deed shall share in the purchase, and we are drawing up the deed to carry this out. Under this deed two or three London Trustees will be nominated who will represent the contributors, but the land notes can be held by American citizens in New York nominated by and subject to the directions of these London Trustees. We understand that a fresh foreclosure suit will sooner or later be instituted in due course for the purchasers of the land notes based upon the Company's default in payment of installment due November 1, 1886, and we shall be glad to hear from you as to the proper time in your opinion for taking this step. Of course, it could not be taken until the sixty days of grace has expired. Mr. Kingsmill cabled to you on the 29th October for a complete list of the bondholders' names and addresses so far as they may be known. If it has not already been despatched we shall be much obliged if you will send it on, the best list you can, immediately on receipt of this letter. We shall also at the same time be glad to hear from you generally on the business and the manner in which it is proposed to carry it forward.

During the latter part of November, 1886, Francklyn Company matters shifted to England. On November 18 Benedict arrived in London, where he spent several days in consultation with the newly appointed British trustees. The visit of Benedict had a threefold purpose: First, a personal meeting with the British bondholders, which had become necessary in order to explain to them in detail the actual conditions causing delay, confusion, and conflict at White Deer; second, establishment of a legal and harmonious working relationship between the New York and the London trustees in the management and control of the Texas properties; and third, agreement on a long-time program in order to make constructive progress in the Company's affairs.

On November 13, 1886, Foster wrote Benedict in London:

I had a letter from Stickney suggesting my resignation as Trustee, the

[2] One hundred fifty-one thousand, four hundred sixty-four pounds, six shillings and sixpence.

winding up of the Company, and the necessity of inviting all the bondholders to participate in the land note purchase. Whittock came in on Wednesday to find out for Bache Cunard how things stood, and I told him of the purchase of the land notes and the course which, as Trustee, I deemed proper for the purchasers to pursue.

Foster reported also that Francklyn had sent over by one John R. Smith a complaint on the Company to recover $165 for services in obtaining judgment against the Bassick Mine out in Colorado for the Francklyn Company, and that he hoped to collect the amount from Francklyn. Foster then referred to the letter he had received from Godden Son & Holme and advised Benedict that:

> I shall answer it in general terms and mention your visit to London, advising them to confer with you. George Allen representing the Balfours has called upon me. I told him of the land note purchase and of my request to purchasers to let in the other bondholders and of the probable action of purchasers in that regard. Fry notified me today that he intended to sell his bonds at auction tomorrow. At my request he adjourned sale one week. I shall telegraph you concerning this matter and regret exceedingly that this letter will not reach you before the adjourned date. You see if Francklyn should purchase these bonds for a song he could use them to pay his debt, or rather square his account. While I should be glad to see him come out all right, I do not want him just now to be in a position toward us more independent than his present one. I hope notwithstanding the lot of things you will have to do that you will have some little chance to enjoy yourself, and that I may soon see you looking as brown as a sailor.

During the negotiations at London, Foster and Benedict kept closely in touch with each other by cablegrams having to do largely with the sale of Fry's bonds. Benedict notified Foster of his arrival in London, November 18, 1886, and added, "Have seen Kingsmill. Everything seems pleasant." Foster cabled Benedict, November 22, 1886, to "Please answer cables concerning Fry's bonds. Everything going well here. Have all patents here now." Benedict on the same date cabled:

> Linen[3] sick. Could not submit Fry proposal until today. He declines further purchase after two days explanatory conference with lawyers held

---

[3] Lord Rosebery owned a string of banks known as "the British Linen Company." Their code name for cable purposes was "Linen London," which had reference not only to Lord Rosebery but also to Andrew Kingsmill.

first general meeting. Williams Linen lawyer. Today your cables October 19th and 21st were understood to mean that any surplus arising on sale under the land notes would be distributed to contributing bondholders exclusively. It was this which mainly induced purchase. Did you intend this? Have explained you intended that at sale in present suit they could probably purchase for amount their present holdings of bonds subject to their first lien thereby acquiring clear title, but any other purchasers would be obliged to raise amount of first lien as well. Have told Linen your intention to resign at once. He approves. Both parties have confidence in you but unwilling to expend more from income of property. . . . Am revising bondholders agreement. Will bring it over with me. Send order publication to Godden with instructions for service. Would Van Zandt be willing to act as Trustee without compensation if necessary going to Texas? Have just learned Alaska deferred one week. No other desirable Steamer Saturday. Shall I remain? No extra cost except maintenance.

On November 24, 1886, Foster replied to Benedict by cable:

Linen has misunderstood cable. You mention how you can explain how surplus above first lien would be distributed. See section 11 of mortgage. . . . Other publication goes to Godden tomorrow. Will cable concerning Van Zandt when he arrives here. Alexander & Green today asked me to cable inquiring what sum Linen will take for his stocks and bonds and land notes. I asked them to make offer, adding Linen not desirous to sell.[4] Communicate with Linen. Mr. Kempland wishes to know whether you have seen, if not, to see Gen. Fitzgerald in regard to taxes, and whether you have any word for him in regard to three loans on November 9th, and cable reply. Regret decision on Fry matter. Have adjourned his sale till tomorrow week. Await my letter last Wednesday and cable if decision changed. Fry says his friend, Col. Jennison, worth $300,000 to $400,000, and another man looking at the property. May wish purchase or lease. Perhaps only talk.

Benedict notified Foster by cable, November 24, 1886, that: "Explanation satisfactory. Linen cannot name selling price of bonds, but will telegraph any offer to India. [Lord Rosebery was in India.] Letter

[4] There was much at stake in the sale of Fry's bonds. Ownership of the bonds carried an appointment on a five-man Board of Directors of the Bondholders, which determined the policies of the organization. It was somewhat similar to a seat on the New York Stock Exchange.

sent today. Linen declines further purchase. Probably no money except expenses until February."

On the same day Benedict also sent Foster a detailed written report of the meetings with the British bondholders in London. He began with this explanation:

By the time this reaches you you will probably have received a general view of the situation by cable. In the first place by way of premise I would say that these Englishmen do not devote their entire attention to business, and if you have any business with them you have to do it when they are ready and stop when they get tired. I cabled you on Monday that I had just had the first general meeting with all the parties. The meeting was arranged with great ceremony and was held at the office of Williams, Deacon & Co., the bankers. There was present the Earl of Leaven, Mr. Williams, Mr. Deacon, Mr. Fletcher, Mr. Courthorpe, representing Wm D & Co.'s firm, Mr. Kingsmill, Mr. Godden Son & Holme. Mr. Holme had prepared a synopsis of the matters for consideration relating chiefly to the value of the land and to the expenses of holding it and the profit derivable therefrom. I was cautious not to go too much into detail as these London bankers are accustomed to leave details to their agents and derive only results. They asked me many questions on their own account, which, however, I endeavored to answer.

It became quite evident that they had made this joint purchase of the land notes unwillingly, especially as it is not such an investment as Williams, Deacon & Co.'s bankers are accustomed to make, and had done it chiefly on your telegrams which they did not wholly understand. They thought from your cables of October 17th and 21st, and Kingsmill's cable intermediate, that you advised them that they would be entitled to any surplus arising from sale under land notes to the exclusion of other (non contributing) bondholders; and from their inquiry to you and your reply of the 21st, such I think would be a reasonable conclusion *for them* to draw. I explained it as best I could and Kingsmill asked me to take the cables to the hotel and look them over and give them further advice on the following day.

The main point of that interview was that they stated that they would be willing to let the mony lie in the land until such time as it could be sold. They do not wish to run a cattle ranch either with their own cattle or other peoples. *This is very clear to them.* I told them that I believed the whole tract could be leased at 6 to 8 cents per acre which would make about $40,000. They were disposed to question the desirability of retaining Tyng, if the land should be leased, but after I had given them some idea of his worth and the necessity of the case, they finally agreed that he would have to be retained. *This they are also convinced of.*

They wish to have the cattle sold as quickly as possible and the money deposited in Court with Gordon Cunard's assent, which I told them could be done. Gordon is on very friendly terms with Williams, Deacon & Co., and Mr. Fletcher will undertake to get his consent to this and give it to us either directly or through Gutherie (who by the way has not turned up in London yet). Kingsmill then talked about the present foreclosure suit and they seemed to drop it and get a little by the short cut under deed to Evans. They wish to make no unnecessary expenditures and save every penny possible. I told them that it would be unwise thrift to do this, except by a suit in equity. After a little talk about trustees etc the meeting adjourned to meet on Tuesday.

After the meeting was adjourned, Kingsmill invited Benedict to dine with him at the Conservative Club, where they discussed matters further. Benedict said that Kingsmill was very pleasant and that:

I gave him some points about your position. He seems to feel as though you ought to act as the attorney for R & Wm D [Lord Rosebery and Williams & Deacon] and not for the minority bondholders. I assured him that you felt so too and had simply taken the Trusteeship for the purpose of acquainting yourself with the real condition of affairs and would resign it at once. He seemed to like this and we had further talk about the position. I suggested that occasion might arise for R to need an English solicitor to look out for his interests in the new Bondholders' Syndicate. He said that he had not thought it best to consult R's Solicitors as they were old and fussy and he had great confidence in Godden & Holme. I assured him that I believed from what I had seen of G & H that they had acted fairly by R & Wm D. He said if I thought it best he would have his cousin, Mr. Burt, to whom he presented me, act for R. *I shall advise this,* and at the same time do a little looking out on my own account although it seems unnecessary. I broached the subject of money. He said he did not feel authorized to make any payments for services until R returns from India in February and hoped you would be willing to wait until then. I shall, however, see what can be done through G & H, and, in any event, will get money to keep your disbursements paid.

On the following day, Benedict went by appointment to the Williams, Deacon & Co. Bank again, where he held a two-hour con-

White Deer Lands Emerge from the Wreckage

ference with the people who had been there the day before. His account follows:

The bankers are all old men (except Courthorpe). The interview was very satisfactory. I first submitted the statement which I enclose as to what your cables meant. I did this not as representing you as Trustee, but, at their request, gave them private advice on the point. It was not submitted in writing but was read to them. The interview was substantially similar to the preceding one. On the other point which I have mentioned and the conclusion reached at the first meeting were confirmed at the second. (Let me remark here that I submitted your cable about Fry's sale to Kingsmill when we were together, but he was convinced that R would not make any further investment. He holds R's letter of attorney to do anything necessary. I shall try to see if he will not buy.)

The other matter which was discussed at the second meeting related to the question of trustees etc. I found that Kingsmill had been almost committed to appoint Cuyler as Trustee for notes, and Paton's letter, which I have read, shows an intense desire to get hold of the business. Kingsmill places a good deal of confidence in Paton and this has controlled Wm D. I have, however, *prevented all this* and done it in a legitimate way. I suggested that if a new trustee comes in he will have to employ an attorney to study up the situation. This would be a repetition of our work and would be very costly. I therefore, suggested Van Zandt who, Kingsmill felt, would act without compensation and *under your direction*. Kingsmill first objected that Van Zandt is too far away to be of use, but after some discussion of the way to foreclose they determined to follow my advice and having a suit in equity, meanwhile allowing the present suit to stand still. Kingsmill's brother [Henry Kingsmill] is to be alternate Trustee appointed in a separate instrument, which I am to prepare. He is in Van Zandt's employ and is a naturalized American. *The new syndicate deed creates a trust in the bonds and the land notes to be endorsed to them.* They will be Englishmen (Godden and some others). I advised them that English Trustees could hold the notes but the legal title to the trust must be an American citizen.

We then discussed the existing trust of bondholders' mortgage and that remains undetermined upon. It is possible that the program will be for you to be the Trustee of the land notes and Van Zandt of the bondholders, and that minority bondholders will be permitted to name a Co-Trustee. Your name was received with great favor by both sides, and they were kind enough to ask that I act as Trustee in the place now occupied by you. As this suggestion was spontaneous on their part I think you will see that I made very good progress toward gaining their confidence for you. I thought it a great victory. Even the suggestion.[5] Of course, I told them I could not accept it without consulting you and considering whether such a step would be beneficial to them. So it was left open and the meeting closed.

Benedict's last act in connection with these meetings was attendance at a conference at the Holmes Chambers, to correct and revise the new Syndicate deed in an effort to make it satisfactory to all parties concerned. "The document is ten pages in length, folio," said Benedict, "and is a masterpiece. It was drawn by a celebrated counsel. It provides, after copying nearly all the foreclosure bill, 21 recitals." These recitals are listed in numerical order. The most important of them permitted each of the bondholders to contribute his proportionate share toward the purchase of the land notes and bonds, a provision which gave Lord Rosebery and Williams, Deacon & Co. a majority in value of the bonds. Another stipulation was that none of the parties were to sell their bonds until foreclosure, "Provided Wm D & Co. may sell theirs if they give other signers opportunity to purchase." A third provision was that "The Trustees shall take such steps as the majority in value shall determine." In commenting on the document, Benedict said:

There are several points of detail which I have suggested might be altered with benefit, and Holme and I will meet the learned counsel at his chambers tomorrow afternoon for the purpose of submitting these points. There are two important questions affecting Rosebery, individually. First the deprivation of power of sale of his bonds until foreclosure, and second the majority question. This last I have advised Holme should be a simple majority, not as he desired a two-thirds majority, so as to give other signers a voice. I put it to him that R was the largest interested and that he should be permitted to dictate more than anyone else. A majority in value will be constituted by R and Wm D. They are very friendly and undoubtedly will remain so. (Kingsmill approves this plan). I have personally suggested that Wm D sell their bonds and buy them in. They seem reluctant to do so, but I think are willing to do as I advise. Godden & Holme seem disposed to be guided by us to a surprising degree.

Benedict expressed great disappointment at being delayed in Eng-

---

[5] Benedict proved his unusual ability as a lawyer many times in dealing with the affairs of the Francklyn Company and their bondholders. He observed his twenty-seventh birthday while on this mission to England.

White Deer Lands Emerge from the Wreckage 211

land, but he thought the longer stay was very kindly received, "by the other people as they do not have to hurry so much":

They are all agreed that the bondholders' deed must be sent to Rosebery at once for signature and have asked me to approve it without taking it over to you. It seems so much like what we should have prepared that I have consented to do this at Kingsmill's suggestion. If it is made perfectly satisfactory to Kingsmill, his cousin and me, I believed you would be satisfied at not seeing it before signature, especially as it in the main follows an informal instrument already signed by R and Wm D. There are several bondholders here who have expressed their readiness to sign and contribute. You are to get the signatures of the New Yorkers and Americans. The Balfours and Sir B Cunard will all sign; also Fenneck. Your cablegram about Francklyn may change the situation again.

Later—5 p.m. Have been to see Kingsmill and showed him your cable about Alexander & Green. He said that he should advise R to accept a small (very small) discount on bonds provided the purchaser should take up the land in full with interest and all costs. He suggested that if any proposition anything like 100 per cent were made he would telegraph it to R with his approval of acceptance. I shall telegraph you accordingly. Kingsmill recognizes that the entire force of your suggestion that it would be well for them to hold the bonds, but says that R was so utterly discouraged with the bad investment and intimated his intention to burn up his bonds. Kingsmill says that if it had not been for his urgent solicitation Wm D and G would have paid the 100,000 and let it go, or let it go without payment. Kingsmill says he feels better about the investment than he did before I came and they all seem to be glad that I am to be here another week. I spoke to him about the terms of the new deed and that if I should approve it without consultation with you, L & R[6] might in the future be inclined to blame us. He replied that he would be personally responsible for no blame attaching, and also that it is desirable to send it to R for his signature next week. I then went to Holmes and went over the deed again making numerous pencil notes which he will have written up in red ink and send the deed and notes to the counsel tonight so that he will have had time to consider them against tomorrow afternoon when we shall see him. When the general form is approved there will be a third general meeting to discuss such points as need it. I suggested that the deed be printed and sent to the bondholders and this will probably be done. I must stop this rambling now. You can attribute any

---

[6] L and R refers to Andrew Kingsmill, whose code name was Linen, and to Lord Rosebery.

wanderings to the fog which has prevailed here for two days to an alarming degree. If it continues I shall be ready to commit filo de so by tomorrow.

Benedict's business in England was now completed. Since his return to New York was delayed for a week, he now had an opportunity to attend some social and religious meetings, and to accept invitations to dine with several influential persons at various places. Among these occasions was a dinner with a small party at the Crafton Club. "Last Sunday," he said, "I went to St. Paul's and heard Canon Wittingham and to Westminster and heard Archdeacon Farrar; also to the Zoological Gardens and saw the elephant. Theodore Roosevelt is stopping at this hotel but I am not acquainted with him."

Finally the machinery was set up by which the British bondholders could legally own and operate their Texas properties. With these changes the Francklyn Land & Cattle Company passed out of existence, and a new organization, yet to be named, took its place. Among the names suggested by the Englishmen were: The Primrose Plateau, The White Deer Estate, and Carrobgrahut. It was only natural, however, that the new company would take the name of the fertile White Deer Valley that had nurtured the Francklyn Company throughout its hectic history, and it came to be known simply as "The White Deer Lands."

CHAPTER 14

A New York Yankee Takes a Look
at Texans and Texas

ONE OF THE MOST interesting and significant aspects of the Great Plains is the reaction it creates in the white man. When the first adventurers and explorers began to push their way up the western tributaries of the Mississippi River, they found themselves in an entirely new and different world. The great wide open spaces appealed to their imaginative and daring spirits and created within them an insatiable desire to learn what lay ahead. Once seen, the plains were irresistible in their compelling power.

Not only did the unknown west appeal to adventurers and explorers, but it also made a strong impression on the travelers and would-be settlers who first came from the East to penetrate these "Western wilds." This impact is sharply defined in the recorded impressions of hundreds of travelers and prospective settlers who dared to penetrate this strange new land with its "ever-receding horizons." The vast reaches of unobstructed view on the flat rolling prairies excited the curiosity and wonder of these Eastern visitors as they gazed at the panorama stretched out before them. They were awed and almost overwhelmed. They could not fathom this strange and mysterious distance. At the same time the far-reaching plains, teeming with millions of birds, reptiles, and animals, made a deep and unexplainable appeal to these uninitiated visitors as they trekked out into a new world. The plains held them within a physical embrace and whetted their desire to learn more about this strange new world.

Benedict Learns about Texas

It is not surprising, therefore, that Russell Benedict followed the general pattern in his spontaneous reaction to Texas during his first visit to the state, in 1886, when he was sent to investigate and evaluate the prospective value of the lands inherited from the Francklyn Company. In his first letter to Foster, June 8, 1886, he declared:

This is a great country in more ways than one. I have learned more about the country at large, its progress, dangers and accomplishments in these three days of Texas life than I should in three years of life at New York. To start at the beginning and give you a brief outline of our journey is all that I shall attempt until another time.

We left New York June 2nd. Landers proved quite an agreeable companion on the way down and gave me many suggestions which I hope will prove valuable in the future management of the Company.[1] So you see I look to the future prosperity of the Company already. The prospect is very flattering and I am disposed at the present time to be enthusiastic. The enthusiasm, however, is not on account of the cattle business, but on the future of the lands which the Company is supposed to own. This briefly is all I can say now and may be summed up in that way. . . .

We reached Fort Worth on Saturday at 8 p.m. and went to the Pickwick Hotel where I found a telegram from Van Zandt saying he would get there on Thursday morning. I wired him to come to Dallas and also wired you. At 7 Sunday morning we left Fort Worth which is a mining camp on a large scale, and reached Dallas about 10 o'clock. (I meant to have said that I sent you a telegraphic cipher code by the porter of the Pullman car who promised to deliver it to you at the office. Let me know if it reached you).

[1] No further mention is made of Landers in Benedict's letters. He was evidently connected with the Southern Kansas railway in some way, perhaps a conductor.

A New York Yankee Takes a Look

Benedict was much less impressed by the Texans he met than he was by Texas itself. He thought Texas lawyers, as measured by New York standards, were much inferior to lawyers of the Empire state. Even though he placed George Tyng Atkins at the top of the list of Texas lawyers, the man impressed him as rather crude in personality. In recommending Miller to Foster in his report of June 8, he quoted Atkins' language in describing Miller:

"He is incorruptible, straightforward, honest, industrious, clear headed, and by G—— a d——d able lawyer. He has no equal by G—— in the state. He has no address by G——, no address sir, but by G—— sir he is a d——d smart little lawyer." And such is my impression too after seeing him today. That is a sample of the style of conversation here. . . . As Atkins says, "He is a genius by G—— versatility of genius sir."

By contrast Benedict's enthusiasm for the land caught fire rapidly as he approached White Deer Lands. Even before he saw it, he waxed strong in his estimate of the future value of the property. He asserted that:

The time will shortly come when $25 to $50 can be easily got for the best of this land from actual settlers. We must hold on at any cost if we have a title. I shall try to get at the bottom of the facts. I mean to search every section and see what the title consists of. I believe from present appearance it is perfect to all the 500,000 acres of the International Railroad grant, and very shaky as to the school sections amounting to 140,000 acres of the International & Great Northern grant. We are almost the only company in the Panhandle which got the International Company lands in solid blocks. The rest got alternate sections from the Houston & Great Northern grant and they are very much mixed. I saw Miller today and laid the whole matter before him. He was a classmate of E. D. Bettais of New York, at Cambridge. I am satisfied he is the right man. . . . His partner is Seth Shepard ex-state senator. They are hard workers and able men. Tyng has just said that he has gone through all the new states and new countries for twenty-seven years past and that these lands are bound to make the fortunes of everyone fortunate enough to own them. I have now told you everything as fully as I can at present. Miller thinks our mortgage covers the cattle and that the brand marks go for nothing.

Benedict was enthralled as a result of his visit to the Texas Panhandle. In his report of June 22, 1886, he gave Foster a rather detailed account of his observations in Texas and of the conclusions he had reached up to that time. Again he depicted the future of the Lands in glowing terms:

I arrived at Dallas last night after a journey of 200 miles by buckboard and stage from Mobeetie to Harrold. I was rather tired as there was no chance to sleep for three days except such as could be snatched in a jolting wagon. . . . I found your kind letter and also Smith's, together with the express package upon my arrival. Your reference to my letter I presume referred to the first one I wrote dated at Dallas June 8th. It was of course not very satisfactory as I had really accomplished but little, but I can assure you that in regard to the land and its prospective increase I did not over rate the opinion of the people in all parts of the country. I believe the future for the owners of the Francklyn Pasture will be very bright inside of five years. At Mobeetie I talked with all the men of intelligence and all said that we had one of the finest blocks of land in Northwest Texas and that it is worth today, taking it by and large, $2 per acre with much that is worth $5 at the present time, especially around White Deer Creek, a fine stream always full of water enough to run many mills. It has never been known to go dry and we have fifteen miles of it in our lands. It would suffice, they say, to thoroughly irrigate 20,000 acres of land. If so the land could be worth as much as Kansas land, say $30 to $50 per acre. The whole pasture is said to be superb. Of course, the cattlemen are intensely prejudiced against all agricultural interests and decry any attempt to introduce immigration or nesting, as they call it, by small farmers.

Benedict called Foster's attention to some rather significant social and economic changes with reference to Texas lands, their uses and future prospects. In discussing the matter he said:

I wish I could give you some adequate idea of the state of society in Texas. I mean the relative power of the different interests, but cannot without too many words. The old idea of holding the land in vast cultivated tracts for the benefit of a few "cattle barons" is slowly but very surely passing away, and with it the stupendous squandering of public lands for the construction of railroads and improvements of all kinds. Not that railroads are not needed. They are the greatest possible benefactors in the state, introducing Northern enterprise and capital, but the state has wasted *millions* of acres absolutely and received nothing in return. All this, however, has gone by and another policy now predominates in the state legislature, Viz: the encouragement of the granger classes, the "actual settler" theory. I am sure the state will prosper if she maintains this policy. Kansas is overcrowded and if you will look at a map of the Southwest you will see that the overflow must be Texas and New Mexico. Ten years from now will see the *Panhandle* covered with farms. The soil is far more abundant and fertile than Kansas, and as the country is broken up, rain its only drawback, will certainly follow, as it has in every state where similar climatic conditions existed before settlement.

I could go on sounding the praises of this significant country for a long time, but I know how busy you are and will spare you. I am enchanted with it and have tried to get at the bottom facts in regard to its future. I have not yet seen our lands. Perhaps Tyng will tell you a far different tale, but I think not.... It is expensive to do anything here. Everybody wants to make money out of you.... All Southern lawyers whom I have met seem to be looking out for No. 1.... I have spent lots of money for traveling expenses. I have tried to be as prudent as possible, but it costs a great deal to do any traveling here.

During these few days in Texas, Benedict and Junkin[2] had learned much about the ways of Texans, and had also come to understand better the conditions in the state in general. Moreover, they had ingratiated themselves into the good graces of many of the people with whom they were to work during the next few weeks. Benedict wrote Foster that "Junkin has developed into a social favorite and is doing the entertaining business handsomely."

During the months of June and July, 1886, Benedict and Tyng were kept busy gathering up the loose ends at White Deer in order to shape up affairs for a new program. Benedict worked mostly from his Dallas headquarters in his investigation of land titles at Clarendon, Mobeetie, and Austin. He succeeded in getting Tyng appointed as manager at White Deer, June 25, 1886. He then wired Foster that he would finish the examination on Saturday and that he believed the title was good. Foster wired back, July 3, 1886, requesting Benedict to come home after he had seen Tyng, "if you think wise. My reason is I want to talk with you before acting." Benedict, on his way home, wired Foster from St. Louis that he would reach New York on July 7, 1886.

During the next few weeks Foster and Benedict worked out a program for the future management of the White Deer Estate. Tyng re-

---

[2] Junkin was connected with Foster's law firm in some capacity.

mained at White Deer, where he arranged with LeFors and Frazer to manage the properties during the winter of 1886–1887. He also furnished Foster and Benedict much valuable information and advice in relation to the new program. Benedict, after his visit to Austin during September, 1886, to examine titles and his trip to London in November, 1886, to sell the program to the British bondholders, returned to Texas early in 1887, when he gained deeper understanding of the ways of the West.

Benedict Returns to Texas to Evaluate the White Deer Lands

Benedict, accompanied by Junkin, went by way of Dodge City and Topeka, Kansas, on his way to Texas in the spring of 1887. Nothing impressed Benedict as unusual until after they left Dodge City. In fact, on April 15, 1887, he wired Foster from Topeka, Kansas, where he stopped to see railway officials: "Arrived here last night. Leave for Kiowa tonight. Interviewed officials. Nothing new." From Dodge City they went by train, stage, and mail hack to Mobeetie. On this end of the journey Benedict found everything so novel and exciting that he felt compelled to describe some of his new experiences immediately. On April 16, 1887, he hurriedly wrote Foster from the terminus of the Southern Kansas Railroad:

Here we are at the end of all things. We are intending to pass the night in a construction camp about twenty miles from Camp Supply and sixty-eight miles from Kiowa. We left, you remember, on Tuesday reaching St. Louis on Thursday morning. Breakfasted at the Southern Hotel in grand style and left St. Louis at 9 a.m. and arrived at Kansas City at 10:45 p.m. and reached Topeka at 12:50 a.m. . . . Spent the day at Topeka and left at one o'clock the following morning via the Atchison, Topeka, & Santa Fe road. After changing cars several times today, we finally reached Kiowa at one this afternoon. We then just had time to get into the construction train (through Mr. Kingsmill's courtesy) and after five hours and forty minutes ride have reached the terminus of the road. As above mentioned, we had traveled steadily since Tuesday with the exception of one day spent at Topeka. Tomorrow morning at six I hope to leave here for Camp Supply in a six-mule wagon with military escort under command of Lieut. Bishop, 5th U.S. Cavalry, who, fortunately for us, was here waiting for twenty horses, the first freight carried over the new line. If we have good fortune we shall get to Supply at 2 p.m. tomorrow and there get a stage or conveyance of some kind for Mobeetie. It has been raining very hard here all day, and there have been constant showers for a week past so that the rivers may detain us. We have been very well thus far and I have enjoyed Junkin's society very much.

On the way to Texas, Benedict and Junkin spent one day in Topeka, Kansas, in consultation with Santa Fe officials about right of way across the White Deer Lands. Benedict concluded his letter with a report of that meeting:

I saw Mr. Smith by appointment and then found out I didn't want to see him. Mr. Robinson, the Chief Engineer, treated me very nicely and said that Mr. Welch was authorized to make any arrangements with me necessary. So I simply talked generally and reserved everything for Welch. Robinson said if we wanted to do anything about selling it would be necessary to do so outside the Company, either through the attorney and their agents or by conferring with the President at Boston who would refer it to them. I am satisfied that Welch is the man to do this business, that is to start it. Junkin is almost wild over Kansas towns, and I confess that I am not far from it either—their growth or "boom" is something marvellous. I fear that the track will be washed out by today's rain. I am tired now and shall say goodnight as I have to get up early in the morning. Will write fully soon as I have seen Welch.

Benedict wired Foster, April 19, 1887, from the construction camp in Kansas: "Reached here safely. Leave tomorrow for Mobeetie." On April 21, 1887, Foster acknowledged receipt of Benedict's message and expressed surprise "that you write in such good spirits after such a journey," and commented further:

I note what you say concerning your interview with the great men of the Atchison, Topeka, & Santa Fe, and expect good results from your negotiation with Welch. I enclose copy of a letter I received yesterday. White of the Texas Land Company tells me the writer is a straightforward man and much thought of by Ira H. Evans. I met White in the street this morning. I shall have a letter written by Mr. Angle to Frost saying that you are absent and that his letter has been forwarded. Van Zandt arrived here yesterday and sailed for Southampton yesterday afternoon.

After Benedict reached Mobeetie he wrote Foster on April 21, 1887, telling him of further exciting incidents on the trip to Texas:

After much tribulation we arrived at this interesting town and are waiting momentarily the arrival of Welch. I wrote you from the construction camp at the end of the Southern Kansas road on the south bank of the North Fork of the Canadian, and I expect that you received the letter. We left camp at 6 a.m., on April 17th and rode into Camp Supply in a mule wagon accompanying a detachment of Cavalry. The railroad is constructed about eight miles beyond the Canadian but the construction train does not run there yet so that we had a ride of about twenty-four miles into Camp Supply. The railroad will not pass nearer to it than about eleven miles. Arriving we found that the stage from Kiowa would not get to Supply until Monday afternoon (the 18th), and we were obliged to remain until seven p.m. Monday before leaving. As the stage station is most uncomfortable, we subsidized the cook who caters for the Government teamsters, to exert himself in our behalf. While the company was not over refined nor the viands very delicate, we enjoyed the three meals which we took there considerably. We succeeded in gaining the confidence of the man who dispenses beer (at 35 cents a bottle) to the defenders of the Union, to such a degree that he permitted us to sleep in his room. He was happy in the possession of two beds, the cleaner of which (save the mask) he offered to us, and for which we were devoutly thankful. We became acquainted at the camp with all of the officers at the Post, and if adverse fortune should ever again lead our unwilling footsteps into that sample of Mars, we might not fare so ill.

We left Camp Supply Monday evening (the 18th) in a heavily loaded stage, technically known as a "jerky." We were due at Mobeetie at 2 p.m. on the 19th. We did not get there. Our horses were willing but weak, our driver was loquacious and incompetent. The jerky had as much as it could hold. The roads were soft from the recent rains, and, worse than all, the rivers were "up." We traveled along until about one o'clock at night, the rain falling at intervals. We reached Wolf Creek. The driver headed the horses for the opposite bank, and in we plunged. As soon as we had left the bank he became frightened at the depth of the water and communicating his fright to the horses, they refused to advance. The great danger in these streams is the quicksands. He then managed to get the horses around to the side of the wagon and cramped the pole [wagon tongue] so that we could not stir. There were four of us: the proprietor of the line, the driver, and Junkin and myself. The driver suggested that we get out and push

A New York Yankee Takes a Look

which we did, first removing our shoes and stockings. This was of no avail. So finally he took out one of the horses and crossed the stream and went to the nearest station, called "Buzzard's Roost." Here he found the north-bound stage and returned with it. That stage had two good mules for its motive power. It became stuck in the stream about ten feet from us. The passengers and freight were removed on horseback to the bank. The mules were whipped up and that stage was pulled out of the water. The mules were then used with like effect on our stage, after we had been removed with all our traps to the further bank, and once more we started on our way, both wetter and wiser, than we were before. The most pleasing part of the experience was the waiting in the stage during the absence of our driver, occasionally striking a match to see what progress we were making into the sand.

We were obliged to travel all the following day until 3:30 a.m. on the 20th before reaching Mobeetie, very much fatigued from the loss of sleep. We found that B. B. Groom had left here Sunday night for Carson County where he is speculating in school lands. Yesterday Tyng came in and I had a long talk with him. He is enthusiastic over the value of the land and thinks we ought not to sell it yet. He does not think we could get over $3 now, but says that in five years the property will be worth from 15 to 20 million.

Junkin gave his version of the trip in a letter to Foster, April 23, 1887, as follows:

The twenty-four hours of our stay at Topeka were very profitably spent. . . . Our whole trip was an enjoyable one to me. Mr. Benedict was "a little out of sorts," as he said, until we had crossed the Mississippi River, but since that time he has been as well and bright as can be. . . . The comfort and se-clusion of our compartment and the opportunity it gave Benedict for lying down during the day made our journey through St. Louis anything but an unpleasant one. The only mishap of our trip occurred at Wolf Creek, a wild western stream which our road crossed at one point twenty-eight miles southwest of Camp Supply, Indian Territory. As there was no assistance to be had for miles around, we had to wait in an unhappy frame of mind as we slowly sank deeper and the water rose higher, until the stage from the op-posite direction came up. But even that is a very pleasant experience now to look back upon and one which will become swollen as the river, I fear. Today being Sunday we went to church in the morning. In the afternoon we dined with Dr. Newton Surgeon at the Post at Fort Elliott, a mile or two from the town. He is a most hospitable and cultivated gentleman, and his wife is a charming woman, so that we enjoyed the evening very much. They are people to whom this isolated life must be very trying, and I think they enjoyed having us, or anybody else from civilization and wearing a white shirt.

Benedict, still optimistic about White Deer Lands, advised Foster from Mobeetie, April 24, 1887, that he had not yet seen the land, but:

Tyng fears when I do it will turn my head. From what everyone here says, I believe it is a wonderful country and there is not a great deal like it in Northwestern Texas. I know that there is not in Western Indian Territory.... Our pasture is better land than most of Southern Kansas, and there is no reason why the property should not be worth 20 million within half as many years.

After Benedict had seen the White Deer Lands, he wrote Foster from Dallas, May 2, 1887:

I have never seen better land anywhere and I am beginning to be affected by the immensity of its value.... I think it is going to make Lord Rosebery richer than his alliance with the Rothschilds did; that if he can be made to appreciate it correctly, and if our friends can be *compelled* to hold on for a while longer, they will get such a taste of its value as will convince them that they never made a better investment in their lives. It is, in my judgment, safe to predict that within five years the entire tract will be worth 50 millions or more. That is, you see, less than $100 an acre. This would have seemed absurd and visionary to me until I had seen the land and heard men talk about it. Every man who has seen it says that it is the finest quality of land in Texas, and that it is infinitely better than Southern Kansas.

Benedict's novel and exciting experiences on this trip to Texas stirred within him a deep and abiding interest in the British bondholders' newly acquired property. He also gained a deeper insight into the complicated problems involved in working out a safe and sound program for the management and administration of the White Deer Lands. His brief acquaintance with George Tyng convinced him that Tyng's years of experience on the plains were an indispensable aid in working out their problems. Furthermore, Benedict now envisioned the immense potential values, economic and cultural, of the White Deer Lands. Convinced of the wealth inherent in the land he spent many anxious years with Foster in the service of the British bondholders in helping administer the property for the benefit of the British owners. Benedict, like hundreds of other Eastern visitors, forever felt the fascination of the plains.

His immediate work in Texas, however, was to assist Tyng in the Francklyn foreclosure suit.

CHAPTER 15

The Francklyn Foreclosure Suit

THE RAPID SHAPING UP of events at White Deer in 1886 made it necessary to press the Francklyn foreclosure suit as fast as possible in order to protect the British bondholders in their Texas properties. They owned approximately 90 per cent of the bonds, while the Francklyn Company held possession of the trust deed and land notes. In addition, Gordon Cunard held against the Francklyn Company a lien of $139,400 that was secured by 5,000 cows and calves in the White Deer Pasture. The Francklyn Company also owed $100,000 on a note due November 1, 1886, plus $21,300 accrued interest. In case of default in payment of these sums all of the land notes of the Francklyn Company, aggregating $711,000, as well as the accrued interest, would become due and would have to be paid under the trust deed executed by the Francklyn Company in 1882.

Preparations for Foreclosure

Distance and lack of understanding still plagued the British bondholders. They were much disturbed by delays and conflicts between the Texas and the New York officials as to a definite plan of procedure. The bondholders themselves were not united as to purpose, and were agreed only on the matter of disposing of the cattle as soon as possible. Consequently, when Frederic de P. Foster was notarized as trustee of the bondholders in September, 1886, his immediate job was to bring all the parties involved into a united group to protect their common interests. Cunard had to be pacified. The American attorneys had to come to an agreement as to procedure. Foster, as trustee, must devise a program that would win the approval of Andrew Kingsmill, who represented the British bondholders, and more particularly the approval of Lord Rosebery and of Williams, Deacon & Co., who owned more than a majority in value of the land notes of the Francklyn Company.

In September, 1886, Foster wrote Andrew Kingsmill, in London, that he was determined to keep all the cattle on the ranges holding them as security for the lien upon them and for any claims which Gordon Cunard might establish, either by adjustment or by litigation. He also stated that it was his purpose to carry through the foreclosure and avoid, if possible, contests with any of the creditors of the Company. "To that end," he wrote Kingsmill, "we desire that you send immediately . . . for the facts as to Cunrad's transactions with the Company to enable us to come to an adjustment with him."

Foster cabled Kingsmill, October 8, 1886:

Van Zandt has advised purchase of the $100,000 note due November 1, 1886. This is impractical. I deem it essential to purchase all of the notes. They are prior lien and this is the only way in my opinion to control the situation and secure your interests. . . . If you purchase it seems to me essential to offer opportunity to other bondholders to join in the purchase in contributing forthwith their proportion of purchase money and all moneys already and hereafter advanced. Please show this despatch to Williams & Deacon for whom it is intended and cable. Have attempted to get extension of land notes and find it impossible.

Foster in further explanation cabled Kingsmill, October 13, 1886:

By purchase of all land notes you obtain assignment of first lien on property thereby getting the best security. . . . If you pay single notes as they mature you only satisfy so much of the Company's debt and do not get security. Holders of land notes decline on payment of single notes when due to assign any interest under the mortgage. Whoever holds the land notes controls the entire situation. If the Company defaults in the November instalment, he can then proceed to acquire clear title under the land note mortgage. If you do not purchase some other party may. In my opinion immediate action is desirable to secure your interests. If you wish, Benedict who has complete knowledge can come to London.

Foster was especially anxious to have the support of Williams, Deacon & Co. in his proposed program. He had heard rumors that Francklyn and his English friends were attempting to form a new company in England. He feared that an alliance might be formed between such a company and Williams, Deacon & Co. which, he said, would work great injury to the interests of the bondholders. Therefore, on October 15, 1886, he wrote the British Linen Bank of London, of which Andrew Kingsmill was manager, telling them of the meeting of the Board of Directors of the Francklyn Company at Jersey City, New Jersey, on October 12, and stating that the Board of Directors of the Company would be retained for the present, "until their services can be dispensed with altogether." He estimated the total value of the land at $1,502,632, and the cattle at $80,000, and observed that, "Until the advent of railroads, which another year will bring, there seems to be little chance of getting the land to more lucrative use than by leasing it, and the 15,000 cattle should increase $20,000 a year, barring extraordinary casualties."

The following notice, which appeared in a Waco newspaper, September 18, 1886, had already convinced Benedict and Tyng of the urgent necessity of getting the foreclosure suit under way as soon as possible in order to forestall the Cunard suit. The notice read:

Gordon Cunard of the Cunard Steamship Company, a resident of Market Harborough, England, filed a suit today in the United States Circuit Court against the Francklyn Company on a protested note for $139,400

The Francklyn Foreclosure Suit

secured by mortgage on 5000 head of cows and their increase in the counties of Carson, Gray, Roberts, Hutchinson and Greer.

After Benedict had urged Foster to make some decision immediately, Foster notified Kingsmill, October 15, 1886, that:

Gordon Cunard claims that the Francklyn Company's lien is superior to the bondholders. I have made him a party to the suit commenced by me. Unless he defends in the latter suit his right will be foreclosed. . . . There is in my judgment only one way by which the present holding which you represent can be most thoroughly protected. This is by acquiring title to the land, including the bonds now outstanding, either by purchase of the lien upon it or require other bondholders to contribute ratably to its purchase. . . . As yet the title is in the Francklyn Company and until a sale under the deed it will remain there.

As a result of the efforts of Benedict and Tyng matters were speeded up and Foster wrote Kingsmill in London, November 5, 1886, that the purchase of the land notes had been completed:

I have handed to Mr. Paton, as you requested, all the securities and papers received from the purchase of these. . . . The purchase puts you in possession of all the lands covered by the land holder's mortgage except one section of 640 acres [which was retained by B. B. Groom]. These notes and securities purchased constitute the lien retained by the New York & Texas Land Company, Ltd. for the unpaid balance of purchase money upon the sale by it to the Francklyn Company.

In preparing for the foreclosure suit the question immediately arose as to whether receivership should be sought. Benedict advised Foster, September 7, 1886, that receivership, by giving title, would make a speedy sale of the cattle possible. "However," he said, "it would entail a heavy expense because of the large bond which would be necessary." On the other hand he assured Foster that a receivership would not be necessary, unless Gordon Cunard made it so. "If you compromise Gordon's Texas creditors, shall negotiations commence immediately?"

Benedict believed that Tyng could adjust all claims of the Texas creditors by agreement at from twenty-five to fifty cents on the dollar, and at the same time save the heavy expense of a receivership. Foster himself in writing to Kingsmill, September, 1886, said of Tyng, "He is a man of fine mind and education, and great energy, and in situations like the present a better man to collect and preserve and further our interests in Texas is not obtainable."

Cattle in the Suit

A question of greater importance in connection with the suit was whether the cattle should be included. Foster wired Benedict at Dallas, September 9, 1886, not to include cattle, saying that "Shepard has been looking up the question and advises that no danger is apprehended in taking this course." Upon receiving Foster's message Benedict and Tyng became seriously disturbed. Benedict felt strongly that it would be imprudent to omit the cattle from the suit, "as the mortgage's title is not divested upon default except after foreclosure proceedings, and no cattle sales could be made if omitted." Benedict further advised Foster:

> Two separate foreclosure actions are improper. Texas creditors likely to attach cattle on waiver theory. No appreciable difference in Gordon's position. Either way he can delay if so disposed. Miller strongly counsels against separation. Trustee ought not to risk losing any part of security, even to expedite proceedings. No blame if usual methods are followed. Great [blame] if cattle lost by waiver. Answer speedily.

Not yet satisfied that he had convinced Foster, Benedict again wrote him from Dallas, September 12, 1886:

> In filing foreclosure suit at Graham [Texas] Stickney insisted that the suit for cattle and land notes be separated. Miller says that if you relinquish the mortgage on the cattle it is doubtful if you could reassert it on independent action. This is a phase of the question that none of us in New York looked at and it seems under Texas decisions to merit attention. I sincerely hope that you will adopt his view; that even though you should sacrifice every dollar of the security in litigation it would be better than to have the bondholders charge you with throwing away $80,000 worth of security. The former would be their misfortune, the latter your fault. Miller thinks Cunard should not influence you in the slightest. I can only add that in questions of this nature, I think his judgment is reliable. He is credited down here with considerable sagacity in such matters.

The Francklyn Foreclosure Suit 229

Matters were fast coming to a climax by September 13, 1886, when Benedict notified Foster from Dallas that:

> Tyng just served with process issue September 6th equity suit, Gordon against Company returnable Waco next term. Is there doubt about the necessity of making Gordon party defendant? There is no time to be lost, so I shall proceed including him as originally proposed filing bill here at once. Receivership and injunction probably necessary to protect property against creditors' attachments.

Foster wired back immediately, "Do not file bill until notified. Telegraph me any cases in point explaining why no difference in Gordon's position."

In his reply to Foster's message, September 14, 1886, Benedict explained:

> Gordon's bill simply asks foreclosure of his chattel mortgage and judgment for deficiency. Claims lien on 2000 head. Alleges Company pretends that other mortgages exist against cattle. Asks discovery concerning such encumbrances. Miller and I convinced that only possibility maintaining possession cattle is by foreclosure and receivership. Taking possession without foreclosure suit is ineffectual; that only one foreclosure suit can be maintained as there is but one indebtedness and one indivisible cause of action; that divided judgment taken in one suit would bar any other recovery; that if bondholders elect to charge indebtedness on land alone they relinquish claim on chattels as against the Company's junior encumbrances, and probably general creditors; that the Company can't give consent which would prevent this as to Gordon; that even where possibility of loss exists, Trustee not justified in carrying risk; that Tyng should be appointed receiver Gordon suit and other action restrained in your foreclosure suit. Unless this is done Texas creditors will take cattle out of Tyng's hands by legal process and sacrifice them in sale. Miller does not regard delay by Gordon as serious as risk of losing cattle. Tyng agrees with me that situation becoming critical in extreme. Every hour's delay dangerous. Your representative here should be authorized to decide these questions with aid of local counsel without embarrassment from lack of confidence in his judgment as apparently this exists now and submit that my longer stay here undesirable.

Benedict expressed the hope that:

> ... these unfortunate delays and doubts will have been resolved into cer-

tainty and action by the time this reaches you. My telegrams seem to have been so extensive that nothing remains to be said upon the vexed question, except that I hope every word contained in them all will receive attention, as they were sent only after careful preparation and revision. I only add this; that in case neither argument nor entreaty prevail, I must ask to be relieved from all responsibility for action which I cannot but believe disastrous.

Benedict then submitted the following plan of procedure:

(1) Bring suit to foreclose upon all real and personal property.
(2) Get Tyng appointed receiver, so as to prevent Cunard and other creditors in New York, Kansas City, St. Louis, and Texas from taking cattle out of your possession *as they are liable to do at any moment now* unless you extend the cattle the protection of the Federal Courts.
(3) If possible in the foreclosure suit restrain the further prosecution of Cunard's foreclosure.
(4) Agree with Cunard if possible that your decree shall provide that the land *first* be sold, then the cattle upon which his chattel mortgage is charged.

Benedict insisted that if this procedure were not followed the cattle would be quickly swept from the range and sold at ruinous prices.

Foster now realized the danger of losing the cattle. He wired Benedict the next day to "file bill as drawn, including cattle and Gordon. Use your discretion as to injunction and receivership. . . . Need you in Texas for present negotiations with Gordon, but push foreclosure. Entire confidence in you."

On September 15, 1886, John H. Finks, Clerk of the United States Circuit Court at Waco, wired Foster as follows:

By request of Russell Benedict, Dallas, I telegraph bill Cunard v Francklyn Company. Plaintiff prays for discovery by defendant of prior lien, if any, and in whom vested; also that account be taken under order of the Court ascertaining amount due plaintiff; also for foreclosure of lien on 5000 cattle with calves evidenced by note for $139,000 to discharge said amount and for costs and for judgment for any balance, if any, and for any other relief.

In defense of this action Benedict explained to Foster, September 15, 1886, that "Stickney's claim for his subject is that it would prevent

The Francklyn Foreclosure Suit

delay in getting title to the land. This delay could hardly extend beyond a year and it would be paying too large a price to buy peace at $80,000."

Since the suit, including the cattle, was filed, and since Cunard's suit did not attack the land notes, both Benedict and Tyng felt that the bondholders' property was much more secure. Benedict wrote Foster from Dallas, September 16, 1886:

> I assure you that there was great rejoicing here yesterday, and Tyng who lingered until this morning awaiting your decision seemed like a different being. You ought to rejoice that you have found him. His discovery was most fortunate, and as I have got to know him better I feel as though the most unstinted praise could be heaped upon him and be far less than his merit. I trust that his predictions in regard to the value of our lands will be as accurate in other cases of which he tells me. By the way the reason of his present position is that he put his savings of six years, about $40,000, into the development of a Mexican town, and when it became valuable the Mexican Government appropriated it. He sued in the Mexican Courts and has a heavy judgment against the Government which they have not paid, but he thinks they will some day. He has made and lost several good fortunes—the last in this way.

Judgment

The Francklyn suit was set for a hearing on January 9, 1887; but, because there was not sufficient time to get legal papers properly signed and to get the approval of the bondholders in London, the case was postponed until the October term of the Court. The Court was convened October 24, 1887, with Judge A. P. McCormick presiding. Frederic de P. Foster, as trustee, was plaintiff in the suit, while the Francklyn Company, Gordon Cunard, and the Western Mortgage & Investment Company were the defendants.

The Court gave a detailed report of its findings under the trust deed and liens of 1882 and 1883, which were signed by Charles G. Francklyn, president of the Company. After reviewing the issues involved, the Court decreed that the Francklyn Company's coupons amounting to $1,718,000 were due and payable; that the trust deed of 1887 should read in the same manner and with like effect as that of the original trust deed of 1882 and 1883; that the Francklyn Company should pay such sum in gold coin of the United States, plus the cost and expenses of the complainant; that the land should be sold in one parcel, and the cattle at public auction. The lands were to be sold subject to the unpaid purchase money amounting to $711,000 and accrued interest. Alfred Sully's lease contract with the Francklyn Company was recognized and ratified by the Court. Thomas S. Miller of Dallas was appointed commissioner of the cattle sales.

As a result of the Francklyn foreclosure suit the British bondholders now held legal title to all of the Francklyn properties in Texas. However, the decree of the United States Court presented many difficulties for Tyng and Foster in carrying out the orders of the Court. Their most important immediate problems were the sale of the cattle as the decree provided, and protection of their range from outside graziers who had to have grass.

CHAPTER 16

Cattle Controversies Ended by Foreclosure Sale

THE FRANCKLYN FORECLOSURE suit brought into prominence the scarcity of grass and the fight to obtain it by whatever means necessary. Thus grass became the dominant issue in the immediate execution of the judgment of the U. S. Circuit Court in 1888—with cattle playing a vital role.

The Foster-Sully Controversy

In his attempt to carry out the provisions in the verdict rendered by the United States Circuit Court in the Francklyn foreclosure suit, Foster, as trustee for the bondholders, entered into an agreement with Alfred M. Sully of New York, on July 28, 1887, by which Sully purchased all of the Francklyn Company's cattle on the White Deer and other Texas ranges, the greater part of which were branded, "either Bar X on the left side and hip and Bar X on the left jaw, or Diamond F on either side, with a crop of the left ear." The cattle were estimated to number 6,038 head, consisting of various classes and ages, including Polled Angus and Durham. The purchase price of the common stock was $11.25 per head, while the blooded stock was priced at $25 and $50 each. The sum total of the purchase price was $72,812. Sully agreed to pay the purchase money in cash on October 3, 1887, meantime giving his note, dated July 28, 1887, and placing $30,000 worth of first-mortgage railroad bonds as collateral for payment of the note. The cattle were to be counted, gathered, and delivered at the earliest possible date after twenty days from the date of sale. Sully agreed to receive the cattle at the White Deer Pasture "in such numbers as shall be delivered to him, or his Agent, and at such time as Foster could make deliveries." Sully also agreed to "put some distinguishing brand upon the cattle" and pay for them at the prices stipulated in the agreement as they were delivered, "whether they exceed or are less than the estimated numbers." The sale was not to include the brands used by the Francklyn Company upon their cattle, but Sully was to take all such cattle delivered to him.

Sully was given a two-year lease on Block 5, estimated to contain 107,000 acres, which were fenced. The lease rate was four cents per acre, payable in advance, beginning January 1, 1888. None of the cattle were to be removed from the White Deer Pasture without payment unless Foster gave his consent. Nor was Foster to release his lien upon the cattle or give a bill of sale until payment for the cattle was made. Moreover, after delivery was made to Sully, the British owners were no longer responsible for loss or damage to the cattle, and no claim for rebate, discounts, or deductions was to be allowed. Sully was the owner of the Clarendon Cattle Company, with headquarters at the village of Old Clarendon, known to Panhandle cowboys as "Saint's Roost." Henry W. Taylor was Sully's Texas manager.

This unusual cattle agreement resulted in much delay and discontent before the deal was consummated. Sully used every means possible to delay deliveries so that his payments could be extended and his lease prolonged. Foster and Tyng on the other hand wanted deliveries made as fast as possible in order to get the cattle off their hands and save the expense of carrying the cattle through the winter. The agreement was made late in the season and every day's delay was important for both Sully and Foster. Three months passed and little progress had been

Cattle Controversies Ended

made in cattle deliveries. By November extremely cold weather had set in. Tyng wrote Foster at New York, November 16, 1887, that the men had 378 cattle collected when the cold spell struck and forced them to turn the cattle loose on White Deer Creek:

> As the season is now too far advanced for safety in keeping cattle under close herd, it may not be possible to get them all together again for delivery to Sully's Agent this Fall, but we will do our best. I enclose herewith another letter on this subject, as you may have occasion to further upbraid Sully. If you instruct me to take full possession of the cattle, I ought to know your subsequent purpose in order to intelligently carry out your instructions. My view is that if we take absolute possession and later undertake to have Sully receive them again, he can call on us to again deliver them to him on actual count. We cannot do this before next Summer. Meanwhile many of the cattle would have died during the winter on *our* hands and Sully would make no end of defensible pretexts for delaying. The cattle cannot now be sold for anything like the money Sully agreed to pay. The cattle here have been very badly managed and are *not* in as good condition for winter as at this time last year.
>
> I do not know anything more than a "bluff" at Sully; a threat to sell the cattle for cash and to keep out the $30,000 paid by him, the difference between his price and the price you expect to get, as also costs and damage. Such threat to be made *after* title to the cattle is carefully and fully protected by record etc. He knows that you *can* sell by making the price low enough. I should prefer tying up his title to the cattle and suing him for the amount due upon them, to having us meet expense and risk of the cattle all winter and have him sue us for value of cattle short. If we take the cattle and hold them till next summer for a market, at expense and loss, we might as well compel Sully to hold them for us at *his* own expense and risk recovery of the cattle by process of law, and *we sue him* next year for value of cattle short.
>
> I have been careful to preserve our legal possession without affording any pretext for a change of interference in management. Influenced by such views, by our total want of forage and preparation, I have allowed Sully's Agent to remove the seventy Durham cows and the ten Polled Angus cattle to the Clarendon Company's headquarters where they can be given hay and shelter which the season now demands for them and which we cannot give. It was either this or a large mortality and expense in trying to prevent it. I have been fearful that something might transpire to throw these fancy cattle in our hands again. . . . Henry Taylor will be as thankful and happy to get rid of them as I have tried to be.

By the time this letter reaches you, you will have been able to fully judge what Sully proposes to do. That nothing has yet been said about the Head and Horn liens of record, raises a suspicion that Sully expects to make them a pretext for more delay after exhausting that of the certified copy of the decree approving sale. I really believe that the best to be done is to leave the cattle in his material possession on *our* land (except the fancy cattle) in Dixon Creek Pasture and keep one reliable man in our employ to tie up the title and to keep notices published in the Clarendon and Mobeetie papers to the effect that the cattle aren't yet Sully's because we have a lien on them till he pays the money. It seems to me that while Sully is worrying us dreadfully, that we can worry him still more, even without suing him. He can make us wait for the money anyhow and laugh while we are stewing. If we can make up our minds that we *must* wait, and can worry him into being glad to pay and buy off with damages. If you decide upon retaining the cattle, please dissimulate Sully until I *can* take them before he prepares to defend them. I will take them anyhow, but we can do it more easily if Sully is unprepared.

On November 17, 1887, Tyng notified Henry Taylor of rumors he had heard of moving Bar X cattle from the Dixon Creek Pasture to the Clarendon range and advised him that he should:

Take notice that I hold legal possession of cattle under fence and on land lawfully in my charge and that if any of said cattle be removed without my employer's consent they will be recovered by process of law and criminal proceedings will be instituted against all concerned in driving them. In support of these assertions your attention is called to Sully's agreement of July 28th, and to the Statutes of this State.

On the same date Tyng notified Foster in New York of these rumors.

There were several factors that caused conflict and delay in the cattle deliveries. Tyng, Foster, and Benedict were busy preparing for the foreclosure sale. Moreover, the growing scarcity of grass and the near approach of winter intensified the rivalries among all the cattlemen on the crowded ranges. Tyng wrote Foster, November 20, 1887:

I omitted to inform you this morning that there is now much demand for grass, owing to the destruction by fire, of all ranges around us. The Manager of the Frying Pan Ranch has been to see me for grass for 7000 or 8000 head of cattle. Your address has been given by him to his principals—Glidden & Sanborn. Sully's Clarendon range is in a bad way for grass, and he must have it or lose cattle heavily. The Espuela Company has turned its 5000 head onto the Bar O range, blocks 3 and B-4 adjoining us on the south and west. The Bar O range is already overstocked. I fancy it is expected to turn cattle into this pasture as a sort of abandonment commons.

On that same November 17, 1887, Tyng advised Foster that no more cattle could be delivered until the following summer on account of the weather:

> Taylor comes to White Deer today. My messenger will wait at Mobeetie for telegrams till Thursday night in case you decide that 300 more cattle will not prejudice. Taylor wants to drive beef next week from Dixon Creek Pasture. Your consent first necessary by telegram Saturday at latest. The difficulty of handling stock and men here in winter needs little explanation. We have 300 cattle and 78 calves in the valley of White Deer and shall be able to collect and deliver most of them this week if you judge that such delivery can be prudently made. If Sully pays balance on note, the lien on *all* of the cattle would compel him to pay for the 300. If we can take possession of 5800 we can also take possession at the same time of the additional 300. If Sully pays, nothing more will be required. If we have to take possession we shall do so in full form with fuel, forage, and shelter for the winter. Sully has been so strongly urging Taylor to drive and sell Bar X beeves from Dixon Creek that he may undertake it.
>
> Legal proceedings here are too clumsy to prevent removal of cattle conveniently. Panhandle lawyers seem to have no idea beyond injunction. The Judge lives at Mobeetie. He fixes bond at stiff figures. The clerk to approve bonds lives at Clarendon [65 miles from White Deer], and the cattle are in Carson County. . . .
>
> I am indeed glad not to have to take back the fancy cattle and heartily approve your determination to let Sully hold them. He cannot sell them *now* owing to the lateness of the season and the utter lack of possible buyers with hay enough to winter them. . . . I have really determined to tally to Sully's name the 300 cattle and to add them to those already in the Dixon Creek Pasture. The contract calls for delivery by us of *all* of our range cattle. Sure it leaves to us the time for such delivery. But these 300 head in this huge pasture will entail on us as much expense as would ten times as many and will prevent us from cleaning out the pasture should our neighbors and others without grass begin to turn their cattle in here as upon the commons.
>
> A very peaceful way for me to settle my perplexities is to throw all re-

sponsibility upon you, and wait for you to order further tally of the cattle. But such tally is already nearly impossible and may at any moment become entirely so until summer through inclemency of weather. The ground is now covered with snow and sleet, and horses under saddle have to be fed grain. . . . The matter would look more simple if I believed Sully would pay, even on presentation of the certified copy of the decree, but I think he will seek to make further pretext for further delay. Unless *absolutely necessary* for proper protection of your responsibilities, I would advise against taking such possession as maybe later would make us responsible to Sully in damages for losses in number of alleged bad care and management.

On November 28, 1887, Foster notified Godden & Holme that the special commissioner would shortly begin advertising the foreclosure sale, which was to take place at Dallas on the first Tuesday in February, 1888, and that in view of the small number of encumbrances there would be little prospect of outside competition, and that, therefore, the bondholders would be forced to buy in the title for their own protection. Foster then called attention to the following questions relative to the sale:

In whose name shall the purchase be made? In whose name shall the title subsequently be held? At what price will the property be purchased? As there is no right of redemption required by the Texas law, it would not be essential that a large bid be made. If such a right existed, the Francklyn Company might afterwards redeem it by paying a comparatively insignificant sum to the purchaser if only a nominal amount were paid by him on the sale. Again if the bid should approach the amount of the judgment lien, $1,718,000, it is apparent that each bondholder would be entitled to a distribution of the share of the proceeds almost sufficient to cancel it. If the property should be sought for all the bondholders this would not matter very much, except that it would render it impossible to take a judgment against the Francklyn Company for a deficiency as provided for in Article thirteen of the decree. But as some of the bondholders have not qualified themselves by contributing toward the land note purchase to share in the advantages of the foreclosure sale and will not contribute their bonds toward the purchase, it is evident that their interest must be recognized. They will be entitled to the same proportionate amount of the purchase as their holdings of bonds bear to the total issue. . . . It will, therefore, be advantageous to the bondholders who do contribute to obtain the title at as low a price as possible. . . .

I offer a few suggestions for consideration. The bid should be taken in the name of a private person as an American citizen. I send you herewith a copy of the Railway and Corporation Law Journal. On page 433 is published the opinion of the Attorney General of Texas upon the right of foreign corporations to purchase and hold real estate in Texas. In my judgment this opinion is conclusive, and in view of it, it would be unwise to attempt the formation of a new company having for its object the purchase and holdings of their lands as was suggested by Paton and Cunard and several of the American bondholders. If this view is adopted some person or persons should be designated and clothed with power to bid at the sale, and he or they should be placed in possession of all the bonds outstanding in order that the provisions as to payment in bonds may be utilized and the bonds stamped by me as provided in Article 25 of the decree.

Foster suggested next that Van Zandt be appointed as the purchasing committee. He suggested further that if Elgood and Godden concurred in this a circular be sent out notifying the bondholders of his appointment under the trust deed of December 1, 1886, and that they be required to forward to his address all the bonds held by them. In addition he suggested:

A simple form of power of attorney to act in making the purchase to be executed by the Trustee and forwarded to him in my case should also be sent over. . . . These suggestions as to Purchasing Committee apply to the third query above. . . . I have not heard whether all of the contributing bondholders have taken advantage of the latest opportunity to subscribe nor whether Francklyn has paid in his shares as yet. In case he and they do not come into the arrangement before a sale takes place, arrangements should be made for paying to them their distributive share of the proceeds of the sale. The cattle have all, except 5000, been delivered to Alfred Sully and are now upon our Dixon Creek Pasture. He has paid on account, irrespective of certain horses, $2850, and he promised to pay the balance, about $40,000, as soon as we should furnish him with a certified copy of the petition and order of the Circuit Court approving the sale. I hope to get the rest of the money in a few days.

Foster did not have to wait long on the money yet due on the Sully contract. He wrote Godden & Holme on January 23, 1888:

I am glad to say that since my letter of January 5th Sully has paid the balance due by him upon the sale of the cattle and also the rent for Dixon

Creek Pasture for the half year beginning January 1, 1888. The entire receipts from Sully for cattle amount to $72,584.30; rent $2140 making a total of $74,724.30. We still have about 300 head of cattle to be delivered to Sully in the Spring at $11.25 each, and a remnant of horses the exact number of which I cannot state just now. In addition to the horses, Tyng has disposed of at good prices horses, mules, and cattle to the amount of $7,263.46 since November 22, 1886, making the net cash of proceeds from sales of cattle and horses to date about $80,000. I believe that the receipts from future sales will aggregate $5000 more. The prices paid by Sully for the cattle are probably the highest which any similar cattle have brought this season, the ruling market having been between $7 and $8 which is about the figure offered by Schneider and to me by several others. Upon getting the final payment from Sully I delivered to him a bill of sale of the cattle paid for with a grazing right agreement covering Dixon Creek Pasture for two years at a yearly rental of $4280. . . . I am greatly relieved at the successful conclusion of the sale, and more especially so in view of the extreme cold weather which has recently visited the Panhandle and which, I fear, will cause some losses to Sully.

The Tyng-Sanborn Range-Cattle Dispute

However, there was yet more cattle trouble in store for Foster and Tyng. Tyng had scarcely settled the Sully difficulty when Glidden & Sanborn leased seventy sections of school lands in Block B-2 and turned 3,000 cattle into Block 7 with, as Tyng reported to Foster from White Deer Pasture on December 19, 1887, "as many more coming in a few days." In a letter to Foster, December 19, 1887, he stated that Frazer, with his outfit, was at White Deer ready to assist in driving these cattle to the east side of Block B-2. "The cattle," he said, "have been collected to the extent possible in the storm." Tyng, anxious to have instructions from Foster, informed him that important despatches could be sent to Miami in care of Bennet Bros. Livery Stable and could be forwarded to him from there "by wagon or saddle."

In the meantime the situation on the range, as herein described by Tyng, seemed amicable:

The word "assist" is used but Glidden & Sanborn's men understand and acquiesce in the situation. . . . We mildly forbid it and reserve enforcement of that prohibition until we see whether or not we make satisfactory arrangements with Sanborn. Meanwhile Sanborn's men ride and keep up the east

Cattle Controversies Ended

and south fence of Block B-2 and keep out other cattle, all in their own interest and incidentally in ours. I am informed that the O-Bar range is nearly all burned out. It is also the Half Circle K range. They took in 5000 cattle which we refused, and will probably undertake to encroach upon our grass. The Clarendon Company turned several thousand of their cattle into the V-V range which were turned back into the Clarendon range again. I fear we must keep up a small outfit, at least until February, to protect our range.

Tyng, having arranged everything possible until after the sale, left Frazer in charge during the month of January, 1888, and went to Victoria for a visit with his family. From there he traveled to Mexico City to look after private business. He advised Frazer to report to Foster at least once each week regardless of whether anything of importance occurred. He assured Foster that he could be reached by telegram at the Iturbide Hotel in Mexico City, and that he could reach White Deer in eighty-two hours from that place, "only one day longer than a trip from New York to White Deer. I do not think you need worry. All seems to be in safe condition during my absence." Continuing his explanation, Tyng reported:

We shall have nothing disagreeable from Sanborn's outfit I fancy. I expect to see Sanborn at Dallas or Houston and will report to Foster as to telegram received from him this p.m. transmitting one received from Glidden & Sanborn. . . . A good beginning has been made at collecting the Sanborn cattle and tomorrow they begin to *go*. Sanborn's men and ours are now "chumming" quite socially yarning and listening to a vile fiddle that fittingly accompanies their scrawl.

On December 3, 1887, Tyng informed Glidden & Sanborn at Dallas that:

You are hereby notified that you have made entry without my consent upon the following described parcels of land, the same being known and assigned as Block nos. 2, 3, 4, 5, and 7, I & G N RR Co. surveys, situated in the counties of Hutchinson, Gray, Carson, and Roberts, State of Texas, and as Block B-2 H & G N surveys situated in Gray County, Texas, known as the pasture heretofore used by the Francklyn Land & Cattle Company, and you are hereby notified that your cattle are now trespassing without my consent upon the above described lands. Now, therefore, this notice is to direct you to at once remove said cattle from said land and to at once vacate same. Otherwise I shall proceed at law to eject you therefrom.

Tyng wrote Foster from Victoria, December 27, 1887, that he arrived at Dallas on the twenty-third, and gave this account of his conferences with Sanborn:

H. B. Sanborn was there to meet me, but in spite of protracted discussions, no hope appeared of effecting any arrangement satisfactory, or even equitable. He has admirable control of his temper and could with difficulty be goaded into exposing his hand. The gamut was exhausted from courteous expostulation to brutal cinnation, somewhat scandalizing T. S. Miller who was present at one of the milder discussions. Sanborn's ultimatum was an offer of $200 per month accompanied by a proposition to refer the matter to arbitration. Whereupon was handed him written notice (a copy of which is transmitted herewith) prepared from Miller's dictation. . . .

Sanborn attempts to find pretext for his unjustifiable trespass in a misconstruction of some letter or telegram from you and in perversion of a conversation had with me by his Foreman. His real purpose appears to have been to pasture his cattle on our land as long as we could be entertained with delusive promises, and then fall back on a lease of the forfeited seventy surveys of school land in Block B-2. I am not clear as to what are all our rights in the block. Neither is Miller who promised to look it up. As I hope to be absent a few weeks, it seemed unwise to leave Sanborn under any impression that he must prepare a defense against our aggression or retaliation at White Deer. I was, therefore, talked into amiability and into not disputing whether harm or trespass had been intended, or was really being done after all. He paid drinks and my omnibus fare, accompanied me to the train, used his acquaintance with the Agent in my favor to deprive another passenger of a secured lower berth, and shook hands *almost* effusively enough to engender suspicion of his doubting the sincerity of my amity.

The school lands are a thorn in our side. The Clarendon Company has intended to occupy them and has only refrained from doing so because of the dreadful loss that can be easily caused among the cattle by our retaliation for any hostile occupation of them. I do not think this Sanborn matter can be a cause for anxiety, though it affords ample ground for indignation. The loss to us as the matter stands is in the expense entailed by keeping up an outfit for resisting this trespass—and others possible. In winter horses have to be fed and men cannot work efficiently. Personally I am much hurt by

Cattle Controversies Ended 243

Sanborn's actions, and as I cannot advise you yet to seek legal satisfaction, I will feel grateful to be allowed to help myself in ways that will cost no money on my return to the ranch. . . . Our horses are fat on good grass, and where ice will be chopped out for them. The best thing to be done for them now is to let them alone. For the Sanborn cattle we are doing the worst thing, handling and driving them.

It seemed to be the irony of fate that severe seasonal extremes of weather, either cold or hot, or wet or dry, should follow the misfortunes of the Francklyn Company's cattle during the entire four years in which they grazed upon the Texas plains, and then perhaps the most severe blizzard of them all struck as the Company closed out. Tyng wrote Benedict, December 20, 1887:

A fierce norther set in here yesterday afternoon, making the night piercingly cold. I slept in Lofan's bed, he turning in with another man. Two men slept in my little shanty and fourteen slept in the house. You can see how like pigs in a sty we all were. All were men who could not be turned away into the storm. This morning there was at least three buckets of snow in my shanty drifted in under the *two* doors. In the house were fully twenty buckets of snow, and in the shed used last summer as a kitchen (when you were here) the snow averaged six inches all over with drifts of nearly two feet. In the stables the snow was up to the mules' bellies. . . . The storm increased in the night into a blizzard that drifted and scattered the Sanborn cattle. This morning it took some punching to force the men out into the storm, and altogether I did not feel satisfied to leave here until my operations can get into motion beyond backsliding. The wind has swept the snow from enormous patches of plains, thus exposing grass for present use of cattle and piling it up in the draws where it will make abundant water, if it does not melt too slowly when the weather changes. The grass will not be injured at all. . . .

Do not fear loss of cattle by this storm it did not last long enough. . . . Since noon the wind has entirely died down, the weather has greatly moderated and stars and moon are making a glorious night. . . .

This morning I wrote a few hours, keeping the ink stand on the back of the cooking stove and frequently holding the pen on the stove to melt gobs of frozen ink, feet wrapped in quilt and pair of blankets, two wool undershirts on, leather jacket overcoat, and cap. By staying in the house I could punch the men out and once *out* they had to ride or freeze.

Oddly enough some 500 of the Sanborn cattle drifted against the storm and were today brought from along our south fence near the breaks of White Deer. . . . Was out a few hours today but was without snow glasses so that my eyes warn me to cease infliction upon you. There is grass enough exposed by the wind and the cattle will eat snow if the water is frozen. . . . Sanborn's 3000 cattle were being driven to the east part of Block 2 when the severe storm scattered them. His 4000 cattle enroute for White Deer were caught by that storm out on the plains in Potter County and scattered and drifted so that they are not likely to be collected again before Spring, even if range owners should consent to allowing the ranges to be worked —not probable.

The Foreclosure Sale

The Francklyn Company sale was held at Dallas, February 7, 1888. Foster attended the sale and Henry Kingsmill acted as purchasing agent for the Company. Since there was no outside bid for the land notes, the property was bid in for $53,564.86, which Foster said (in a report to Godden Son & Holme on January 23, 1888) was:

. . . the estimated difference between the total cost and expense attending my administration of the property and the total receipts from sales and rent as shown upon the enclosed statement. This amount will be paid in by the bondholders proportionately and will, therefore, be disbursed as in the enclosed statement. It will be approximately $35 per bond. Lord Rosebery will furnish about $18,025 and will be repaid $50,940. He will also hold fifty bonds. Williams, Deacon & Co. will furnish about $10,925 and will be repaid $7215.75. The other bondholders will subscribe directly or through the firm of Elgood & Godden. . . . Now that the cattle have been cleared off the property, the force of men may be reduced to Tyng and two assistants, the latter being only to keep squatters out and to keep the fences in repair and the fireguards protected, so that outside the salaries of these men and maintenance, there need be no expense in the next year at the ranch.

As to the expense of carrying the property during the two years past Foster said:

I believe that Tyng has been as economical in his expenditures as the nature of the case permitted. The fact that this property is so vast and difficult of access has magnified the cost of every step necessarily taken in the business, and the disposition of our neighbors to encroach upon us, and the unsettled conditions of the country produced by the advent of railroads and the influx of prospectors have increased the necessity for adequate expansion and its resultant costs.

Foster presented a bill of $50,000 for his services in the foreclosure suit, in which he said:

... that the cost of foreclosing the mortgage, had I employed reliable counsel in Texas, would have been $15,000, that suit being the most important one ever brought in the state for such a purpose. This business has required, as you know, four journeys from New York to Texas besides constant attention at my office during the past two years. The correspondence has been exceedingly large, the question novel, and often requiring solutions without the possibility of consultation with my clients, and the entire matter was one of a character not usually managed from a lawyer's office. ... I shall be very glad notwithstanding to learn the views of Kingsmill and Williams, Deacon & Co., as well as your own and will meet these views in the fairest possible manner.

In discussing the final act of the sale Foster reported to Godden Son & Holme that it was made subject to the first lien notes of $711,000 and accrued interest; also subject to the right of way of the Southern Kansas Railroad across the land, and also subject to the lease of the Dixon Creek Pasture to Alfred Sully. "There was but one bid made," he said:

Having previously had the Commissioner's report of the sale prepared, I obtained the signature to it, and the United States Circuit Court being then in session at Dallas, we had the report judicially confirmed upon notice to the attorney for the Francklyn Land & Cattle Company. Thereupon the Commissioners executed a deed of the real estate and a bill of sale of the personal property to Van Zandt and Henry Kingsmill, and subsequently Henry Kingsmill executed a declaration of trust to the effect that Van Zandt and Kingsmill were acting in the purchase as the agents and attorneys for Elgood & Godden Trustees of the trust created by the indenture of December 1, 1886. The foreclosures made by these purchases brought the suit to a conclusion and nothing remains to be done, except the authority of my accounts and the endorsement of the proportionate share of the bonds, if any, in the proceeds of the sale.

Foster recommended that the recording of these sales in the counties in which the lands were situated be postponed until the counties where the land lay were organized.

Upon the completion of foreclosure proceedings and the cattle sales it became incumbent upon the White Deer officials to work out and put into operation a long-time constructive program in the management and sale of the lands. This procedure required time, patience, and understanding on the part of the British bondholders.

CHAPTER 17

Ancient Grasslands and Modern Beef Production

FROM THE EARLIEST TIMES to the latter part of the nineteenth century the history of the Plains region of the Southwest was built upon a foundation of grass and water. Nature carpeted this region with a great abundance of nutritious grasses. The roots held the plains earth from destructive winds and produced grasses that built up from the waste accumulated through the ages a rich alluvial soil. The plains grasses made possible the development of three distinct plains cultures and valuable additions to a fourth culture.

Nature was much more sparing of its water than of its grasses. However, for centuries both grass and water were provided in sufficient quantities to give life and sustenance to the Plains Indians. As a result, one of the oldest as well as one of the most mature cultures of antiquity was developed on the plains, that of the sedentary Indian. Because of isolation, sparse population, and the vast distances over which the Indians were scattered, warfare among these savage tribes was confined to local areas. Since the physical environment of these various Plains tribes furnished no other resources than grass and water, they were forced to provide their own tools, weapons, clothing, and other necessities of life from the materials at hand. Consequently, they developed into an independent and resourceful people whose handiworks were made from stone, bone, wood, and hides, and whose places of abode were fixed firmly in the soil of their surroundings. This age-old hand-made culture was developed to a comparatively high degree. Nature imbedded and preserved this old culture beneath a plains soil rich in minerals.

The Spanish invasion into the Southwestern Plains in the sixteenth and seventeenth centuries brought about a new order of things among the Indian tribes. A number of factors contributed to the new era. Perhaps the introduction of Arabian horses into the region by the Spaniards in the sixteenth century was the most important. These horses, which were lost and abandoned by the Spanish conquistadors, multiplied and grew wild on the plains for more than a century. For ages past the Indian's only means of travel, with resulting communication, was on foot, but this situation was drastically changed when the Plains warriors caught up this hardy stock and adapted it to their use. So well did they adapt to the horse that they became some of the most expert riders of all times. Indeed, the Spanish horse revolutionized the whole manner of living among the Plains Indians: it greatly enlarged their range, it intensified their warlike traits, and it made them masters of the plains for almost two hundred years. These Indians developed on the plains during the seventeenth and eighteenth centuries a nomadic horse culture that became a vital factor in the transition from an Indian to an Anglo-American culture. The Indians' method of mounted fighting was perfected to such a degree that the United States government had to reorganize completely its methods of warfare on the plains in order to cope successfully with the Indians. Science came to the aid of the Anglo-Americans. With machine-made weapons and improved methods of transportation and communication, the white man outdistanced the red man and forced him onto the reservation to bring to an end the period of Indian culture.

The establishment of the cattle industry on the Plains in the decades of the 1870's and 1880's produced a new semi-Plains culture. Here on the Spanish borderlands of the Southwest the Spanish dons with their longhorn cattle met the Anglo-Americans with their blooded stock from the East. Since the Spanish stock was not adaptable to fenced ranges, to rail transportation, and to the production of corn-fed beef, the Spanish system had to give way to the new order. The change, however, was not so thorough as it first appeared to be. The Texas cattle culture, laid upon the foundations of the Spanish system, instilled the romantic flavor of the Spanish period into a vital and permanent part of the culture of Texas and the Southwest. The cattle industry of the period added greatly to the state and national wealth. The Anglo-American and the Spanish cultures blended in this decade to produce on the Plains a new culture which was unique in that it was more or less incidental and was produced unconsciously as a result of its unusual environment.

To the Francklyn Company the passing of this nomadic culture was deeply significant, for its end came during the trying days of the 1880's, when this company and other similar companies were making a desperate effort to survive. A distinct transition from the nomadic to the sedentary and agricultural era marks this decade. Barbed wire completely transformed the old methods of handling cattle. Moreover, grass was becoming scarcer with each passing year. These conditions forced the ranchers whose cattle fed on grass alone either to go out of business or to compromise with their former antagonists, the so-called, "Nesters," and supplement their grass with forage crops. The day of the small rancher and stock farmer was at hand.

The growing scarcity of water in the Panhandle in the 1880's proved to be a much more serious question than grass. The rapid influx of settlers into the region posed a water problem that has challenged the best efforts of the Plains people to this day. After the settlers invaded the area, tanks, dams, and living streams could no longer provide a constant water supply for either stock or for domestic purposes. The need for water on White Deer Lands was accentuated by its vast area and by the plains nature of the property. Tyng informed Foster, April 7, 1888, that: "There is no living water on the plains. In 1886 the accumulation of rain water in natural and artificial reservoirs should have carried through the winter at least 25,000 head. In 1887 there was less. Now there is virtually none." Tyng pointed out a few spots of water, such as Red Deer Dam, Spring Creek, and a ditch at the west side of Block 7, but, he said, "they are almost dried up." He further explained the water deficiency:

> By looking over the map you can judge what an immense proportion of the range is now without stock water. In fact the main source of water is provided by parts of two windmills put together over a 450-foot well two miles from the White Deer farm which had been used by the Francklyn Company and rigged with a pump that drew water for travelers and railroad builders for miles. The outfit held together and worked well much longer than we had hoped. It was a splendid advertisement as far as it went. I had hoped that timely rains would make it unnecessary for me to again repair this pump or well, particularly as it is two miles away, out of sight from here, and as we have not the requisite material. But as we are on the verge of being driven off the plains by thirst, which *would* be an irish advertisement of the property, we are trying the well again. . . . The water question has become a serious one, and likely, if not corrected, to have given this plains a bad name. The expense of hauling it continues until residence and water supply be made neighbors. . . . This question, because unsolved, has summarily closed discussion of the value of White Deer Lands. I propose to sink ten or twelve wells, at intervals of a couple of miles upon the plains, preferably along the line of the railroad and where, being in sight, they will best advertise the property and its abundant water.

In a letter to Foster, April 29, 1888, Tyng deplored the fact that five of the wells:

> . . . were sunk in ravines much below the level of our plains. They all reached abundant, pure water, but they are remote from our large area of choice arable lands. You will find them located near our exterior fences. The ravines are in our broken and least valuable lands. A well in a ravine appeals to the imagination as one to surface catchment water, and not as one to an inexhaustible subterranean supply. They will some day sell our grazing lands around them. We look for the big money from our farming lands on the plains.

Tyng made a careful study of land formation on White Deer with a view to determining the sources and potentialities for water. He observed that water had been found in the wells already sunk at an average of from 400 to 450 feet with some 30 feet of water standing above the bottom of the well. He said these wells were invaluable demonstrations, but that they did not "reasonably prove abundance accessible to good water to underlie any considerable part of our hundreds of square miles of arable lands, nor does its cost afford any basis for estimating cost of other wells."

As a result of his observation and study, Tyng became convinced that there was an inexhaustible supply of water that could be had from underground streams far beneath the top layers of the plains soil. In discussing this matter he said:

Water in our 450-foot well on section 25, block 7, was found at 400 feet in gravel *under* impervious clay (which held the water down) and rose in the well about forty feet to where it has since stood. In a limited way this is an "artesian well." In August, 1886, I reported some of these facts . . . but also reported that I saw nothing upon which to base a reasonable expectation of getting surface flowing wells upon our plains. The water flowing from every deep canyon at bases of our plateau was attributed to percolation of local rainfalls. This impervious character of many of the strata had not been determined. . . . My opinion has so been changed by additional facts since observed, that I now believe that surface flowing artesian water can be certainly had upon any part of a very considerable area of White Deer plateau from a probable depth of about 1500 feet. . . . For our use we do not need a surface flowing artesian well. A pumping well will answer all our demands for occupation. . . . A surface well of good water on White Deer Lands upon "The Great American Desert" will afford a news item that will appear in nearly every newspaper in the United States. Every owner, dealer, or shark in North Texas lands will strive to give it publicity in his own interest. A flowing well appeals to the imagination of every man who does not pay the cost of it. . . .

It would directly add largely to the sale value of White Deer and would enormously contribute to ease and readiness of sales. Outlay for ten wells can be suppressed for the present. One or two wells can be started by some one possessing a portable horse power outfit who will do the work for $1.25 per foot, we furnishing the casing and other things, making these wells cost about $1000 each, if no bad luck is encountered to cause abandonment of casing in a partly completed well. I have shrunk from employment of well drillers with inadequate outfits or experience. Any failure of this will be attributed to the dangerous and impossible character of our formation for well drilling, and not at all to their lack of skill, or their defective apparatus. It has seemed better for first wells to employ experienced men with strong outfits who will make no failure. Their demonstrated success would thereafter silence all adverse criticism of our sedimentary formation, and would be worth to us higher prices they might charge. The outlay would be temporary. The lands with water will soon sell for additional price equal to wells upon them. It is worth a great deal to White Deer to prove water. When the interest account is $150,000 a year, it is also worth more than it will cost to prove that neither flowing water nor pumping wells can be depended upon.

If White Deer has water it will sell for several million within a few years. If no water for farms can be had upon it, it had better be sold en bloc and without unreasonable delay. Default in water will certainly give it a black eye—a very bad one, but no intelligent man will fear that if he will take time to look the country over thoroughly. . . . *One well* on these plains is worth more to the property than a town like Miami, and fifty acres in sight of the railroad is of more value right now than a town like Panhandle.

Tyng wrote Foster, September 6, 1888, that a grazing contract on White Deer had been made with Goodnight and Taylor for $15,000 a year. He said, however, that the land could be leased for grazing at a higher rate per acre, but that "The entire tract consisting so largely of valuable plains land, is completely destitute of surface water proportioned to the great extent of grass."

The Southern Kansas Railroad was also faced with a serious water problem. The Company drilled a well at Panhandle in 1888, but failed to find a sufficient water supply. Foster reported to Godden & Holme, September 12, 1888:

> The railroad appears to have given up its well after fooling away over $9000 for which they attained a depth of 340 feet. At this depth water was encountered in porous dolomite. It is probably the same inefficient supply which we found in our well at 338 feet, and through which our well was sunk to 404 feet, at which depth we struck our present supply which appears to be inexhaustible.

The railroad engineers failed to concoct a pump that would bring sufficient water to the surface, and for a time no further drilling was done. Baker, the resident engineer, "loudly and emphatically pronounced against the practicability of wells on the plains. . . . I think he urged upon the railroad company the construction of dams for storing rains," said Foster. Water prospects for the Company, however, were greatly improved when Mr. Avery Turner took charge of the Texas Division of the road. Turner wrote Tyng, September 6, 1888:

I desire if possible to meet you and have a talk with you concerning the water question. I believe, as you do, that a good well can be sunk at Paton[1] with a sufficient flow to give us a fair supply. . . . Recently I made a survey of the two ponds near our line. I find that the one near the breaks of Red Deer Creek does not contain a sufficient supply of water to experiment with. The lower pond five miles west of Codman . . . contains plenty of water, and if Goodnight and Taylor do not object, I should like very much to set up a small pump and temporary tank there to test the water. . . . I will also send a man to the well near Paton for a jug or two of water in order to make a chemical analysis of it.

On October 1, 1888, Tyng advised Foster:

The determination of White Deer Lands to put down ten wells was given publicity throughout this part of Texas, and has stimulated well boring. H. B. Sanborn has let contracts for wells on his lands in Potter County . . . W. M. D. Lee . . . passed a day here with me to talk over the well and water prospects of the plains. He left here resolved to have a number of wells put down on his land in Oldham County. . . . The Fort Worth & Denver road now has a fine well at Washburn at a depth of something over 500 feet . . . and it is now reported that the railroad has ordered that the well at Panhandle be dug down to water by hand by three shifts of men to work eight hours each throughout the twenty-four.

Tyng reported to Foster, November 5, 1888, that two of the new wells had been put down to water, and that the new pump was put down within twenty-two feet of the bottom of the well, that a hand pump was rigged to it:

. . . upon a 9½ stroke, 34 strokes to the minute. The cylinder sucked in air for 39 minutes condemning that water supply as insufficient. The ease and

[1] In 1892 when application was made for a post office, the name "Sutton" was sent in, but disapproved, because so many post offices in the United States carried that name. The name "Glasgow" was sent in, and refused, for a like reason. Then Mr. Tyng sent in the name "Pampa," which was accepted. Pampa already had its post office before the townsite was laid off in 1902. M. K. Brown to L. F. Sheffy, August 8, 1961.

rapidity (12 to 13 days) with which these wells have been drilled has already done much to dissipate the alarm as to water on these plains. . . . Sights are in full view of the railroad on surveys 38 and 56, Block 7, and upon survey 204, Block 3. Survey 56 was selected, not only as a demonstration for the western part of Block 7, but also for the lands adjoining whose early settlement it is our policy to encourage. . . . The windmill now in use at these headquarters was quite liable to breakage at any time. . . . A new and complete outfit has been obtained from which good results and effective advertisement is expected. The outfit will be put up more for advertisement than merely meeting our requirements for water.

Water prospects were also given a boost by J. R. Busk, a New York City capitalist, who had recently purchased eighty of the Francklyn Company's bonds. After Busk visited White Deer, in the fall of 1888, he became enthusiastic about the prospects and possibilities of the property. In a letter to Tyng, December 12, 1888, he made inquiry about the wells, saying:

Please let me know about this as soon as you can, as I want to write the other side about it. . . . I hope we shall have the pleasure of seeing you here before long so we can talk over our matters. In the meantime I have done everything I can to get everything in good shape with our English friends and expect to hear from them in the course of a few days.

Tyng enclosed a copy of the letter to Foster, December 19, 1888, with this comment:

This will perhaps explain to you my delay in reporting upon wells and land matters. Results definite and final have not been reached in either matter. . . . I prefer reporting results *practically* demonstrated, to predicting those probably demonstrable, but I fear that winter is about to cut me off from further practical proof of wells and drive me into "scientific use of imagination" in the unavoidable report for the end of 1888. The wells have not realized my hopes, although they have demonstrated results better than predicted. The work was necessarily begun late in the season, since when progress has been slow, owing to the difficulty of holding men and animals to their work in cold weather. . . . The wells are far from failures and are not yet proven to be fully successful. . . . The other wells must go over till Spring.

Tyng ended his employment temporarily at White Deer in December, 1888, and went to Victoria to await further developments. Before leaving White Deer he made arrangements with A. A. Holland and W. R. Frazer, who were instructed to report conditions on the Estate to him regularly. Tyng, on his way to New York, made a brief visit to White Deer in mid-summer of 1889. On July 15, 1889, he reported to Benedict:

> Everything looks far more prosperous along the Fort Worth & Denver than on the Southern Kansas line. The state lands are being taken rapidly and will soon be out of our way.... The settlement over that way inspires even me. Very heavy rains fell yesterday over most of White Deer Lands. Grass and water fine. Goodnight and Taylor have some 14,000 to 15,000 cattle here, but they hardly mark the grass.

Holland and Frazer, in their report to Tyng September, 1889, stated that everything was in good shape. "Crops planted and up.... Two windmills up and the third on the way at the switch.... The finished wells doing excellent work."

The problem of water was closely tied in with the leasing of White Deer Lands for grazing purposes, as well as with settlement. Tyng's leasing program was fairly secure in 1888 and 1889. With the grazing problem temporarily settled, he spent much time during these two years in shaping up the lands for sale. All interior sections were surveyed, and exterior fences were placed on correct boundary lines. Farming on a small scale was continued, but for demonstration purposes only. Much work was also done on wells, windmills, and railroad development in order to encourage settlement. Tyng in his annual report, December 1, 1889, said:

> As during the past year White Deer Lands have been under lease, operations on the property have been chiefly confined to further proving its adaptability to a given culture, and to increasing the number of wells on the "plains" part of it.... The lease enables the Trustees, should they find it best to do so, to dispense with all employees and to cut the current expense down to nothing. It relieves them from the care and expense of keeping out trespassers and squatters, and of maintaining fences and fireguards, and it provides a substantial revenue from which can be met any outlay on which the owners may later determine for advertising or other purposes. The one serious objection to the lease is that in spite of its being subject to any sales

that the owners make, in the lease we have in our camp a party who is antagonistic to ours, in that he wants to continue occupying the land with his cattle, while we want to sell it out to the purchasers who will turn his cattle off the land they buy.

As to progress made in the use of wells and windmills, Tyng concluded:

Settlers are now living upon the "plains" in such numbers, and have put in so many little crops, that it seems not necessary for the Trustees to any longer keep up the White Deer Farm merely for advertisement. . . . It is probable that a well and outfit big enough for all uses of a settler upon a section of land can be put in for $640 . . . probably less. Settlers with their families are scattered over the plains and have put in wells and windmills enough to dissipate all doubt as to obtaining abundant good water. The contractor who drilled the new wells at White Deer, has put in 102 new wells in the Panhandle during the past eleven months, and besides his, several other outfits have been at work.

By 1890 the windmill era had arrived on the plains, and with it small ranchers and stock farmers were destined to follow. Ever since the Texas Legislature passed the lease laws of 1883, 1884, and 1887, the large ranchers on the plains had been struggling to survive. They appealed to the Legislature to enact laws that would ease them over the difficult times which the decade had produced. They succeeded only in part. The lease law of 1887 was something of a compromise between the ranchers and settlers in their efforts to secure lands and grass, in that it gave the rancher temporary use of the grass lands, but at the same time made these lands subject to sale to the small ranchers and settlers. It was, therefore, inevitable that in this highly competitive fight for grass some of the large operators would be crowded out, while others were able temporarily to tide themselves over the crisis and divide their holdings into small ranches and stock farms according to the trend of the times.

Tyng in reporting to Foster on affairs at White Deer, February 17, 1887, commented:

I cannot recommend the establishment of any part of the White Deer Pasture a *permanent* cattle ranch. Range cattle must go. . . . Many corporate and individual owners of range cattle are this year going to be driven out

Ancient Grasslands and Modern Beef Production

of business by curtailment of their grass privileges and by financial difficulties. Many of the ranges are upon lands to only part of which cattlemen have title, and the intersituate lands are being rapidly located or squatted upon by actual settlers who let fires get into the grass by accident or purposely to drive the cattle away from their unfenced or weakly fenced crops.

In further discussing this matter Tyng advised Foster, March 1, 1887, that:

The market for stock cattle has not been made, but the outlook is not encouraging. The embarrassments of cattlemen are more general than I have represented them to you. Maturing obligations and occupation of ranges by actual settlers are going to force sales of stock cattle, and to a lesser extent may affect the price of beeves.... A called meeting of the Panhandle Stock Association has gathered here many of our neighbors. They are all anxious to sell their she cattle to meet necessities, and at the same time more anxious to effect arrangements that may bridge them over to another season.... In response to any criticism that may be made upon prices set upon she cattle, attention may be called to the losses in Montana... which have disabled and discouraged the purchases of Texas stock cattle at the prices anything like those heretofore paid and to the fact that plenty of she cattle are being offered at less than our prices.... Curtis & Atkinson have plenty of money, but their range is on alternate lands along Red River. The Fort Worth & Denver railroad is being graded through their range and settlers are occupying the school lands therein, thus breaking up their facilities there.

Tyng was by no means alone in his concern about the growing scarcity of grass. Goodnight, Simpson, and many of their contemporary ranchers were vitally affected by this crowded range environment and they were the first to propose remedies for the situation. *The Texas Live Stock Journal* in reporting the annual meeting of the Texas Cattlemen's Convention at Dallas in February, 1887, made a strong plea in behalf of the cattlemen. The *Journal* declared:

The prudent economical ranchman who uses proper energy will profit by the pressure on the country.... He will know that so long as this country continues to grow, beef will be in demand, and that they who own the grazing lands must produce the beef, and when the next generation of cattlemen hold control it will be seen and realized that he who owns the land and produces the beef will be the well-fixed independent man of the country. We refer you to older countries than ours to see the value of grass lands. In many states you find districts where extensive farming is carried on. There you can see a dependency on one industry. Turn your attention to districts where farm and grass lands are held and used together. You see a different show of prosperity. If farm products are short or low priced, you find the owners economizing and nursing the stock held on the grass lands. He has two strings to his bow. Here in Texas we find the agricultural lands in great abundance, and the grass lands lay right along beside them. If not, it is but a short distance away. Many of our ranchmen have good lands that will produce rich feeds for cattle. Hold it for the day when thrifty wide-awake ranchmen will see the necessity of growing on it such crops as will help to keep and fatten his stock. The time is coming when the land you have and the feed you will make, will make our country prosperous. Today it is plain to the observing farmer that he who plants his crop with an idea of feeding it to the cattle makes more money and easier money than he who ignores that plan.

Therefore, how necessary the good feeling between farmer and stockmen. The day will soon be on us when the Western range steers of New Mexico, Colorado, Wyoming, and Montana will not be on the range. They will be raised there, but will be carried to the farm districts, there to be prepared and fattened for the markets. . . . When such is so, we can have fatter and better beef at home, more money to the ranchman, and more money to the farmer. How bad to see our beef shipped to the Chicago market and there bought by the beef dressed ring at just what they may offer. It is then slaughtered. Such as is suitable to sell is set aside and shipped over the country to hotels and customers. Some of the same steers that we send over the lines to Chicago ride back to be hashed up to our home people, having stood shrinkage, heavy expense, rate of shipping, feeding, yardage, and commission all tacked on, and come back to us, to the steers' native land to be paid for with all this string of costs. Can it be that our people will stand such a state of affairs much longer. We hope not.

The Live Stock Journal urged the cattlemen to build their own "cooling houses" where they are needed in order to sell refrigerated beef:

If something of the kind is not done, then you must make up your minds to raise cheaper beef than you have been selling for those who have pressed you to where you can scarcely endure it. . . . We would recommend that this Committee would ask the legislature to enact such laws controlling the school lands as will not work a pressure on the stockmen. Let them consider the difference in the grazing lands. All sections are not worth the same price, though the Land Board has been requiring pay for all alike. This should not be. The Land Board should demand of the stockmen pay for the land in proportion to its value for grazing.

The Live Stock Journal gave an extended report on a paper which was read at the Cattlemens' Convention at Dallas in February, 1887, by Colonel W. E. Hughes, one of the leading cattlemen of the Southwest. Colonel Hughes gave such an excellent analysis of the cattle situation in the preceding year that it deserves to be quoted here at length. He began by saying:

The ranchman as we view him, has been an important factor in the settlement, development and civilization of the state. His domain was the arid stretch of country extending from the Gulf Coast north and south across Western Texas. Adaptations to his environments, to surroundings, was the law of his existence, as it is the law of all animate things. The environment best suited to him was the vast grazing belts, the temporary use of which, in the beginning, was to be had for the occupancy. Dry climate and thin soils did not early invite the agriculturists where the thin grass grew and cured upon the stalk, were especially adapted to his wants.

Given the usufruct of such lands, the crops of grass that otherwise wasted and went annually to decay, and it was possible for the pioneer ranchman to fulfill this mission in the social organization. He was a civilizer, a benefactor. If he did not make two blades of grass where one grew before, by utilizing and saving from waste those already grown he furnished food for thousands and added materially to the state and national wealth. He caused the deserts, plain, and waste places, while awaiting the husband-man's hand, to contribute to the food supply of the world. The ranchman of the plains was not to be a permanence. He never so considered himself. His mission was to precede the agriculturist and stock farmers, and until a changed order to things should make agriculture profitable, or possible, it was his to establish and maintain, with profit to the state, a valuable industry. He represented as it were, an era—an epoch—a step in social progress. In fact every weapon, tool, or dwelling of man, every occupation, trade, or calling, indicates a certain stage in civilization. The rough arrowhead of the savage fashioned without tools from the rock, the hunter's rude shelter of dried skins, the shepherd's tent, the ranchman's dugout, the plow and the farm house of the agriculturist, all bespeak the age, the physical characteristics of the surroundings.

Colonel Hughes emphasized the effects of a constantly changing physical environment on all forms of life and its relation to the plains. He stressed the fact that:

For the time being no other industry is so profitable to the state, because none other is so well adapted to the particular surroundings. It is well when the governing powers of a state recognize these truths. That they were not so recognized by the governing powers of this state from 1883 to the present, with other causes, cost the cattle industry of this state over $100,000,000. What a vast sum! Think of it more than one-half the value of the entire cattle industry of the state as it stood in 1884, completely wiped out within three years. No wonder the one-half of those engaged in the business for the past five years are bankrupt. In 1884 the number of cattle in the State of Texas, from the most reliable attainable statistics, was not far from *ten million head,* worth at that time $18 to $20 per head. The difference in value of this industry alone from three years ago was worth more than three times what it is today according to these figures is over $125,000,000. In other words the cattle industry of Texas three years ago was worth more than three times what it is at present.

Gentlemen, the ranchman of the plains is fast passing away. . . . Pressure population, increased value of lands, the gradual disappearance of the wild grasses from overcrowding, railroads and telegraphs, must soon transform the rancher into a stock farmer. The active forces that surround him, as we know, are changing, and he must change with them or cease to exist. In his interest and for the good of the state, we hope that a more enlightened state policy will allow these changes to come gradually, as surrounding forces change, and that further shocks, depreciations and losses will be avoided.

Colonel Hughes then referred to a compact between the cattlemen and the state and discussed it in these terms:

To our view, the mission of the ranchman, as we knew him, is well nigh ended. His compact with society and the state is very nearly performed on his part. That compact was that if he redeemed the lands from savage occupancy, and passed them to his successor in the march of civilization, he should be given their temporary use. How well he has, upon his part, kept this compact is evidenced by the vast sums he has added to the state and national wealth. By utilizing waste forces he has produced the only product that has ever made Texas known to commerce in the food market of the world. The policy of the general government Viz: that of allowing the free use of public lands for grazing had always worked well. It settled the country from ocean to ocean. It had always prevailed in Texas as elsewhere. The pioneer ranchman did not dream of innovations and changes at this late date. He supposed of course that the grass upon the public domain and upon outlying lands would always remain free until withdrawn from the public use by the rightful claim or fence of the owners. Upon this tacit agreement he performed his part of the compact and redeemed and occupied with his herds what was then a desert waste, peopled only with savages.

What has the result been? A sudden and complete change of state policy found him expanded with large interests and their attendant liabilities. The state legislature in 1883 imposed a heavy tax by way of a coercive lease for holding cattle upon the public lands, and compelled its payment under penal laws. A bureau composed of state officials, unfortunately, was entrusted in carrying out the legislative will. This bureau, called a Land Board, under assumed power in the face of the law, more than doubled the already onerous burdens. The result has been that the ranchman finds himself today stripped of the earnings of years and he is either bankrupt, or his possessions are reduced by one-third of their former value.

In concluding his discussion Colonel Hughes listed some of the most pressing problems facing Texas cattlemen. He called first for the protection of the general government against "that disease pleuropneumonia," which he said existed in many states and threatened the destruction of the cattle industry. He declared that the federal government should be given authority to act at once in this matter. He also suggested that the state government be given power to declare quarantine against the disease if necessary. "We also want refrigeration establishments at home," he said, "or, as it was forcefully expressed by a friend of mine . . . we want to quit sending a steer half across the continent for sombody to kill him." Hughes appealed for cheaper transportation, declaring:

From the most reliable attainable statistics the number of livestock that go annually to market from Texas is nearly a million. All of those transported by rail cost in transportation nearly $8 per head—one-third what they would bring at present prices. The saving of freight in this industry alone, with twenty-five feet of water on the Texas Coast, would in five years pay the cost of deep water. . . . We do not want forces antagonized. We have heard that the ranchman was antagonistic to the farmer, and will with force resist his approach. In other words that the cowman with the aid of his cowboys and his carbine will be an obstacle and block civilization's path. This is but idle talk. Those who speak so are not adept in observational science. A little time and patience will show them in Texas the rough ranchman transferred and softened into the stock farmer and agriculturalist as naturally and as quietly as the Winter softens into Spring. . . . We desire complete abolition of all bureaus that assume legislative powers, and the repeal of hurtful laws born of popular prejudice in time of great excitement.

As to the Permanent School Fund and the public lands Hughes advised that:

If the mandates of the constitution are to be carried out and the public schools and university lands are to be sold to raise a permanent fund for the establishment and maintenance of public schools as was the intention of the framers of the constitution, we ask that the second industry in the state, the cattle industry, be allowed to purchase lands in quantities suitable to its needs. The unlawful fencing should be prohibited by penal laws in order that the owners whose lands are in alternate sections may be able to fence and utilize their own possessions. Some system of exchange of sections should be provided for by law. If on the other hand it is to be the policy of the state government to reserve the few lands that are left for the people, we suggest that in the meantime it may be better in the future to allow nature's forces to be utilized and one industry to live while another is being born.

The Committee on Improvement of Stock ended its report to the Convention assembled with this advice:

A common native animal eats the same grass as an improved one, and the difference in price in favor of an improved steer is from $5 to $8. This speaks for itself in thunder tones not to be misunderstood, and those who do not improve their stock and keep pace with the necessities of the times will, as the cars of progress pass along, be side tracked and left to perish by the wayside.

The Committee on Public Lands also called for a just and equitable division of the public lands between ranchmen and settlers, and for laws that would protect the interests of both groups. Said their report:

We beg to call your attention to the fact that about 25,000,000 acres of our public domain are to this state a barren waste, and under a just system of leases can be disposed of so that a revenue of near $1,000,000 by leasing the same can be secured for the state. . . . To avoid all friction between the stock raisers and the actual settlers we recommend that no lands suitable for farming shall be leased, but reserved entirely for actual settlers.

As the plight of the cattlemen continued to grow worse, Tyng declared that "This year of 1887 is one of enforced liquidation for the range-cattle business. . . . Prices of stock cattle are practically at bottom, but little above their cash value for hides, tallow, bones, and fertilizers." Tyng further declared in a letter to Foster from White Deer, June 17, 1887:

The railroad construction while greatly enhancing the value of the land, has still more injured the range cattle business in this pasture, fully doubling current expenses, dispersing cattle, and demoralizing laborers. We cannot afford to keep our little bunch of cattle in this huge pasture, churned up by our new fellow citizens and other new railroad accompaniments. . . . The White Deer fence encloses 600,000 acres, including school lands in Block B-2, indifferently watered for 15,000 to 20,000 cattle, but too large a single enclosure for economy or success in cattle, even if it could be continued an unvisited, untroubled range again. Approach of the dry season . . . gives prominence again to the fears of fires in dry grass. The success or danger having been multiplied by an influx of small farmers and home seekers, adventurers, tramps, and other natural enemies of the cowmen and large land owners, and all careless about the risk of fires in the other fellow's grass.

There was much evidence in 1887 that the cattle business was undergoing a complete transformation. Many factors were contributing to this change, such as extremes in climate, overcrowded ranges, glutted markets, and new methods of transportation. Fisk & Keck, commission men of Kansas City, explained the situation as follows:

Because of the lack of markets in Wyoming, Montana, and Dakota, 50,000 cattle headed for the region were turned back to Texas, 20,000 having already entered Wyoming. This action practically removes from existence forever the long used cattle trails for the transportation of cattle. The cause of the trouble is principally in the exaggerated nature of the information threatening the stock market. It was thought that the hard winter had made cattle scarce in Wyoming, Montana, and Dakota, and it was not learned that Wyoming wanted no cattle whatever until the herds were started. For fourteen years cattlemen have used the trail to the northern markets without a season's interruption and many millions of dollars worth of cattle have passed over it. Last year 300,000 cattle were driven over the trail. This year about 70,000 have been started and two-thirds of these are now turned back. Theodore Ives of Fort Worth declares that the disastrous result of the failure to get cattle to market will have the effect of putting two million dollars worth of beef back into Texas which is already overstocked, thus driving prices down to a ruinous figure. . . . The settling up of the Western country is what played the mischief with the raising of cattle in large herds. The trail has been gradually growing narrower until last year it was but three miles wide, and now it has been thrown open to settlement.

The organization of counties in the Texas Panhandle in the 1880's and early 1890's reflects the rapid influx of settlers. For example, the *Panhandle Herald* under date of July 28, 1887, announced the organization of Hemphill County, which at that time was the terminus of the Southern Kansas Railroad. The new officers were E. E. Polly, county judge; T. T. McGee, sheriff; John Gerlach, treasurer; J. H. Hopkins, clerk; and S. S. Straughan, surveyor. Canadian was the county seat. Other counties followed Hemphill's lead, and within three years more than half of the Panhandle counties were organized. In order to stimulate immigration, a celebration was held at Panhandle, Texas, in February 22, 1888, which announced a

Mammoth Excursion to Canadian and Panhandle. Round trip tickets at half fare rates will be sold on February 21st and good until February 25th, 1888, from Kiowa, Kansas, to Panhandle, Texas. The Immigration Association of the 19th Senatorial District of Texas, and the Editorial Association, and the Medical Board of the Panhandle, will hold conventions at Canadian on February 22nd. A grand ball will be given in the evening in the court house. Brass and string bands have been secured.[2] Extra coaches will be put on by the Railroad Company. 5000 people for Northern Texas expected to be present. (Signed) Featherston, Chairman, Hemphill County Immigration Association.

The excursion was planned despite a severe storm raging in the Panhandle at that time.

[2] These bands added much festivity to the occasion. They were organized about 1912 and were probably patterned after an earlier band which Alex Schneider organized at Mobeetie in the early 1880's.

On February 28, 1888, Tyng warned Foster:

You may this summer be beset by speculators and offerers for "options" unless this Spring sees the inevitable crash which will close out mortgaged farmers in the West and bring them to Texas with *some* money left, good teams, implements and intention to *settle*. We cannot afford to be regarded as a "foreign monopoly" nor as land misers. Neither can we sell at prices still current. My own answers to inquiries is that you are preparing to sell out the land in any sized tracts, preferably in small parcels to actual settlers on long time and moderate interest: that the land is being surveyed and prepared for that disposition as rapidly as possible, and the price will be whatever similar lands may then be selling for.

On January 5, 1888, Foster made a report to Godden Son & Holme on conditions in Texas generally, and particularly on White Deer Lands. He said:

Grass in the neighborhood of the White Deer range is unusually scarce and many cattle in the vicinity will perish for want of it during the winter. . . . The work of surveying the entire pasture and marking out the various sections by driving pieces of iron pipes at section corners is, in my judgment, essential to the development of the property and its sale. It is the opinion of almost all who are acquainted with the land that it will be sold in small quantities to actual settlers rather than in bulk to speculators. The coming Spring will unquestionably bring to all of the Panhandle counties of Texas a heavy influx of settlers. The question of immigration is receiving earnest consideration throughout the state, and numerous conventions and meetings have been recently discussing measures and adopting means for hastening this influx in co-operation with various railway systems of the Southwest. If, as now seems probable, two railroads will be bringing settlers into our pasture within the present year, it is none too soon to have the property in a position for sale in small quantities as required, and the work of locating of section lines can be done to far greater advantage and with much less expense if the entire work is done at one time and not allowed to wait until an actual sale is made to a settler, when the land sold to him would have to be surveyed, and when any uncertainty as to the exact boundaries of his holdings would lead to endless difficulties and involve all concerned in litigation.

This work is made more needful on account of the absence of natural monuments, such as hills, streams, trees and the like, on the greater portion of the tract the uniformity of which can scarcely be appreciated unless seen,

Program
OF THE
Pampa Band Concert
GIVEN AT THE AUDITORIUM ON
Friday Night the 18th December, 1914

PART ONE

1. Granite State March, ... Pampa Band
2. Nevada Overture, ... Pampa Band
3. Overture, The Lion's Bride, ... Pampa Orchestra
4. Cornet Solo, Lizzie Polka, ... J. Butschi
5. Violin Solo, the Son of Puszta, ... Roy Tinsley
6. Cornet Duet, Side Partners, ... Schneider and Butschi
7. Aroua Waltz, ... Pampa Band

Interval.

PART TWO

8. March, Selected, ... Pampa Band
9. Song, Chain of Memories, ... M. K. Brown
10. Tuba Solo, Bombardonia, ... Pampa Band
    John Hamilton, Soloist
11. (a) On Desert Sands,
    (b) An Indian Sagwa, ... Pampa Orchestra
12. Musical Recitation, How We Kept the Day,   DeLea Vicars
13. Cornet Duet, Selected, ... Schneider and Butschi
14. Medley March of Southern Airs, Introducing Dixie, Old Black Joe, My Old Kentucky Home, Massa's in de Cold, Cold Ground, Arkansas Traveler, and Maryland, My Maryland, ... Pampa Band
15. Eldorado March, ... Pampa Band

Leader, Alex. Schneider.   Accompanist, G. W. Buckler
Piano kindly lent by the Baptist Church
Commences at 8:30 p. m.
Prices of Admission:—Reserved Seats 35 Cents. Admission 25 Cents
Tickets obtainable from the Pampa Drug Company and the
First National Bank

and over which thirty miles of railroad is now constructed without a single curve or deflection. . . . This work is of incalculable value and when finished will never require to be done again by us. It has already resulted in very material recoveries of land from would-be invaders of our territory, and has compelled surrounding neighbors finally and forever to relinquish claims and remove their fences from portions of our land which they had usurped. I have opened negotiations with the Southern Railway looking to joint action with them for introducing immigration, and this subject I hope to have in good shape for final action by the bondholders in June. I have in preparation an article for publication in the leading Fort Worth papers upon the subject of sale and settlement of these lands which will indicate the intension of the owners to welcome the actual settlers, and their repugnance to tying up so great and valuable tract of country in the hands of a syndicate of non-resident owners. By this means I hope to allay in some measure the feelings of hostility and cupidity which the owners of a large tract of land in a desirable location invariably produces and gives public notice that these lands are not being held for speculation or rise in value, but are in the market for any man who wishes to buy and improve them.

The whole trend of affairs in 1888 presaged a new era on the Texas Plains. Large cattle operators recognized the change and put forth their best efforts to adjust to the new order. But the free-grass epoch that had produced millions of dollars' worth of grass-fed beef, with its attendant trail-driving transportation as an outlet to hundreds of thousands of Texas cattle, had definitely passed away. Rail transportation made possible the substitution of improved stock, fattened on both grass and corn, for the inferior grade of Texas trail-driven common stock. It is significant that grass roots that had furnished life and sustenance for millions upon millions of animal, reptile, and other wild life for eons past, and upon which hundreds of thousands of buffalo and other wild life had fed for centuries, had finally laid the basic foundations for our Plains culture and development.

With the fulfilment of the Sully contract Foster and Tyng had some three hundred cattle and a number of horses left. They now began their most difficult task—working out a program for the disposition of White Deer Lands that would satisfy the British bondholders and at the same time recover their doubtful investments in the Texas property.

CHAPTER 18

Tyng Proves Agricultural Value of White Deer Lands

THE DECREE OF THE United States Circuit Court, October 24, 1887, ordering the sale of White Deer Lands, presented many difficult problems to Foster and Tyng. The British bondholders were anxious to sell the lands in order to recover, in part at least, their investments in the Texas property. However, much preliminary work had to be done to get the lands ready for sale. The land survey had yet to be completed, and the title to the lands had to be recorded in such manner as officially approved by the state land commissioner. A working agreement dealing with both transportation and land values had to be made with the Southern Kansas Railroad. Land values had to be elevated from estimates based on grazing to those determined by agricultural production. Above all, the lands had to be proved capable of agricultural production by actual demonstration. A constructive program for land sales had to be worked out, one that would meet with the approval of the British owners.

The Court decree of 1887 had ordered that the lands be sold "in one parcel." Since large cattle operations on the plains were no longer profitable, it was impossible to find investors who were willing to risk the large capital required to purchase 631,000 acres in one block. To add to the problem cattlemen preferred to lease rather than purchase grasslands so long as dull markets prevailed.

A solution of these and other questions must be found before any land sales could be made. No satisfactory program could be effective without time and meticulous effort, since the bondholders had only a vague understanding of the actual conditions on White Deer Lands.

The Program for Land Sales

Benedict initiated the program with a letter, March 28, 1888, to Howell Jones, the attorney for the Southwestern Division of the Southern Kansas Railway, at Topeka, Kansas. He informed Jones that the White Deer Lands had been sold under foreclosure; that the owners of the property favored a speedy settlement of the lands in small parcels to actual settlers, and that:

Every concession and advantage that will induce immigration on the part of thrifty settlers will be furnished them. The owners are advised and believe that their lands are the best adapted of any tract of similar size in Texas for cultivation and improvement. As one of the factors in this they recognize the potency of the railroad companies. . . . But unless the right kind of immigration is obtained they feel that it might prove worse than none at all. They, therefore, would like to be put in possession of full information as to the means Purcell and his associates[1] propose to employ in bringing any part of the property into the market, if any contract should be made with them. . . . This matter is of so much importance that I hope for an early reply and will bring it at once to the attention of the owners.

[1] The Purcell Company was a Kansas corporation that acquired exclusive rights to build town sites along the Southern Kansas Railway at Canadian, Miami, and later at Panhandle. Tyng was strongly opposed to this practice. He bitterly criticized the Purcell Company for exploiting these towns instead of making investments to improve them. He claimed that the families of this corporation lived in luxury in Kansas, and that whatever profits were made by the Company were sent to Kansas and, therefore, the Panhandle towns received no benefits from them. Believing that every Panhandle town should have control of its own affairs, he appealed to the officials of the Southern Kansas Railway to co-operate with him in bringing into the Panhandle settlers who were essential to the growth and improvement of towns.

Foster wrote in the same vein to Godden and Holme, April 3, 1888, stating:

It is not likely that the entire tract, or a large portion of it, will be sold at one time, and a town or two can be started under proper auspices and thrifty settlers induced to buy and improve some small quantities. It will be the best means we can take to advertise the lands.

In a letter to Foster, April 29, 1888, from Topeka, Kansas, where he had gone to meet Benedict, Tyng explained that he had delayed in making suggestions as to the early and profitable realization of the White Deer Estate in order to learn first the intent to which the land and town organizations of the Santa Fe Railroad Company:

... are likely to carry out their implied promises to demonstrate capabilities of and bringing farmers to the Panhandle lands of Texas, thereby relieving us of much of the cost of doing so in our own interests, and finally to learn the wishes of the new owners of the property. Land seekers are swarming into our country, sales are increasing, and prices are rising in other parts of Texas, and very much so in Western Kansas immediately north and a hundred miles or so from us. Shrewd practical farmers with money, looking for farms larger than they have in older states have examined our land critically, extolled its soil, inquired about water and crops, and then have gone and bought no better land in Central Texas at $10 to $40 dollars an acre. Such men feel uncertainty as to the possibility and cost of getting water on the plains and uncertainty as to the capability of the plains soil and climate for producing paying crops. Observation and limited experience have removed every doubt in *our* minds, but they will not invest on deduction. They require palpable visible demonstration. ...

If we owned a small tract, surrounded by other small tracts, our neighbors would make some demonstration of water and crops that would also prove our lands. But we own a province, the lands around us are held in large tracts, to a great extent. Their owners live elsewhere, and are waiting for us and for each other to demonstrate. We have no neighbors in this sense. The town and land concerns in the Panhandle appear to be a part of the railroad companies when invoking the name of the great corporations for threatening or cajoling. For any real improvements of or advancement of our country they disclaim all right to commit those corporations to action or outlay. The men supposed to represent the land interests of the Southern Kansas Railway have owned lands and town sites in our country for over a year and a half. . . . Thus far they have done little but "boom" and "hurrah" small towns and to sell lots on promises of what the railroad is going to do. . . . The men who splendidly managed the Santa Fe railroad lands in Kansas are now rich and are occupied. Their successors or assigns in Texas have not yet forwarded development of crops or water in a way to do us much good.

We must work out our own salvation, or wait for time and other people to do it for us. Benedict informs me that among the owners of White Deer some diversity of opinion as to the manner, and prices at which the land ought to be handled and marketed; that some object to outlays which others think is not essential to early and profitable realization, and, in fact, that general objection may be made to any considerable outlay whatever, and possibly a disposition to realize now, even at a loss, rather than later without loss or profit. . . .

But Benedict informs me of your wish for data upon which to at once formulate some program for disposition of the property. If it is intended to get rid of the estate at the first opportunity in blocks. . . . Lease the property from year to year, sell personal property to save cost of caring for it, suspend all operations and outlays, discharge all employees, cede town sites to railroad companies. All companies want us to sell out cheaply, particularly to settlers, at once. It is to the interest of all of them to discourage us as to price, and to bring to notice every low quotation of Texas lands regardless of title, quality, or location. Some of them acquired their interests cheaply and could get profit that would be a heavy loss to other owners. The former may press the latter to realize at once. The occupation and development of our lands by actual settlers by vile prices would enormously enhance the value of the lands of Tyler Tap and others.

Tyng called attention to the fact that the state was selling all of its land, regardless of quality or location, at $2 per acre, which, he said, was not too high. He suggested that a classification of the White Deer Lands be made, and recommended a considerable outlay to enhance the Lands' value by proving them and getting water on them. He commented further:

We live one and a half and two miles from our farms. All we do in proof of our lands' capacity should be done as an advertisement, near the railroad, and in sight of all passers. This outlay need not be large. A large outlay would overdo and defeat the purpose. A house of four rooms, wood shed, and barn for about four work animals, and a few cows would be enough.

Some kind of shelter at water will have to be constructed upon the plains anyhow, if you hold the land through next winter and keep employees upon it. If we abandon the plains we set a poor example to new comers whom we are inviting to buy our lands and live there. Our head quarters there are virtually untenable any longer. . . .

If it is determined to sell the land in parcels, some office will be needed for making a showing of maps, for correspondence, preservation of books and papers, for chaffering and transportation of business, and for your Agent to sleep in. Also a farm for animals and a light wagon in which to take purchasers to view our lands. . . . To avoid confusion a complete record of transactions must be scrupulously made and preserved. You will need at White Deer an office to make and keep it in. Such an office would be at Paton or Glasgow,[2] close to the railroad, the mails and to telegraph. . . . As to demonstration of fruit and timber very fine peaches are raised in Wheeler County. . . . Two varieties of wild grapes grown in profusion in the canyons, three varieties of palatable plums, cottonwood and bois d arc etc. . . .

It will take some time to survey, demonstrate, and get ready to sell upon some well defined system. The demand will have reached our price by the time we can get ready to meet it, be we ever so diligent. It must be hard for our owners to comprehend how rapidly a dry buffalo country changes to one of farms and villages. . . . The villages are emerging from board and canvass shanties and going into brick and stone. No prediction or "scientific use of imagination" is required for placing an evaluation on White Deer Lands. Within a hundred miles of this there is a country that by comparison does that for us. It puts evaluation high, as high as $10 per acre for our plains land, barring the question of drinking water, which in Kansas is at convenient depth. This question of water is a bug bear here because it is *uncertain solved*. . . . The estate has a good future with only the one road it has now. Other roads will be built in.

Tyng cited the "Neutral Strip," which separates Kansas from Texas, as a physical barrier to settlement in the northern part of White Deer Lands. He was convinced, however, that the Southern Kansas Railroad, already completed across the White Deer Estate, and other roads that were building into the adjacent territory would overcome this physical deterrent. In support of his theory he submitted a late map of Kansas to Foster with the following comment:

[2] Later named White Deer and Pampa. See Chapter XVII.

Agricultural Value of White Deer Lands

Its southern boundary is just seventy-eight miles due north from our north fence in Roberts and Hutchinson counties. It is separated from Texas by the "Neutral Strip," a strip just thirty-three miles wide, in which there is no law, order, nor jurisdiction. A strip which is like a wall to keep immigration out of Northern Texas. Congress is now trying to humanize the Strip by attaching it to Kansas for judicial purposes. You will note the present terminus of the Atchison, Topeka & Santa Fe branch railway at Englewood, on the 100th meridian, which is also the eastern boundary of our Panhandle. Englewood is just thirty-six miles from Lipscomb County, Texas, and a short 100 miles from the northeast corner of our pasture and is filling up with settlers at a marvellous rate, whose land is not so very good, but water is handy. You will see the terminus of the Rock Island at Liberal in Seward County, Kansas. Liberal is near the 101st meridian, thirty-six miles from the north line of Ochiltree County, Texas, which is next north to our Roberts County. The 101st meridian passes about eight miles east of White Deer Creek, whose valley offers a fair route upon which a railroad may ascend to our plains, and good routes are scarce for getting on the plains from a crossing of the Canadian River. In calling your attention to these railroads the point sought to be made is this: the roads would not have been built there from and in the directions they have taken, unless that country would support farmers and give traffic. They are not on transcontinental or interstate lines. They are branches or feeders for trunk lines. Well, the farmers are there, lots of them, and more are coming.

White Deer Affairs Shift to London

On May 14, 1888, Foster addressed to Godden and Holme a letter in which he enclosed a letter from Tyng containing Tyng's view as to the best method of bringing White Deer Lands onto the market. Foster agreed with Tyng's views.

Foster then made the following observations concerning a letter which J. R. Busk had written to Godden and Holme:

Referring to the suggestions contained in Busk's letter on the subject of getting a bill through the legislature incorporating the property as a land company in spite of the general law of Texas, it seems hardly possible that such a plan should succeed. In the first place the present special session of the legislature, as you have noticed from the "Panhandle" was called by the Governor of the State to consider certain specific questions, and it has no power in general legislation, except upon those subjects. It would be wholly futile to attempt any thing of this sort, therefore, with the present session. The next regular session will come in January, 1889. It may be worth while to attempt to pass a bill granting to non-residents of the state privileges and powers which the state has seen fit to withdraw from its own citizens, but I am very much in doubt of the success of such an attempt.

Even if it should be possible to obtain from vile and ignorant law makers chartered privileges of this kind by improper use of money, the very rights granted to the owners of the land would attract public opinion in a highly unsatisfactory manner to them, and newspapers, thinking to please their immediate neighbors, would make the matter the subject of unfavorable comment, and could hardly fail in creating a public sentiment prejudicial to your interests, and which in case of unscrupulous attack upon our title, or invasion of our lands, might result in serious harm. All danger of this has been thus far prevented through the friendship which Tyng seems to have inspired toward himself among his neighbors in the Panhandle. As it now rests the title to these lands is, in my judgment, unquestionable, and I shall greatly deplore any proceedings wherever complications might be involved. The management of the property is now very simple, and is besides under the control (as it should be) of the persons holding the largest interests vested in it.

In the matter of reorganizing the White Deer Lands, Foster and Busk took opposite views. In commenting upon Busk's proposal to incorporate the White Deer Lands, Foster listed the following objections to the plan:

Among the disadvantages of incorporation are these: it would involve the abandonment of the existent trust arrangement which has voluntarily received the almost unanimous approval of the "contributories"; it would convert these contributories into share holders whose shares probably inalienable at will might introduce new members without the consent of the remaining members, thereby the control and changing the policy. It would vest the powers of management in a board of Directors, a majority of whom would probably have to be American citizens. This might result in the rule of the minority in interest. It would be likely to engender a hostile local public sentiment which, in many ways must be apparent, might operate to your prejudice, especially in such an unsettled state of society as exists in the Panhandle of Texas. It would not be obtained without a large expenditure of money.

There is also the objection to the corporate management of such an enterprise as ours. The owners are far removed from their property, and if merely holding securities issued by a corporation would be tempted to postpone, or waive personal supervision of the property committed to the charge of their directors in New York and servants in Texas, whereas, if the account and expenditures are controlled by the owners, their interest in the details of the management would be more alert and keen. I think, moreover, that the employees in Texas would work with more diligence, and spirit of faithfulness for individuals as such than for a corporation. These objections seem to me to outweigh the advantages which a corporation by the vesting of the title in a mode not affected by the death of individual owners of trustees affords.

As to Busk's suggestion that the title to the lands should be put in the names of two well known and responsible New Yorkers, I may say that I entirely agree with him. As you know, the purchase was made in the name of Van Zandt and Henry Kingsmill acting under the letter of attorney from the Trustees. . . . It is obvious that the persons holding the title should live in the same place, and it seems desirable on many accounts that the place should be New York. The owners, or ostensible owners, ought not to reside in the jurisdiction where the property is situated. Service of process upon him would be made so easy that it would invite litigation, and ordinary conversations on his part of a mere social character might be readily used to base claims for damages and for compensation for fictitious service and commissions for any sales of property.

Foster was opposed also to Busk's suggestion of the appointment of a general manager in New York to act as custodian of documents and to keep accounts:

The accounts and money should be kept and distributed just as readily in London as in New York. . . . The Texas Manager could send his monthly reports and vouchers to the English Trustees and draw upon them for whatever funds might be required in the business. This would eliminate any intervening Manager in New York and bring the Texas Manager under the direct control of the Trustees in England. It is highly important that the Texas Manager should be a man of good judgment. . . . I think it is wise to give him general instructions and empower him to act upon his own judgment, within certain limitations, rather than to hamper him by requiring matters of petty detail in the management to be submitted to the Trustees in London. . . . I have every reason to confirm the opinion of Tyng's character and fitness for the position he now holds expressed in my letter to Andrew Kingsmill last December. . . . The Texas Agent must be in a position to give him either a deed, or else a contract which would bind the Trustees to give a deed in thirty days. The farmer must not be allowed to go away and wait for his offer to be accepted by some man in New York or London. The bargain must be clinched on the spot. . . .

I should before leaving this subject call your attention to the necessity for very great care on the part of the owners to avoid any action upon which the real estate brokers or agents might claim commission upon sales of land. In Texas it is not unusual for brokers to be paid a commission as high as twenty-five cents an acre for affecting [effecting] sales, and the usual charge is ten per cent. Your Manager should be the only person through whom any offers to purchase should be accepted. He being salaried should not be entitled to a commission. There will come a time when you will be favored with innumerable propositions and offers to purchase made by real estate agents in Texas and elsewhere merely as a basis for presenting claims for commissions upon the completion of actual sales by your Manager. . . . The fact that the land note trust is still outstanding as a lien on the property and that the release from Van Zandt, the Trustee, will be required for every purchase should not be overlooked.

Busk aspired to become manager of the White Deer Lands, while Foster was extremely anxious that Tyng should remain in that position. In a letter to Godden and Holme, September 11, 1888, Foster enclosed a letter from John Paton of New York City. Paton, the New York correspondent for the British Linen Company Bank, was somewhat leary of Busk, who had recently purchased eighty shares of the Francklyn Cattle Bonds and who, it appeared to Paton, aspired to become Texas manager of the White Deer Lands. Therefore, Paton warned Kingsmill that Busk "might throw his influence in support of a sale of the bonds at a price which would repay his investment with profit and yet which would not enable other bondholders to come out without considerable loss, if unlimited discretion be left to him."

Tyng Makes Improvements on White Deer Estate

With reference to Tyng's work at White Deer, Foster explained to Godden Holme & Co. on September 12, 1888:

Tyng will expend about $2,500 on the house and outbuildings, of which sum $1,100 will be spent for the house and the balance for buildings and fence for the protection of stock. This outlay is not so much needed for

Agricultural Value of White Deer Lands

Tyng's personal comfort as it is for the purpose of illustration of what can be done by farmers who settle on the estate at a moderate cost.

Tyng in a letter to Foster, September 12, 1888, advised him:

Our expenditure here is coming all in a heap, but in a few weeks it will also terminate rather abruptly. It all has to be made sooner or later and is very proper, and I am glad we *are* making it. Although authorized by the English gentlemen, it will shock them a little. However, time and results will vindicate it. . . . I think matters here are getting shaped up so that we shall need here this winter only a caretaker to hold things level until events force action say next year sometime. My continued presence here will not be necessary. My absence will cut off some expense, and at the same time, if not formally relieved, I can come here for now unforseen emergencies. . . . We want to hand the property over properly and in good fix for *progressive* management. If the fellows will not then "progress" the fault will not be ours. Much was hoped for from the railroad people, but their omission has caused hopes for the four counties to center upon us who own so much there. . . . The buildings will be run up rapidly and will be completed before frost. . . . The two buildings are not pretentious but they are not going to be blown down by anything but a cyclone that would blow down a stone house.

Busk visited White Deer in November, 1888, inspected the property and expressed his approval of the work that was being done by way of improving the estate. On November 8, 1888, Tyng gave Foster the following report on Busk's visit:

Busk has come and gone. I hope and believe that he is now willing to endorse your judgment in your selection of the Trustee's Agent on White Deer Lands. Life here is monotonous enough to make such a visit an "event." So forgive me if I expatiate. I felt certain that upon inspection Busk would corroborate and confirm to the other English owners the representations of this property that I think you have made to them. For this reason I looked forward to his visit with eager interest and with preparation for giving him as thorough a view of the estate as possible in whatever time he might be able to spare for it. In the bucolic simplicity of my heart I complacently viewed the tent, mess wagon, ten dozen eggs (imported from Kansas), ham, lemons! raisins! ten pounds of butter!!! (oleo) and other "fancy chuck" which I had collected for regaling his party, and the new "guilds" (see Mittenhall's bill) for lodging it, and thought what a bully good time I was going to give them all.

As drops the peacock's feathers when he sees his feet, so dropped my complacency into utter abasement, when Busk and his two friends were side tracked at Paton in a palatial private car with state rooms, baths, servants, and a Delmonico larder. The friends were Mr. Agassiz of Boston or Cambridge, and Mr. Davis of Newport, both very agreeable, and both of good judgment as proved by their appreciation of our good land of which they saw all that good teams could show them during the two days of their visit, and all that could be seen from thirty-three miles of railway by daylight.

The farm of course, like all farms in November, did not show at its best, but Busk is an observant man and I think its promise surprised his expectations. . . . He examined our buildings and looked over everything pretty closely. The nature of his questions and his comments showed a faculty for quick observation that made me anxious as to his final criticism. They passed two days here during which the weather was glorious, exhilerating enough to make one "holler." . . . Yesterday morning they pulled out. Toward noon a norther sprang up, increased during the night, and today is a howling gale of snow and sleet triluated to dust. They got off just in time. One room of the new house was finished and fitted with a stove. It is not very elegant but *so* comfortable that it makes me laugh with content. As the carpenters cannot work out of doors, they are at it inside, partitions, floor, overhead, etc. So that it is not a bit lonesome nor like a solitude in here today. . . . I hope by the middle of December to have everything puckered up into compact shape to virtually run itself, and go to Victoria for the Christmas Holidays. Then if you have nothing special for me here. . . .

Knocking about for a month or two will dissipate my accumulated *restlessness,* a feeling which respectable, dutiful citizens can ill comprehend, but is as nearly uncontrollable as a migrating bird's instinct. The remedies are periodical sprees, travel under some privation, and (best of all) plenty of work that counts—that shows results. Before concluding anything definite I will submit a situation and program for affairs here for your instructions. I cannot go contented if ought remains insecure or incomplete.

Tyng was delayed in closing out White Deer affairs by complications at the General Land Office. He complained to Foster, November 15, 1888:

Disappointment meets my hope of putting our business speedily through the Land Office in the shape most desirable for us. The Commissioner is a man of small caliber, like all men whose both eyes look out through one hole. His rulings in some phases of our affairs are absurd and illogical, but it is cheaper to humor him than to fight him, and we shall carry all our points anyhow by practicing good nature, patience and diplomacy. Fortunately I brought Omohundro[3] down here with me and he is now at work on the changes in our paper work made necessary by the Commissioner's fickleness.... The Land Office is nearly a year behind in its work in the office, and it won't do to simply file our work in the office and let it await its turn. I want to avoid all questions to be submitted to legal advice and hope to succeed in doing so without sacrificing any advantages to which we are fairly entitled. Extremely pleasant relations have been established with Major I. H. Evans and with employees of the New York & Texas Land Company. The latter will do platting etc for us, which is very satisfactory, as they are all recognized experts in their several lines.

Prospects for Agriculture on White Deer Lands

Tyng visited with his family in Victoria for a few days while Omohundro was engaged in making revisions in the legal records of the White Deer Lands at the Land Office in Austin. On December 3, 1888, Tyng reported to Foster that the work at Austin was completed except the commissioner's signature, and that he was returning to the Panhandle. On December 5, 1888, Tyng notified Foster from White Deer that he had:

Arrived here this morning. Weather has been charming ever since and White Deer begins to have a homestead look like a Pennsylvania Dutch farm. *Red barn,* big haystack, good corral, fat stock, good poultry, and a house unpretentious but comfortable.

He also called Foster's attention to the fact that the name "Paton" had been changed to "White Deer."

February 1, 1889, found Tyng again at Victoria, where he reported to Foster:

During the Spring and Summer next White Deer will need very little attention so expensive as mine. Some garden and small crops, a very few more wells, and *judicious* letting alone, are about its requirements.... Prospects for Northern Texas are excellent. It would be worth your while

[3] Phil Omohundro was the state's official surveyor of both the New York & Texas Company's lands and the White Deer Lands.

to make an early trip down there to note the great changes since you were there last, to enable you to compare present conditions with those sure to exist next Fall. The brilliant future of White Deer seems to me very real. . . . I have feared that the foreign owners might be alarmed by the recent outlay, might sniff about my promises about White Deer as those of an interested or visionary enthusiast, or, worse than all, upon the eve of a decent success, might prefer the clipping bird in the hand to the drove of turkeys in the bush, and sell out just too soon. It is hard to foretell millions just to a day. A year or two may seem little to me for other folks to wait for them, and will not to them. The property is now in excellent shape and on the high road toward success. . . . I am inclined to think I could make a record in 1890 that would make the owners forget all dissatisfaction for 1889. However, White Deer is allright for awhile, and there will be time enough for anything new, deliberately and reflection.

Tyng left Victoria April 4, 1889, "for a flying trip to Central America." He expected to be in New York in May, but he was delayed at Juancito, Honduras, and did not reach New York as soon as he expected. On September 14, 1889, he wrote Benedict from Liverpool, England, that he was sailing for New York, September 21.

After several months' absence from Texas, Tyng then wrote Foster from White Deer: "I am glad to be back here. It is the best air I have tasted since I left, and not a human thing up there makes grateful impressions upon the senses."

On October 14, 1889, Busk advised Tyng from Milwaukee, Wisconsin, that he would not get to the ranch but was returning to New York. On October 22, 1889, Tyng, acknowledging receipt of Busk's letter and expressing regrets that he was unable to make his contemplated visit to White Deer, promised:

A little later I will try to give you detailed and accurate reports on conditions and prospects of White Deer Land affairs. . . . Our crops are fairly good. . . . Grass is good and water is more abundant than I expected on all that I have yet seen on White Deer Lands, and it is reported to be the same all over them. A number of wells and small crops are reported to have been successfully made the past summer by new comers on lands in our general vicinity. If these reports are correct it may be safe enough for us to considerably curtail expense of well sinking for mere "demonstration." But before so advising or reporting to the Trustees, I had better ride a few days over the country and see what has and is really being done. At the same time I will learn all I can and let you know as to the prospects of selling Dixon Creek and other lands.

Tyng in his report, November 9, 1889, informed Foster:

So many farms are now being undertaken in this vicinity that perhaps it will not be necessary for the Trustees to again put in a crop merely for demonstrating the agricultural value of these lands. . . . I leave here tomorrow to pass the week in seeking possible buyers for the Dixon Creek Pasture, and other information that may be of use to you in judging the prices of these lands. Unless you have other work for me after settlement of taxes and closing up a number of trifling matters here, I see nothing to justify my employment after the latter part of this month until next Spring. I shall be in Victoria and will hold myself at your orders should you have further work to be done.

In discussing the value of White Deer Lands in his report to Foster, December 1, 1889, Tyng suggested that a fair evaluation of these lands could be determined by comparing them with land prices adjacent to and in the vicinity of the estate. He cited figures to show that land lying along the Fort Worth & Denver line, and extending from Wichita Falls into Potter County, were being sold at from $2.50 to $16.00 per acre. These lands, he said, were producing from fifteen to twenty bushels per acre, although they were inferior to White Deer Lands. As further evidence of the increasing demand for farm lands, Tyng referred to the lands in the Indian Territory, which were being opened up to white settlement. He observed:

These things have kept away *bona fide* settlers who neither want to squat and provoke contention, nor to buy a title that can never be perfected. . . . Heavy storms and cold weather set in early in November making it difficult to collect in volume and in detail information for this report. But it is clear that a rapid occupation of $2 and $3 state land is fast taking them out of competition with White Deer Lands. . . . A beginning was made for laying pipe for a sale of the 107,000 acres of the Dixon Creek Pasture. The only purchasers for that land en bloc are speculators and cattlemen. . . . All indications now point to the beginning in 1890 of a satisfactory demand for land sales at retail prices which will give the largest returns, but also take for disposing of the entire estate a longer time than the Trustees or owners may be willing to wait. The actual purchase and occupation of some part of the estate by settlers at retail prices will make quotations and also stimulate the demand for the land in blocks.

During the years from 1890 to 1893 Tyng gave much of his time to the observation and study of White Deer Lands as producer of wheat crops. In response to an inquiry about the cost and profits of wheat farming on the Texas Plains, Tyng wrote Foster, January 1, 1893:

I cannot give specific answers to your inquiries as to the cost and profits of raising wheat on White Deer Lands, nor as to the probable rise in value of said lands in consequence of the 1892 crop there. The succeeding facts here related will enable you to judge the accuracy of conclusions from them on which are based these general answers. On White Deer Lands the average farmer can make the same or better average profits than he is making at raising wheat on the much higher priced lands of other states already recognized as big producers of wheat. The present owners of White Deer Lands are not likely to make any direct profit, nor aid their current outlay by farming wheat or anything else on that land. . . . If the 1892 crop be accepted as proof of the land's capabilities, it has probably raised the value of two-thirds of White Deer Lands (421,000 acres) from the present market value of merely grazing lands at $1.50 to $2.50 per acre up to between $5 and $25 per acre depending partly on nearness to the railroad as well as demand for land.

Tyng pointed to the operations of the Holland Bros. on White Deer farm to show that farming on the plains made only small profits. He declared that these men could have made about as much money working for wages and hiring out the teams they used in farming—all without any risk. On the other hand he was convinced that in larger units of from 2,500 to 3,000 acres, farming could be made a profitable business, but he warned:

The White Deer proprietors cannot undertake it. They cannot wait seven years to recoup a farming investment. . . . It appears to me that the inquiry of the Committee and proprietors should be satisfied as to why any farming whatever is done on White Deer at their expense since such farming entails direct loss in money. Why, if such farming is necessary, the inevitable loss therefrom is not lessened by limiting the operation to areas smaller than those we have been cultivating? And why we cannot make a profit from cultivating White Deer Lands if an average farmer can make on that land such profits as would justify his paying $5 to $25 an acre for it.

By way of explanation Tyng gave the following answers to his own queries:

Our 631,000 acres are in a country little known until within the past five years, and is popularly considered even yet as a part of the "Staked Plains" of Texas. It was admitted fit for cattle ranching and for that business the land has, and has had, a market value fluctuating in proportion to the prosperity of that business from $1 to $2 an acre. It was and is of the greatest importance to the White Deer proprietors to *know* whether any considerable part of their land has such value for other purposes than cattle ranching as to reasonably justify them in expecting to obtain for it higher prices than those named. . . .

On American farms distant from large cities the cash crops are mainly cotton in the South, and wheat elsewhere. On White Deer it will be wheat. The 3,000 to 3,500 feet elevation and meteorological characteristics of the White Deer country appear to especially favor wheat farming. . . . I believe that the first farming of any kind on plains land of similar elevation and character within 500 miles in any direction from White Deer was done in 1885 by the Francklyn Company. It was confined to the production of forage for that Company's local use without including any products that can be generally and profitably exported from White Deer. Though the Francklyn crops were planted and put in at seasons of the year not conforming to White Deer requirements yet, because of the exceptional weather of 1885, it was a grand success and consequently all the more misleading. Practically no farming was done on the plains in 1886. . . . During 1887 and 1888 enough experiments had been made, on small but sufficient scale, and at no very great outlay, to enable us to assure you that White Deer Lands have a positive value for agriculture. . . . In 1889 there was expressed a preference for suspension of farming on White Deer at their expense. . . . The first comers were speculators mostly who occupied the state lands at $2 and $3 an acre for the purpose of selling them again to farmers at an advance. Some of them made money and some did not. None of them made improvements or plowed land more than barely enough to meet requirements of the state law. . . . The fact remains that there must be continuously kept on White Deer ground visible proof that farmers can safely buy at farm prices from whomever is induced by such people to buy large parcels from us. . . . But until the property can be sold farming must be "kept in sight" on White Deer Lands, even at considerable cost.

Tyng declared that the 1892 crop on White Deer produced eighteen bushels per acre while at the same time he said yields in the older wheat-growing states, as well as in Great Britain and France, the yields ran from fourteen to seventeen bushels an acre. He considered it:

> ... an unfortunate fact that none of the farmers who have yet settled on land near White Deer have come from the wheat growing area of America, and none of them know any more about the area covering implements and labor saving methods of the northwest than do the wheat growing peasants of Europe. They work two or three teams of little animals to the man and appear to regard forty to seventy-five acres large wheat fields. This year, 1892, our country was for the first time, inspected by 1000-acre farmers from the Northwest and California; attracted by 335 acres of wheat on cheap lands at White Deer railway siding. On such small crops the expenses are larger per bushel, and while the profits help to support the family they do not pay for the land. So far our neighbors are from the cotton country chiefly, or from Tennessee, Kentucky and Virginia; good people but trifling wheat farmers. ... Now from the actual farmer's point of view, wheat raising at White Deer assumes a different aspect. 160 acres in wheat is a small average unit in wheat countries of area for the work of one man with one team. Of the $2,130 worth of work above figured the actual farmer would count that he and his team would do all the labor of hauling, fence building, plowing, harrowing and seeding and part of that of harvesting. ... The personal equation of health and other factors not mentioned in the White Deer statements for public use, make the results vary. I have said enough if I have shown that two-thirds of White Deer Lands, about 450,000 acres, are good for wheat, can be sold at $10 per acre, and that, therefore, you can expect to sell at wholesale for a price greater than that of land merely fit for cattle raising.

In continuing his report Tyng called attention to the similarity of climate and topography of the White Deer Estate to that of the plains region of the Southwest which made its farming operations more adaptable to the plains than to the older settled regions of the East. He continued:

> Now as to the area to be kept in farming the White Deer properties regard must be had for the condition at White Deer which differs greatly from those on farms in the older and thickly settled states, and somewhat resembling those in the wheat growing Northwest and of the interior valleys of California. In the older states a patch of wheat is a side show, and farms whose nearness to the market encourages reliance on other crops,

Agricultural Value of White Deer Lands

sheep, beasts, dairy, poultry, etc. The patches here are two small and labor is too cheap to justify the use of big implements and big teams. Right now in the State of New York the farmers cannot compete in raising wheat with the broad-acred and broadguaged men of the West, notwithstanding our handicap of greater freight charges. It appears to me to be the same in England. The explanation lies probably in the direction of insufficient areas of virgin cheap lands for use of labor savings.... If we are going to retail the land to wheat farmers it would be enough for them to see the crop. Its cost to us would cut no figure. They know what it would cost *them* to do the work, but we have got to sell in large blocks to men who expect to sell to farmers, and are not themselves practical farmers. If they were they would not have money enough to buy large tracts.... The most profitable unit of labor for working lands like those of White Deer is composed of the biggest implement that can be drawn by one man. Cheaper work is done elsewhere by outfits ranging from eight to sixteen and up to twenty-eight mules hitched together, but are suited to areas larger than it is prudent or necessary for us to cultivate, and demand more talent than can just now be secured in Northwest Texas for wages. On White Deer Lands once subdued a six-mule outfit appears to be enough for 300 acres of wheat. It will add much to the value of White Deer Lands to give buyers proof of that fact. A small field of wheat attracts little of the interest which we want to attract. The 335 acres of 1892 wheat at White Deer did more to advertise our land and the surrounding country, and to restore confidence of the railway officials who had condemned our country for several years because of its having produced no agricultural freights. They have since, for the first time, discussed plans for making our country better known to the people, and for encouraging its development. That crop has been an object lesson to our neighbors that has stimulated them to enlarge their fields and to adopt broader methods. Nothing will so quickly and so generally make White Deer known as the heart of a choice wheat country, as shipment of wheat from that country.... I strongly advise that no less than one hundred acres at Pampa and the same at White Deer siding be thoroughly prepared as soon as possible after April 1st for sowing wheat between August 15th and September 15th.

Eight years of observation and study had convinced Tyng that White Deer Lands were capable of producing wheat in paying quantities when Western techniques were applied to farm operations, thereby establishing land values based upon agricultural production rather than upon grasses used for grazing. He realized that it would require more time for land values and prices to become adjusted to the new economic order of things in the Texas Panhandle. His immediate problem was to keep the shaky bondholders contented enough to wait for these developments to materialize.

CHAPTER 19

Boom Towns Boost Northwest Texas Lands

DURING THE 1880's AND 1890's settlers continued to move into Northwest Texas in rapidly increasing numbers despite severe drouths, financial difficulties, and other uncertainties of the time. Settlers followed closely behind the railroads extending into the region, and established farms adjacent to the railroad lines. Soon these farmers were producing wheat, forage crops, and other supplies for shipment to the state and national markets. These conditions revived Tyng's hopes of developing White Deer Lands into farm lands sufficiently proven to enable him to recommend sales at prices profitable to the bondholders.

Activities of the Townsite Companies

However, progress was slow and difficult. Tyng encountered strong opposition from land speculators who attempted to establish townsites ahead of settlement, a program that retarded his plans for several years. In 1886 a group of Kansas capitalists under the name of the Purcell Company purchased 30,000 acres of land, known as the Tyler Tap Lands, adjoining the White Deer Lands in Carson County. This company also acquired land for a townsite at Canadian and another at Miami. It sold out these townsites and the one at Panhandle to another subcontracting organization. The officials of the Southern Kansas Railway, hoodwinked into these townsite schemes, unfortunately gave their apparent approval to the work of these organizations.

In a letter to Foster, April 7, 1888, Tyng complained bitterly about the false boasts of these townsite companies. He declared that the Purcell Company:

... has not even yet surveyed its Carson County lands, nor otherwise spent money on them during the sixteen months of its ownership. The Subtown Company spends nothing to improve the towns. It merely takes advantage of or stimulates an existing town. Its every dollar of receipts goes to Kansas. Not a penny to develop or demonstrate values. It is not so very wild to compare their business to a bunco game and them to its steerers. They certainly are working up a little town at Panhandle, *but* they are largely aided in it by the expectation that *we* are at once going to put our lands on the market they so represent. *Our* well is *their* advertisement for water. . . . Lands in Carson County are being sold and the hopes of a town at Panhandle are being fed on *our* demonstrations of soil values at this farm. Several times a week a hack load of prospectors are brought here—12 miles —to be enthused by conditions of soil now being turned by *our* plows. By examination of grain rubbed out at *our* hay stack and plants already sprung from *our* seeds, despite the dry Spring. We dare not stop merely because others are also deriving free benefits from our work. Our interest accounts are accumulating at over $150,000 per year. Until we can adopt some system and method, we must continue with our pitifully wasteful make shifts, but we cannot stop. A minimum was suggested for the seventeen sections. If that contract is carried out it looks as if that outfit will simply pay us the named price (some day) and then simply hold the land until our work or that of others on adjoining lands, raise the value of all of it, and enables them to work off a little town. The railroad company has to put in a small station and telegraph operators at Glasgow anyhow for operating the road. It also has to put in a section house at Paton which it is now doing. The Land Company is not selling nor offering its Tyler Tap lands in Carson County. It is waiting for others to develop value for it. If it acquires our seventeen sections it will be urging us to sell at once, at any price, to settlers who may nourish towns on *their* seventeen sections. . . . Yet this Land Company has a stronger motive for developing its own forty-seven sections there than it can have in improving its half interest in our seventeen sections here.

By way of further explanation of the situation at Panhandle, Tyng in a communication to Foster, May 13, 1888, commented:

About May 1st in writing you I disapproved of the "town forming" methods of the gentlemen into whose management have been placed the towns of Canadian, Miami, and Panhandle and who fully expect to handle the land at Paton and Glasgow upon this property. Herewith are transmitted a few newspaper excerpts in which appear an effort to criticise the "town company" without giving too heavy a black eye to the town in which the newspaper's patrons own property. Panhandle is a town that has been a fair prospect. Its growth is assured by circumstances and would be rapid under management similar to that which has done so much for Kansas towns. But its growth has stopped. It is stunted and choked by a narrow minded skinning policy of its Managers. Their other towns are also at a standstill. The Managers and Agents still live in a tent, retail coal at a big profit, and sell water at thirty-five cents a barrel. They undertake no improvement, promote nothing of public utility and in no way show confidence in the town or country, and in every way show their purpose to skin the hide off of everything they can and leave the country. Their homes and families are in Kansas.

I made no mistake in recommending co-operation with the Santa Fe railroad in protesting against relations with the two-for-a-nickel razoopers into whose hands the Company seems to have been committed in forming these "towns." The local manager triumphantly informs me that "we" were only waiting for you people to "back out" of that section proposition; that "we" would have given $5,000 rather than not to have "you people" back out, and similar statements are made to which of course no reply is to be made by an employee of gentlemen. . . . Since Purcell has sublet or sold out the Texas town part of the Santa Fe Railroad business (as appears to be the case) it will be unfortunate for this property if the propositions made at Topeka by Benedict are rejected. . . .

It would be premature to undertake towns here before next Spring or before lands around them and upon which they must live are in the market to settlers. By next Spring . . . the Santa Fe railroad will be ready to make overtures which you can entertain. Even with another survey outfit in the field, it would take all of this Summer to get the lands here ready for retail sales. We want depots and when the time comes we will have to have them. Beyond present convenience we can get along very well as the stations are, for a year. When our lands begin to produce the railroad company will provide facilities for handling the products. It wants traffic as badly as we want depots. By the time our lands are in the market and producing crops, other railroads will be upon our lands then the road providing the best facilities will get the business. . . .

Mr. Howell Jones is a strong man. He is Purcell's attorney. He protects Purcell's interest and those of Mr. G's sub-contractors and of theirs perhaps. In doing so he bluffs at us all the mighty power of the Santa Fe Railroad Company to punish or reward. But it is only a bluff. It isn't loaded. The Santa Fe is a big concern. So is White Deer a big concern. Our interests are identified and we shall work together when the time is ripe for it. . . . Benedict's propositions at Topeka were liberal, justified in being so by the fiction that they were asked for the Santa Fe Railroad Company and by the wisdom of showing a disposition to meet that corporation half way upon any proposition for getting settlers and railroad traffic on White Deer Lands, but those propositions contemplated that *some thing* should be given as well as received. "Giving" is what the razoopers have no use for.

Foster agreed with Tyng on the townsite question. He wrote Godden and Holme, May 16, 1888:

I do not think that the town site plan contained in the tentative agreement with Purcell of April 25, 1887, ought to be adopted. On this subject Benedict recently went to Topeka, Kansas, where the headquarters of the Atchison, Topeka, and Santa Fe road system of which the Southern Kansas Railway (the only road which as yet has reached the White Deer Estate) is a part. After mature deliberation with Tyng who met him there, Benedict, under instructions from me, made the proposition of which a copy is enclosed. This was done upon the conviction that to ratify the former proposals would be highly injudicious and without any adequate benefit for the loss of so large a tract of valuable land.

I would suggest that the Trustees be authorized to make some arrangement with Purcell and his associates and be given a grant of one section of land at or around each of the stations of "Glasgow" and "Paton" for a nominal consideration, but on the best terms as to a share in the proceeds of sales of town lots that can be obtained. Tyng's letter will give you a pretty accurate idea of the difficulties and dangers of any arrangement that may be made with the Agents of the Town Site Company, and in conformation of this I send you a marked copy of the *Panhandle Herald* this day received, and which shows the plan of action which these gentlemen have adopted is beginning to be appreciated by the people of the town of Panhandle and is working out its legitimate and necessary result of disaster to those who confided in the vague promises of land speculators. All this and very much more with which I will not trouble you, has made me extremely cautious in my negotiations with these people who, while entirely sincere and honest themselves, have been unfortunate in the selection of their Agents in Texas, among whom is Col. Groom the former Manager of the Francklyn Company.

Development of the Panhandle

Judge J. C. Paul, who established the first bank in Northwest Texas at Panhandle in 1888, was greatly interested in the growth of the town and made valuable contributions to its development. He was anxious to bring more settlers into Carson County who would develop the lands along the Southern Kansas Railroad. Paul reported to Tyng at New York City, September 24, 1889:

Our town is quiet. Have just secured an addition in the way of drygoods store. We have secured too an Academy. The building is to be finished by December 1st. Some settlers have come into the southern part of the county and withal we feel somewhat encouraged. Our bank has grown in business considerably. I was elected Secretary and Treasurer of the Southern Kansas Railway of Texas when the general offices were moved here, so I get all the business as far up as Higgins. There is no big salary, nor very much honor about it, but I'll get free rides and additional business to pay me something. I am just in receipt of an inquiry from a friend from Richmond, Virginia, wanting to invest in Panhandle lands. He has means and I hope to interest him in Carson County. When you come I'll get some figures from you. . . . We hope you will bring us some good hotel news. We need a hotel badly.

On July 7, 1890, W. S. Decker, a real estate agent of Claude, advised Tyng:

If you make an effort this Fall toward the settlement of your lands, it is the general opinion here that you will be in the midst of a "boom" this country received last Spring. Everything is pointing to that at the present time. Carson and Armstrong counties have been thoroughly investigated and more eyes are turned on them than any other portion of the state. . . . The influx of settlers in this community has been good, not a school section to be had within twelve to fifteen miles of here. Claude got up a picnic July 4th celebration, held it several miles out of town, and to my surprise not less than 100 vehicles and 500 people attended. Nine months ago there were not forty people in this county. Prospectors are going and coming every day. Some buy others defer until later. All, however, have a favorable impression of the county. Real estate men think that the rush will begin as early as September.

On December 1, 1889, Tyng gave Foster a detailed report on the progress that had been made in settlement and in building in Northwest Texas during the years from 1886 to 1889. He advised Foster that until actual sales were made of White Deer Lands, or until *bona fide* offers were received for part of them:

It will be difficult to declare their exact market value, but a brief review of changes in Northern Texas that have taken place since you took possession three years and two months ago, and a comparison between then and now, justify our expectation that within the next two or three years they will be saleable, if not sold, at a price quite satisfactory to the owners. In 1886 it was still rather generally conceded, even in Texas, that our Panhandle country held out little promise to agriculture; that its only value was for grazing and that even this value was sharing the depression then beginning to overshadow the cattle industry. In all the forty-one counties of Northwest Texas there were then but three villages. There was not a mile of railroad, not a bank, and but three little weekly newspapers. The villages were first and most important, Mobeetie in Wheeler County, created and chiefly supported by the Government outlay upon the garrison at Fort Elliott, a post to check and overawe the wild Indians. Second was Tascosa in Oldham County first built as a base of supplies to buffalo hunters, and after 1879 supported by the trade and recreation of scattering cow men. Third was Clarendon in Donley County originally brought into existence for a model home of religious cranks; in 1886 barely living upon a small trade with cattlemen and still retaining its nick name of "Saints' Roost!" These villages were all located in the shelter of canyons upon streams. Upon the "Plains" proper which comprise the best soil of the forty-one counties (and the chief part of White Deer Lands) not a soul was then even pretending to make a permanent residence. Cowmen camped upon the "Plains" every summer near collections of rain water in natural or artificial catchments. But the absence of full and permanent water, and the then popular belief that men and animals could not endure the severities of winter storms upon the broad, unsheltered plains, and that good crops could not be grown there have deterred all attempts at permanent settlement. The then recent construction of the Fort Worth & Denver Railroad to Harrold in Wilbarger County was regarded as a move so reckless that for awhile it seriously affected the Company's credit. Twelve miles northwest from Harrold was the new little hamlet of Vernon, the nearest town to the Panhandle containing but one two-story house and a population of less than 200 people. There was then but one mail route into the Panhandle, mails and occasional passengers being carried in a light wagon from Harrold to Clarendon and Mobeetie, and thence on a buckboard to Tascosa. From the north and west the nearest railroad was Kiowa, Kansas, 225 miles from White Deer. Since all that, in three years, the changes have been so great that any detailed enumeration of them becomes tiresome. Good crops have been successfully raised upon the plains, as also on the sandy bottoms along the streams. Owners of cattle ranches have had forced upon them the value of their lands for farming, and instead of trying longer to drive back "the man with the hoe," they now look confidently to sales of their lands to settlers to restore to them the fortunes lost in cattle. Population is fast flowing into the country, opening up new farms and building thriving towns. Who should now repeat the dicta of 1886, that the Panhandle-Plains are uninhabitable or unproductive, would be laughed at. They produce and people live on them.

Tyng claimed that the White Deer Farm was the pioneer in farming on the plains and said that it had set an example which was worth following and was followed. He recited further growth and development:

Since last December Potter, Hansford, Randall and Roberts counties (all near White Deer) have been organized with a full quota (120) each of legally qualified voters, since augmented by later arrivals. Benedict will remember Vernon as the little village where in 1886 we bought grain and coffee for a journey to Mobeetie, at a little shanty which contained its only store. Vernon has now a population of over 3,000, blocks of brick buildings, two banks, two newspapers, is grading up its streets and doing a big business. The country around it is now a wheat field. The average in wheat in that county (Wilbarger) being three times greater than last year, when the crops ranged from 20 to 35 bushels per acre. Its railroad station does a business of $25,000 a month. In October it was $27,000. Quanah in Hardeman County has store building, two churches, newspaper, a national bank in a two-storied store building and is in every way a thriving town with fifteen new business buildings and over 100 dwellings built since last August. Childress in Childress County, Salesbury[1] in Collingsworth, Claude and Washburn in Armstrong, Panhandle in Carson, Miami in Roberts, Canyon in Randall, Higgins in Lipscomb, Mangum in Greer, Canadian in Hemphill, and Timms City[2] in Ochiltree are now superior to the three villages of 1886. Clarendon has grown to be twice as big as all those three towns in 1886. So has Amarillo in Potter County. Tascosa has grown greatly, though Mobeetie has not, and all over the forty-one counties are scattered a number of little villages that compare with Clarendon three years ago.

With reference to railroad building and mail service in Northwest Texas, Tyng made this comment:

A year ago the Fort Worth & Denver had traversed the Texas Panhandle from the southeast to northwest, and the Southern Kansas had reached its center from the northeast. The former road has done a good business which has put its securities above par. The present year has not favored railroad construction anywhere, but the prospects were worse three years ago for construction of the railroads first named than they are now for an early building of the St. Louis & San Francisco through White Deer to Albuquerque for a continuation of the Kansas & Nebraska (Rock Island) from its present terminus at Liberal (less than 100 miles from White Deer) southward through the Panhandle toward El Paso, or for realization of the declared intention of the Fort Worth & Denver to extend a road southwesterly from its present station at Washburn in Armstrong County. The new banks at Mobeetie, Canadian, Clarendon, Panhandle and Quanah are doing business from fair to good enough to invite competition. . . . Daily mails are now distributed by saddle or wagon in every county in the Panhandle, except possibly into one or two owned by the Capitol Syndicate, along the New Mexico border. We have daily mails at our new office on White Deer Lands, 22 hours from Fort Worth, 24 from Kansas City, 48 from Chicago, and 72 from New York.

[1] The word *Salesbury* correctly spelled is *Saulsbury* and is located near Memphis in Hall County.
[2] Timms City also was in Lipscomb County.

Tyng Proposes Plan for Sale of White Deer Lands

In this 1889 report Tyng gave a detailed analysis of the land situation in the Texas Panhandle as it affected the sale of White Deer Lands. He cited a number of sales in the local area made recently at prices ranging from $2.50 to $16.00 per acre, depending upon the quality of the soil and the distance from the railroad. He declared that these sales had delayed the sale of White Deer Lands, but contended that such sales would soon be exhausted, and that the increasing demand for lands would soon bring his Company's lands into the market at prices for which they could afford to sell. Giving examples in proof of his statements he said:

As reported to you in 1888, the present year (1889) has not offered inducements for putting White Deer Lands upon the market, but indications now all point to the beginning of 1890 of a satisfactory demand for them. Sales at retail will give the largest returns, but also take for disposing of the entire estate more time than the Trustees or the owners may be willing to wait. The actual purchase and occupation of some part of the estate by settlers at retail will make quotations and also stimulate a demand for the land in blocks.

Large prices should not be asked for the first settlers but they can be raised as fast as the demand may justify. Disappointment has followed the hopes of the town-and-land side show of the Southern Kansas (Santa Fe) railroad company. . . . A sort of dry rot seems to have pervaded anything connected with the Atchison system and it made an unhappy selection of agents for working up its Panhandle interests. Its inside officers have bought up a large interest in the Tyler Tap lands adjoining us in Carson County on the west and it was proposed to make of Panhandle City the leading town of that country. An enthusiastic public, having faith in the Santa Fe's Town Company was ready to back it to the extent of its capacity, for awhile buying its town lots at $200 to $500; lots 25 x 140 feet.

But the public seems to feel that it has been exploited on a petty larceny scale and that the Town Company is a "pizen" to all it touches. It would now take little to start in Gray County an independent town that would draw away some of the population of that Company's towns of Panhandle, Miami, and Canadian. At the coming of the railroad we were already established in a small way at White Deer Farm and some difficulty would then have attended any change of base by us, nor was any such change thought desirable. That point was developed because it was on the railroad and conveniently accessible from our Carson County lands which it was then supposed would first come upon the market following the Tyler Tap lands expected to be well advertised and whooped up by the Santa Fe Town Company. But Carson County, the best in the Panhandle, is not keeping up with the procession. We are not ready to go into town making as a speculation, but we want some kind of village from which to sell lands in Roberts and Gray Counties. These lands are not conveniently accessible to White Deer Farm, nor from Miami and not at all so from Panhandle, but they would be very easily got at from a village at Sutton, on the railroad laid out on survey 103, block 3 in Gray County.

Tyng went further into detail about the proposed town at Sutton saying:

From our new map you will see that two-thirds of our land in Block B-2 in Gray County is absolute "plains" and that the most of the balance is not too broken for agriculture. The school lands have been fraudulently taken by speculators. A little moral support and encouragement would soon induce settlers to squat on them, particularly if we could give them temporary use of a few wells on that block and options to buy such wells and the patented lands on which we might have drilled them. We want all the state lands near us occupied by actual settlers about as badly as we want to sell our lands. The first will promote the second.

The lines of the St. Louis & San Francisco (Frisco) railroad have been surveyed through the White Deer Lands as a tangent cutting through survey 8 block 3 passing within one and one-half miles of Sutton and striking the Southern Kansas Railroad at Paton whence it is proposed to use the Southern Kansas Railroad in running trains westward. It is a little gauzy to suppose the one railway would so closely parallel another for twenty miles over "level" plains, if after that, it expected to use the latter's road bed for the next thirteen more miles. It is far more probable that any such junction if ever made, will be at Sutton [White Deer] . . . where the latter road *first gets up onto the plains*. The Frisco road gets onto the plains from the Sweetwater, and a different water shed. The topography of the country forces its line onto the plains and it cannot well make a junction with the Southern Kansas further east than Sutton, because here is where the Southern Kansas first strikes the plains. The breaks of the North Fork of Red River along the south line of our block 3 forbid the running of a railroad line that far south. . . . While all this is still in conjecture, it is "good enough Morgan until after the election," and if backed by the placing of a sale of 50,000 acres or so of the surrounding fine lands would afford plenty of reasons for the birth and existence of a little town at Sutton.

A boarding house, livery stable, and grocery and variety store are great helps to the sale of nearby land, backed by a railroad station, telegraph and Post Office. They would all come quickly enough if we let down the bars and give invitation. . . . It will not cost very much to plot and survey out a town at Sutton, and not so very much more to drill a well there for supplying free water to travelers, visitors, and first residents. Probably no direct great profit could be made out of the town; nor should that be the intention. The motive should be that of adding value and hastening sale of surrounding lands. From the land of a town site a good fair price can be obtained and recovery of all outlay on it in improvements, even by donating lots to the first ones that erect buildings on them.

Gray County has already enough qualified voters to enable it to separate organization as a county. It is not to our interest nor will it be for awhile to the interest of the first residents of the projected village at Sutton to have the county prematurely organized. The state taxes are much less than would be the county taxes on taxable lands in our Block B-2. The proper place for the county seat of Gray is upon the railroad at Sutton. The lawful place for it is at the center of the county, except upon two-thirds majority of all the voters of the county. Chiefly because of our large land holding in Gray County at present, nearly all the residents are in the south and east parts of the county, and of course want the county seat established near them—to our injury. By starting a village at and near Sutton a considerable number of votes can be quickly obtained to delay organization until we can control it, and when inevitable, to compel the county seat upon our land.

Perhaps this sort of business is new to the Trustees and owners and may appear visionary, but I have been surrounded by it for the past thirty years, so that to me it looks very real, even when I recognize my lack of the peculiar abilities for developing the possibilities of Sutton and adjacent country. But given a large body of fine land, much of it non taxable, all of it proven adapted to settlement and to agriculture, a railroad running through it, a railroad station upon it, no villages nearer to the station than Miami, by rail twenty miles northeast, Panhandle by rail twenty-six miles southwest, Mobeetie fifty miles east by wagon, and Clarendon fifty miles south by wagon, in a country soon to be organized, a junction imminent upon it of two important railroads, and a public hungry for homes upon new lands, given all this (and it is certainly beyond question) and I think the Trustees can find no difficulty in securing a competent real estate agent for booming settlers into a county seat railroad junction and a base for a good sale of their lands in Roberts and Gray counties.

In White Deer Farm the Trustees have still retained an excellent base from which to sell the Carson County lands as soon as they begin to move. A prudently liberal policy at Sutton would put back into the town, in improvements, all the profit made from it, then distribute several times their amount in added selling price of the surrounding lands. Nothing kills a town quicker than squeezing it. That is what the Santa Fe's Town Company did to Panhandle, Miami, and Canadian. A slower game makes bigger winnings. . . . Herewith are submitted some of the "high falutin" advertising being done. It might be more effective if less offensive. You are not likely to require much of that kind.

Sutton, however, was not destined to be the junctions of railroads building into the Texas Panhandle. The topography of the High Plains lying between the rough Canadian Breaks and the forbidding lands of the Palo Duro Canyon at the head of the Red River forced the railroads pushing toward the Southwest up onto the level plains. During the decade of the 1890's the Santa Fe Railway extended its line to Roswell, New Mexico, to connect the Pecos Valley and Southern Pacific lines. Consequently, settlers and large cattle operators followed the railroad and were turned away from White Deer Lands. By 1900 settlers had reached the Texas-New Mexico line in the western Panhandle.

Foster and Tyng Investigate Possibility of a Town at Pampa

On March 23, 1898, Tyng sent Foster a newspaper clipping from the *Globe Democrat* of Wellington, Kansas, under the date of March 18, 1898, which stated:

Pres. E. R. Ripley of the Santa Fe, and a party of officials of the road, passed through here this morning on his way to Panhandle, Texas. It is understood that the mission of the party is to locate the junction point of the Santa Fe and the Pecos Valley extension, soon to be built from Roswell, New Mexico. While here Ripley gave out the statement that the construction of the Pecos Valley would begin in thirty days.

And on May 6, 1898, Tyng notified Foster from Pampa that:

During my absence at Trinidad active work has begun on extension of the Railway from Amarillo to Roswell, New Mexico, twelve miles already having been graded out from Amarillo yesterday morning. The present result is to draw the attention to the country west of us and draw away laborers and teams. The latter result will be highly beneficial to the interests of this property.... Money is abundant again and is being loaned freely-seeking borrowers. The drouth in this part of the Panhandle is fairly broken and plowing for the summer crops is now general. These facts alone are enough to considerably advance land values this summer. If the corn crop also turns out generally good, there is nothing to stop the beginning of a boom in land and everything else. All ill effects of war [Spanish-American War] have been discounted west of the Missouri, a country that is substantially out of debt, and that has capital enough to work up a boom without calling on the East for a dollar. The outlook for this property is better than for years lately passed.

As a result of these glowing reports, Foster sent Benedict to Texas in November, 1898, to investigate the possibilities of establishing a town at Pampa in Gray County. Benedict and Tyng spent a month in traveling over the White Deer Estate and adjacent territory in the Texas Panhandle. After the investigation was completed Benedict gave Foster a detailed account of the trip, from which a brief digest is given here. He began his report with these general comments:

Acting under your instructions received from you to investigate the present outlook for sales of White Deer Lands and the general situation with regard to the development and settlement of the surrounding territory in the Panhandle of Texas, I left this City [New York] November 5th ultimo, accompanied by Tyng, and returned on November 27th. The following is the general outline of the route traveled and incidents and results occurring on the trip.... Arrived at the town of Panhandle in Carson County ... on the line of the Southern Kansas Railway in Texas.... It has not fulfilled the expectations attending its organization and has struggled against adverse circumstances ever since the advent of the railroad more than twelve years ago. For about six years prior to last May there was practically no activity in real estate in the surrounding territory.

In making his investigation Benedict visited and talked with a number of settlers on White Deer Lands, with railroad officials, and with large operators, particularly in the western Panhandle. He learned from real estate agents that lands were selling rapidly in the vicinity from $2.00 to $2.50 an acre. He recommended the sale of Dixon Creek Pasture if approximately $3 per acre could be secured, "As it seems improbable that enough can be realized from the small proportion of good land to equalize the price for the whole pasture, in view of the very low price at which a great proportion of the land would have to be sold." Benedict spent three or four days traveling over the White Deer property to examine the land, and talked with a number of the earliest settlers there, including Perry LeFors, Jesse Wynne, "an exceedingly desirable man to have permanently settled upon the property," and David Somerville at Pampa headquarters of the Matador Company, "who used our White Deer Lands for steer cattle exclusively." They also visited with other settlers. Among these was Henry Thut. Benedict thus described Thut's farm:

... a small section or two just east of our easterly fence at the northwest corner of our Block B-2, and leases three sections outside of our lands of us. He has been there since 1885. He is a German Swiss and came there without any money. He now has a house, well, and windmill, fences, 147 cattle and about 80 calves besides some horses. He is the Postmaster and is generally respected and liked by his neighbors. . . . Drove to Henry Lovetts about five miles from Thut's. He desired to buy the section which he leases from us. Drove thence to Hopkins. He has a good house and other improvements and is doing considerable farming. . . . Drove to Owens . . . from Owens to Fritz's house. . . . On the way over we saw four large wagon loads of feed going from Groom's pasture to the Choctaw railroad construction camp. Fritz told us that Groom had sold 100 tons of feed at $12.50 a ton besides 1,000 bushels of oats at sixty cents per bushel delivered at the railroad. Fritz and his brother are the sons of an architect in Kansas City. They have recently been married. Since last summer they have built what is probably the best house in this part of the Panhandle, and when we were there were engaged in putting in a well. Whether they are likely to be the kind of settlers who will permanently remain in the country is a little hard to say. There is so little in the way of social life to attract people of their class that I should think it unlikely that they would remain long unless conditions change.

The men then drove from Fritz's about eleven or twelve miles, to the headquarters of the Mortimer Land Company on Survey 19, Block B-2. At this place they met Colonel Groom and Harry:

... who were formerly connected with the Francklyn Land & Cattle Company, and who manage the business connected with the Mortimer Land Company, or rather by Van Beuren who is the owner of the cattle and subtenant of the Mortimer Land Company. The Grooms have built very large and good looking improvements upon the property consisting of five or six large barns and numerous other buildings. I learned from other persons with whom I talked concerning them that their herd of cattle is among the best, if not the very best, in Northwestern Texas. It consists of between 700 and 800 head of high class cattle, mostly Herefords. The Grooms showed me some excellent bulls which they had brought from Kentucky. . . . The herd, I was told, is in much better condition than when it was first brought from Kentucky, most of the poor and weak stock being weeded out.

After touring the White Deer Lands Benedict and Tyng went to Amarillo and Claude, where they talked to a number of the leading men, including W. H. Fuqua. They found much activity in land sales at both towns. Benedict declared:

Amarillo is now the largest and most promising town in the Panhandle District of Texas. . . . It has three railroads running into it and another which will soon reach it. It has two banks and a large number of stores. It has several hotels and a population of about 2,000 persons. We were introduced by the Judge of the District Court to the President of the First National Bank. This gentleman, Mr. W. H. Fuqua is, owing to the nature of his business which involves lending money to persons engaged in the cattle business and making loans on land notes and other similar securities, very conversant with the value of lands around Amarillo and in the Panhandle district generally. He is acquainted with almost every cattle raiser and farmer in the entire territory and necessarily understands the conditions which now exist as well as anyone whom I could have found. In the course of the conversation, he told me that the last four years had been years of exceptional advantage to the Panhandle, and that rainfall had been reasonable and in sufficient quantities to produce excellent crops. He gave me many interesting illustrations of the manner in which farmers had prospered, and he told me, incidentally, that in the last year the profits of his bank had been seventy-five per cent upon the capital. He has deposits of more than

$500,000. . . . Fuqua intimated that, as he had considerable business all the way along the line of the road from Miami down to Amarillo, he might consider the establishment of a branch bank if we should start a town at Pampa. . . .

I talked with several persons who desire to buy one or two sections of our lands as soon as they are placed on the market. One of these persons is a Mr. Hill, who desires to buy about four sections somewhere near Pampa. Hill has built a very good business at Panhandle. He has two stores, one a general merchandise store and the other a hardware store. He owns considerable land around Panhandle as well as some cattle. He is energetic, pushing, is said to be honest and to have made considerable money. He seemed the right sort of man for us to have a general store at Pampa in case the town should be started there and I spoke to him about it in a general way. He said he would look into the matter and give it careful consideration.

The Capitol Syndicate, a British corporation, had recently placed upon the market a solid body of land situated in the extreme northwest corner of the Texas Panhandle. Since this land possessed many of the characteristics of the White Deer Lands, Benedict was instructed to make inquiry regarding the manner in which these lands were being sold, and if possible to look at some of the land. In this connection Benedict reported:

On this day I called upon Mr. Boyce, who is one of the Agents of this property and who is a practicing lawyer in Amarillo. Boyce's father is the General Agent for these lands and the legal representative of the Farwells. Boyce gave me copies of a printed pamphlet, one of which I enclose herewith. . . . Boyce informed me that they had, during the present year, sold over 700,000 acres at a uniform price of $2 per acre, both plains and broken country. . . . Called on Lieut. Governor Browning, whose firm is the legal representative of the Choctaw Railway, concerning the changing of the right of way of the road. . . .

I obtained from Mr. Starkweather, Superintendent of the Southern Kansas Railway, free transportation for Tyng and myself to the New Mexico line. We took the train from Amarillo in the morning and rode entirely across the Capitol Syndicate lands to Portales, New Mexico, covering a distance of about 232 miles. . . . We saw on this line three new towns, one nearly south of Amarillo called Canyon City, another a short distance east of the Capitol Syndicate lands called Hereford, and the third being Portales in New Mexico. None of these towns is more than three years old. They all look to be flourishing. We were told that there had been about 550 separate sales of lands at Hereford within the last six months. Of course, this included many small plots. The Capitol Syndicate lands that we saw are, like our own, practically barren of population, and are used exclusively for the business of cattle raising. Canyon City and Hereford are on plains land, but, by their establishment, people have been attracted to their vicinity and scattered farms can be seen from the railroad showing that settlers are beginning to occupy the adjacent territory....

I call your attention to that feature of their method of sale which provides that purchasers, at their option, may not pay less than ten per cent of the purchase price in cash, and the balance in equal payments extending not over nine years, with interest on deferred payments at eight per cent per annum. This is a method which might be adopted with advantage in the sale of White Deer Lands, as it enables the intending purchasers to put more money into improvements than if a larger proportion of the purchase money were required to be paid down.

At Amarillo I had another talk with Starkweather and conferred with him regarding the establishment of a town at Pampa on the line of his railway. As was natural, he favored the plan and said he believed the time was ripe for such an improvement.... He wished me to see Mr. Nichols, the General Manager of the Southern Kansas Railway in Texas, whose office is at Amarillo and who has had much experience in the development of railway towns....

Had a long talk with H. E. Hoover, who is the attorney for the Southern Kansas Railway of Texas. Both seemed fully alive to the importance of starting a town at Pampa as being the best place for us upon their line, and spoke of the good desirability as having that place selected as the County Seat town of Gray County when the county should be organized.... I learned that the people who are building the Choctaw road south of our property, are endeavoring to have the County Seat town located on the line of that railroad.... Hoover advised me that it would be of very considerable advantage to us in the sale of our lands if we should establish a town at Pampa and obtain a location for the County Seat.... I found that his views were entirely in accord with my own on these points and he agreed to give us the benefit of such assistance as he could render in the matter.

I had been thinking over the general plan for laying out a town at Pampa in case this course should be decided on. I went over the ground there very carefully with Tyng in order to determine the exact lines where it would be best to begin the work. The railroad has built at Pampa a section house,

PAMPA IN 1902

station, two wells with steam pump and a very large tank or reservoir for storing water. . . . I told Tyng in a general way how, in my opinion, the streets should be laid out and where land should be reserved for the Court House. Talked with Somerville regarding the Matador Company's improvements and wrote to Mr. McKenzie at Trinidad to say that we would be at that place about the end of the following week. . . . The object of establishing the town at Pampa is to furnish a base of supplies to settlers and a convenient location from which they may examine the lands offered for sale and not being, as is usually the case, merely a scheme to make money out of the sale of town lots.

Benedict and Tyng traveled to Trinidad, where McKenzie gave his hearty approval to the plan of establishing a town at Pampa. From there they went to Chicago to confer with the general superintendent of the Santa Fe Railway, who also offered every assistance possible to the town plan at Pampa. From Chicago, Benedict returned to New York, while Tyng left for the Panhandle to begin work in laying out a townsite at Pampa.

CHAPTER 20

A Decade of Leasing White Deer Lands

THE LAST DECADE of the nineteenth century was the most decisive and uncertain period that Tyng had encountered since he began the management of the White Deer Lands. The period was characterized by severe drouths, a financial panic, economic changes in ranching operations, a bitter controversy over the gold-and-silver question, and a change in national party control. For Tyng this period presented the problem of retaining leases on 631,000 acres of White Deer Lands at prices sufficient to maintain the property and, at the same time, to pay for gradual improvements that would enhance land values sufficiently to justify land sales. Because of dull markets and the uncertainty of the times, little movement in either land or cattle occurred during the decade. Leases were hard to make under the best of circumstances. Tyng also had to keep the British owners confidently looking ahead to prospects for better times. Boom towns and the race in the 1880's for land sites had subsided and railroad building was temporarily slowed because of financial difficulties.

Problems in Leasing

Tyng traveled continually over the West and kept in close touch with cattle traders in order to determine the trends in land and cattle prices. Despite the recurring downward trends, he was convinced that prices would soon take an upward turn and again reach the boom proportions of the 1880's. He was hesitant, therefore, to set definite prices on either leases or sales of White Deer Lands. He followed a policy of extreme caution in making commitments of any kind. He reduced expenses at White Deer to a minimum (except for emergencies), even cutting out the expenses of his own salary. During periods of his unemployment Tyng usually went to his home in Victoria, making only periodic visits to White Deer to investigate conditions which might require his services.

In February, 1893, Tyng was in San Juancito, Honduras, but was "anxious to get back to Texas." On his return trip, he wrote Foster from New York, March 27, 1893:

For reasons circumstantially given you at this time, it seemed well to eliminate from White Deer the expense of employing me from about January 1st to May 1st. I still hold that opinion, but will start for Texas via Chicago, St. Louis, and Topeka, stopping at these points to carry out your instructions, to measure the probable early demand for land and grass; to obtain categorical demand for grass from Niedringhaus, and close matters pending with the Santa Fe Railway. I think you need have no fear of being unable to lease all unsold White Deer Lands after the expiration of the present leases July 1st. The only uncertainties are as to price and as to length of time you are willing to have leases run after July 1st. I have already received inquiries for more than twice as much land as we have. . . . No cattleman wants to rent lands from which he can be ejected between September and May. To move cattle at that time is most damaging, even if the owner has other land on which to move. To gather and move from 5,000 to 30,000 head of cattle, after cold weather begins, and before good new grass, is something that no man will do and no lease or contract can be drawn to compel him to do. Practically it cannot be done at all. . . . I advise no precipitancy in the matter of leaseing. The expectant attitude of the prices for land must continue until the advancing season shall have indicated prospects for 1893 of crops and cattle. I think it will be May before these can be predicted. . . . I have several inquiries for 20,000 acres and upwards, to which it has seemed best to give evasive replies for the present. . . . I am told that the loss of cattle in the Northwest has been enormous, because of bad weather. This may affect Niedringhaus' plans, but it would improve prices and improve credit of Texas cattle owners. Congress is about to acquire 6,500,000 acres of the Cherokee Strip. The cattle there would then be forced to seek other pastures by July and August.

On April 15, 1893, Tyng reminded Benedict:

Pray bear in mind that I have thus far been evading applications for grass since last Fall, then consider that we have bids for about 2,000,000 acres of grass; then imagine how it might be were I to turn loose to seek tenants, or advertise for them. I can already guarantee that we can lease at not less than five cents, but it is yet too soon to predict a higher price. . . . If it were not for scaring and fretting our English friends, I would advise 18 Wall Street to refer applicants to Tyng and for Tyng to go and hide somewhere until June. . . . Just the same about making sales. However, I suppose it is necessary to fly around and fuss just to *show* interest and activity. Probably the Britishers would feel safer in renting to a British Company at five cents than to a bloody Yankee you know at ten. So I won't go home for a couple of weeks anyway, nor until I have worked some of the towns.

Cow business is experiencing a revival. The advance in beef cattle is considerable but may be fortuitous. Not so, however, is an advance averaging twenty-six per cent in prices of range cattle, yearlings, and feeders, and this before any human being can tell what is going to be the crops of hay and corn in the feeding states. . . . I ought to have stuck it out and refused to take White Deer wages before May anyhow. But it made me hot to have 34 Old Jewry express a hint that Foster might lose a sale or lease by neglect or by absence from Texas and his employees. So here I am compounding with conscience by personal mortification.

While waiting for crops to mature and for possible land sales, Tyng was negotiating for leases with several large cattle concerns, including the Matadors and Niedringhaus Bros., whose lease was to expire July 1. As to possible sales, he advised Foster, April 30, 1893:

I had several talks with Goodnight. He sold 150,000 acres of the Quitaqua Ranch for $2.50 an acre. . . . There was some question over part of the titles which delayed the transaction and affected prices. Some technical irregularities in the certificates when issued. . . . Goodnight says that this question, as also the distance of the land from the railroad, prevented him from getting what he considered the land worth. He said he was compelled

A Decade of Leasing White Deer Lands   309

to sell because of his losses on his Mexican mining properties, and because of the necessity of raising more money to rescue that property. . . . Paul's $2,000,000 trade is still alive but expectant. . . . The offer to pay is modern business, but confirms my opinion that Paul represents the Tyler Tap lands. While he was East he investigated to some extent the ability of the putative purchaser to command and pay over $2,000,000 cash for the land. He thinks that it is all right and that the trade will be made if the season favors crops. . . . Ten days ago the prospects were *brilliant* for grain crops. Now they are getting mixed. The dry weather and high winds have continued so long that three more days will wreck some crops, and I think another week of such weather will catch them all. . . . This watching of the sky and of crops is harassing. It is like watching at the bed side of a dear friend hovering between life and death. The least cloudiness revives hopes; its dissipation draws heavily on cheerful courage.

With reference to the effects of the dry weather on leasing lands, Tyng said:

Each days continuance of this weather makes a lease of 350,000 acres to the Matadors at five cents a better "hedge." The grass on our land is good enough right now and will not be damaged by drouth. Water is scarce and will be till it rains. That is why I appointed Amarillo for meeting the Matadors instead of citing them to Pampa. I guess Johnstone is a good fellow but he must be some kind of an office man or he would have better sense than to agree to talk a big trade for cow grass anywhere except upon the ground itself. This acceptance of Amarillo means that they want the grass badly enough to "must have it." If it was an American outfit they would pay six or seven cents, but I guess it has taken them several months to work up Scotch consent to five, and it would take more to screw it up another cent or two. Coggin of Brownwood is a banker as well as a cattle owner and is just as sound financially as the Matadors. Hoff and brother of San Antonio are Jews but responsible. They both want 350,000 acres on the same terms as the lease now expiring.

The proposed lease to the Matadors was typical of all leases made during the decade, except as to price, which varied with conditions at the time, and size of area leased. This lease was to contain 348,000 acres and was to run for two years from July 1, 1893, with option to renew for another year, with rental at five cents per acre per annum paid quarterly in advance at New York. The lessee was to keep all fences, windmills, dams, and other improvements in good repair, plow and burn out existing fireguards annually, and return the property in as good condition at the expiration of the lease as when received. The lessee could remove all fences when he left if he desired, or sell to the owner upon agreed prices. Any part of the land could be sold during the continuance of the lease, except watered lands, but such lands as were purchased had to be fenced. Railway rights and townsites were excluded from the lease. Tyng was always anxious to lease White Deer Lands, not only because of the revenue they produced, but also because the lessees would protect the property from intruders in their own interest.

Special Problems at White Deer

In a letter to Foster, June 3, 1893, Tyng explained his problems at White Deer:

> Block 7 has no living water and has not this year had rain enough to store water in the tanks or dams. There are five wells in that pasture as fenced which would ordinarily water 2,000 to 2,500 head. Two of them are now choked by entry of surface dirt made possible by neglect. They are being restored, but even so its scarcity of water makes that block hard to lease until good rains. . . . As you know, breeding cattle cannot be placed in considerable numbers on land of short or uncertain tenure. This fact limits rental of White Deer to steer cattle, mostly handled by men who buy to sell again after one or more years growth. There appears to be plenty of men willing to buy steers and lease land who ordinarily could get what money they need for that business. But for the past couple of weeks a difficulty in borrowing money has checked speculation in steers and grass, notwithstanding apparent refutation of my already expressed opinions. I cannot help believing that grass with water will soon be worth more money. . . . Showers have made fair grass, but have accumulated no stored water in block 7, nor in the western two-thirds of block B-2. This scarcity of water has deterred several people who have looked that land over with a view to leasing.
>
> You will probably soon be wanting to make a report for the annual meeting at London. I should like to defer writing a report as long as possible in the hope that the situation and prospects may become clearer than they now are. Though there is little movement and though there are many individual discouragements, I think that the general sentiment is one of hopeful of better times as soon as the country's financial condition settles. . . .

Up to April 20th we were all right on season. Since May 1 the season has been Hell. Cattle are fully twenty per cent higher than last year and can afford to pay forty per cent more for grass. Speculators are anxious to buy cattle, but cannot borrow money. This fact limits bidders for grass. The flurry in money matters you know all about. It has choked off large land buying. Either a dry season or tight money might have proved me a liar. Both together so far have made me a regular Ananias if judged by my positive predictions of March and April. Both together ought to make White Deer prospects look badly for the rest of 1893. Had I remained here on the land I should have thought so myself.

But after seeing many people and hearing them talk, I think there is a general conviction that this part of the country is all right. I cannot define this thing. But you may have, or not, noticed some such inexplainable sentiment toward real estate in some part of your world. It is the feeling that makes "booms" when fully developed and that cut no figure in reports to unhappy owners. Whether this feeling will grow, or whether it will die out for lack of facts to feed upon I cannot yet guess. . . . I expect to stick it out until the property is in possession of tenants approved by you, say July 10–15, and longer if immediate prospects justify. Otherwise I expect to put up shutters, stop expense, and go somewhere not yet determined. This will give you a clear opportunity for subsequent changes that may look desirable. If London grumbles say "All right I'll put another of my men on the Texas outfit."

General conditions continued to grow worse at White Deer with each successive season. Tyng wrote Foster, July 1, 1894, that "Hard times still prevail sufficiently to extinguish purchases of lands here for the present." And on September 20, 1894, he declared to Foster while he was in New York:

These conditions do not justify my employment or any immediate outlay in advertising or demonstrating the value of that land. On survey 25, block 7, the headquarters building will be occupied by the Matador Company till June, 1895, at a rental sufficient to cover repairs, taxes and insurance. . . . At Pampa in Gray County you have a modest improvement, of which photographs are handed to you herewith. It is near the Railway, near the wagon road through that county and attracts much attention from all passers, and is an ideal advertisement. An arrangement has been made with S. C. Case and family to occupy the place at Pampa and is to furnish food and lodging for their own account to travelers and visitors. They pay no rent . . . because they have a small house of their own unoccupied upon the station ground belonging to the Railway Company. They are decent conscientious people who will faithfully care for the property there. This arrangement is only for the term of the lease of the surrounding land by the Matador Company. Case is section Foreman of the Railway. The presence of decent families goes far to dispel the otherwise easily acquired impression that this great property is merely a vast wilderness fit only for wild cattle and nomadic cowboys. . . .

Under circumstances herein first mentioned it seemed best to undertake this year no demonstrative farming whatever. But later it will be profitable to do it, charging the direct loss to an advertising account. On the State lands in Block B-2, the Mortimer Company of which B. B. Groom is the Manager, have this Fall introduced a large steam plow, and plans to do farming on a large scale. Whatever success attends that operation will correspondingly affect the outlay on farming needed for advertising your lands, whenever a renewed inquiry for land shall have made advertising useful. . . . Harry Taylor has been on the property for several years, has assisted in all surveys, and has usually accompanied me in traveling over the estate. He knows every watering place and can show the land to its best advantage to prospective lessees or buyers. After the next leases are made, he can be dispensed with if thought best. He will reside at Pampa and will there receive instructions from you by mail. . . .

Viewers of the land can get board and lodging at Pampa from the Case family. You have there a pair of horses, a light wagon and camping outfit with which Taylor can convey people over the property. Taylor writes with difficulty but he will get Case or Lane to write for him communicating anything important for you to know. There is plenty of forage to meet all requirements for next year. In case of fires Taylor will employ any men who happen to be available to help extinguish them and report the outlay to you. While it is true that the grass belongs to your tenants, the effects of fires is so bad on future crops of grass that you cannot afford to conscientiously abstain from helping to put them out. . . .

Wells and windmills were put in perfect order last year and so delivered to lessees with expressed condition that at the expiration of leases they be returned in as good order as received. . . . The western two-thirds of Block B-2 are without sufficient water for cattle, except in years of abundant rain. Moreover, as each alternate section is subject to occupation, and as a large number of them have been occupied by settlers and others, this land would

A Decade of Leasing White Deer Lands

be less easy than your others to lease in large parcels. A number of the settlers have cattle which graze upon your or any other land in the Block. There is no practical way to prevent this nor to collect from these settlers any rent for the grass. ...

The Manager of the Mortimer Company has talked of leasing some twenty sections near the southwest part of this block. As the other leases do not expire till next June, it is doubtful if any successful inquiry for new tenants can be prosecuted before the cattlemen begin to make their plans next Spring. It would be well to begin to advertise next March in newspapers of Kansas City, Dallas, Fort Worth and Chicago.

Tyng, on April 13, 1895, in acknowledging receipt of a letter from Benedict, said:

Yours of April 10th came this afternoon while I was packing up for a trip to Ann Arbor, Michigan, to see one of my boys. I shall have the pleasure of seeing you within a few days after your receipt of this. If I can be of any use in the White Deer matters I shall be very glad to be so, and I think I shall be foot loose for awhile. In this part of Texas the prices of cattle have been rising rapidly. If this be due to confidence it will help White Deer. If due to actual scarcity of cattle, it may or may not be of help.

On May 11, 1895, Tyng advised Benedict:

By this mail I write to Foster my views *to date* upon the leasing of these lands. Herewith is a copy of my letter to Paul which I hope will brace him up a little. He has been hearing only one side of the grass question and is a little inclined to fall down too soon. He is anxious lest the land remain tenantless. If you agree, I had best be his boss during the few weeks that it will take to arrange this business. If you should close any lease at New York please telegraph me in *care of Panhandle Bank* as Paul will have my changing address. I do not think that Paul's advertising has been effective. I enclose one sample. All of them have expired but one which is like sample and [in] which I have suggested interpolation of "631,000 acres" after the words White Deer Lands. If any further advertising we want to call attention to these lands as "solid" and not alternate like most of Texas lands; as fenced into large pastures, well watered and convenient to railroad shipping facilities, to attract owners and dealers in large herds. I am going to Fort Worth, Dallas, Houston, and San Antonio, stopping two days at Victoria. Down in that country are owners of herds that must now leave Indian Territory after having been there long enough to comply with sanitary requirements for their introduction into this Panhandle. Whether to draw from New Mexico or Colorado cattle will be determined later.

Tyng's letter of the same date to Foster made the following report:

From Chicago and Kansas City to the Panhandle the general opinion as *expressed* by dealers and others interested, appears to be that cattle are scarce, and that pastures are in excess of all requirements, and, therefore, to secure tenants for Texas pastures these must be afforded at lower rentals than heretofore paid. In support of this opinion is quoted the fact that by recent act of its legislature, the State of Texas has reduced the minimum rental of public lands from four to three cents per acre per annum. As Paul of Panhandle shares this opinion, I have given it much consideration and have been slow in presenting to you my own belief that nothing yet justifies our *asking* lower rentals than have been paid for these lands during the past two years.

No man can yet correctly declare a surplus or deficit of good pasturage in Texas, or in the West. All that depends upon warmth and rains yet to come. The Indian Territory has been occupied by settlers whose small holdings make it impossible to keep there the large herds by which it has until recently been occupied. In Texas and all over the West the lands have been subdivided and fenced into smaller enclosures. Consequently the number has become greater, but correspondingly smaller of large pastures like ours available for large herds. The State of Texas has millions of acres of public lands that are sterile, broken, unfenced, destitute of water, and of little value for pasturage or anything else. That land is in tracts of 640 acres alternating chess-board fashion with like tracts granted as subventions to railway and other enterprises. It is likely to remain tenantless at any price for some years. You have failed to lease some 70,000 acres of alternate land in Block B-2, even at three cents per acre during the two years that five and six cents have been paid for the solid lands of this estate. The State is receiving rentals at from four to twenty cents an acre for some of its public lands. Considering these facts the recent act of Texas is good "for talk," but can have only a temporary and sentimental influence upon rentals of large good pastures like these. . . . If cattle are really scarce their value will rise enough to cover a higher cost of grazing them.

As we want to lease this enormous tract in as few subdivisions as possible, only for short terms, and subject to sale, we must to a great extent seek tenants who are able and willing to buy cattle on a large scale for speculation for such turns of their money as can be made in one, two, or three

A Decade of Leasing White Deer Lands

years. Such tenants must be sought at and around the main centers of cattle trading. To a great extent the rental and leasing of this land will depend upon its grass and water. It is yet a little early to determine what these will be as the Spring has been cold and backward, though the prospect is very good at present.

Before consenting to reduction of rentals, I should like to look around for two or three weeks among cattle dealers, to give the grass time to grow, and to determine with some certainty the prospects of speculation in cattle. . . . It is easy enough to lower prices whenever it becomes necessary to do so. It would be hard to get them up again. It is worth while to make some effort, and even to risk loss of a few weeks rental, before yielding to interests that are not ours.

The Search for Lessees

Tyng scouted around for several days surveying the cattle situation and searching for lessees. He wrote Foster from Fort Worth, May 25, 1895:

Any reduction of price will not expedite the making of new leases. Cattle dealers on a large scale must first be certain as to how they are coming out of their present holdings and of their chances for borrowing money for carrying new purchases before leases of large pastures can be much in demand. Large numbers of cattle will soon be ready for market and the crowding of them for sale, to meet maturing notes will probably check the present disposition to stiffen prices and to delay sales of young cattle. Rains have been general over the state and grass is very good wherever I have been.

Tyng felt confident of renewing rental of White Deer Lands to Niedringhaus, a large manufacturing concern in Kansas City, who had rented the lands in 1893, "Because their owners do not have yet any good place to take them, and because we do not want to crowd them into ejectment." Tyng also had hopes of leasing these lands to McKenzie of the Matadors, but said: ". . . he has been flitting about so much that my efforts to see him have thus far failed. . . . I will leave here by train tonight and catch him on the train to Trinidad tomorrow morning."

With reference to the Niedringhaus lease Tyng on June 8, 1895, explained to Foster:

I wrote you of my visit to Niedringhaus. As I staid two days in Kansas City, Heinrich Niedringhaus arrived in Panhandle before I did. I did not know of his coming there until I saw him. He is not the rich brother of F. G. and Wm. F. by whom he is employed but with whom he has no very responsible position nor partnership. From Panhandle he was driven in a buggy part way down to the White Deer headquarters, but had to return because of bowel trouble. Realizing the propriety of confining himself to light diet, but feeling hungry after the ride, Heinrich loaded his stomach with cabbage. The doctor unraveled his organs out of that tangle. Thursday morning Heinrich felt well enough to go down to the saloon and fill up on iced lemonade. I left him too cramped up to talk or to consent to my bringing him down to Pampa when he can travel. I do not know his intentions other than to get back to St. Louis without delay. He can know nothing of the condition of the pasture except through such information as has percolated to his mind through cabbage and lemonade; I had no business talk with Heinrich. Paul asked him if he was looking for pasturage. He answered "no" and said that his company was expecting to get out of the cattle business altogether.

In commenting further on the leasing situation Tyng advised Foster, June 27, 1895:

Goodnight very earnestly advises that the owners of this land stock it with cattle. This would probably be a profitable operation under management of an experienced cattleman like him, and give returns much larger than mere rentals. Whether the owners would on top of what is already locked up here, put up $200,000 or more in the purchase of cattle, is another matter. As I promised Goodnight to present this matter to you, I beg you to briefly communicate to me your opinion on it. I am bottled up here at present, waiting for Goodnight and also for McKenzie as this week terminates the Matador lease.

Tyng continued to negotiate with Goodnight, McKenzie, Creswell, and others for leases, but he said, "There has been little inquiry for the 348,000 acres recently leased to the Matador Company; too large for most men at present." He attributed the lack of activity to tight money and the gold-silver controversy. On July 22, 1895, Tyng expressed surprise to Benedict concerning Foster's position on money:

Foster seemed a little shocked by my advocacy of the greater use of silver in coinage. The enclosed excerpt does not prove my views to have been cor-

A Decade of Leasing White Deer Lands

rect, but it does appear to show them to be more or less shared by the British Linen Co. and by Williams, Deacon & Co. and by other notables commonly reputed to be fairly honest and to possess practical intelligence. I believe the outcome of White Deer Lands to be mostly if not entirely controlled by that of the money controversy.

Tyng was in New York, April 15, 1896, where he advised Foster of his plans for the immediate future:

It is possibly a little early in the season to secure grazing tenants for White Deer Lands, but with your approval I shall start for Texas this evening or tomorrow, stopping at Chicago, St. Louis and Kansas City on the way to place advertisements in the live stock papers, to gather information at the stock yards as to the condition and prospects of the cattle business and to confer with agents of the larger cattle concerns, or with such of the larger operators as may happen to be in from their ranches. Later and after brief inspection of grass, water, fences, etc. on White Deer Lands, doing about the same at Fort Worth, Denver and other centers of cattle business. After acquiring fresher information as to prospects and actual conditions, I will submit to you by mail such opinions as I may form respecting rentals and terms to be demanded and as to concessions likely to be asked and that could be properly granted in order to secure good tenants.

Tyng's hopes, however, were dampened by continued inactivity and by increasing demands for improvements at White Deer. On May 5, 1896, he informed Foster:

Since my last communication to you little has come to my notice that develops the outlook for leasing pastures. Dealers in cattle occupy a more prominent position of expectancy than I had supposed, waiting for some modification of the relations at [of] present high prices on the range to almost unprecedented low prices for slaughter.

In addition to the question of prices Tyng stressed the damage by fires, need for fence repairs and fireguards, the difficulty of keeping traveling herds off Block 5, the demand of the public for gates on White Deer, etc. However, on June 13, 1896, he declared:

Inquiries for large pastures have not passed beyond the stage of inquiry, although several parties profess to want them in case they buy cattle for stocking them. . . . The cattle situation is uncertain. There are for sale plenty of young cattle of the kind adapted to be held on these lands for later shipment to Montana and Wyoming, but money lenders appear unwilling to make loans except for periods too short to enable cattle buyers to make the turn. The number of floating herds sponging around railroad termini is unusually large.

On June 23, 1896, Tyng was at Denver where he reported to Benedict that:

I have got here some men whose talk sounds sincere enough to induce me to wait a week for them to get information on which to decide whether to lease or not. . . . It has been dry, dry for many weeks. The newspapers here are frantic about gold-silver politics which I trust disturb your serenity as little as they do yours sincerely.

Tyng found the same conditions at Omaha. On July 21, 1896, Tyng advised Foster:

I do not think *any* result of the two conventions now at St. Louis will at once affect White Deer prospects in any way. . . . Feeders cannot borrow money for buying cattle. It's a craze. Despair maddens the silver men, rancor and distrust pervert advocates of gold. Good sense as well as calculating honesty will eventually recover control. Meanwhile it calls for some cheerful courage to predict much immediate good fortune for White Deer.

Tyng continued in a letter to Foster, August 28, 1896:

The prospect for satisfactory leasing all this land this Fall continues uncertain. A number of propositions and much correspondence have not resulted in leases, mainly because of difficulties in raising money. . . . *Big* leases appear out of the question and I am continuing to fish for smaller ones.

Tyng wrote Benedict, August 26, 1896, that:

You asked for my views of the political situation in the West and South. The majority of the voters are honest and sincere, and *anxious* for reliable information upon which to decide their votes for or against free coinage and legal tender of silver. Nearly all the leading newspapers of the South and West, like those of the East, are against it. Instead of procuring and publishing exact and impartial information, and logical consistent reasoning, the sound money publishers are pouring out conflicting and padded statistics, wild prophecies, denunciation, ridicule, and a lot of Sunday School primer tommy rot that sickens men who want light and not insincere guff.

A Decade of Leasing White Deer Lands

The voters cannot talk much but they think a heap and are richly endowed with common sense. They hear a false ring in the silver talk, without being able to define it. But the gold literature flung at them is too rotten to swallow.

Tyng concluded his remarks on the subject of sales in a communication to Foster, November 28, 1896, from Victoria, saying, "Prospects of early sale of the lands are not just now brilliant. The Country must recover from its recent depression before there can occur much demand for unimproved land at fair prices."

Waggoner Bros. were negotiating for a lease of White Deer in the summer of 1897, which, Tyng said, "is the only chance I have seen this year for leasing 555,000 acres to one tenant."

Hopes for the Future

The last two years of the nineteenth century brought brighter prospects and more activity in both land and cattle in Texas and the Southwest. Tyng's hopes were revived. On February 12, 1898, he wrote Foster from Victoria:

Though nothing has been said since my employment terminated last Fall, I have assumed that you would want me to again take hold of White Deer, whenever something to be done might justify the expense. Under this assumption I have continued to act as if I might have been in charge and am about to thrust myself actually into your service. If in this I am too cheeky you can easily choke me off by telegram to Panhandle or by mail to Pampa. Having stuck to it during three years of despair I should like really to be kept on a little longer, at least until the now brightening prospects shall have materialized solidly enough for everybody's hind sight to become as good as have been we'll say *my* foresight. If we have no drouths this year, White Deer comes out on top. Should we have one it will be forgiven by next year if the coming "boom" does come. American folks are built that way. You may have noticed it even in New York. . . .

Inquiries for lease and purchase of these lands have been increasing greatly during the past thirty days. Few have been for as much as 150,000 acres, on lease, most are for smaller tracts. Some are for more efforts to tie up tracts under lease and options of purchase, and other inquiries from real estate brokers that show awakened activity in land dealing. An epidemic of land hunger appears to have set in all over the Southwest and is possibly more general than I have yet had opportunity for observing. The entire history of Texas and Western development is of alternating booms and "debacles." The breaking of each wave has left values unrealizable for a time, but to be picked up and carried higher by the following wave. We now seem to be fairly emerging from a period of great depression. . . . While we ought not to sell at still low (though rising) prices nor tie up the lands for too long periods at current rentals, we do not want to arouse or confirm any local hostility against "land monopolists" by refusing to discuss propositions nor by *naming* prices too far in advance of the present market. . . . Fort Worth is just now a "storm center" of dealings in land and cattle, two and one-half million being the published aggregate of such transactions there last week.

On February 28, 1898, Tyng added the following transactions for Foster's information:

Ninety per cent at least of the State lands within 100 miles of here are already off the market, some gone to lessees, mostly to purchasers and they are going fast. The Agent of the New York & Texas Land Company tells me that he has sold more land within the past sixty days than altogether during the previous six years and at from $1.73 an acre for one tract of 16,000 acres up to $2.25 an acre. His sale has been of grazing lands only.

Tyng in his report to Foster in October, 1898, advised him as follows:

A period of much promise being followed by some years during which it was impossible to sell White Deer Lands and difficult to lease them, and another period of promise apparently now coming on, a review of some facts and of public opinion will be helpful in determining what now to expect from the property and in judging its depression has been due: to mistaken management, to demerit of the property itself, or to general conditions that are passing, that have passed or that may occur. The management has been based upon an expectation of selling the largest part of the property as farmland, sooner and at higher prices than has yet proved possible, and it has been influenced by the expressed wish of the proprietors to avoid tying up its property by long leases. Depression of similar property in Texas and throughout the Western states have afforded no prosperous standards with which to adversely compare effects of White Deer Management. Minor and local errors do not appear to have materially affected general results. It does not just now seem advisable to abandon the expectation upon which the management has been based, nor to tie up any considerable part by long

A Decade of Leasing White Deer Lands 321

lease merely for the higher rental thereby obtainable. The ebb of depression has already turned to flood of enhancing values, both for farming and grazing lands.

As to the merits of the property itself, some are patent and generally admitted, while others are still discussed. ... It has been pleasing during the past ten years to observe in the vicinity of White Deer the evolution of wretchedly poor settlers on State lands (forty years credit) beginning in dugouts, living on their own crops, pigs and chickens with few or no bought groceries, and now owning lumber buildings, orchards, fences, good cattle, horses and implements and paying their bills by check against bank deposits. ... They have grown also to lease patented land from you, and they live and have prospered on some of the worst and most broken land we have along the east edge of Block B-2. ... Such facts are a warning against superficial or too general classification of our broken lands as "valueless except for grazing," and against too hastily [sic] assumption that they will be saleable only in large tracts for cattle ranchers and at relatively low prices. ...

The best demand and the best price is and will be for small tracts. However, excluding consideration of price at which the rough lands might be sold in small parcels, it is well to consider their probable value as large grazing lands. A first and most important difference in values of land for large grazing lies in whether it is "alternate" or "solid." ... Of the White Deer estate about 550,000 acres are solid tracts, and about 76,000 acres (in Block B-2) are of alternate land. Other factors of value being equal, the solid lands are worth more than the alternate for large pastures. ... When patented sections are leased on alternate lands settlers have free use of grass on alternates and their too frequent wrong branding of ranchers' stock and running their stocks [according to source].

With the exception of one 150,000-acre tract no large parcel of grazing land was sold in the vicinity of White Deer after the beginning of the depression of 1893. Tyng reported that a number of 20,000- to 25,000-acre tracts were sold at $2.50 per acre, but, added in qualification:

Large parts of it are, for good grazing of modern cattle, too far from permanent drinking water. This defect is a serious one to a tenant on short lease who cannot afford to put in wells, windmills, or to construct reservoirs for storing rain water, nor to subdivide large pastures into more controllable ones by fences.

The immediate demand for a much greater water supply was discouraging, and Tyng became weary of the continued "ebb and flow" of high hopes and depressing defeats from year to year and from season to season. His sale-lease program had not produced satisfactory results after ten years of operation. With the rapid influx of settlers into the Panhandle it was evident that leasing lands on a large scale was at an end, and that a definite trend toward stock farming was emerging. With the sale of Dixon Creek Pasture in 1903 the White Deer Lands were practically without living water, with the exception of White Deer Creek, which has an abundant flow of living water. Tyng, therefore, was compelled to turn his attention to the problem of providing more water on the plains portion of the property.

CHAPTER 21

More Water for White Deer Lands

THE OLD ADAGE "Time and tide wait for no man" was amply demonstrated on White Deer Lands during the last decade of the nineteenth century. *Time* was what Tyng needed most of all in carrying out his program on the White Deer Estate. Surveys must be completed and fence lines must be built and properly placed, more wells must be drilled and windmills repaired and erected, and old dams must be scraped out. In short, more water must be provided, particularly on the plains portion of the property. Time and money were required to make these changes and improvements. Tyng was convinced that he could finally succeed in making such improvements if he could persuade the British owners to hold on until the uncertainty of local and national affairs ended and conditions returned to normal. He staked his hopes on his combination program of the lease and sale of lands to provide the necessary funds to meet the outlay in effecting his program. However, ranch affairs got caught in the swirl of rapidly changing conditions during the closing years of the century. Time rolled swiftly on, while lease and sale of lands became stagnant.

The Need for a Demonstration Farm

In 1893 Tyng was confronted with the problem of convincing the British owners that farming had to be carried on at White Deer even though it meant a definite loss. In an extended explanation of this question in a report to Foster, January 1, 1893, he said:

> With such a factor frankly and truthfully stated, I admit the difficulty of convincing men strange to our western country that they will make big negative losses if they do not, and big positive gains if they do pay out good money to raise wheat at a loss and to raise truck they have no use for and cannot sell. It is like advertisements that cost money in that its results are hard to measure in money figures. The negative losses are all of the money we might have received but do not get; the positive gains are some part of the money we *shall* get for the land, never to be measured with precision, and not to be measured at all until the money is paid.

Tyng believed that successful farming as already demonstrated on lands adjacent to White Deer was not enough, and that it was necessary to give visible proof that the land itself was capable of producing crops, under favorable climatic conditions; that crop failures were not caused by any soil deficiency but were due to the lack of sufficient rainfall. He insisted that a small farm sufficient to demonstrate to prospective purchasers the value of the lands as farm property should be maintained at White Deer, even though at a money loss.

The Critical Water Situation

Tyng felt fairly secure as to leases of the Company's lands, though he was not too optimistic about the price of rentals. However, conditions were greatly changed by late spring. In a letter to Benedict from Victoria, May 3, 1893, Tyng declared:

> If the weather keeps dry until June the Matadors would not sell their lease from us at even 20 cents an acre. Their own range gave out entirely last year and is no good yet. I do not feel proud of the Matador lease. It was a tribute to timidity and safety. You can scarcely imagine how much

More Water for White Deer Lands

White Deer correspondence is piling in on me—in most of which there is little good for us, but which has to receive long-winded perfunctory attention. . . . Most applicants for grass need it, but they are hard up for money and their cattle are not fit to ship or sell. If I were in a fix to rent all of White Deer Land and to run it, I could clear from $25,000 to $40,000 a year by taking and keeping outside cattle in lots of 2000 and upwards. The cattle would then be ample security for grass and outlay. My correspondence proves this. But we are limited to a few responsible owners of large herds. . . .

Eighteen hundred ninety-three was a hard year for Tyng on White Deer Lands. In addition to the confusion brought about by the national election of 1892, followed by the panic of 1893, the weather was extremely dry all over the Southwest, and drouth conditions extended even into England. The problem of water supply became critical.

On July 6, 1893, Tyng wrote Foster:

No objection to be made as to price or conditions—the questions are water and credit. . . . The Spring Creek dam on survey 6, block 7, was the last remaining water available for block 4, and the western two-thirds of block 3. On going over there about three weeks ago to make some measurements found that it had gone dry for the first time in years. Sniffing the dry wind were about 200 head of Matador cattle left here from the lot put in last Winter so gaunt and thirsty that instead of running from a man on foot, as usual with range cattle, they came around me lowing and moaning for help. That sort of things do not help the making of leases.

As a result of the continued dry spell, farming was also at stake on White Deer farm. On August 27, 1893, Tyng wrote A. A. Holland from New York:

I depend on you to see that while I am gone no human neglect or carelessness mars that crop. You know whether or not I understand a square friendship. If that crop makes, White Deer is a farming country, and worth big money, and you will not lose anything. If she fails I will not be given another chance at grain on White Deer. If she fails White Deer goes for a cow range at $1 an acre, and I go out in disgrace as a fraud and a liar. Carson County gets another black eye and you will want to pack your grip. That's the size of it.

Tyng's Discouragement

White Deer affairs continued to grow worse in 1894. Tyng lamented to Foster in a letter from New York, September 20, 1894, that:

> Continuance of general business depression and the lowest prices known for over forty years of all general agricultural products have, for a time, suppressed all demand for western lands. No prospects now appear for a satisfactory sale of any considerable part of White Deer Lands during the next one or two years. . . . For mere exhibition of water no further outlay is required. That question is now thoroughly settled throughout the country. . . . As to farming there does not appear to be any way in which the owners of White Deer Lands can raise crops for their own account without direct loss, except by undertaking it on an extensive and permanent scale not to be considered.

A further discouraging note was sounded in a letter Colonel Goodnight wrote to Benedict, July 30, 1895, relative to the lease of Block B-2:

> As it stands today it will take a good deal of money to put it in condition to use. The fence all needs repair. There are but three waterings in it which all need work before they can be depended on. They are too near the fence to be valuable, so shallow that they will always have to be scraped. One broken windmill, one well that seems to have never had a mill on it. By the time it is put in condition to use it will cost as much as the lease is worth. It would then be good property. But little or no water in tanks. Do not want it.

Tyng was not occupied at White Deer during the years from 1894–1896, due to the stagnation in all business affairs. During most of this time he was in Old Mexico, where he was employed as representative and agent of a multi-million-dollar mining concern composed of New York capitalists. Before leaving White Deer he arranged with J. C. Paul of the Panhandle Bank to disburse all necessary funds for the protection and maintenance of the property. He left A. A. Holland in charge of the White Deer farm, and Harry Taylor was hired to live at the Pampa station to protect the property there and to show the lands to any prospective purchaser who might appear.

More Water for White Deer Lands

When business affairs began to show some improvement in 1896 Tyng wrote Foster from Victoria, April 7, 1896:

I have at present no other plans. If, therefore, I can be of use to you for a month or two in White Deer, or in any other matters, it would please me greatly. The winter in the Panhandle has been a mild one up to a couple of weeks ago, since which I have had no advice from there. It may be well that you have made or have in view some other arrangement in regard to White Deer. In such case it will gratify me very much to write you all the information and suggestions that occur to me as likely to be of value. Prospective tenants are likely to make objections in regard to the fences which are not in good condition, windmills, water etc. Such objections can be successfully met. It is also probable that some subdivision of the 350,000 acre tract will be demanded. It will be less easy to agree upon such a subdivision as shall not give to one lot undue control of water etc. to the prejudice of other lots. Like cutting the heart out of a melon.

On April 15, 1896, Tyng advised Foster that:

The general conditions that kept so much of the property idle last year, as set forth in former reports, have practically continued through the winter. It is reasonable to expect some changes in them with the opening of Spring. It is not likely that my absence from the business has lost the owners any opportunity of leasing or selling during the past few months, because of the general depression that has kept the demand for any prices of Texas land too low for any proposition that could have justified you in selling.... I will report to you from White Deer after fresher knowledge. I hope to find that such outlay can be met from advanced rentals and that there will be no need of any considerable immediate expenditure. This last will depend somewhat upon demands of prospective tenants. I have no plans that will interfere with my devoting time to this business. In fact I feel under obligation to do so while my services can be of any use. But if by July 1st I should not have realized expectations, it may be indecent to receive compensation for unproductive efforts.

Traveling Herds Deplete Water Supply

When Tyng again took charge of White Deer Lands, in 1896, he was having considerable trouble with herds of outside cattle and traveling herds seeking purchasers. Every herd drinking water and eating grass added to his problems. He reported to Benedict, June 12, 1896, that these herds:

... have been causing damage and much annoyance while making themselves at home on these lands. Our distances are so great that it has used up much of my time to eject them. To not have ejected them would have been to invite cumulative multiplication of the evil. To have employed an efficient ejector would have entailed the risk of notoriety and expense of backing an employee who might get into powder smoke–perhaps justifiably. At present the nuisance is abated and permits are being asked for crossing these pastures and for watering therein. But in the case of some *very* truculent trespassers, the hitherto successful blending of "fortites with suaviter" may prove ineffective. Then too respect for property must be established against my absence and against the chance of some of the land not being leased this year. The collection of a fair charge for reasonable use of grass and water, and a punitive charge for stolen grazing and water for damages would solve some difficulties, if and whenever practicable.

A noisy and advertised entanglement of a trespasser in meshes of law would for a long time induce prompt payment of fair charges and other attempts at imposition. It would put us to trouble and expense—once. The local Jim Crow attorneys are two-edged implements dangerous to use. Texas statutes do not fully meet our needs, except as to flocks of sheep or as to cattle within half a mile of our inhabited houses. Our problem is to give some one trespasser a maximum of trouble and cost with minimum of same to ourselves and without throwing any boomerangs.

Common sense in absence of definite statutory provisions must exempt this great tract of nearly 1000 square miles from the privacy secured by general law to ordinary fields or enclosures. The public must have some passage across it for persons, vehicles and herds. No public roads have been declared and marked over it. The passage may be in any direction convenient to the passer, and unfenced roads would be like none or like commons. Yet such passage should be made with reasonable diligence and without injurious loiterings. Grass along the roads (or in this case along the route) is unavoidably eaten and trampled, and natural waters can be drunk by herds without liability. Water stored at great cost in troughs or in artificial reservoirs is certainly property which may not be taken away in cows' paunches or otherwise without the owner's consent. If so taken, can it be proved to have value sufficiently so proved to constitute the taking of it a theft to the satisfaction of a Panhandle jury, and to justify criminal proceedings? Probably not. But in civil proceedings I think the same jury would award punitive damages and costs to the victim of flagrant imposition, similar to those frequently inflicted by traveling herds on small ranches, with impunity.

Tyng warned Foster that such matters would involve court proceedings, possible lawsuits, and counter suits and delays, and then asked, "To what extent, if any, am I empowered to bring suit in representation of Foster and Cuyler without special and previous authorization in any given case?"

In presenting his bill for expenses, Tyng on October 28, 1896, explained:

A hope that personal interviews might prove more effective than writing letters toward making leases, has led to much traveling which the long distances render expensive. A considerable part of the expense was also caused by policing the property and by supervision etc, of employees on various repairs and fence lines. The unoccupied state of the property has in itself (as with isolated vacant buildings), tempted trespass and trepidation, aggravated by the unusual arrival of small herds of cattle from Old Mexico, driven by rather tough citizens of Arizona and elsewhere, of inferior quality and stealing grass while waiting for buyers. The loud talk of political campaign has also intensified a disposition to disregard property rights of "alien landlords," "land monopolists," "plutocrats" etc. It seemed best to divert this disposition as to White Deer Lands and to cause it to be generally recognized that the White Deer owners take pleasure in fair treatment of everybody, and are prompt and also able to protect themselves against opposition. It has been politic to publicly demonstrate that the trouble made by us for offenders and trespassers has been in defense of our rights and not for money. For this reason a refund has been made of petty sums collected, as also to avert ill opinion of neighbors and reputable cattlemen. For sometime now no one has attempted to even enter our lands with stock without first asking permission, notwithstanding that this large tract must be traversed for passage between important points.

Inevitability of Stock Farms and Small Leases

Concerning the subdivision of White Deer Lands, Tyng wrote Foster from Victoria, January 10, 1897:

In case of White Deer Lands it is not possible to subdivide it into tracts of 20,000 acres more or less without cutting off many larger areas from access to water, the latter being rendered valueless, without making large outlay for making water available in them. Present values of grass do not justify this outlay and that upon subdivision of fences. . . . Some subdivision may soon become advisable or even necessary, but at present the prospect seems to me good for leasing the land this year in larger tracts. . . . I have been naming the price of five cents per acre per annum for tracts of 100,000 acres and upward for periods not exceeding three years and with the provisions hitherto incorporated in your leases.

After attending a cattlemen's convention at San Antonio in March, 1897, Tyng advised Foster:

The general financial disturbances of the past few years have curtailed credits and compelled breeders to get out of debt by selling cattle in number to offset low prices of a forced market. As a result the total number of range cattle is smaller than that of a few years ago. Pastures are not overstocked, breeders are comparatively out of debt, able to hold for higher prices and are doing it, and prices are 75 to 100 per cent higher than two years ago. . . . For the past two years because of tight money such transactions have been on a smaller scale than formerly and have required only pastures much smaller than ours. The facts above cited, however, brought the business of breeding cattle to a profitable condition such as it has not known for several years.

Consequently there is a growing disposition to buy small herds and establish them on pastures under comparatively long lease. . . . I should not hesitate to advise lease for a few years to a good lessee of a large tract, or even some rebate to a tenant who would take all or most of the land without further cost or care to the proprietors. Last year most or all of the land might have been leased had it been practical to have it fenced off into pastures of 50,000 to 100,000 acres each with abundant water and broken land enough in it to afford shelter to stock during winter storms. Irrespective of the considerable outlay on fences and water that such subdivision would have required, there were other reasons for not recommending it to you. Until our election excitement completely tied up money, there were several large operators wanting to buy cattle and to rent pastures, to whom I had hoped to lease, even at some reduction of rental, in view of our having to make no outlay on interior fences or otherwise. It seemed undesirable to begin splitting the property up for small tenants as long as there was a fair chance of selling it to a few big ones.

Tyng contended that it would cost just as much proportionately to provide water and shelter on small plains tracts as on larger areas.

More Water for White Deer Lands

Moreover, he estimated that it would require about $6,000 to drill an artesian well to provide sufficient water, since lessees of pastures of any considerable size usually borrowed money, and therefore, could not afford such outlay, even though it would greatly enhance the value of the land and would also increase rentals. "I believe we have a tenant for about 150,000 acres at a rental of $7500 for the first year and $9000 for the second year by expending about $5000 on fence and water," he said.

Tyng advised Foster, April 21, 1897:

The question of water is a vexatious one. Wells and windmills are all right for small herds and small pastures, but to supply this great area with sufficient water during dry times it would require a too costly lot of them. If the owners would consent to gamble $10,000 or $12,000 on artesian water, I do believe they would win. The land would lease and would sell enough better to recoup them manifold. The alternative is to wait for another coming of the rainy seasons we used to have here, and then for the folks to forget the dry seasons we have been having.

Land leases on White Deer were almost nil in 1897. One of Tyng's best prospects was a Mr. E. D. Wight, a large operator from Trinidad, Colorado, who came to the ranch to inspect the property with a view to leasing it. Tyng was anxious to make the lease and he provided every comfort possible for the inspection trip. In his report of the trip to Foster, May 10, 1897, he said:

Had a rough four days with Wight. Rained every day, at times hard with much wind. Took him out in a buggy from Panhandle with bedding and cooked grub from there. Got wet and did not get dry, having to favor him as older and visitor and possible customer. He has had dyspepsia but would sup heartily on cold fried beef. Then he would grunt, groan and roll all night, rolling the bed clothes away. He is adipose anyhow. Had to sleep on ground with him, as could not carry in buggy clothes enough for two beds, besides grub, oats etc. for the horses. He got so much the better of trading that I was not very sorry to have him break off. . . . In view of the required outlay of improvements, Wight's offer would net but three and a half cents per acre for the two years, and a part of the land more rentable than other parts. It will "keep" a little longer.

Tyng informed Foster from Victoria, December 16, 1897:

A general abundance of grass, a comparative scarcity of cattle, and a greedy demand for restocking vacant pastures and feed lots in other states have made large pastures in Texas difficult to lease out at fair prices, and a number of them are still vacant. . . . Water is our weakest point. Without sufficient and available water, however good the grass, pasture land is not rentable at fair price. That is our fix at present. The larger part of these lands depend for stock water absolutely on rain water collected in tanks or dams of which we have a good many today. The winter has been very mild and dry, exceedingly favorable to cattle but exhaustive of stored water. . . . The demand is for long leases of solid land at the low prices lately prevalent . . . with improving rentals wells could be restored by us or by our tenants. We can lose nothing by waiting till Spring rains and for new grass. In view of the rapidly increasing sales of land and of the very probable rise in rentals, it seems best to avoid long leases if possible.

In the spring of 1898 a number of offers were being made for White Deer leases. Among these was that of Murdo McKenzie of the Matadors, who offered five cents an acre for 200,000 acres. Gutherie Nicholson of Kansas City offered to build the required fence himself if given a five-year lease. J. D. Jefferies, a cattleman from Clarendon, offered five cents per acre per year for 100,500 acres of Block 7. Waggoner Bros. were also bidding for the lease of Dixon Creek Pasture. Tyng told Foster, March 8, 1898, "I have avoided offering the land and do not report a number of tentative offers positive for small (20,000 to 50,000 acres) tracts."

Tyng attended the cattlemen's convention at Fort Worth in March, 1898, and in a letter to Foster, March 8, 1898, he declared:

The attendance at this convention is very large—an immense mob intoxicated with cow trading—as bad as a stock exchange. Money is in unlimited quantities and credits of immense sums are given with an eagerness actually reckless by agents from Kansas City, St. Louis and Chicago. . . . Any of our lands not leased during this week of fever had better be withdrawn from market until after good rains. They are too scant of water and too burned off to bear inspection at present. I do not think rentals will go down. On the contrary they will go up whenever there is water enough for the grass.

In October, 1898, Tyng made a detailed report of the land and water situation at White Deer, somewhat in defense of his administration of the property during the 1890's. He maintained that his program was determined by the British owners' desire to sell the land as soon as possible—that the heavy outlays necessary to improving the property were limited by short-term leases for which large operators were unwilling to pay sufficient rentals to make such improvements. He admitted that grazing land on a large scale was a "disappearing business" and that future sales and leases would have to be made to settlers in smaller tracts. Moreover, he called attention to the state's policy of selling land at $1 an acre on forty years' time and leasing its public lands at three cents per acre, which, he said, had greatly retarded any prospects of improved sales and leases of his Company's land. He cited figures from the report of the Department of Agriculture to show that there were 17 per cent more cattle in the United States in 1884 than in 1898, but 20 per cent more people in 1898, a large percentage of whom had occupied and fenced the open ranges of the West. This, he contended, had resulted in the introduction of a new type of cattle better adapted to the closed ranges and at the same time had greatly reduced the amount of grazing lands. In short a new era of meat production was at hand.

This situation presented to Tyng an even greater problem of water supply on White Deer Lands. In his report he gave an informative, though brief, analysis of his problem:

Considering White Deer, all of it, as grazing land only is admitted to be well grassed and not to have been short of grass (except when burned off) during any of the driest periods known here. But large parts of it are not good for grazing of modern cattle, too remote from permanent drinking water. This defect is a serious one to a tenant on short lease who cannot afford to put in wells, windmills and troughs, nor to construct reservoirs for storing rainwater, nor to subdivide our large pasture into smaller controllable ones by fences. This defect was less marked during earlier years of our possession. There had been no long periods of scanty rainfall and as apparently a sufficient supply of rainwater was maintained in natural and artificial reservoirs theretofore made by the Francklyn Company. There were many large herds of traveling cattle to occupy our large pastures of 150 to 540 square miles to graze out on the drier parts whenever rainwater became scarce. For instance on blocks 2, 3, and 4 we have had one pasture of 540 square miles on which there was no living water, except one mile at the extreme southeast corner of block 3 and for two miles along the extreme west edge of block B-2. Taking five miles as a maximum distance to which modern cattle can properly graze from water, we had on that pasture 420 square miles of grass wholly dependent on stored rainwater, and a few wells. In Block B-2 (alternate lands) we own one-half of its 238 square miles with living water only at spots along its eastern edge. . . . Block 5 is better although its stream failed last year for the first and only time. There having been for the last two or three years few or no large steer herds to risk the confusion and annoyances of leasing a large pasture in common. A natural suggestion was to cut, by interior fences, the larger pastures into smaller ones of size to suit the demand, at the low rentals lately prevailing. The cost of such interior fences would for sometime have eaten up the income. A more serious objection is that, by cutting up the land among a number of lessees, a few pastures would have living water, while most of them would be wholly dependent on stored rainwater or wells of which the absolute reliability is still distrusted; that the present number of these would have to be largely increased and that their cost would compel the proprietors to make cash advances to be slowly recouped from rentals. . . . The question of rainfall on White Deer reliable enough for successful farming is a vital one on which public opinion has swung from positive affirmation to positive negation, and is at present divided.

A sufficient water supply was available for nineteenth-century needs, but it flowed too far beneath the surface for Tyng's windmills and well drills. White Deer Lands were on the verge of a revolution in well drilling and water production. But with public opinion divided on the water question and with inadequate outlay for drilling and fencing, time was about to run out on Tyng, and the search for water to meet the constantly increasing needs was to be passed on to future generations.

CHAPTER 22

Tyng Bids Farewell to White Deer Lands and the Panhandle

THE OPENING YEARS of the twentieth century presaged better days for the White Deer Lands. Land sales and leases began to move rapidly in 1900 with settlers closing in fast on lands adjacent to the White Deer spread. Large cattle owners, encouraged by the prospects, took their grass problems to Washington and appealed directly to President Theodore Roosevelt for aid and relief. Numerous land agents attracted to the area got busy "listing"[1] saleable lands and seeking both lessees and buyers. A spirit of optimism seemed to pervade the entire country. The strong national sentiment to maintain the gold standard, plus the trend toward a change in national party control, stimulated a move toward a new

[1] Land agents would frequently exploit landowners by getting them to list their lands for sale at a price mutually agreed upon, which was usually about $2.00 per acre. The agent would then sell the land for as much above the price agreed upon as he could get and put the profits in his own pocket. It was conditions such as these that caused both Tyng and Hobart to oppose the sale of White Deer Lands through anyone except the legally appointed agent, who was paid a salary commensurate with his duties. As a result of this no commission was ever paid for the sale of White Deer Lands after the sale to S. B. Burnett in 1902.

order of things. As a result of these conditions, Tyng believed that another land boom was in the offing and that the time had arrived for opening White Deer Lands to settlement. With this in mind he conceived a plan which was calculated to combine both leases and sales of land, and by which the White Deer Lands would ultimately fall into the hands of farmers and small ranchers. To accomplish this he set up, during his last years of service with his Company, the machinery for a program of disposing of the property.

Tyng Gives Advice on the Establishment of a Land Office

In order to prevent too sharp a break from the old order, Tyng believed that the first sales should be the cheaper, rough lands, most suited to grazing, and should be made to the large cattle owners. The Dixon Creek Pasture was well suited for such a program, since it had sufficient living water and both grass and shelter adequate for grazing large herds.

As a result of these projects, Tyng was called to New York in October, 1900, to consult with Foster and Benedict on future plans for the White Deer property. There is some evidence to show that this meeting was not entirely harmonious. In the Texas Panhandle at that time rumors began to fly that Tyng was contemplating the severance of his connection with the White Deer people. These rumors were confirmed by Tyng upon his departure for Texas. Just before sailing from New York he sent a message to Foster, October 29, 1900, saying:

A multitude of petty details incident to getting off have cheated me of the satisfaction of taking orally my leave of you. Your note enclosing a $5 check was duly received. I am sorry to have unwittingly caused you the annoyance. The "Lampasas" is to sail today. She should reach Galveston next Monday. . . . I shall be at Victoria two or three weeks probably. . . . Please give my adieus to Benedict.

Upon reaching Victoria Tyng found a letter from Foster to which he made a lengthy reply, on November 12, 1900. In this letter he further confirmed his intention to leave White Deer Lands. The letter reads in part as follows:

Tyng Bids Farewell to White Deer Lands

Awaiting my arrival here was your letter of October 30th, covering the one of October 20th from Godden Son & Holme, and asking the approximate cost of establishing an office for the sale of White Deer Lands, and the cost of surveys preliminary to such sales. Sufficient surveys have already been made and have been approved and adopted as official by the General Land Office of Texas. . . . The cost of further surveys need not be considered.

The establishment of an office on the land itself is also a small matter. You have at Pampa a nearly perfect equipment for that purpose and at the best point for it on the property. It was put there some years ago, not long before the flood of demand for land turned to ebb. (N. B. That ebb turned to flood a year or so ago and is again a rising tide.) At Pampa you have room for lodging and feeding visitors, barn room for your and their animals, good wells and excellent water service to settle all doubts about getting water. You used to have (to less extent the Matador Company still has) continuous demonstration of forage and good crops raised on the land itself, a railway and telegraph Station, post office and daily mails. To again equip Pampa as an effective land office you would need only three horses costing about $175, and about $175 outlay for sundries; say a total of $500 exclusive of repairs to building, probably necessary by occupancy of the Matador Company.

Pampa was established to meet conditions at that time, when the cost and practicability of getting water anywhere on that land were yet in dispute, when lodging and food were obtainable only at long intervals of distance. Even now the nearest place for that is 14 miles from Pampa, the next nearest is 18 miles and the third is 28 miles, when a stream of land seekers was flowing into Texas—a stream that soon dried up. Among the objections to establishing at once at Pampa a land agent of your own are: terms of the Matador Company's lease, they have full control and occupancy of your premises, and the difficulty of escape from running a sort of free inn and stable for everyone arriving with pretext or intention of looking for land. A custom of the country is for everyone to pay his own way at any village or town, but to receive free hospitality at isolated ranches, especially when arriving at the latter with any pretense of business. This would involve at Pampa, besides food and forage, the cost of servants for house and stable and other outlays petty in detail but large in their aggregate.

If you should decide to employ your own agent, I think, as things now are up there, you had better establish him at the town of Panhandle. If a suitable office and residence cannot be rented there for about $15 per month, one can be built, costing for lot $75, house of two rooms and shed $300, stable and fence $125. Other outlays would be $500 as at Pampa—a total of $1,000. The lot and improvements would sell for about their cost when no longer needed. The current expenses would be far less than at Pampa. It would probably be per month wages and board of a helper $50, fuel, forage, horse shoeing, repairs and incidentals $35, agent's board and provision for trips with land buyers $30—a total of $115 per month. During the winter or less active months the current expense would be reduced. Much of the land which you would probably like to sell first is as accessible from Panhandle as from Pampa. At Panhandle are a hotel and public stable where visitors can pay their own way while talking about land and while deciding whether or where to buy. Panhandle is an advertised railway town to which land seekers are likely to first go to make inquiries before going to Pampa, a town at which they can be steered away to look at other lands as easily as toward the White Deer Lands, at which they can be told that there is no use looking at lands which are not for sale anyhow.

We have never before been in a position to advertise the lands for sale. We have asked for offers, but a vendor must be able to state price and terms and to close a trade at its "psychologic" moment. Your agent's salary would be fixed by yourself. Plenty of men can be employed at wages you like. Of more petty stealing there need be little or no risk, but at such a distance from Texas you would want to feel reasonably safe against deliberate deception or treachery of an agent in collusion with buyers of land. The selfish interest of everyone on White Deer now is, of course, against your selling to others, against recommending the land, against advanced prices and toward discouragement of new comers. Your tenants do not want any disturbance of their lease or intrusion into their pastures. Those of them who want to buy land want to buy it cheap and without competition from outsiders. An agent on the ground or near enough to catch land seekers, show the land and quote prices, and not interested in selling other lands, can offset that opposition after familiarizing himself with the character and advantages of the property.

Tyng then listed a number of reputable local agents who would be available for selling land to settlers, and also proper agents for the sale of larger tracts.

The nearest professional land agents are: McClelland Bros. (whom you know of) at Clarendon 20 miles south of the south line of your block B-2. There are others at Clarendon, but McClelland Bros. have as good reputation as any. At Miami about 11 miles east of the east line of block B-2 is an

Tyng Bids Farewell to White Deer Lands 339

agent named Coffee of whom I know very little. At Panhandle is Dan Leary, a very energetic man. There is none now at Claude, 7 miles south from the southeast corner of your block 7. All the lands in Armstrong County have been sold to occupants except some held at $4 and upwards per acre and represented by McClelland Bros. at Clarendon. At Canadian 25 or 30 miles from your nearest land is T. D. Hobart, a man capable and trustworthy in every respect. You may remember him as having presented to you, a few years ago, a letter of introduction from me. He is not a general land agent, but is Agent for land belonging to the estate of W. W. Phelps. His office is at Canadian though he has a ranch of his own down on the Little Washita. As he has a young family an increase in pay would justify him in leaving Phelps and coming to White Deer. Agents in Amarillo are rather far away for effective service. For selling in parcels to speculators Kansas City or Fort Worth are the best points at both of which are a number of reputable agents.

The customary commission for selling lands are five per cent of the price where the sales are made for large sums and entail little outlay of time, trouble, or money, and ten per cent where the transactions are smaller and more troublesome. For instance to sell 640 or 2560 acres of White Deer Lands from Clarendon might require several fruitless trips of two or three days each with a buggy and pair of horses. Special arrangements can be made for smaller commissions, as where an agent at Fort Worth happens to run across a buyer for 10,000 or 100,000 acres of cheap land and can effect a sale without leaving his office.

The expense of advertising is one on which you can determine. Except at some of the nearby towns and by sign boards or posters at Panhandle and on land along the railway, I do not think there is much to be gained by outlay at present in this direction. Large buyers of cheap lands can best be reached by advertisement in city papers, but you want the home makers who buy at better prices, and whose presence on the land attracts other buyers and stimulates advance in prices. This class usually starts out by rail or by wagon to look for land when it gets ready to buy. It can be bagged on the wing, but is not easily flushed from home by newspaper advertising. The railroads are anxious to have the land settled along their lines and will cooperate with you in attracting the attention of small land buyers at little expense to you. It is difficult to steer clear from on one hand from antagonizing the professional land agents, and on the other hand from giving them pretext for "listing" your land on their books and thus demanding commission whenever the land is sold by anybody. Some buyers do a lot of preliminary looking about and inquiring of different agents, each of whom is apt to claim that it was his talk and recommendation that effected the sale. One reason why the commissions are so high is that they usually have to be divided with other agents.

A description from memory of nearly 1,000 square miles of land must necessarily be a general one. I regret not having at hand a map of White Deer Lands on which to make shadings or other marks for clearer illustrations. Whenever propositions of sale shall be submitted for authorization, a detailed description of the land can accompany them, opportunity for making a description being afforded while showing a particular tract to the prospective buyer. Meanwhile the following together with the map will give the Committee a fair idea of the general character and intrinsic value of the different parts of the land. Block B-2 contains the only chess board or alternate land. All the rest is solid. All smooth "plains" lands are upon a table or plateau lying at higher elevation above sea level than do the broken lands which slope downward from that plateau for several hundred feet. The plains are of rich, deep soil, a sort of "loess" deficient in grit, varying in color from dark brown to black—mostly black. . . . The broken lands nearest the plains are clay with some limestone gravel; lower down they become sandy. Having little rock they have been deeply gullied by rains, although scattered through them are many rich flats or valleys and slopes gentle enough for plowing. All these plains, slopes and flats appear suited to farming, and similar land in the vicinity is in fact being farmed successfully. . . .

The value of White Deer Lands, meaning only the price at which they can be sold, is a value subject to changes to an extent that must be difficult of appreciation by men accustomed to stability of values in older communities, or unfamiliar with the violent extremes of "boom" and collapse common to our newly-settled West. . . . Last summer George B. Loving tried to float in New York a combination of a number of large ranches comprising several million acres and several hundred thousand cattle, the owners of which were to take a large part of the securities. Those owners appointed a Committee from their own number to value the several properties to be put into the combination and among the latter being the White Deer property. Besides two land and cattlemen equally prominent, that Committee contained Chas. Goodnight, whom you know, whom perhaps Cunard knows. Although Loving only offered $2 an acre all around for all the land, conditioned upon the floating of the new concern, that Committee valued your land at $2.35 an acre for all of it. . . . In viewing that land that Committee valued it for grazing purposes only, and not for farming nor for sale in parcels. Loving's failure to float the new enterprise is ascribed to unwillingness of capital to go into new enterprises until after the election. He is now again at New York and may call on you with some new proposition. Winter is not a favorable season for roughing it and camping out in search of land. Then also many farmers count upon the sales of cattle for meeting recurring payments on land and like to wait and see how their stock gets through before committing themselves. Demand for Panhandle land may slacken during the coming few months or it may not. But I trust the proprietors will see in facts coming to their knowledge good reasons for recovering a confidence in their property that must have been shaken during the recent bad years.

Tyng Evaluates the Land Situation

In reporting further on land conditions in the Southwest Tyng reported to Foster from Houston, March 11, 1901:

The enclosed clippings are mere samples of items appearing in daily papers. They indicate continuance of interest in Southwestern lands which will increase with the passing of winter's uncertainties and upon appearance of fair prospects for coming crops. I shall go back to Victoria by the end of this week and again be ready for whatever may turn up.

Tyng appeared to be optimistic of the outcome as stated in a letter to Benedict from Victoria, April 7, 1901, in which he said:

Yours of April 4th was received yesterday evening. I will answer it more formally from the Panhandle after getting in touch with affairs up that way. From here it looks to me as if no great difficulty will be encountered in carrying out instructions beyond some delay in the mere getting around over that country and to the fact that the usual cattlemen's conventions at which that folk meets and makes most of its trades for the season, are over, and that farmers and stock farmers are now about planting corn and are not likely to leave home until crops are laid by.[2] I was packed up for leaving here tomorrow and can, therefore, start in the morning for Panhandle without bother.

When Tyng arrived at Panhandle he reported to Benedict on April 20, 1901:

I sent you the memo to show you how rents have jumped there from 6, 8 and 10 cents. They will soon rise greatly around here also. Your small

---

[2] This term was used by farmers after the last plowing or cultivation of their crops before they were harvested.

tenants are *not* indisposed to buy their holdings, nor is there any lack of interest in lands—quite to the contrary. Most of your small tenants began where they are with shirt-tails sticking out and have prospered but are not rich yet. Fifteen hundred dollars is a right smart money to 'em yet. Outsiders have been and are buying right along where lands are on the market. Are the White Deer Lands on the market? If so at what price? On what terms? What rate of interest? What kind of deed? What conditions? What sort of title? Can you show abstract of title? Does the record trace back to the State?

In a report May 2, 1901, Tyng continued:

Land dealings appear to be daily increasing in number and, gradually in value per acre. I am puzzled by the difference paid between those paid here and those paid fifty miles or so to the east and southeast—a difference of $2 to $4 per acre. Several theoretic explanations present themselves but I propose to drive on and investigate before reporting to you. . . . The speculative craze beginning to pervade the whole country from Wall St. to Texas oil is not likely to cease before touching Texas and Western lands. I hope you will not find me too deliberate or slow, but the present movement around here looks to me like only the scum and froth of an incoming tide spreading its force as it emerges from a narrower to a very broad surface.

A big factor in the spreading of this "incoming tide" was the extension of railroad lines, into and in the vicinity of White Deer Lands. Tyng in a letter to Foster, May 16, 1901, had the following comment on this subject:

The Choctaw Oklahoma & Gulf Railway Company has determined to issue $2,000,000 of new common stock, subject to approval of the stockholders, at a meeting called for that purpose July 9th for construction of 112 miles from the terminus of its actual graded dump at the State line to Amarillo. The common stock is quoted at $112, the preferred at $136. Control of the stock is held by the management—probably the Missouri Pacific outfit. Non-issue of bonds for above use is not satisfactorily explained. The line believed to have been adopted is nearly a straight one through the southern edge of Wheeler, Gray and Carson, part of the way within two miles of these White Deer Lands. I made a wagon trip over the adopted route and over those previously surveyed to come west through these lands.

Some difficulty is being experienced in getting right of way and town sites along the alleged adopted route. I hoped we might yet be in time (and justified) to offer inducements sufficient to cause enough deflection in the route to bring the same substantially within our lands. ... The route adopted cannot be much more cheaply followed than those surveyed through our lands last Summer, but the annual cost of maintenance would be very much less. So the routes appeared to me upon examination merely visual. But this Choctaw outfit seems to have inner wheels like construction schemes, town site booming, and passing the hat for aids, gifts, and inducements. These gangs often override the judgment of engineers. You can probably come in contact with the proper men to talk to by inquiring at the Missouri Pacific offices in New York, if you think it worth while. I am disappointed that no one from that outfit has called to see you on a begging errand. We expected much from the Santa Fe gang. That powder is burned. The Choctaw men are with a new, fresh and enthusiastic following. Times are also favorable to excitement in any direction.

These improved conditions brought about renewed activity on White Deer Lands and Tyng's hopes were again revived. On July 2, 1901, he advised Foster:

I went to Fort Worth yesterday mainly to catch some of the large cattlemen who must shortly be out of the Indian Territory because of the opening to white settlement of 2,000,000 acres of that country. The ones I want to see will not be there till next Sunday. John Andrews has wiggled in and got the Connell Bros. and me balled up so that he can plausibly demand a five per cent commission in case they buy the 107,000 acres of Dixon Creek in ninety days from June 30th inst. I wrote the letter to you yesterday in Andrews' office and read it to him in order to finally and effectually end his pretensions. Connell will probably write you, as I told him I had no authority to name price or terms, $1.50 having been tentatively suggested. I permitted myself to state that any price you would likely consider must be much higher than that. Jeffries was not at home but seems to have left word that he would give $1.50 an acre for the land leased by him. Paul says that Jeffries will pay $2 an acre for Dixon Creek. There is no need of hurrying. Land prices have begun to move, will be higher before Winter, and much higher by Spring if weather conditions should not have been extraordinarily adverse.

As to actual land sales Tyng wrote Foster, July 22, 1901:

Within the past year there has been a feverish demand for land. Every acre of public land has been bought in our vicinity on easy terms granted by the State—good, bad, and indifferent, dry or watered land. Most of it has been sold at an advance, locally called a "bonus." The State sells land at $1 on forty years time allowing four sections to the purchaser.... If it is advisable to allay impatience by making sales at once, this might be done by advertising for sale some part of the property "in tracts to suit" naming the terms and price of payment.

Tyng Suggests Plan for Sale of White Deer Lands

In June, 1901, Tyng made a detailed report to Foster in which he suggested a method of procedure to be followed in the sale of White Deer Lands. He said:

As reply has not been given to my inquiry as to prices and terms at which sales may be made, it is possible that some difficulty is experienced in deciding these points. First as to terms. It is customary to sell Texas land for a small payment in cash, the balance being paid at intervals existing over a term of three or more years and represented by promissory notes bearing interest at six per cent, or even five till paid. A deed is given to the vendee who thereupon executes to a Trustee of the vendor a deed which becomes void on perfect payment of the notes which empowers the Trustee to summarily sell the premises upon default of payment of any of the notes. As such notes are readily saleable to investors the sale of land for the vendor virtually a cash transaction if he prefers to forego the interest by selling the notes. Until recently rates of interest were at eight to ten per cent. Money is cheaper now.

In the case of practical settlers of some means, it might be advisable to demand a small first cash payment, or to distribute the deferred payments over a longer term, conditioned upon his making a well, erecting fences, buildings etc. ... Beyond giving minimum prices at which any particular part, quantity or class of the lands may be sold, revising and changing the minimum from time to time as circumstances may render advisable, it seems as if you may have to leave this matter largely to the discretion of the local agent upon whom you would have to rely anyhow, for description and value of any land in question, especially so in the case of buyers of only a few square miles. The buyer of a large tract expects to consume time in cheapening and in correspondence back and forth, and generally wants to deal directly with the principals. But the man who comes 200 or 300 miles looking for a square mile or two on which to make a new home, though he will pay more per acre than the big buyer, has no time to fool away on correspondence. He goes forward where the land is for sale and the seller knows his price.

Prices have fluctuated and always will. They are on the upturn now, will go higher than ever, but will never again get lower than they are now. . . . One reason why lands of the same good quality are higher in Oklahoma than in the Panhandle is because there it is not so deep to water. The best lands of the White Deer property are on the plains, where the average depth to water is 350 feet. This handicaps sale of plains land in small parcels nearly $2 an acre.

Tyng listed a number of necessary improvements that had been made on White Deer Lands, such as wells, pumps, steel windmills, new fence, dam repairs, and new tanks. "No more wooden towers or windmills are advisable," said Tyng. "They rot, catch fire, and get broken by gales . . . galvanized steel tubs are wholly satisfactory. But when rains fill ponds and water holes, some tenants neglect pumps. Wooden tubs dry out, fall apart or warp, and sometimes burn."

In a letter to Foster written in New York, December 22, 1901, Tyng seemed somewhat annoyed at Foster's continued delay in stating prices and terms of sale of White Deer Lands. He spoke with unusual frankness in presenting the problems which were delaying land sales and proposed a remedy for the solution of his difficulties. There is a note of complaint in this letter in which he said:

So little and direct information regarding sale of Texas land has been received since I was at White Deer last May, that I have tried to get some by correspondence before replying to your inquiry. Hence, the delay. The result is not very satisfactory, my correspondence showing more anxiety to earn a commission for selling land at prices low enough to make sales than to give me detailed information. Changes in the general situation have occurred since May which must affect land sales. . . . If the proprietors really want to make some sales, they must give definite instructions to that effect; setting a minimum of price and terms and trusting to their selling representative to do as much better as may be possible. If their minimum is too high for immediate realization, they must wait until the demand reaches it; as it will. If I speak frankly, I do so without disrespect.

In the matter of White Deer Lands, no price has yet been asked. Were an offer now procured that might merit your approval, you could not accept it. The offer would properly be submitted to Godden Son and Holme, who in turn would feel bound to consult the Committee, who again would feel a delicacy in acting without ascertaining the wishes of other parties in interest; particularly so if the price appeared low as it properly would appear if the rough, poor land were sold first, as I should advise. In the older and more settled parts of the United States, it is expected to use up weeks or months in negotiating a large land deal. Not so in the Southwest. Land there is too abundant to be fooled away on any one parcel. It would be easier to make sales through some representative on the ground. The prospective buyer wants to at once know the price and terms, to be carried over the ground to view its character, to be shown its boundaries. The seller should be able to point out its advantages, to skip its demerits, and to readily find or re-locate survey marks.

To sell lands so far from towns and inhabitants involving travel of 30 or 40 up to a total of 150 miles, one must have wagon, horses, bedding and provisions for camping out. A number of trips over the same land with different customers may be needed before a sale of it can be effected. It is, as you know, difficult to effect sales without sharing compensation with professional land agents who are in a position to send buyers toward or away from any given tract of land. In view of these facts the customary commission of five per cent on the amount of sale is not exorbitant in the Southwest if the agent is active and is honest in getting the full market price without collusion with the buyer.

Texas lands are nearly all sold on deferred payments, the latter represented by promissory notes bearing interest and secured by a recorded lien on the land in favor of the vendor. The notes are freely bought by banks and investors. . . . An attempt to departure from established customs would probably frustrate sales. The smooth, level lands of White Deer may, in small holdings become very valuable. I think they will. But to develop and expedite [that value] people must be living on them. A beginning of sales should be made at current prices without concern as to the future value of the land so sold.

My view is that at least 20 sections (640 acres) each should be sold to actual settlers at $3 as a minimum, one-fifth cash, balance in four annual payments with six per cent interest. . . . Rough grazing land in large tracts will not go very much higher for some years; smooth plains land will. The best season of the year for selling large pastures has nearly passed. Winter is a bad time for that. Buyers rich enough for taking them do not like the exposure of camping out in winter for land viewing. Nevertheless, I think the 107,000 acres of broken land in block 5, or 100,000 acres of the roughest land block 2 can be sold before Spring at the price and terms I have named.

Several professional agents would undertake it at their own expense and risk for the customary five per cent commission. I would undertake it myself. Whatever the proprietors may decide to do at present, they should bear in mind that, in the West, land prices ebb and flow; that they are now on a rising tide that may reach its highest point within a year or two, and then ebb. So much land cannot be easily sold at once in the limited time during which the top prices may hold good.

Conflict between Tyng and Benedict

As the program of White Deer Lands unfolded, the conflicting opinions of Tyng and Benedict were brought into bold relief. On December 24, 1901, Tyng wrote Foster from Miami, Texas:

I came here last night to recruit my horses and for mail. I have your letters of 11th and 17th urging the location of the county seat at Pampa, and stating that you rely on me to secure that result. Gray County has *first* to be organized into an independent corporate existence on petition signed by 150 voters qualified by twelve months in residence in the state and six months in the county. Such signatures are being secured as rapidly as possible. This is slow work. Many voters have been talked into opposing our move in the interest of a new town on the Choctaw Railroad. The entire 150 (votes) may perhaps be obtained in time for presenting to the meeting of Roberts County Commissioners Court the second week in February in which case an election can be ordered for about March 15th. As it is planned to contest our petition, we cannot "pad" the petition, but must have 150 *bona fide* signatures of qualified votes. Hoping to expedite [matters] I sent out several copies of the petition I am carrying around, but none got a single signature except. . . . Perry LeFors who got twelve names in three weeks and then gave up. I have taken up all the petitions in order to control the movement.

LeFors made the same mistake we did. He talked county seat too soon. He is for the Center. It was he who "inspired" the various newspaper items which you have possibly ascribed to my talk. I have promised *nothing* even by implication, and shall not except as instructed by you to do so. Nothing in print will come from me unless my name is signed to it.

Statutes are complicated, but the Supreme Court of Texas has decided that it takes two-thirds of the entire vote cast to locate the county seat at any one point more than five miles from the center of the county. Pampa is nearly twelve miles from it; Choctaw town nearly sixteen. . . . A north-south line through the center runs along our east fence one and a half miles from it. The county contains about 175 qualified voters. One hundred and fifty may go to the polls if the weather be fair. Men in the territory tributary to Choctaw will vote Choctaw; in that handy to Pampa will vote Pampa (if there be any Pampa at election time).... The more populous west half of Gray County contains, Pampa 55 votes, Choctaw 61, Center (at most) 20 with a total of 175 votes.... This is the situation stated as accurately as is now possible. It was different when I wrote you last Spring.

You rely on me to change it. The difficulties make the task attractive and too interesting to be dropped, even for Christmas at home after an absence of nine months. But in justice to your interests, I shall employ or recommend the first man equally or better qualified to secure the result of your desire.... Miami is the trading point of most of the Gray County people north of McClelland Creek. Those south go to Clarendon now, later to the Choctaw railroad. Miami people are against Pampa, fearing to lose trade. ... Miami took new life as soon as the Santa Fe got out of it. Miami now has three hotels, 120 children at school, and does a good business. Panhandle is still dying of Santa Fe dry rot.... Newspaper gossip mentions "active building operations" at Pampa.... In view of the law and the probable facts, it might have been worth considering to throw our weight toward locating the county seat at Center, with a view of moving it to Pampa after the Choctaw boom fizzled out and until voters came into our uninhabited lands. Benedict objected forcibly to that idea and I dropped it *absolutely*. Since receiving your letter of December 11th, I am, of course, working actively against it. The *Panhandle Herald* item was based on LeFors' talk, not on mine. I am sorry you and Benedict thought otherwise. I comprehend perfectly that I am to rise or fall on the results of my efforts to locate the county seat at Pampa. But if I fail to get two-thirds of the votes for Pampa, and if the law then declares for Center, whatever you may think of my ability, I trust you will not have suspicion of my disloyalty.

It is unnecessary to build court houses now or in the future. LeFors' people of Galesburg, Indiana [Illinois], are promising to do that and more. It is wise to stick to selling land and to avoid offending independence of people who *do* need civilizing by trying to force them into neater living and aesthetic surroundings: all *that* comes.... As to Pampa, we were beaten before we began this fight, but are slowly recovering ground. Benedict advised against "too much talent," and in favor of "coming out in the open." I prefer that also but it cannot be. This is a still hunt and a hard one; it must not be made with a brass band or torch light. The problem now is to get 150 good names. It must not be further complicated by county seat discussions before its solution. When I get them I can hold elections back *sometime* to enable you to get Pampa ready. I prefer not to tell you my plans. Some of them do not deserve my own approbation. *I shall spend no money without first asking for consent.*

Gray County was organized in 1902 with LeFors as the county seat. Tyng in analyzing the 175 qualified voters of Gray County evidently believed that with uncertain vote for LeFors, together with the rapid increase in settlers along the Santa Fe Railway, that he would be able to carry the two-thirds vote for Pampa. In this he failed.

At this time (1902) Russell Benedict worked out in his New York office a detailed plat of the townsite of Pampa and sent it to Tyng, requesting him to get James L. Gray of Panhandle to make a survey of the site.

Tyng lost much of his enthusiasm for the White Deer program after his month's association with Benedict in their inspection of the Texas property and adjacent territory in November, 1901, with a view to determining the advisability of establishing a town at Pampa. This trip brought into bold relief the conflicting ideas of the two men in working out a program for the future management of the White Deer Estate. Both were capable and aggressive, and each had strong convictions as to the policy to be pursued in disposing of the White Deer Lands. It is interesting to note that, since Benedict was second in command in the administration of White Deer affairs, he, as emissary of Foster, should naturally take the initiative in questioning all parties contacted on the Texas trip. Tyng on the other hand, recognizing his subordinate position and respecting Benedict's talents as a brilliant lawyer, remained silent on the entire trip. However, as the journey proceeded he felt more and more that, since he was on the ground and had acquired a detailed knowledge of White Deer matters, and since he had a lifetime experience on the Western frontier, his advice should still be sought in determining these matters, as it had been considered for the past seventeen years. It should be noted here also that Benedict was viewing matters from afar in his New York office, with practically no knowledge of the actual conditions on the Western frontier.

Tyng Resigns

Tyng's program was real and practical, but severe climate and bad weather conditions continually plagued him in his program. He finally gave up in despair. He had on many occasions been very positive in his declarations as to the future value and sales of White Deer Lands, especially in years of abundant rainfall. But each time periodic drouths kept recurring to defeat his plans. Finally it became evident to him that much more time was yet required and much more work was necessary before land values could be raised to a point at which he could recommend sales. Moreover, he had other plans made urgent by his advancing age, and he felt that he must provide for the security of his family. However, despite these unfavorable conditions, Tyng continued a diligent search in his efforts to find lessees, and perhaps buyers, for at least a portion of the White Deer property, hoping that he could tide matters over to better times, and retain the confidence of both Foster and the British bondholders in his program.

In Washington the fight for grass which was being made by the large cattle owners became entangled in a contest between Senator Joseph W. Bailey, who represented the cattle owners, and Congressman John H. Stephens, who championed the cause of the settlers and small ranchers. This postponed the sale of the Dixon Creek Pasture. For Tyng this was the last straw.

On March 12, 1902, he wrote Foster from Fort Worth:

Your invitation to make some proposal to work for you by the year was received February 19th. It could not have been expressed in a manner more gratifying to me and it clinches my sentiment tighter, if possible. Because I do not expect to go to New York for a long time, it seems proper to write some reasons for refusing and for this delay in answering you. Texas has suffered from a long and destructive drouth, the effect of which you can guess from the extraordinary jubilation over yesterday's rain in so staid a newspaper as the Dallas News which I send you herewith. In our White Deer vicinity no great harm has been done beyond drying up stock water and checking eagerness for land. With the outlook growing worse every day it was no time for me to talk of quitting. But yesterday's rain has broken the deadlock and land will again move, and to an extent that I do not think you believe possible. Continuous employment on White Deer under instructions from your office will not be worth half the wages that have been paid me from time to time. Many difficulties have disappeared and living there has become less squalid. A while ago the successful issue of so long and discouraging a pull would have been inducement enough to hold me to White Deer irrespective of compensation.

But recently there seems to be slipping from me the enthusiasm in White Deer work without which I could not make a good employee there. I am mortified by having misunderstood Benedict's plans in November and having permitted myself to run on a wrong trail from then until receipt of your letter February 19th. His recommendations are based on his own observations and on information given him by many persons out here. You and your clients approve them; in many respects I approve them myself, and he is away ahead of me in cleverness. It does look as if I ought to fall in line, but I do not. The county seat is not at Pampa. I did not in November display sagacity enough to refuse to touch this project. I am ready, therefore, to take what comes to me. Five years ago T. D. Hobart of Canadian, Texas, presented to you an introduction from me. You may remember him. Men are not made more trustworthy and conscientious than Hobart. Everyone who knows him, friend or enemy, would tell you the same. He has been selling land all over the Panhandle for sixteen years or longer and knows land and land buyers. The lands in his charge are nearly sold out. . . . He would be moderate as to wages and would be well worth what he would ask. There is your man. Should he decline there must be others. The Cattle Raisers' Association here will scatter tomorrow. As I have not seen my family for eleven months, I want to go to Victoria tomorrow night, starting back to Pampa Sunday night. I will do my best at Pampa until replaced— even well into May should you be delayed in getting a suitable person.

Changes in Land Titles and Management

In 1902 Lord Rosebery sent Andrew Kingsmill to Texas with instructions to find out whether there was any possibility of making sales, and also to expend money as he deemed it fit in connection with buildings in the town of Pampa. On arriving in New York he visited with Mr. Foster and explained to him Lord Rosebery's wishes in connection with the development of the White Deer Lands and the expenditure of monies. Mr. Foster told him that Mr. Tyng had recently reported a prospect, a wealthy cattleman in Fort Worth by the name of Captain S. B. Burnett, who wished to purchase the Dixon Creek Pasture, comprising 107,520 acres.

In October, 1902, before Tyng left the Company, Andrew Kingsmill of London, England, representing Foster & Cuyler, and S. B. Burnett of Fort Worth, Texas, entered into a contract by which Burnett was to buy Dixon Creek Pasture, consisting of all of Block 5 and three westerly tiers of surveys in Block 4, in Carson and Hutchinson counties, adding up to 168 square miles or 107,520 acres. The contract said:

The agreed price is at the rate of $2.65 per acre, amounting to $284,928. The vendor is to furnish the buyer with a complete abstract of said lands without delay and the buyer is to have twenty days from delivery of said contract . . . for examination of the title. If the title is approved by Burnett's lawyer a contract will be made and executed for carrying out this agreement under which Burnett will pay to the order of said Foster & Cuyler, at the First National Bank of Fort Worth, Texas, on the execution and delivery of such contract the sum of $23,750 and the further sum of $1,250 to the order of C. B. Willingham, as earnest money to be forfeited by Burnett if Burnett should fail to carry out the contract, and Burnett will obligate himself to pay to the order of Foster & Cuyler on June 1, 1903, the further sum of $3,750 which shall be in full of a commission of $5,000 promised to C. B. Willingham by Kingsmill for effecting the purchase. . . . Burnett will further make notes, of the form commonly used by Foster, payable to Foster . . . reserving the vendor's lien for unpaid parts of the price and bearing six per cent annual interest as follows: $192,464 payable *on or before* June 1, 1904, [and June 1,] 1905, and Foster & Cuyler are to allow Burnett a rebate at the rate of six per cent per annum on the $25,000 to be first paid, if paid, from the date of its payment until June 1, 1903, to be deducted from the $71,250 above mentioned. Pasture to be delivered June 1, 1903, now leased by Harrison & Popham.

Russell Benedict was selected by Godden Son & Holme "successor and substitute for Trustee and alternate Trustee." The lien was to be released for each $2.65 per acre paid to Benedict. Hunter & Flood of Fort Worth approved the deed November 6, 1902, and the deal was closed.

On returning to Pampa, Kingsmill bought for Lord Rosebery, at $5.00 an acre, a section of land on which he had a water well drilled. The land, located just a few miles from Pampa, was to be held in trust by Foster & Cuyler of New York. The present village located there bears Kingsmill's name. At this time Kingsmill met with T. D. Hobart, who had been strongly recommended by Tyng to take his place in the management of the White Deer property, and Mr. Kingsmill, representing the proprietors in England, agreed to his employment.

Tyng Bids Farewell to White Deer Lands

On November 26, 1902, Hobart wrote to Major Ira H. Evans, President of the New York & Texas Land Company, at Austin, Texas, tendering his resignation, effective February 6, 1903, when he began his employment with the White Deer Lands.

Tyng's Public Farewell

On March 8, 1903, Tyng published the following farewell in the *Miami Chief*, Miami, Texas. [3]

I had intended before leaving here, to devote a couple of weeks to making farewell visits to the people of these counties, who have always treated me so kindly since May, 1886. Circumstances compel me to forego that pleasure and to take this method of expressing my appreciation and of wishing them continued prosperity.

During the seventeen years I have attended no social gatherings, made no social visits, nor amused myself in this part of Texas; but have stuck to my employer's business and have acquired no private property or interests of my own. This has not been from pride, or moroseness, or want of confidence in the country. Far to the contrary.

This people is my people; the kind I like; the kind I have been with from boyhood; with this difference, that the hard times of a few years ago weeded them out and left here a more select community than is usual in a frontier country, of as fine a people as anyone could wish to live with. I am not seeking votes and I fear I may not see you all again; so this is not taffy, but is only a fact that a great many other people have also noticed.

This country has a bright future and I have often wanted to share in it. But it seemed right to let my employer always feel that his business here was not neglected through my using time that he was paying for, on any private business or amusement of my own. My temper is quick and is apt to lend more energy than courtesy to my language. Where it has hurt any good man's feelings, I beg him to accept my regrets and to forgive and forget. I have (thank God) two or three enemies, of the kind a man ought to have, with whom I should like to converse a little before going. But we all have to give up some little pleasures. The property in my care has always been respected, without recourse to Courts or Rangers. The good will of a good community is the finest of protection, and nowhere on Earth are just rights better respected than here. In seventeen years no one has, in word or tone, shown me even any disrespect that a reasonable man could resent.

[3] Courtesy Mrs. DeLea Vicars, Pampa, Texas.

Last year, in circulating a petition, I went around to our people's houses for the first time; it was just like visiting kinfolks. Now, with all that experience, how could I help taking away with me the warmest kind of friendship for you folks?

I do take it and sincerely desire God's choicest blessings on you. Goodbye.

George Tyng was an honest, hard-working man, dependable and efficient in every way. He was a "rugged individualist," a sage philosopher, a prolific letter writer, a self-made linguist and master of frontier lore who had a prophetic insight that few men ever attain. He was patriotic and he was a true friend. If George Tyng had any traits of character that stood out prominently among his many fine qualities, they were strict devotion to the task at hand and absolute loyalty to Foster and the British bondholders.[4]

---

[4] On January 30, 1906, T. D. Hobart received the following telegram from J. Peters at American Fork, Utah: "George Tyng was in his office at Wyoming Mine American Fork Canyon when a snow slide came and smashed the office building killing him instantly. He is being buried today near the mine. This was his request sometime ago." An account of the tragedy in the American Fork *Citizen* of January 17, 1906, said in part:

> Mr. Tyng had just gone into his office which is a leanto built at one end of the house. He had sent word to Mr. Kruse to join him to talk over some matters, but before he could reach the office the slide started. Without hardly a second's warning it struck the office crushing it from the main building, breaking it into splinters. Mr. Kruse was in another building in the course of the slide and was caught also. Kruse, however, was thrown on top of the slide and rode with it for about a distance of 75 feet, escaping without serious injury. . . . Mr. Tyng was evidently killed instantly as he still grasped a lead pencil when found.

It took twenty-five men about twenty-four hours to find Tyng's body. In further commenting on the tragedy, the paper stated that:

> If there is a man in American Fork who ever had a business dealing with Mr. Tyng and could not understand his great nature we have failed to find him. His life was simplicity itself and the request made in his will only shows how true to nature he aimed to live. Therefore the body of this great frontiersman lies on a little knoll on Kalamazoo Flat where he had often remarked: "What grander monument could a person wish than to be surrounded by the beautiful hills and scenery."

One is strongly tempted to conjecture that Tyng might have perhaps recorded another large volume of memoirs of his life of adventure and achievement on the Western Frontier had this tragedy not occurred.

It is interesting to note here also that Tyng had planned to visit in Pampa in 1904, but other events forced him to write Mrs. Jesse Wynne that it was necessary to postpone his visit "until next year."

Courtesy Mrs. DeLea Vicars, Pampa, Texas. Mrs. Vicars holds possession of the source for the information given in this footnote.

CHAPTER 23

The White Deer Lands, 1903–1957:
A Summation

WHEN GEORGE TYNG took charge of the White Deer Lands in 1886 a transition from the old ways of doing things to a new social, political, and economic order was in progress. Several factors contributed to these changes. One of the most important was the advent of railroads. The natural topography of White Deer Lands made them the strategic spot for connecting lines and for extending them further toward the Southwest —even to the Pacific Ocean. Transportation into the Texas Panhandle by rail made the migration of settlers into the region much faster than it had been in the old days of slow, covered-wagon travel. Settlers could reach their new homes almost within a matter of hours. Moreover, a greatly increased amount of household supplies, even a few cows and horses, could be shipped in the railroad car to add more comfort to the new homes on the frontier.

Another major factor in the process of transition was the new method for securing water with horse-drawn well drills. An abundant supply of water for household and domestic purposes could be reached within a few days, and windmills of the knock-down variety could be easily and cheaply erected by following the directions accompanying the shipments. In addition, barbed wire, now made with machines, was being introduced at this time into the Texas Panhandle. It brought fenced enclosures within the reach of all farmers and small stockmen.

Blooded stock, well suited for these small enclosures, could be shipped from the North and the East to supplant the Texas Longhorns, which had already prepared the way and had laid so well the basic foundations for better beef. Beef could be produced faster, nearer the home owner, and more cheaply, and at the same time the producer could add his surplus to the cattle markets and increase gradually his small margin of credit at the bank.

Gardens surrounded by irrigated trees and shrubbery, with the windmills which made them possible, could be seen for miles, small oases on the level prairies adding much to the beauty of the Texas plains. A few cows, pigs, and chickens, supplemented with a great abundance of the choicest meats of birds, wild animals, and native-grown fruits, filled the larders of these frontier settlers and made them a happy and contented people.

George Tyng, during his seventeen years of labor on the White Deer Estate, saw all these changes taking place around him. He came to feel himself a part of the Texas Panhandle as he played a strategic part in its development. Although he had contemplated resigning as agent of the White Deer Lands for some months, when the time came he took leave of the property with regrets and disappointment. His years of hard labor in restoring the estate and putting it on a sound financial basis had thoroughly convinced him of its latent possibilities for agriculture and stock raising. Moreover, his greatest desire was to convince the British creditors of that fact by actual demonstration. He realized, however, that this would require time, patience, and considerable money. Tyng had neither time nor patience. He was a man of action; his mature years were passing too rapidly, and he felt that he must provide for his growing family. He was greatly pleased when Andrew Kingsmill employed T. D. Hobart as his successor. The two

The White Deer Lands, 1903–1957

men saw eye to eye on the program for White Deer and they worked together as long as Tyng remained in the Panhandle.

The Hobart Administration

PROPOSAL FOR LEASE AND SALE

When Hobart took charge of White Deer Lands, Foster and Benedict had not yet worked out a definite program for disposal of the property. Hobart's long years of experience in selling Texas lands fitted him well for the work that was ahead of him. However, he approached his task with extreme caution and care in order to learn exactly what his official relations with the Company would be. Therefore, on April 3, 1903, he wrote Godden Son & Holme that he had offers for sale of large tracts, but that he was "not in a position to give . . . any explicit information about the land." He also requested the London solicitors to send him copies of the leases which Foster had made up to that time. "Some of this information I can get from Tyng," he said, but added:

I understand that several leases of White Deer Lands would require that I should receive definite instructions in regard to these matters at as early a date as practical . . . so that when occasion presents itself for making or renewing a new lease I may act promptly and intelligently for the interests of the Company without unnecessary delays and without having to be referred to the Committee.

Hobart also made inquiry in this letter as to the policy the Company approved with reference to the development of the property. With reference to the 107,520-acre tract of rough lands in Blocks 4 and 5 in Carson County, he said:

If it is the wish of the Company to begin development of that part of the estate in the immediate future, it would of course be very poor policy to tie up the land with a lease which quite likely would prevent such development. I do not feel that at the present moment I have any authority from the Committee which would warrant such action on my part. Now, if the Committee does not wish to begin development of that part of the estate in the near future it will, in my judgment, be better to make an absolute lease for a period of one, two, or three years, and secure the highest rental possible. I think the Committee would readily understand that an absolute lease of lands in a large body will command a better rental than land which is leased with the right to sell and deliver possession of the land so sold at any time. I am not arguing in favor of an absolute lease, but, as already stated, if the Committee does not desire development in that part of the estate at present, then it would seem better to make an absolute lease and derive corresponding benefits from the same. In my judgment, development in that part of the estate should be begun in the near future, but having expressed my views, it of course remains for the Committee to decide what shall be done and I shall endeavor to carry out their wishes. . . .

The enclosed copy outlines in a measure my views in regard to leasing this land, provided, of course, you wish to begin development in the near future. In that event I think no restrictions should be placed on selling and delivering possession in small lots of say one to two sections, or possibly more under exceptional circumstances, with the exception of sections on which wells and tanks are located and reasonable protection to the lessee during the winter months against being deprived, of say one-fourth of what might be left of his range from November 1st to May 1st. . . . It is quite possible that a better way to develop this part of the property would be to make a few small sales and then to make a few small leases to such purchasers of lands adjacent to their purchase. This will at the same time allay public sentiment against the holding of a large body of land and leave the way open for the proprietors to receive the benefit of the enhanced value of the lands leased to settlers. I enclose two forms of leases for your inspection, one of which is absolute, and the other for use in cases where lands are subject to sale. The leases have been used quite successfully in Texas for many years, and I invite such instructions as you may think best in regard to them.

HOBART—BENEDICT RIFT

On February 13, 1903, H. E. Hoover, of Canadian, made application for one of his clients for the purchase of from 100,000 to 200,000 acres of land, "in a solid body," for $2.50 per acre. Hobart made a lengthy study of the matter, and advised Godden Son & Holme that this would not be a good time to sell. "I think the land can be sold to better advantage," he said, "and the payment of commission can be avoided. . . . A little later I shall have much to say about the large tracts of rough lands as well as other matters." This was the sale made to S. B. Burnett of Fort Worth in 1903 at $2.65 per acre, an increase of fifteen cents per acre over the Hoover-proposed price. Benedict

The White Deer Lands, 1903–1957

came from New York to Panhandle, Texas, to close the deal. As a result of Benedict's visit a rift developed between him and Hobart over the question of power of attorney and other matters. Hobart, who was watching affairs closely on White Deer Lands went, without invitation, to Fort Worth to close the Burnett deal. In a letter to Tyng at Pampa, July 31, 1903, Hobart said that he went:

> ... to see that all matters we agreed to about the fence were reduced to writing. Benedict is here now. He is crazy to have the Panhandle editor to move his plant here (to Pampa). He wants to guarantee the editor $20 to $25 per month for a year, all of which I decline to do. Benedict says we should have an "organ" of our own so to speak. I will encourage the laity to come by using any reasonable means. But I do not want to *own* an editor at least at this stage of the game. I tell Benedict that the most effective mode of advertising really is to do what we have agreed to and do it at once, and a simple announcement of that backed up by the facts will do more good than all of the whooping up that he proposes.
>
> I have been pointing out a few of the defects in the power of attorney to him. He said it was intended that I should execute leases, but that the deeds should be executed in New York. I told him that was not the intention of the Committee, as they had made their intentions very plain. As we were riding along on the train he said that I needed a clerk. I knew what was coming and told him that I had a fellow working for me by the name of [M. K.] Brown that I thought would fill the bill. Brown met us at the train and when I introduced him as Mr. Kingsmill's nephew, I think Mr. Benedict turned just a little pale. I shall treat Mr. B nicely, but will have him distinctly understand that I am the *Committee's employee*.

Hobart wrote Tyng again, on August 30, 1903, that he was much annoyed at not having received deeds which Benedict had promised to send him on his return to New York, and that Benedict would be in trouble if they did not come soon. He commented further:

> I at one time was quite inclined to your view that it would be just as well, perhaps better to have the deeds executed in New York. But innumerable delays of the past, and what will likely occur in the future, if I have to depend on New York for the deeds, have incited a fired determination on my part to have a suitable power of attorney to enable me to deal with the property.... Just as soon as this is settled you may look for my advertisement in the papers.... I received another very satisfactory letter from Mr.

G. S. & H. [Godden Son & Holme]. The Company seems inclined to trust me as far as I could wish and I certainly appreciate it. I fully appreciate what you say about Mr. Kingsmill, and I feel confident that he will stand by me. My task is difficult as it is, and would be much more difficult if it was not for him.

HOBART TAKES HIS PROBLEMS TO LONDON

Hobart realized that the British creditors understood nothing about conditions in Texas and that they were interested only in transferring White Deer Lands into cash in order to satisfy the first lien on the property. He was also convinced that his task would require interminable delays at best, and that the holders of the lien would have to understand and approve of his program if he was to succeed. He determined, therefore, to sail for London, where he could explain his plans directly to the Directors.

Hobart never did things on the spur of the moment. He always looked ahead and planned every undertaking in detail. Before sailing for England he secured letters of introduction from United States congressmen, and other influential leaders, to the American ambassador and other high officials in England. He also wrote his kinsmen and his former employer, Major Ira H. Evans, for advice. The Major was pleased that Hobart was going to make the trip, for he believed that it would clear up all possible misunderstandings between Hobart and his new employers. He advised Hobart:

> Dress is very important with Englishmen and in London. You will need a Prince Albert suit and silk hat over there. Foster is strong socially and you will have to be ready to hold your own with him. You should take along full data as to deeds etc. to support your statements, copies of Tyng's letters etc.

Hobart, dignified and versatile man that he was, could mix and mingle with the utmost ease and composure as a peer among the socially elite. He made all due preparations for his journey, and, on June 8, 1904, accompanied by his young son Warren, he sailed on the *Teutonic* of the White Star Line for England. He was well received in London, both lien holders and bondholders giving their hearty approval of his program for the disposal of White Deer Lands.

While Hobart was in England he spent several days in the home

The White Deer Lands, 1903–1957 361

of Brown's relatives, who lived near London. During his stay there he wrote Brown commending him for managing the ranch so well during his absence and added, "Your family have shown me every courtesy and have given me a royal visit. I will tell you more about it on my return."

HOBART STUDIES LAND TITLES

Hobart's chief objective, and perhaps his greatest contribution to White Deer Estate, was the removal of all possible defects in titles to the property in order to prevent any possible law suit, either in state or local courts, against prospective clients who might make purchases on the lands.

In a letter written to Godden Son & Holme, January 24, 1906, Hobart explained the problem:

> I thought we had the question in regard to the title of White Deer Lands pretty thoroughly settled, especially after the sale of the Dixon Creek Pasture to S. B. Burnett, the title being passed on and approved by Messrs. Hunter & Flood, but it appears that there are still some matters that need clearing up. You will remember that I reported the sale of the S. W. quarter of survey No. 89 Block 3, to H. B. Hendricks of Miami, Texas. Hendricks is a well known lawyer of this locality and the title was passed on by his firm (Hendricks & Ewing). Mr. Hendricks made a very careful examination of the title and the result of his research of the records is embraced in an opinion which is herewith enclosed. It seems that the notes originally given by the Francklyn Company to the New York & Texas Land Company Ltd., were transferred without recourse by that Company to the Farmers Loan & Trust Company by the latter Company to Mr. Benedict and by Mr. Benedict to Messrs. Elgood & Godden, Trustees. In order to place these notes of record in the various counties where the land is situated Judge Hunter suggested, that Mr. Benedict acknowledge those transfers to Messrs. Elgood & Godden before a Notary Public and this was accordingly done and the notes placed of record, you observe that Messrs. Hendricks & Ewing held that it is necessary to have a regular transfer of the notes and lien that existed upon the land, that they also hold that the appointment of Mr. Benedict as Trustee is void under the Texas laws. I was considerably troubled at the result of their conclusions and hoped that they might be mistaken in the position they have taken; I accordingly decided to lay the matter before Messrs. Cochran & Penn lawyers of very high standing at

Austin, Texas, and they substantially agree with Messrs. Hendricks & Ewing, as will be seen by their opinion which I herewith enclose. In laying these matters before Messrs. Hendricks & Ewing as well as Messrs. Cochran & Penn, I in no way disclosed to them the relations that exist between the Holders of the notes and Messrs. Foster & Cuyler, preferring that they should examine the matter as any outside lawyer might be called on to do. These gentlemen not only hold that a regular transfer of the lien is necessary, but they also hold that the endorsements of the notes referred to by the New York & Texas Land Company, Ltd., to the Farmers Loan & Trust Company by the latter to Mr. Benedict are not legally of record in the different Counties for the reasons that these endorsements were not acknowledged as above cited. I am fully convinced that these matters need careful attention. Fortunately the New York & Texas Land Company is still in existance [sic], though in strict confidence I will say that I have it from good authority that this Company will be a thing of the past very shortly, consequently I felt obliged to act quickly so far as that Company was concerned and employed Messrs. Cochran & Penn to procure a transfer of the lien referred to in proper form from that Company, which I also herewith enclose for your inspection. This matter may be somewhat delicate to take up with Mr. Foster, still I believe he will realize the importance of it when he has all the light before him.

We are making quite a number of sales and you can readily understand what a set back it would give the White Deer business if some one of the parties to whom we sell land should employ an attorney who would raise these questions. As you are aware a great deal of talk was indulged in, in the past in this country to the effect that the title to White Deer Lands was defective, several parties have consulted Messrs. Hendricks & Ewing, and these parties have been assured that they would probably have no trouble with their title, that there were some irregularities which would doubtless be cleared up all right. Messrs. Hendricks & Ewing have given this assurance to people upon my assuring them that I would do all I could to have these matters straightened up on the record.

Another point which I have perhaps overlooked is, that the original deed of Trust provided that the land could only be released from this lien in a certain specific way and the lawyers referred to, you will note hold this course must be followed or, that the entire lien must be released. . . . What further action is taken in the matter of course rests with the Committee and yourselves. I have employed Messrs. Hendricks & Ewing to prepare a complete abstract to these lands to which they will add their certificate that they consider the title absolutely clear if the matters referred to can be straight-

The White Deer Lands, 1903-1957 363

ened out. This abstract I wish to have published so that I can place a copy of it in the hand of every purchaser.

The death of C. C. Cuyler in 1910 caused Hobart much trouble and anxiety in clearing up the legal difficulties involved in probating Cuyler's will. He sought much legal advice from Cochran & Penn, Austin attorneys, before he succeeded in having the will probated and recorded in Carson County, July 26, 1912. He also carefully examined all deeds and abstracts of lands he sold while at White Deer.

Hobart spent more than twenty years of hard but fruitful labor in selling and leasing White Deer Lands. His work, together with that of his able assistants, M. K. Brown and C. P. Buckler, added millions of dollars to the value of the property.

Changes in Administration of White Deer

In 1924, when he was again in London, Hobart tendered, to the British Committee, his resignation as Texas agent of White Deer Lands, and recommended that M. K. Brown and C. P. Buckler be given a joint power of attorney to act in his place. After Brown's retirement, on January 1, 1935, the Committee decided to let the joint power stand and requested Brown to act in an advisory capacity when needed.

Upon the death of Frederic de P. Foster in June, 1929, some changes were made in the administration of White Deer Lands. Mrs. Foster conveyed all her "right, title and interest" to Russell Benedict, who was chosen to act as successor trustee to Foster. In making his income-tax reports Foster had always included Cuyler's property along with his own as a part of the report. Russell Benedict continued this practice and reported all the income from the White Deer Trust, and from other sources, as his own personal income, thereby again increasing the taxes attributable to White Deer income over the amount that should have been paid had the income been reported correctly.[1]

On October 1, 1931, Russell Benedict conveyed one-half interest in the White Deer Trust properties to his son, Williston Benedict, who as the sole American trustee became the taxpayer. Williston Benedict also treated the White Deer Trust property as his own personal income for

[1] Report of Williston Benedict, president of White Deer Corporation, to the stockholders of the corporation at New York City, April 30, 1957.

income-tax purposes, and consequently, the tax had continued to be reported incorrectly. This furnished the basis for the taxpayer's claim for refund for the calendar years 1943–1944.

Discovery of Gas and Oil

In 1919 oil and gas were discovered in Carson County, and soon the field was extended into Gray and Hutchinson counties, and was later pushed over into the border of Roberts County. With improved techniques applied to drilling operations, the field spread rapidly over wide areas. For the British and American owners this was the "boom" that Tyng had predicted fifteen years before. Liquid gold poured into the pockets of alien and American owners in large quantities. People became greatly excited and flocked into these new oil fields in great numbers. Towns grew up overnight where, only a year or two before, lands had been used for ranching and grazing purposes. For example, Borger in 1923 boasted a population of 16,000, with the boom still going. Hobart wrote Foster, June 20, 1919, that "There are all kinds of wild-cat schemes in the air in this country in regard to the oil situation." World War I multiplied the demand for these products, and as a result of improved techniques as applied to drilling, millions of barrels of crude oil were being pumped out of these underground reservoirs into whatever natural storage tanks happened to be near the wells. Moreover, millions of cubic feet of gas was being blown into the air daily and wasted.

As a result of the discovery of oil Foster and Benedict received valuable and substantial income for several years. However, in 1931 American income taxes were greatly increased, and the income from the properties, added to Benedict's other income, put him each year in a higher bracket, "at times as high as 90 per cent. At the same time a relatively small per cent of the income and liquidation proceeds was paid to the owners" (Benedict report of April 30, 1957).

Liquidation of White Deer Lands

Williston Benedict, representing the Directors, made an extended report to the stockholders on April 30, 1957. In his report he informed the British owners that "The fact of non-ownership in the record title was not reflected in the records in Texas; it was a closely

The White Deer Lands, 1903–1957

guarded secret until 1949 when the White Deer Corporation was formed and only after I had deeded all the remaining properties to the new corporation . . . a Delaware corporation [was] authorized to do business in Texas . . ."

Benedict commented further:

Recently, the Bureau of Internal Revenue ruled that with respect to the Corporation's sale of real property relative to its fiscal year ended October 31, 1952, White Deer Corporation was in the real estate business. Accordingly the net gain was taxed at ordinary income rather than capital gain rates, and the net deficiency amounted to $19,066.44 (which deficiency the corporation paid in 1956). The corporation has filed a claim for refund with respect to this payment, and the legal action in the Court of Claims is contemplated, and if the foregoing ruling of the Bureau of Internal Revenue be not reversed, the corporation may be assessed additional taxes for all years since October 31, 1952 in connection with the reported gain on its land sales.

In the meantime, . . . the stock of the corporation has become owned by Americans who are not disqualified from owning the properties by Texas law, as individuals rather than as stockholders. For them, and indeed for all the stockholders, the corporation is but a holding company and now serves no purpose—except that it is possibly a convenience—a very expensive convenience.

Accordingly, all of the directors and many of the stockholders think we should liquidate the corporation. The Directors believe if they should now liquidate, it would be vastly to the benefit of all the stockholders, thus save the corporate taxes, reduce expenses, and permit each stockholder to pay his or her own income taxes on his or her individual share in the former corporate income. . . .

This majority of American citizens owners enabled White Deer Corporation to qualify legally as a domestic corporation (as distinguished from an alien corporation); and thus be allowed to own property in Texas, and to have a minority of alien landholders. . . . What is now left of income and land sales after corporate taxes goes to the stockholders in the form of dividends, again taxable to them as ordinary income. . . . The objects for which the corporation was originally constituted having been wholly carried into effect, and having sold between 1949 and 1956 nearly all of the remaining real estate, leaving only the office building and some town lots not readily saleable, it is desirable that the corporation should be liquidated and its assets distributed among the owners of the stock.

Benedict said in this same report of April 30, 1957:

The practical disposition of the real estate to the stockholders in the event of liquidation has always been a serious problem. Except for cash and oil royalties, distribution of real estate in kind would not be feasible for several reasons. It could not be made to British stockholders for reasons stated above. . . . The real estate could not be distributed as such. . . . If the property be sold within a twelve months period by the corporation to one person in a single transaction, the sale would, in the opinion of the tax counsel, be completely tax free to the corporation and would obviate all these problems, and permit ease of distribution of the proceeds. In overcoming these problems, and in order to facilitate the liquidation and to receive the tax benefit permitted by section 337 of the Internal Revenue Code, Mr. C. P. Buckler, a Director, Vice-President, Agent, and largest stockholder in the corporation, has consented to purchase the real estate for $43,411. (This exceeds the appraised value), and to pay $1550 for the used car, and personal property of a minor nature. In the opinion of the Directors it is believed that it is in the best interest of the corporation for the reasons above stated that this offer be accepted. They believe the price to be fair, and such a sale for cash will solve the major problems in the way of a complete distribution of the assets of the corporation. Anyone of the American stockholders who desires to offer more for all the property than Mr. Buckler's offer, is free to do so on or before May 31, 1957. . . . Certain mineral property of the corporation is not now embraced in mineral leases, because of lack of demand. After the corporation is liquidated the expense of obtaining a lease or leases, on such interest from stockholders would be prohibitive. It is, therefore, believed desirable that a lease be given to Cecil P. Buckler for twenty years, so that if there be any demand for lease, he or his successor can transfer the same to the oil company desiring it. Under such a lease and trust, all payments and royalties, less necessary expense, would be paid directly to the stockholders.

With a view to solving all these problems, a meeting of the Directors was held on February 7, 1957. The Directors adopted resolutions for a complete liquidation of the White Deer Corporation, and notified the stockholders that a meeting would be held at New York City, on May 29, 1957. At this meeting Mr. William Jarrel Smith, a director, presented to President Williston Benedict a sealed bid of M. K. Brown to purchase from the liquidating corporation the remainder of the White Deer Lands and town lots in White Deer and Kingsmill for

The White Deer Lands, 1903–1957

a sum of $70,000, which was considerably in excess of the bid made by C. P. Buckler. Brown said he knew from past experience the value of this property and felt sure he would make a substantial profit at this figure. The Directors approved the $70,000 bid of M. K. Brown, and the property was transferred to him. Hereupon the White Deer Corporation passed into history after almost one hundred years of successful operation.

At the time the liquidation of the White Deer Lands took place, oil production had settled down to a well regulation system, and a strict policy of conservation was being followed. In 1958 Gray, Carson, Hutchinson, and Roberts counties were producing annually 32,850,816 barrels of oil; the grand total produced up to that date was 974,265,960.[2] This was an increase over the production in 1938, when the four counties with a population of 54,202 citizens owned 101,833 head of cattle and produced 36,159,816 barrels of crude oil annually with a daily production of 96,000 barrels.[3] Land values had risen to several hundred dollars per acre. Scientific research had been perfected to the point where the elements of oil and gas could be analyzed and separated into helium gas, sulphur, carbon black, explosives, butadiene, and plastics, to be used in almost every line of human endeavor. It seems safe to conclude that these four counties are yet destined to produce untold millions of wealth in years to come; a far cry from the income from two- and three-dollar-per-acre pasture land in the Panhandle soon after the Civil War.

The Francklyn Land & Cattle Company and its successors experienced many changes in the short period of their operations in the Texas Panhandle. This area was an open range when the Francklyn Company came into it, with more than a dozen large cattle concerns already well established in the region. However, the country was being fenced rapidly. This development encouraged small landowners to settle and engage in farming and stock raising. Stiff competition for grass and the introduction of hand tools and machinery also encouraged use of the land on a smaller scale. The Francklyn Company was forced to

---

[2] *The Texas Almanac, 1961–1962* (as compiled by the State Comptroller of Public Accounts, Austin, Texas), p. 145.
[3] *The Texas Almanac, 1939–1940*, (as compiled by the Texas Mid-Continent Oil and Gas Association), p. 219.

yield to the trend of the times. Then, in 1919, the discovery of oil and gas, aided by the scientific processing of their by-products, made the exploitation of this natural resource the dominant enterprise of the White Deer Lands, while farming and stock raising continued as subordinate to the major industry. Large cattle corporations belonged to the past.

APPENDIX

White Deer Lands Management: Tables of Organization

FRANCKLYN LAND & CATTLE COMPANY, 1882–1886

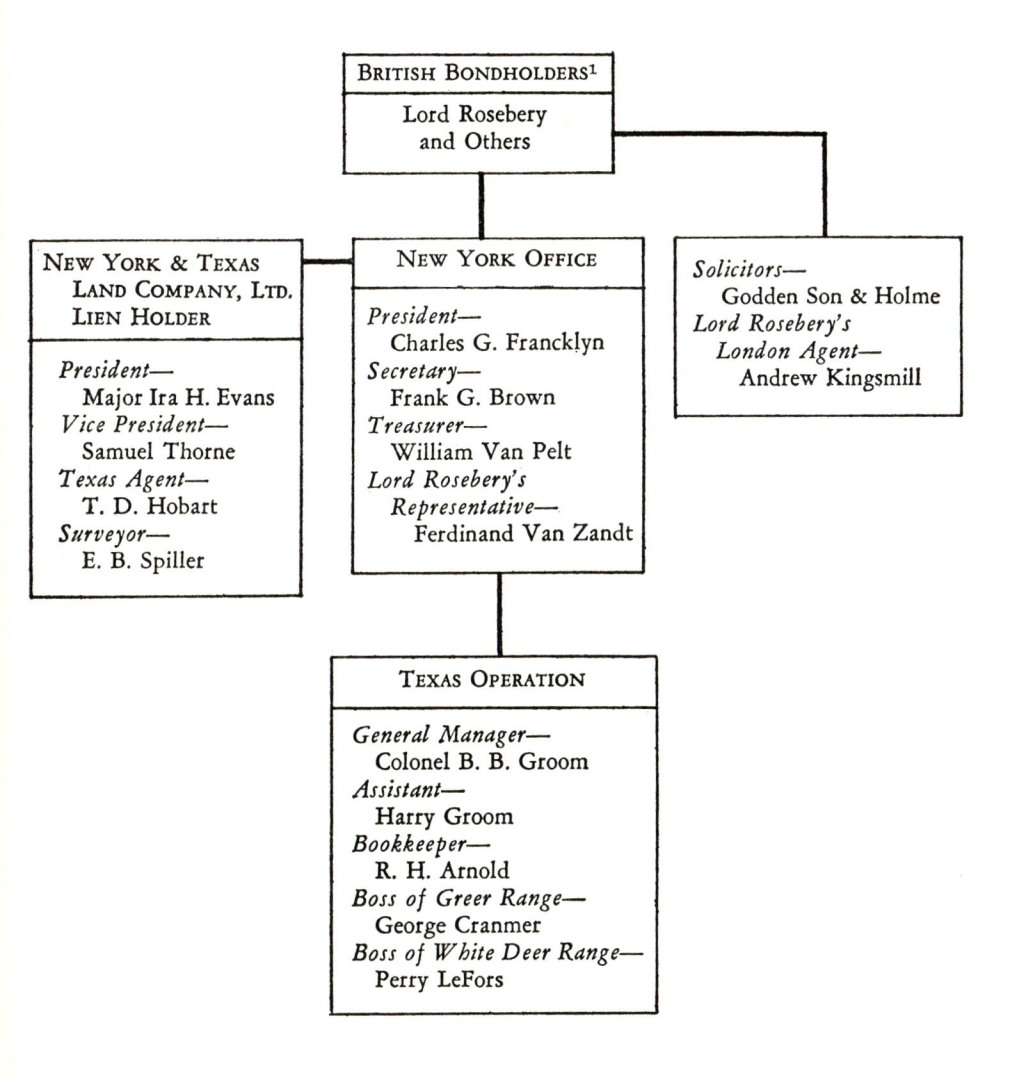

British Bondholders[1]
Lord Rosebery and Others

New York & Texas Land Company, Ltd. Lien Holder
President—
Major Ira H. Evans
Vice President—
Samuel Thorne
Texas Agent—
T. D. Hobart
Surveyor—
E. B. Spiller

New York Office
President—
Charles G. Francklyn
Secretary—
Frank G. Brown
Treasurer—
William Van Pelt
Lord Rosebery's Representative—
Ferdinand Van Zandt

Solicitors—
Godden Son & Holme
Lord Rosebery's London Agent—
Andrew Kingsmill

Texas Operation
General Manager—
Colonel B. B. Groom
Assistant—
Harry Groom
Bookkeeper—
R. H. Arnold
Boss of Greer Range—
George Cranmer
Boss of White Deer Range—
Perry LeFors

---

[1] Because of the Texas Alien Land Law the actual status of the British bondholders could not be publicly acknowledged.

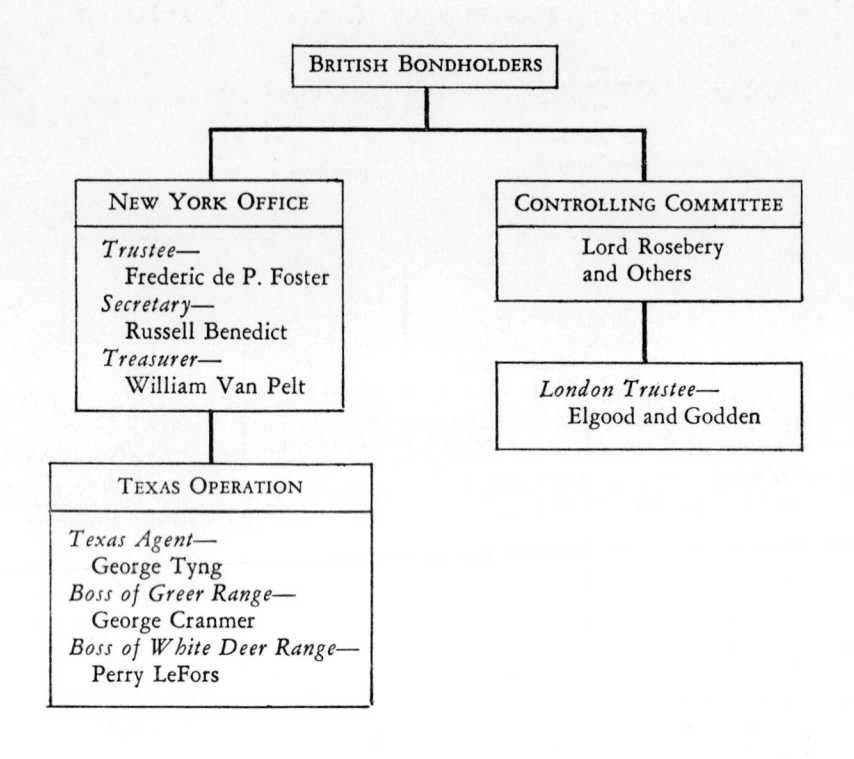

WHITE DEER LANDS, 1886–1903

BRITISH BONDHOLDERS

NEW YORK OFFICE
Trustee—
 Frederic de P. Foster
Secretary—
 Russell Benedict
Treasurer—
 William Van Pelt

CONTROLLING COMMITTEE
Lord Rosebery
and Others

London Trustee—
Elgood and Godden

TEXAS OPERATION
Texas Agent—
 George Tyng
Boss of Greer Range—
 George Cranmer
Boss of White Deer Range—
 Perry LeFors

WHITE DEER LANDS, 1903–1948

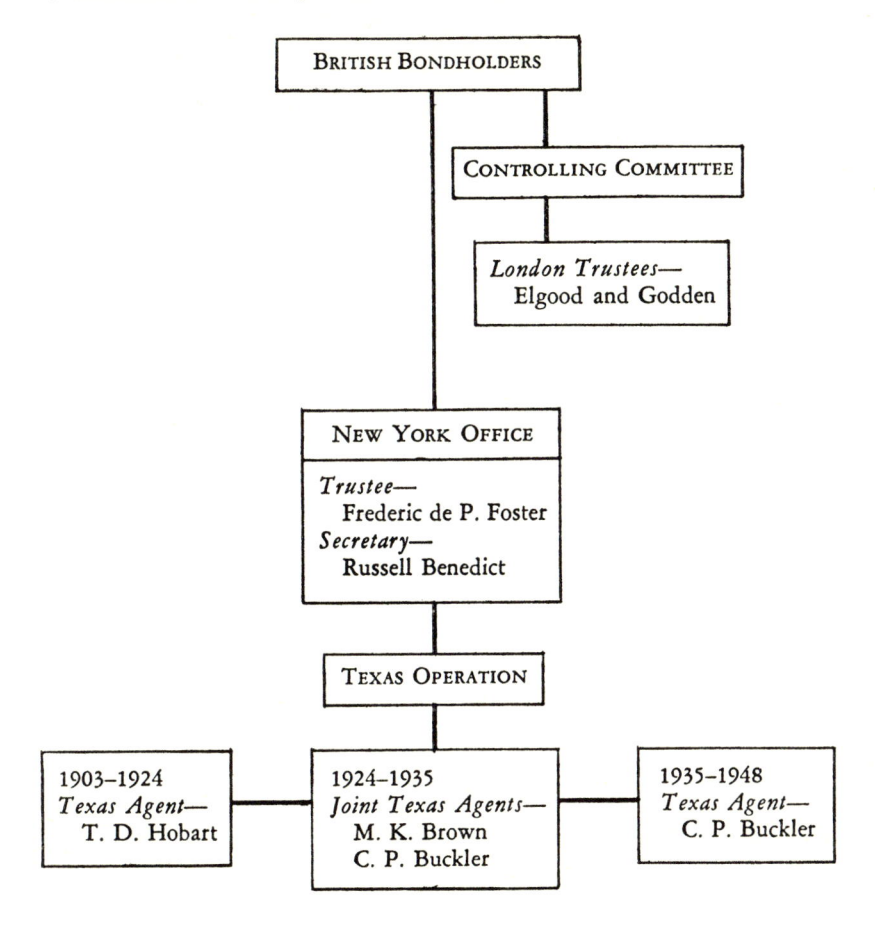

```
                    ┌─────────────────────┐
                    │ BRITISH BONDHOLDERS │
                    └──────────┬──────────┘
                               │
                    ┌──────────┴──────────┐
                    │ CONTROLLING COMMITTEE│
                    └──────────┬──────────┘
                               │
                    ┌──────────┴──────────┐
                    │ London Trustees—    │
                    │ Elgood and Godden   │
                    └─────────────────────┘
```

NEW YORK OFFICE

Trustee— Frederic de P. Foster
Secretary— Russell Benedict

TEXAS OPERATION

1903–1924	1924–1935	1935–1948
Texas Agent— T. D. Hobart	*Joint Texas Agents—* M. K. Brown, C. P. Buckler	*Texas Agent—* C. P. Buckler

WHITE DEER CORPORATION, 1948–1957

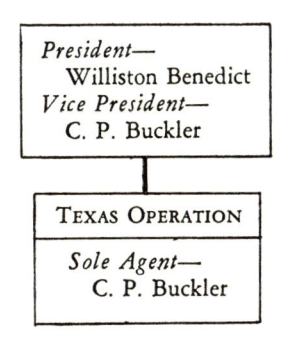

President— Williston Benedict
Vice President— C. P. Buckler

TEXAS OPERATION

Sole Agent— C. P. Buckler

INDEX

Abilene, Kansas: 133
Adair, ———. SEE Goodnight & Adair
Adams-Onis Treaty: 4
Addington, P.: and Indian land lease, 116, 117, 120
Adobe Walls, Texas: 188
Advertiser, Trinidad. SEE *Trinidad Advertiser*
Agassiz (friend of Busk): 278
agriculture. SEE farming
agriculture, commissioner of: Loring as, 121–122
Agriculture, Deparment of: figures of, 333
Albuquerque, New Mexico: railroads to, 294
Alexander (Francklyn employee): 49
———, Charles B.: as trustee, 65, 171
Alexander & Green: as lawyers for Francklyn Land & Cattle Company, 21, 26, 28, 206, 211
Allen (of Standard Cattle Company): 174
———, George: 205
———, Thomas J.: and purchase of Harrold & Ikard cattle, 68, 69, 70
Amarillo, Texas: 302, 309, 339; railroads to, 32, 299; development of, 294; description of, 301; Russell Benedict in, 301
America. SEE United States
American Fork, Utah: George Tyng's death in, 354 n
American Fork *Citizen*: on death of George Tyng, 354 n
Anadarko, Indian Territory: 77; P. B. Hunt at, 104, 108, 115, 117, 118; Colonel Groom in, 109, 110; Indian council at, 109; James Haworth in, 110; McKisker in, 111; George Fox in, 113; Thomas Woodward in, 116

Andrews, John: and sale of Dixon Creek Pasture, 343
Angle, ———: 219
Anglo-Americans: culture of, 248
Ann Arbor, Michigan: George Tyng in, 313
antelope: on Francklyn ranch, 15
Arapahoe Indians: formerly on White Deer Lands, 45; lease of land of, 105, 107
Arkansas River: Atlantic Railroad at, 16
Armour & Co.: 74, 130
Armour Bros.: 74; and Francklyn forgery, 130
Armstrong County: 294; settlement of, 292, 339
Arnold, R. H.: 187; as bookkeeper for Francklyn ranch, 49, 73–74, 189, 191; to Frank Brown, 166
Apache Indians: 109, 110; and George Fox, 113; and Indian schools, 119; agents for, 122
A-sa-ha-be (Indian): and Indian lease, 108
Atchison, Topeka and Santa Fe Railroad: 7, 177, 218; and White Deer Lands, 219, 270, 289, 290; and townsite development, 271, 295, 305; in Neutral Strip, 273; and Purcell Company, 289; and Southern Kansas Railway, 290; progress of, 298; and Pecos Valley extension, 298; and organization of Gray County, 348, 349
Atkins, George Tyng: Russell Benedict on, 215
Atlanta House, Galveston: 132
Atlantic Railroad: 16
attorney general, Texas: on foreign corporations in Texas, 239
Atwater (commission agent): 156
Augur, General C. C.: 112, 113

Austin, Texas: 73, 174; New York & Texas Land Company offices in, 5; Colonel Groom in, 21; Alfred B. Thatcher in, 24; Russell Benedict in, 179, 217, 218

Babcock, Colonel: as agent for Capitol Syndicate, 160–161, 164–165
Bailey, Joseph W.: and controversy over grass, 350
Baker (railroad official): 252-253
Baker and Botts: as lawyers for International Railroad, 24
Balfour, J. A.: visit of, to White Deer Lands, 86
Balfours, the: 205; and syndicate deed, 211
Ball Hutchings & Co.: 132
Bank of London: Williams, Deacon & Company of, 8
Bank of New York: 141
banks: in Texas Panhandle, 294
Barbados: Charles Francklyn in, 68
barbed wire: 84; effect of, 33, 249, 356; for fencing White Deer Pasture, 34; types of, 37
Bar O range: 237
Barton (cattleman): and Francklyn survey, dispute, 38; offers sale of land, 82–83
Barton & Williams: and Francklyn survey dispute, 39
Bassick Mine: 67, 79, 205
Bates breed: 8
Bear Creek: 46, 186
Bear Lake: 49, 54
beaver: on Francklyn ranch, 15
Beck, Senator: and Indian lease, 118, 119
Benedict, Russell: 184, 270, 293; as assistant to Frederic de P. Foster, 171, 172; trips of, to Texas, 173, 175–179, 180, 195–196, 214–215, 216, 218–223, 299–305; on Colonel Groom, 176, 178, 180; and George Tyng, 177, 186, 221, 222–223, 231, 299, 301, 336, 347–349, 351; on school lands, 178; Miller, hired by, 178; and Colonel Goodnight, 180, 181–182, 326; on Gordon Cunard's mortgage, 186; and Francklyn Company finances, 188; visit of, to London, 204–212, 218; and Andrew Kingsmill, 205–206, 208; and bondholders' meeting, 207–208, 208–210; and Holme, 210; character of, 210 n; and syndicate deed, 211; effect of Great Plains on, 214–217, 223; on Texans, 215; on George Tyng Atkins, 215; enthusiasm of, for White Deer Lands, 215, 222; and land titles, 217, 218, 361; and program for White Deer Lands, 217–218, 222–223, 269, 349, 357; and Francklyn foreclosure suit, 223, 226, 227, 228, 230, 231; and purchase of Francklyn land notes, 226; and railroads, 289, 290; investigation of Capitol Syndicate by, 302–303; and establishment of Pampa, 303, 349; on gold-silver controversy, 316–317; as trustee, 352, 361, 363–364; and sale of Dixon Creek Pasture, 358–359; and T. D. Hobart, 359; and discovery of gas and oil, 364
—communications from: to Frederic de P. Foster, 176, 177, 179, 181, 182, 183–184, 185–186, 205, 206–207, 214–215, 216, 217, 218–219, 220–221, 222, 227, 228–229, 230–231, 299, 300, 301–302; to Howell Jones, 269;
—communications to: from Frederic de P. Foster, 180–181, 204–205, 206, 219, 228, 229, 230; from George Tyng, 183, 186, 188–189, 193–194, 194–195, 198, 201, 202, 243–244, 255, 308, 313–314, 318–319, 324–325, 328–329, 336, 341
Benedict, Williston: and liquidation of White Deer Lands, 364–366, 366–367
Bennet Bros. Livery Stable: 240
Bent County Colorado Stock Association: on movement of cattle, 161
Bettais, E. D.: 215
Beverley, ———. SEE Wright & Beverley
Bexar Department: Northwest Texas as part of, 19, 21
Big Tree (Indian): and Indian land lease, 114
Bishop, Lieutenant: 218
Bitter Creek: southern cattle on, 166
Black Bear (Indian): 115
blizzards: of 1882–1883, 72
Block B-2: school lands in, 19, 28, 48, 54,

Index

82, 83; disputes about, 21; Colonel Groom's attempts to secure, 135 n; George Tyng's program for, 199–200; Glidden & Sanborn cattle on, 240, 242, 243–244; Colonel Groom farms on, 312; proposed lease of, 326; water on, 334

Blocker, ———: 164

—, Ab: and movement of cattle, 164–165

—, John: and controversy over cattle trails, 155

Blue Joint: 71

Boaz, W. I.: 149

bois d'arc: on White Deer, 272

bondholders, British: 306, 323; and Charles Francklyn, 7; control of Francklyn Company by, 170–171, 192, 203; appointment of trustees by, 172, 209; position of, under Texas law, 172; and Francklyn foreclosure suit, 185–186; 190, 208, 209, 224, 232, 238; and Russell Benedict, 204, 218; purchase of land notes by, 205, 207, 210, 225, 226, 227; meeting of, 207–208, 208–210; syndicate deed of, 209, 210, 211; and George Tyng, 207–208, 350, 354; creation of White Deer Lands by, 212; and program for White Deer Lands, 267, 268

Bondholders' Syndicate. SEE bondholders, British

bonds, Francklyn: sale of, 8, 28, 61, 64, 65, 146, 181 n, 205, 224, 254

bookkeeping: for Francklyn ranch, 73–74

Borger, Texas: 364

Boston, Massachusetts: 278

Botts, ———. SEE Baker and Botts

boundaries: of Texas, 12

boundary disputes: of Francklyn ranch, 19–30, 38–39

Boyce (Capitol Syndicate agent): 302

Boynton, General: 117, 118

branding: of Francklyn cattle, 73, 76–77, 78–79, 80, 86, 88, 138, 140, 141, 168–169, 193, 196

—, illegal: troubles with, on Francklyn ranch, 90, 93

brands: used by Francklyn ranch, 74–77, 139, 141, 193

Breckenridge, George: and controversy over cattle trails, 155

Bright, Charley: 49, 78; as assistant to George Cranmer, 73, 94

British American Company: 147

British Linen Company Bank: 226, 276; and gold-silver controversy, 317

Britton (banker): 149

Brown, Frank G.: and management of Francklyn Company, 6, 8; and Francklyn survey dispute, 28; and Charles G. Francklyn, 32; and Colonel Groom, 32, 61; on transportation, 35; on fencing, 36; and Francklyn Company finances, 47, 54, 79, 125, 140; on securing water, 50–51; securing of cattle by, 58; and purchase of Harrold & Ikard cattle, 63, 97, 141, 143; on brands, 76, 79; and Carhart lease, 84, 85; visit of, to Texas, 86; on number of cattle, 90, 91; and sale of cattle, 97, 135, 145; and Indian lease, 110, 111, 113; and James Haworth, 111; and Francklyn forgery, 127, 133; on condition of cattle, 144; on Harry Groom's expenditures, 150; and quarantine law, 156; and Stephens and Lytle, 158, 162; school lands in possession of, 178

—communications from: to Charles Francklyn, 28, 36–37, 63, 64, 66, 67, 68; to Harry Groom, 41, 42, 46, 47, 50–51, 71, 76, 83, 85–86, 90, 93, 94, 97, 170; to Colonel Groom, 50–51, 52, 64–65, 66, 69, 74, 79, 85–86, 89, 94, 111, 117, 133, 138–139, 139–140, 144, 147–148, 149; to R. B. Edmunson, 60–61, 86

—communications to: from Colonel Groom, 10–12, 14–17, 20, 32–33, 33–34, 34–35, 37, 38–39, 42, 47–48, 48–49, 52–54, 60, 62, 69–71, 74–76, 76–77, 78–79, 80, 81–82, 90–91, 96, 97–98, 107–108, 108–109, 110, 111, 112, 113–115; 116–117, 117–118, 121–122, 124, 139–140, 143, 145, 152–153, 156–157, 158–159, 162–163, 165–166, 171; from Alexander & Green, 26; from Harry Groom, 36, 39–41, 51, 52, 55, 76, 82–83, 83–85, 86, 91–93, 94, 97, 98, 134, 135, 136–137, 158, 159; from Charles Francklyn, 47, 64; from A. Ripley, 54; from Ferdinand Van

Zandt, 86; from W. B. Kidd, 137; from W. F. Somerville, 146–147; from R. H. Arnold, 166

Brown, M. K.: and T. D. Hobart, 359, 360–361, 363; as nephew of Andrew Kingsmill, 359; as joint manager of White Deer Lands, 363; purchase of White Deer Lands by, 366–367

Browning, Lieutenant Governor: 302

—, J. N.: 183

Brownwood, Texas: 309

Bruner Bros.: as agents for Colonel Groom, 110

Buckler, C. P.: as joint manager of White Deer Lands, 363; bid of, on White Deer Lands, 366, 367

buffalo; hunting of, 13, 16

Bugbee, J.: trade in cattle by, 33, 62

—, Colonel Thomas: cattle of, 13

Bugbee and Nelson: 92

Bureau of Internal Revenue: and White Deer Corporation, 365

Burnett, S. B.: and Indian lease, 108, 116, 117, 120, 121; and Colonel Groom, 116–117, 121; sale of cattle by, 162; sale of Dixon Creek Pasture to, 335 n, 351–352, 358, 361

Burnham & Co., Greeley: 74

Burt (lawyer): 208, 211

Busk: J. R.: 254; and George Tyng, 254, 278, 280–281; and digging of wells, 254; Frederic Foster on, 273–276; ambitions of, 276; visit of, to White Deer Lands, 277

Buzzard's Roost: 221

Cache Creek: 103

Caddo Indians: and Indian schools, 119

California: admittance of, as state, 4; George Tyng in, 176

Camp Supply, Indian Territory: mail route to, 57 n; Russell Benedict in, 196, 218, 220

Canadian, Texas: 294, 339, 358; as county seat of Hemphill County, 264; and Purcell Company, 269 n, 288; mismanagement of, 289, 298; bank established in, 294; emigration from, 295; T. D. Hobart from, 351

Canadian River: 15, 32, 57, 103, 166, 189; cattle on, 13, 95; and transportation problems, 36, 46; Francklyn ranch drained by, 44–45; the Grooms on, 183, 186; Russell Benedict on, 220; railroad crossing of, 273; Breaks of, 298

Cantwell, D. C.: purchase of cattle from, 60

Canyon, Texas: 294, 302

capital, British: investment of, in West, 59–60. SEE ALSO Francklyn Land & Cattle Company; White Deer Corporation; White Deer Lands; White Deer ranch

—, New York: investment of, in Texas, 4–5. SEE ALSO Francklyn Land & Cattle Company; White Deer Corporation; White Deer Lands; White Deer ranch

Capitol Syndicate: movement of cattle into Panhandle by, 13, 160–161, 164–165; sale of land by, 302, 303; investigation of, by Russell Benedict, 302–303

Carhart, J. W.: 41

—, L. N.: 41

Carhart Company: as competitor of Francklyn ranch, 39; lease of land from, 39–42, 54, 84; Francklyn ranch joins fences with, 43

Carpetbaggers: and Ira H. Evans, 5

Carrobgrahut: 212

Carson County: 221, 294, 295, 299, 363; White Deer Lands in, 6, 28, 38, 44, 227, 241, 298, 352, 357; Gunter & Munson in, 8; White Deer cattle in, 237; Tyler Tap Lands in, 288, 289; settlement of, 291, 292; slow development of, 295; farming in, 325; railroads through, 342; production of oil and gas in, 364, 367

Carter (Francklyn employee): 49, 142, 151

Case, S. C.: at Pampa, 311–312

—, Munson T. SEE Case Company, Munson T.

Case Brothers, SEE Case Company, Munson T.

Case Cattle Company. SEE Case Company, Munson T.

Index

Case Company, Munson T.: as competitor of Francklyn ranch, 39; and Carhart lease, 39–42, 84

cattle: prices of, 33, 61, 62, 68, 157, 160, 162–163, 167, 169, 263, 264, 310, 313, 330; improved breeding of, 33, 69 n–70 n, 262, 356; killing of, by fire, 55; and screwworms, 77, 81, 141, 168–169; marketing of, 88–89, 257; diseases of, 95, 105, 122, 136, 145, 160–161; in Indian Territory, 102; in Greer County, 104; killing of, by Indians, 111; movement of, from South Texas, 122, 123–124, 160–161, 164; sale of, 162, 263; scarcity of, 314, 332; proposal to stock White Deer with, 316

cattle, Angus: 139; Colonel Groom raises, 8; on White Deer Pastures, 88, 92, 234; Colonel Groom on, 96

—, Durham. SEE cattle, Shorthorn

—, Francklyn: 30, 71, 112, 141, 162, 185–186, 189; purchase of, 18, 48 n, 58, 60–61, 66, 86, 99, 197; roundup of, 72–73, 97, 137; branding of, 73, 76–77, 78–79, 80, 86, 88, 138, 140, 141, 168–169, 193, 196; movement of, 85, 98–99, 138, 144–145, 168, 188, 192; theft of, 90; sale of, 94, 125, 135, 138, 139, 142–143, 143–145, 148, 154, 157–158, 159, 160, 163–164, 167, 169, 170, 185, 187, 197; location of, 88–89, 95; condition of, 144, 158; numbers of, 144, 174, 189, 190; mortgages on, 179; George Tyng's investigation of, 182–183. SEE ALSO cattle, White Deer

—, Galloway: on White Deer Pastures, 198

—, Keno: purchase of, for Francklyn ranch, 60; gathering up of, 72–73, 80; brand for, 76; location of, 88, 95; number of, 90, 94; counting of, 91

—, Longhorn: passing of, 31, 356

—, Northwest: nature of, 69, 69 n–70 n, 95 n

—, outside: on White deer ranges, 232, 237, 240, 242–243, 244, 317, 327–329, 333

—, Hereford: Colonel Groom raises, 8; use of, in breeding, 70; Colonel Groom on, 96, 99

—, Shorthorn (Durham): 139; value of, 8–9, 92; sale of, by Colonel Groom, 8–9; purchase of, 36, 60–61, 89, 90; on White Deer Pasture, 48, 88, 95, 198, 234; use of, in breeding, 70; in Texas climate, 202; market for, 202

—, White Deer: liens on, 178, 179, 180, 181, 224; collection of, 193, 199, 200–201, 202; branding of, 196, 215; number of, 199, 201; sale of, 199, 208, 232, 233–234, 239–240, 246; taxes on, 201–202; and Francklyn foreclosure suit, 203, 228; price of, 234. SEE ALSO cattle, Francklyn

cattle industry: importance of, 13, 259; and public lands, 13, 262–263; techniques of, 45, 61–62, 96; breeding practices in, 69 n–70 n; driving of cattle in, 98, 157–158; condition of, 101, 263, 308; on Great Plains, 248–249, 256–257; nomadic phase of, 249; of Spaniards, 249; wealth from, 249; and raising of feed crops, 258; Colonel W. E. Hughes on, 259–262; and Texas Legislature, 260–261; and transportation, 261, 263, 267; problems faced by, 261, 263; effect of weather on, 263; and railroads, 263, 267

cattlemen's conventions: 69, 257, 259

Cattle Raisers' Association, The: 351

cattle trails. SEE trails, cattle

cats, wild: on Francklyn ranch

Center, Texas: 348

Central America: George Tyng in, 280, 307

Chase National Bank, New York: 63

Cheevers (Indian): and Indian land lease, 114

Chemical National Bank, New York: 141, 152–153

Cherokee Indians: lease of land of, 105

Cherokee Strip: cattle on, 308

Cherokee Strip Livestock Association: and movement of southern cattle into north, 161

Cheyenne, Wyoming: shipment of Francklyn cattle to, 163; Harrolds' land near, 165–166

Cheyenne and Arapahoe Cattle Association: and movement of southern cattle into north, 161

Cheyenne Indians: 108; on Francklyn ranch, 45; lease of land of, 105, 107
Chicago, Illinois: 305, 313, 317, 332; Francklyn ranch does business in, 74; Colonel Groom in, 144; 157–158; mail service from, 294; George Tyng in, 307
Chick (banker): 165
Chicken Creek: 54
Childress, Texas: 294
Childress County: 294
Chillicothe, Texas: Russell Benedict at, 179
Choctaw Oklahoma & Gulf Railway Company: route of, 302, 303, 342–343; towns along, 347
Choctaw Town, Texas: 347, 348
Cimarron Creek: 46
Circuit Court, U. S.: and Francklyn survey dispute, 21–22; Gordon Cunard's suit in, 226–227, 230; Francklyn foreclosure suit in, 233, 245, 268
Citizen, American Fork. See American Fork *Citizen*
City National Bank, San Antonio: loan from, 165
Civil War: 25
Clarendon, Texas: 49, 178 n, 234, 237, 293, 297, 348; mail route to, 57 n; trial of cattle thieves in, 90; Russell Benedict in, 179, 217; Colonel Groom in, 202; Clarendon Cattle Company at, 234; establishment of, 292; development of, 294; McClelland Brothers in, 338
Clarendon Land & Cattle Company: establishment of ranch by, 13; Alfred Sully as owner of, 234; range problems of, 241; use of school lands by, 242
Clark (Francklyn employee): 51, 52
Claude, Texas: 291, 294, 339; settlers in, 292; Russell Benedict in, 301
Clay, Henry: and doctrine of "Manifest Destiny," 4
Clay County: 71 n, 178; Jack County records kept in, 19
Clements, Erskine: 57 n
Cleveland, Grover: and Indian lands, 108, 112

Click, Governor: on quarantine law, 122
climate. See weather
Coburn, J. M.: and Colonel Groom, 14; and cattle thefts, 90; purchase of cattle by, 162
Cochran & Penn: and title to White Deer Lands, 361–362, 363
Codman, Texas: 253
Coggin (banker): 309
Coffee (land agent): as possible agent for White Deer Lands, 339
Coke, Senator: and Indian land lease, 121
Collingsworth County: 67, 294
Collins, L. B.: Francklyn cattle handled by, 94; and movement of southern cattle into north, 165
Colorado: Charles Francklyn's mines in, 6, 205; quarantine law of, 95, 160, 161; cattle industry in, 258, 314
Colorado City, Texas: 113
Comanche Indians: 109; formerly on Francklyn Ranch, 45; Francklyn cattle on land of, 105; state of, 110; and James Haworth, 110; and Indian land lease, 111, 114, 115, 116, 124; and George Fox, 113; and Indian schools, 119; agents for, 122
Combs, A. B.: 69
Commerce, Committee on: on cattle trails, 121
Committee on Improvement of Stock: report of, 262
communication: problem of, on Francklyn ranch, 18; in West Texas, 31, 248
Compromise of 1850: and settlement of Southwest, 4; and boundaries of Texas, 12
Congress, U.S.: and quarantine law, 121, 156; and Neutral Strip, 273
Connell Brothers: as possible buyers of Dixon Creek Pasture, 343
Conover, W. H.: at meeting with Indians, 115, 116; and Indian lease, 119
Conservative Club: 208
Cooley & Co. See Gregory & Cooley
Coolidge, Kansas: 168
corn: as feed, 158; raising of, in Panhandle, 299

Index

Corpus Christi, Texas: 165
Cotlin, W. L.: 69
cottonwood: on White Deer, 15, 272
counties: organization of, 264
Courthorpe, ————: at bondholders' meeting, 207, 209
coyotes: on Francklyn ranch, 15
Crafton Club: 212
Cranmer, George: 148; as boss of Greer County range, 93, 94, 110–111; to William Van Pelt, 111, 137; on Francklyn cattle, 141; to Colonel Groom, 170–171
creditors: of Francklyn Company, 145–146, 152–154, 166, 171
Creswell, Henry: 93; and Colonel Groom, 14; fence posts owned by, 33; sale of cattle by, 33, 65; Francklyn ranch joins fences with, 43; and cattle thefts, 90; drift fence of, 166; and lease of White Deer Lands, 316
Crooked Creek: 46
Cross S Ranch: and Greer County Notice, 123
Cunard, Sir Bache: 205, 239, 340; and syndicate deed, 211
——, Gordon: and S. W. Morrow, 174; suit of, against Francklyn Company, 175, 183, 185–186, 192, 203, 208, 224, 226–227, 229, 230; lien of, on White Deer cattle, 178, 179, 180, 181, 224; and Gutherie, 181, 182, 186, 208; attempt of, to get lien on White Deer Lands, 182; and Fletcher, 208; and Williams, Deacon & Co., 208; and Francklyn foreclosure suit, 225, 227, 228, 229, 231
Cunard Steamship Company: 226
Cudgell (rancher): 34
cultures: on Great Plains, 247–249
Curtis & Atkinson: 257
Cuyler, C. C.: as trustee, 209; death of, 363. SEE ALSO Foster & Cuyler

Dakota Territory: movement of settlers from, 124; cattle industry in, 263
Dallam County: movement of southern cattle into, 160, 164, 166
Dallas, Texas: 24, 26, 27, 313; Major Evans in, 29; Colonel Groom in, 153, 165; Gordon Cunard's suit in, 175; Russell Benedict in, 176, 181, 214, 216, 228; George Tyng in, 201, 241, 242, 313; Francklyn foreclosure suit at, 238, 244, 245; cattlemen's convention in, 257, 259
Dallas *News*: on weather, 350
Damon, George F.: 85, 86
dams. SEE tanks, earthen
Davis (friend of Busk): 278
Dawson, ————: movement of southern cattle into north by, 166
Day, Doc: and controversy over cattle trails, 155, 166
Deacon, ————: at bondholders' meeting, 207. SEE ALSO Williams, Deacon & Co.
Decker, W. S.: 291–292
deeds: to White Deer Lands, 192
Deep Red Run: 109
deer: on Francklyn ranch, 15
de Forest (rancher): Francklyn ranch's conflict with, 49–50
Denver, Colorado: 317; Colonel Groom in, 171; George Tyng in, 318
"Desert, Great American:" SEE Plains, Great
Desternell, ————: map by, 104
Diamond F brand. SEE branding; brands
Diamond F ranch. SEE White Deer ranch
Diamond Tail Ranch: and Greer County Notice, 123
Dickerson Bros.: 74
disease: in Francklyn cattle, 51, 136, 198; in cattle industry, 261
Dixon Creek Pasture: 44, 236; cattle on, 237, 239; lease of, 239–240, 245, 332; sale of, 281, 300, 322, 335, 336, 343, 350, 351–352, 358, 361; clearing of title of, 361
Doan, C. F.: 109, 113. SEE ALSO Doan's Store
Doan's Store: 70, 76, 109, 133, 164; Colonel Groom at, 111; John Welder at, 113; mail received at, 138, 149; southern cattle near, 166
Dodge City, Kansas: 128, 129, 157;

Francklyn ranch deals with firms in, 18, 34, 37–38, 74, 94; difficulties on route to, 34, 46; mail route to, 57; R. M. Wright & Co. in, 127, 132; Henry C. Young in, 133; trial of Henry C. Young in, 134–135; Harry Groom in, 135; Russell Benedict in, 196, 218

Donley County: 178; organization of, 13; Clarendon in, 292

Donnan, John K.: and Francklyn survey dispute, 28–29, 38

Door Nail, The: 65

drift fence: across Texas Panhandle, 34 n

Driskill, Major: 61, 77

ducks, wild: on Francklyn ranch, 15, 16

Eaton (rancher): 43, 83, 84

economy, U.S.: 59–60

Editorial Association: 264

Edmunson, R. B.: and Frank Brown, 60–61, 86; purchase of cattle by, 60–61

election, Texas: 153

Elgood & Gordon: and Francklyn foreclosure sale, 239, 244, 245; and title of White Deer Lands, 361

Elk Creek: 108, 110, 113

Ellis, ———: and movement of cattle into north, 166

Elm Camp: 86

Elm Creek: 163

Elm Fork: 73, 115

El Paso, Texas: 294

Emporia, Kansas: 156

England: Charles Francklyn in 6, 146; financing of cattle companies in, 59–60, 140; Russell Benedict in, 204–212, 218; Ferdinand Van Zandt in, 219; Gordon Cunard from, 226; George Tyng in, 280; T. D. Hobart in, 360–361, 363

Englewood, Oklahoma: in Neutral Strip, 273

Espuela Company: 237

Evans, ———. SEE Hunter & Evans

—, Major Ira H.: 54, 208, 219, 279; as speaker of Texas House, 5; as president of New York & Texas Land Company, 5–6; character of, 6; and Francklyn survey controversy, 20, 24, 26, 27, 29, 63–64; and Francklyn land notes, 183; as trustee, 185; and T. D. Hobart, 353, 360

Ewing, ———. SEE Hendricks & Ewing

farmers. SEE settlers

Farmers Loan and Trust Company, New York: and Francklyn land notes, 87, 166, 174, 183; and title of White Deer Lands, 361

farming: on White Deer Lands, 255, 268, 271–272, 281, 282–284, 284–285, 293, 312, 324, 325, 326, 340, 368; in Texas Panhandle, 293

Fair, Dallas: George Tyng at, 201

Farrar, Archdeacon: 212

Farwells, the: 302

Featherston, ———: 264

feed crops: growing of, 258

fence posts: sources of, 33

fences: on White Deer Pasture, 30, 33–39, 42, 43, 79, 317, 323, 330, 345

Fenneck (bondholder): and syndicate deed, 211

Finks, John H.: 230

fire: description of, 55; causes of, 55; on range lands, 55, 257, 263; fighting of, 55–56; on White Deer Pastures, 137, 310, 312, 317

fireguards: description of, 55; use of, on White Deer Pastures, 56, 310, 317; making of, 56

First National Bank, Fort Worth: 143, 352; robbery of, 129

First National Bank, Galveston: 132

Fisher, ———. SEE Young, Henry C.

Fisk & Keek: on cattle industry, 263

Fitzgerald, General: 206

Fletcher (bondholder): at bondholders' meeting, 207; and Gordon Cunard, 208

flies: problems with, 145, 169

Flood, ———. SEE Hunter & Flood

Florida Treaty: 4; and Greer County conflict, 102, 103

Folsom, P. H.: as special Indian agent, 118–119

Forsyth, ———: sale of cattle of, 162

foreclosure sale, Francklyn: 238–239, 244, 245–246, 268

foreclosure suit, Francklyn: 185–186, 190, 204, 208, 223; nature of, 209, 227, 228, 229; preparations for, 224, 225; reasons for, 226, 229; cattle included in, 228; hearing on, 231–232; judgment in, 231–232, 268

foreign corporations: in Texas, 239

forgery: of Francklyn Company drafts, 126–135, 136

Fort Bascom, ———: mail route to, 57 n

Fort Elliott, Texas: 127, 132, 292; mail route to, 57 n; Russell Benedict at, 221

Fort Leavenworth, Kansas. SEE Leavenworth, Kansas

Fort Still, Indian Territory: 108, 109, 112, 118

Fort Worth, Texas: 73, 98, 149, 162, 176, 264, 313, 317, 339; Colonel Groom in, 69, 121, 124, 149; cattlemen meet in, 116, 332; robbery of bank in, 129; Harry Groom in, 137; Harrold in, 139, 140; W. F. Somerville in, 146; Russell Benedict in, 214; mail service from, 294; George Tyng in, 313, 315, 343, 350; land deals in, 320; S. B. Burnett from, 351, 358

Fort Worth and Denver City Railroad: effects of arrival of, 16; well digging by, 253; settlement along, 255, 257; value of land along, 281; progress of, 293, 294

Foster, Frederic de P.: as trustee, 171, 172–173, 209; background of, 172; investigation of Francklyn Company by, 173; and George Tyng, 176, 177, 186, 221, 222–223, 227–228, 231, 244–245, 275, 291, 301, 347–349, 350, 351, 354; and Williams, Deacon & Co., 180–181, 208, 245; and New York & Texas Land Company, 181; and Andrew Kingsmill, 181, 225–226, 227–228, 245, 351; and the Grooms, 184, 202; and Godden Son & Holme, 203–204, 205, 238, 239–240, 252–253, 265, 270, 273–274, 276, 290–291; and Lord Rosebery, 208; and program for management of White Deer Lands, 217–218, 267, 273, 357; and Junkin, 221–222; and Francklyn foreclosure suit and sale, 225, 228, 231, 232, 238–239, 244–245, 268; and purchase of Francklyn land notes, 226; sale of cattle by, 233; and cattle controversies, 240; fees for services of, 245; on J. R. Busk, 273–276; on improvements on White Deer Lands, 276–277; on farming operations, 283; on townsite question, 290–291; sends Russell Benedict to Texas, 299; and sale of Dixon Creek Pasture, 351; and leasing of White Deer Lands, 357; character of, 360; and title of White Deer Lands, 362; death of, 363; and discovery of oil and gas, 364. SEE ALSO Foster & Cuyler

—communications from: to Russell Benedict, 180–181, 204–205, 206, 219, 228, 229, 230; to George Tyng, 189–190

—communications to: from Russell Benedict, 176, 177, 179, 181, 182, 183–184, 185–186, 205, 206–207, 214–215, 216, 217, 218–219, 220–221, 222, 227, 228–229, 230–231, 299, 300, 301–302; from George Tyng, 182–183, 184–185, 186–187, 190–191, 193, 195, 196, 202, 235–236, 236–237, 237–238, 240–241, 242–243, 249–250, 251–252, 253, 254, 256–257, 263, 265, 270, 272–273, 277–278, 278–279, 279–280, 281, 282, 288–290, 292–294, 298, 299, 307–308, 308–309, 310–311, 314, 315–316, 317–318, 320–321, 324, 325, 327, 329–330, 331–332, 333–334, 336–337, 341, 342–343, 344–345, 345–347, 347–348, 350–351; from T. D. Hobart, 364

Foster, Mrs. Frederic de P.: 363

Foster & Cuyler: 329; and sale of Dixon Creek Pasture, 351, 352; and Rosebery's section of land, 352; and title of White Deer Lands, 362. SEE ALSO Cuyler, C. C.; Foster, Frederic de P.

Fox, George: and Indian land lease, 108, 113–115, 115–116, 117; duplicity of, 113–115; and P. B. Hunt, 115–116, 117. SEE ALSO Sloan & Fox

Francklyn, Charles G.: 138, 170, 205, 211; and creation of Francklyn Company, 6; background of, 6–7; and Lord Rosebery, 7, 120, 153–194; and Francklyn survey dispute, 26–27; and Francklyn ranch operations, 32, 92, 100, 139, 145; and Frank G. Brown, 32; and

Colonel Groom, 32, 155, 165; and financial problems, 47, 125, 147, 165, 179, 181; sale of bonds by, 61; and purchase of Harrold & Ikard cattle, 63, 68, 140, 141, 143, 147, 148; and Ferdinand Van Zandt, 66, 68; and choice of brands, 74, 79; and Carhart lease, 84, 85; visit of, to Texas, 86; and purchase of cattle, 89; and employees, 90; on Indian land lease, 120; and forgery of Francklyn Company drafts, 127, 128, 131, 135; in England, 146; resignation of, 171, 172, 173, 174; school lands in possession of, 178; and George Tyng, 184; ownership of Francklyn Company stock by, 185; and Francklyn foreclosure suit, 231, 239

—communications from: to Frank G. Brown, 47, 64; to Colonel Groom, 86–87, 99, 100, 153; to Harry Groom, 127–128

—communications to: from Samuel Thorne, 21; from Frank G. Brown, 28, 36–37, 63, 64, 66, 67, 68; from Colonel Groom, 61–62, 98, 119, 120, 141, 143–144, 149–150, 163, 164, 167–168, 169–170, 171, 175, 181; from Harry Groom, 128, 131, 135, 166, 173–174; from W. D. Searles, 164; from Stephens and Lytle, 169

Francklyn Land & Cattle Company: organization of, 6, 17; purchase of land by, 6, 7–8, 20; financing of, 8, 28, 60, 61, 64, 65, 146, 181 n; sale of bonds of, 8, 28, 61, 64, 65, 146, 181 n, 205, 224, 254; and Carhart lease, 39–42; financial situation of, 48, 79, 88, 89, 91, 94, 99, 107, 110–111, 125, 135, 138, 139, 141–142, 143, 145–154, 163, 164, 166–167, 170, 171, 173–174, 178, 181, 188, 190, 192, 224; lease of Greer County land by, 67, 71, 72, 73, 76–79, 80, 85, 86, 88–89, 90, 91, 93, 94, 95, 97, 98–99, 105, 110, 111, 112, 120, 140, 141, 142, 155, 163, 179, 183, 188, 190, 192, 193–194, 198, 202; creation of separate company by, 85; and Panhandle Cattle Company, 94; and Greer County Notice, 123; forgery of drafts on, 126–135; and Indian lease, 105, 107, 108–109, 114, 115, 116, 123, 148, 167–168; holdings of, 153–154; failure of, 171, 172–173, 212; resignation of officials of, 172; trusteeship set up for, 172, 192, 203; investigations of, 173–174, 175–179, 182–183, 188, 193–194; lawsuits against, 174–175, 192, 203; suit of Gordon Cunard against, 175, 182, 183, 185–186, 192, 203, 208, 224, 226–227, 229, 230; mortgages held by, 178; titles of, to land, 179, 361; the Grooms' relationship with, 182, 185, 187–188; fraud in, 182–183; land notes of, 183, 185, 191, 203–204, 205, 207, 210, 224, 225, 226, 227; foreclosure suit against, 185–186, 190, 204, 208, 209, 223, 224–232, 268; inventory of property of, 190; income of, 197; newspaper articles about, 197–198; foreclosure sale of, 238–239, 244, 245–246, 268. SEE ALSO cattle, Francklyn; cattle, White Deer; Francklyn ranch; White Deer Lands; White Deer ranch

Francklyn ranch: 51, 125, 188; purchase of land for, 6, 7–8, 20; surveys of, 14, 18, 19, 20–30, 38–39, 54, 63; description of, 14–17, 44–45; water on, 15, 43, 50; timber on, 15; wild life on, 15–16; value of land of, 16; and railroads, 16, 32; buffalo on, 16; establishment of, 18, 20–30, 32, 42, 45, 51; area of, 18, 44, 69; communication problems on, 18; puchase of cattle for, 18, 36, 58, 60–61, 62–71, 72, 73, 74, 77–79, 80, 85, 86, 98, 99, 180; transportation problems on, 18, 34,–35; financial situation of, 18, 47, 65, 73–74, 85, 110–111, 140, 142; school land in, 19, 28, 38, 48, 82, 83, 135 n; cattle owned by, 30, 71, 72–73, 76, 77, 85, 88, 90, 91, 95, 98–99, 136–137, 144, 147, 198; fencing of, 30, 33–39, 42, 43, 79; effect of weather on, 36, 50, 81–82, 136, 137, 140–141, 143, 158, 197, 198, 243; and Carhart lease, 39–42; and Indians, 45, 105, 107, 110–111, 118, 137–138; creeks on, 45; improvements on, 46, 47–48, 50, 80; and settlers, 48; movement of cattle to, 60, 160–161, 188, 192, 198; and Greer County lease, 71, 72, 73, 76–79, 80, 85, 86, 88–89, 90, 91, 93, 94, 95, 97, 98–99, 110, 111, 140, 141, 142, 155, 163, 179, 183, 188, 190, 192, 193–194, 198, 202; horses and mules on, 73, 89, 97–98, 138; branding of cattle for, 73–79, 80, 86,

Index

88, 138, 140, 141, 168–169, 196; employees of, 73, 89, 90–91, 92–93, 98, 110–111, 142, 150, 151, 173, 188, 189, 190; brands of, 74–77, 139, 141, 193; visit of J. A. Balfour to, 86; visit of Ferdinand Van Zandt to, 86; operation of, 89–94, 226, 367–368; and illegal branding, 90, 93; cattle theft from, 90; sale of cattle by, 94, 125, 135, 138, 139, 142–143, 143–145, 148, 154, 157–158, 159, 160, 163–164, 169, 170, 197; roundup on, 97; and Indian lease, 105, 107, 108–109, 114, 115, 116, 123, 148, 167–168; Quanah Parker employed by, 118; Frank Brown at, 127; shipment of cattle by, 144–145, 163, 168, 186; Texas fever on, 145; protection of grass on, 155; forage crops on, 158; investigations of, 171, 179, 182–183; inventory of, 193; farming done by, 283. SEE ALSO cattle, Francklyn; cattle, White Deer; Francklyn Land & Cattle Company; White Deer Lands; White Deer ranch

Frankfort, Kentucky: Leon W. Moore from, 70

Frazer, William R.: as acting manager of Francklyn ranch, 191, 195, 196, 218, 241, 255

freight wagons: use of, 18

Fritz (settler): on White Deer Lands, 300

Frost, ———: 157, 219

Fry (bondholder): sale of Francklyn bonds by, 205, 206, 209

Frying Pan Ranch: desire of, to lease land, 236

Fuqua, W. H.: 301

Gainesville, Texas: 162

Galesburg, Illinois: 348

Galveston, Texas: Henry C. Young in, 131–133, 134; George Tyng in, 336

Ganky, Gan (Indian): Colonel Groom's meeting with, 115

Garnett, H. T.: 94

gas: discovery of, on White Deer Lands, 364; production of, 367, 368

Gates & Co., J. W.: 74

geese, wild: on Francklyn ranch, 15, 16

General Land Office. SEE Land Office, Texas

Gerlach, John: 264

German National Bank: 130, 135

Gillespie, H. B.: 171

Glasgow, Texas: 272; railroad at, 288, 290; development of, 289. SEE ALSO Pampa, Texas

Galveston *Globe Democrat*: on Francklyn forgery, 132

Glidden & Sanborn: 236; lease of school land by, 240; trespassing by, 241. SEE ALSO Sanborn, H. B.

Glidden wire. SEE barbed wire

Globe Democrat, Galveston: on Francklyn forgery, 132

———, Wellington, Kansas: 298

Globe Live Stock Journal of Kansas City: 196

Glucksen, Paul: 153

Godden (trustee): 206, 209; and Francklyn foreclosure sale, 239. SEE ALSO Godden Son & Holme

Godden Son & Holme: 337; as lawyers for bondholders, 203; and Frederic Foster, 203–204, 205, 238, 239–240, 252–253, 265, 270, 273–274, 276, 290–291; at bondholders' meeting, 207; and Andrew Kingsmill, 208; and purchase of land notes, 210; and Francklyn foreclosure sale, 245; and sale of White Deer Lands, 345; and Russell Benedict as trustee, 352; from T. D. Hobart, 357, 358, 359–360, 361–363. SEE ALSO Godden (trustee); Holme, ———

gold-silver controversy: and White Deer Lands, 316–317, 318–319, 335

Goliad, Texas: 113

Goodnight, Colonel Charles: 83, 93, 340; in Palo Duro Canyon, 13; and Colonel Groom, 14, 182; and Francklyn survey conflict, 54; and well digging, 54; sale of cattle by, 62; on brands, 76; and cattle thefts, 90; building of tanks by, 128; to Russell Benedict, 180, 181–182, 326; on Perry LeFors, 180; on school lands, 196; on state of White Deer Lands, 199; and scarcity of grass, 257; sale of land by, 308–309; and lease of White Deer Lands, 316, 326;

and stocking of White Deer Lands, 316
Goodnight & Adair: fence posts owned by, 33
Goodnight and Taylor: lease of White Deer lands by, 252, 255
Gonzales, Texas: Judge Miller from, 121
Gordon, ———. SEE Elgood & Gordon
government, U.S.: SEE United States government
Graham, Texas: foreclosure suit filed at, 228
gramma grass: 71
grangers. SEE settlers
grapes: on White Deer Lands, 272
grass: scarcity of, 233, 236, 249, 257–258, 265; as foundation of Plains economy, 247; condition of, 255, 280, 315, 332; controversy over, 350
Gray, James L.: surveying of Pampa by, 349
Gray County: 21; White Deer Lands in, 6, 28, 38, 227, 241, 298; Purcell Company in, 295; need for towns in, 296; organization of, 297, 347–348, 349; Pampa in, 299, 311; county seat of, 303, 347–348, 351; railroads through, 342, 348, 349; production of oil and gas in, 364, 367
grazing land: White Deer Land lease as, 199–200
grazing rights: in Indian territory, 101–125
Greeley Burnham & Co.: 74
Green, ———. SEE Alexander & Green
Greer County: 294; hauling from, 49; Harrold & Ikard in, 62–63, 107; Francklyn lease in, 67, 71, 72, 73, 76–79, 80, 85, 86, 88–89, 90, 91, 93, 94, 95, 97, 98–99, 105, 110, 111, 112, 120, 140, 141, 142, 155, 163, 179, 183, 188, 190, 192, 193–194, 198, 202; boundary dispute about, 102–104; Texas cattle in, 104; cattle trails through, 105, 122, 123–124, 160–161; Colonel Groom on, 107, 122, 129, 145; cattle companies in, 107; Indian claims in, 111, 167–168; removal of settlers from, 112, 147; George Fox in, 113–115; division of, 120; and Governor Ireland, 124, 125; and Texas Land Board, 124–125; taxes in, 201–202

Greer County Notice: issuing of, 123

Greer County range, Francklyn: cattle on, 71, 72, 88–89, 90, 95, 97, 147, 148, 227; branding of cattle on, 73, 76–77, 77–79, 80, 86; Colonel Groom on, 73, 110, 163; in separate company, 85; George F. Damon in, 85, 86; Ferdinand Van Zandt in, 86; J. F. Pierce as boss of, 90; Cape Willingham as possible boss of, 91, 93; George Cranmer as boss of, 93, 94, 111; roundup on, 97; shipment of cattle from, 98–99, 163, 188, 190, 198, 202; expenses of, 140, 142; weather on, 141; protection of grass on, 155; George Tyng at, 179, 183, 193–194; financial arrangements on, 188; tools and machinery on, 192

Gregory, ———: 156. SEE ALSO Gregory & Cooley

Gregory & Cooley: 74; and payments for cattle sales, 79, 170; Francklyn cattle handled by, 87, 94, 142–143; and Harrold & Ikard, 117; and George Fox, 117

Gresham, Secretary: 117

Groom, Colonel B. B.: as general manager of Francklyn ranch, 6, 8, 16, 17, 20, 21, 28, 32, 42, 45, 94, 99; lease of land by, 6, 8; tour of inspection of, 8, 10–12, 14–17; background of, 8–9; opinion of, on Texas land, 10–12, 14–16, 16–17, 18; arrival of, in Texas, 13; and J. M. Coburn, 14; and James Goodnight, 14, 182; and Henry Creswell, 14; and Frank G. Brown, 32, 61; inexperience of, with Texas ranching, 32; and Charles G. Francklyn, 32, 155, 165; in St. Louis, Missouri, 34; and Francklyn survey dispute, 38; and Carhart lease, 39–42; techniques of, in cattle raising, 45, 96–97; and Francklyn Company finances, 47, 79, 110–111, 142, 145, 146–147, 149, 153, 162, 164, 165, 167, 171, 173, 197; securing of water by, 50; purchase of cattle by, 58, 60–61, 67, 69–71, 73, 76–77, 77–79, 79–80, 86; Frank Brown on, 61; and Harrold & Ikard, 67, 69–71, 73, 76–77, 77–79, 80, 86, 168; on branding problems, 73, 74–76, 76–77, 78–79, 79–

Index

80, 86; on Greer County range, 76–77, 107, 122; and horses, 81, 97–98, 138, 159; and Francklyn employees, 81, 188; and J. F. Pierce, 90–91; and Cape Willingham, 93; and Captain Knight, 93–94; on Texas fever, 95–96; on Texas cattle, 96, 99; and controversy over cattle trails, 105, 155, 160–161, 166; and Indian Territory lease, 105–107, 108–109, 110, 111, 115, 120–121, 167–168; and Quanah Parker, 108; in Anadarko, Indian Territory, 109, 110; and James Haworth, 110; to P. B. Hunt, 110, 118; and George Fox, 113, 117; meeting of, with other cattlemen, 116–117; visit of, to Secretary Teller, 119; in Washington, D. C., 121; and Kansas quarantine law, 121–124; and Francklyn forgery, 132, 133, 134; and sale of cattle, 135, 143–145; and school lands, 135 n, 196, 221; and Harry Groom, 151–152; activities of, 152; and failure of Francklyn ranch, 155, 171, 182; character of, 155, 186–187; and Texas Legislature, 156; and John T. Lytle, 157; and George Cranmer, 170–171; and Francklyn's resignation, 173, 174; and investigation of ranch, 175, 179, 180; and Gordon Cunard's injunction, 175; Russell Benedict on, 176, 178, 180; and George Tyng, 180, 183, 184, 186–187, 187–188, 188–189, 191, 194, 198, 201, 203; dismissal of, 182, 184, 190, 192; movement of cattle by, 183; and Frederic Foster, 184, 202; interest of, in Francklyn land, 185, 227; salary of, 190; and inventory of Francklyn property, 190; defense of, 197–198; and Perry LeFors, 202; as agent for Purcell Company, 291; sale of feed by, 300; as manager for Mortimer Land Company, 301, 312; farming by, 312; possible lease of White Deer Lands by, 313

—communications from: to Frank Brown, 10–12, 14–17, 20, 32–33, 33–34, 34–35, 37, 38–39, 42, 47–48, 48–49, 52–54, 60, 62, 69–71, 74–76, 76–77, 78–79, 80, 81–82, 90–91, 96, 97–98, 107–108, 108–109, 110, 111, 112, 113–115, 116–117, 117–118, 121–122, 124, 139–140, 143, 145, 152–153, 156–157, 158–159, 162–163, 165–166, 171; to Charles G. Francklyn, 61–62, 98, 119, 120, 141, 143–144, 149–150, 163, 164, 167–168, 169–170, 171, 175, 181; to P. B. Hunt, 110, 118

—communications to: from Charles G. Francklyn, 86–87, 99, 100, 153; from Thomas Woodward, 116; from Frank Brown, 50–51, 52, 64–65, 66, 69, 74, 79, 85–86, 89, 94, 111, 117, 133, 138–139, 139–140, 144, 147–148, 149

Groom, Elizabeth Thomson: 8

Groom, Harrison Thomson: background of, 8; fencing of ranch by, 36, 80; on Carhart lease, 39–41; and M. T. Case, 41–42; and Francklyn Company finances, 47, 148, 150–152, 174–175; description of fire by, 55; handling of cattle by, 58, 60, 76, 80, 91, 138, 139, 160, 183; and R. H. Arnold, 73; and branding, 77; and school lands, 82, 196; and Lovell, 92–93; on Cape Willingham, 93; on need for horses, 98; and Francklyn forgery, 127, 128–129, 131, 132, 133, 134, 135; from R. M. Wright, 129; from William Van Pelt, 142, 150–151; from Colonel Groom, 151–152; activities of, 158; on investigation by S. W. Morrow, 173–174; on Gordon Cunard, 174; and Francklyn's resignation, 174; and lawsuits, 174–175; and investigation of ranch, 175; dismissal of, 182, 184, 190, 192; and failure of Francklyn Company, 182; and George Tyng, 183, 184, 186–187, 187–188, 188–189, 191, 194, 201; interest of, in Francklyn land, 185; duplicity of, 186–187; salary of, 190; and inventory of Francklyn ranch, 190, 193; and Mortimer Land Company, 301

—communications from: to Frank Brown, 36, 39–41, 51, 52, 55, 76, 82–83, 83–85, 86, 91–93, 94, 97, 98, 134, 135, 136–137, 158, 159; to Charles Francklyn, 128, 131, 135, 166, 173–174

—communications to: from Frank Brown, 41, 42, 46, 47, 50–51, 71, 76, 83, 85–86, 90, 93, 94, 97, 170; from A. Ripley, 55–56; from Charles Francklyn, 127–128; from R. M. Wright, 129; from Henry C. Young, 135; from William Van Pelt, 142, 150–151; from Colonel Groom, 151–152

Grothouse, C. A. SEE Young, Henry C.

Gunter & Munson: 49; establishment of ranch by, 8, 13; Francklyn ranch joins fences with, 42–43

Gutherie, ———: and Gordon Cunard, 181, 182, 186, 208

Half Circle K range: 241

Hall County: 294

Hamburg, ———. SEE Rath & Hamburg

Hancock & West: 26

Hansford County: organization of, 293

Hansford Land & Cattle Company: 51; and cattle thefts, 90; building of tanks by, 128

Hardeman County: Quanah in, 294

Harrah (Francklyn employee): 151

Harrison & Popham: lease of White Deer Lands by, 352

Harrold, ———: 85, 97; and sale of cattle, 66, 165; from T. J. Allen, 68; and branding of cattle, 78–79; and Wheeler County lease, 87; and Indian lease, 108; Francklyn Company's arrangements with, 139; and Charles Francklyn, 140, 141, 147, 149; payment to, 143, 153; money owed to, 149–150, 168; from Colonel Groom, 168

—, Doc: and sale of Francklyn cattle, 165

—, E. B.: and sale of cattle to Francklyn ranch, 63, 64, 69, 70–71; to Frank Brown, 97; to Teller, 107; money owed to, 166

—, Elin: money owed to, 153

—, Eph: and branding of cattle, 77; money owed to, 152–153

Harrold Brothers & Ikard: 89–90; Francklyn Company buys cattle from, 62–71, 72, 73, 74, 77–79, 80, 85, 180, 197; and branding and counting cattle, 72–73, 74, 77–79, 79–80, 86, 144; Francklyn Company debt to, 89, 98, 143, 148–149; in Greer County, 107; and Suggs, 117; and Gregory & Cooley, 117; and P. Addington, 117; lien on Francklyn cattle held by, 162

Harrold Bros.: payment to, 143, 167

Harrold, Texas: 171; cattle shipped to, 161; Colonel Groom in, 170, 186; Russell Benedict in, 179, 216; George Tyng in, 186; railroad to, 293

Haworth, James: and Indians, 110; and P. B. Hunt, 110; and Frank Brown, 111; and Indian lease, 119

hay: cost of, 48–49; preparing of, 48–49, 49–50, 80; securing of, 158

Hays, Texas: mail route to, 57 n

Haystack (place): 81

Head, Dick: 157

Head & Horn: sale of Francklyn cattle to, 174, 180, 187

Head, Taylor & Co.: 189

Hearn, ———: 69

Hemphill County: 294; organization of, 264

Hemphill County Immigration Association: 264

Hendricks, H. B.: on title of White Deer Lands, 361

Hendricks & Ewing: and title of White Deer Lands, 361, 362

Henrietta, Texas: 26, 162; as county seat of Clay County, 19; Henry C. Young in, 129; Russell Benedict in, 178

Henry, ———: 27

—, Major: 110

—, Colonel John L.: and New York & Texas Land Company, 30

Herald, Panhandle. SEE *Panhandle Herald*

Hereford, Texas: 302

Higgins, Texas: 291, 294

Highland Farm: 49

Hill (settler): on White Deer Lands, 302

Hobart, T. D.: and use of land agents, 335 n; as possible agent for White Deer Lands, 339; as manager of White Deer Lands, 351, 352–353, 356, 357; and Andrew Kingsmill, 352, 356, 360; from J. Peters, 354 n; and George Tyng, 357, 359–360; and program for White Deer Lands, 357–358; and sale of Dixon Creek Pasture, 359; and Russell Benedict, 359; and M. K. Brown, 359, 360–361; and Committee, 359; power of attorney of, 359; character of, 360; trips of, to London, 360–361, 363; and White Deer Lands titles, 361–363

—communications from: to Major Ira H.

Index

Evans, 353, 360; to Godden Son & Holme, 357, 358, 359–360, 361–363; to Frederic Foster, 364
Hobart, Warren: 360
Hoff, ———: 309
Hoffman, ———. SEE Shattuck and Hoffman
Holland, A. A.: 255; and George Tyng, 255, 325; in charge of White Deer Farm, 326
Holland Bros.: operation of White Deer Farm by, 282
Hollicott, John: 57 n
Holliday (lawyer): 113
Holme, ———: at bondholders' meeting, 207; and Russell Benedict, 210; and syndicate deed, 211. SEE ALSO Godden Son & Holme
Holmes, Sam: 70
Home Cattle Company: sale of Francklyn cattle to, 174, 180, 187
homesteaders. SEE settlers
Honduras: George Tyng in, 307
Hoover, H. E.: of Southern Kansas Railway, 303; and proposed purchase of White Deer Lands, 358
Hopkins (settler): on White Deer Lands, 300
———, J. H.: 264
Horn, ———. SEE Head & Horn
Horn Mine: 65, 67, 79
horses: on Francklyn ranch, 15, 89; securing of, 45–46, 47, 73, 82–83, 97–98, 159; cost of, 98; diseases of, 136; condition of, 138, 144, 145, 158, 159; sale of, 240; influence of, on Great Plains, 247–248; and Indian culture, 248
House of Representatives, Texas: Ira H. Evans as speaker of, 5
Houston, F.: 69
Houston, J. F.: and Francklyn survey dispute, 38–39
Houston, Temple: and Francklyn forgery, 128, 130, 131, 132, 133; and S. W. Morrow, 173
Houston, Texas: Alfred B. Thatcher in, 24; Major Evans in, 29; George Tyng in 241, 313, 341

Houston & Great Northern Railroad: 215; and International Railroad, 5
Houston and Spiller: 128, 131. SEE ALSO Spiller, E. B.
Hudson (rancher): 15
Hughes, W. E.: 69; on future of cattle industry, 259–262
Hughes and Simpson: 70, 165
Hunt, Colonel P. B.: 109; as Indian agent, 104; and Greer County conflict, 104; and Indian lease, 108, 121; and James Haworth, 110; and Colonel Groom, 110, 118; and Indian delegation, 111; and George Fox, 114; attempts to remove from office, 115, 117–118; resignation of, 118, 119
Hunter, Colonel R. D.: 117, 156
Hunter & Evans: 139; and Indian land lease, 108
Hunter & Flood: and sale of Dixon Creek Pasture, 352, 361
Huntley, ———: and Indian land lease, 108
Huselby House, Mobeetie: 86
Hutchinson County: 273; White Deer Lands in, 6, 227, 241, 352; production of oil and gas in, 364, 367

Ikard, E. F.: and inspection of Harrold & Ikard holdings, 70; and branding of cattle, 77; and Indian lease, 108; Francklyn Company's arrangements with, 139–140; payment to, 143, 149–150, 153. SEE ALSO Harrold Brothers & Ikard
Ikard's Peak: 108
Illinois: Harrold in, 66
immigration. SEE settlers
Immigration Association of the 19th Senatorial District: 264
Indian Affairs, Commissioner of: H. Price as, 102; and Indian land lease, 168
———, Committee on: and Indian delegation, 111
Indian agents: appointment of, 122
Indian Bureau: and settlers in Greer County, 112 n
Indian Creek: 45, 49
Indians: retreat of, to Indian Territory,

13; and Francklyn ranch, 45, 105, 110–111, 118, 137; protection of, 102; leasing of land from, 102, 105, 107, 108, 109, 111, 114, 115, 116, 123, 124, 148, 167–168; council meeting of, 108–109; state of, 110; visit of Colonel Groom with, 110; and James Haworth, 110; schools for, 110; in Washington, D. C., 111, 120; and George Fox, 113; and Indian schools, 119; support of P. B. Hunt by, 120–121; agents for, 122

—, Plains: culture of, 247–248; and horses, 248

Indian Territory: retreat of Indians to, 13; Atlantic Railroad in, 16; plans to lease land in, 101–125, 148, 167–168; and Greer County conflict, 102; cattle in, 105, 137, 313–314, 343; settlers in, 112, 124, 281, 314; cattle trails through, 121, 161; and Kansas quarantine law, 122

Interior, Secretary of: H. M. Teller as, 101–102

Interior Department: and Indian leases, 109, 110; and P. B. Hunt, 117

International & Great Northern Railroad: and White Deer Lands, 215

International Railroad: and Houston & Great Northern, 5; and White Deer Lands, 215

Ireland, Governor: and Greer County land, 124, 125; and Francklyn forgery, 134

irrigation: of Panhandle lands, 216

Israel, ———: swindling of, 129

Iturbide Hotel, Mexico City: George Tyng at, 241

Ives, Theodore: 264

Jaccard Jewelry House: and Henry C. Young, 134

Jack County: 25; organization of, 19; Colonel Groom in, 21

Jacksboro, Texas: 26, 38; as county seat of Jack County, 19; Colonel Groom in, 21; records at, 25; Thomas F. West from, 130

J-Buckle roundup: Francklyn cattle at, 193

Jefferies, J. D.: possible lease of White Deer Lands by, 332; as possible buyer of Dixon Creek Pasture, 343

Jennison, Colonel: 206

Jersey City, New Jersey: Francklyn Company meeting in, 226

Johnstone (of Matador Company): 309

Jones, ———. SEE Swenson & Jones

—, Horace: in Washington, D.C., 120

—, Howell: 290; letter to, from Russell Benedict, 269

Jones County: Swenson's ranch in, 173

Joslyn, Assistant Secretary of Interior: 119

Juancito, Honduras. SEE San Juancito

Junkin, ———: and investigation of White Deer Lands, 217; trip of, to Texas, 218, 219, 220, 221–222; to Frederic Foster, 221–222

Kansas: 186; Colonel Groom in, 10; Francklyn cattle in, 95, 138, 163; quarantine law of, 95, 105, 122, 124, 159–160, 161; and Neutral Strip, 104, 273; Governor Click of, 122; Panhandle lands compared to, 216; settlement of, 271; land speculators from, 288; development of towns in, 289

Kansas & Nebraska Railroad: 294

Kansas City, Missouri: 133, 313, 317, 332, 339; Henry C. Young in, 130, 131, 134; Colonel Groom in, 156, 158; Lytle in, 167; Russell Benedict in, 218; mail service from, 294

Ke-che-a-qua-ho-no: as name for South Fork of Red River, 103

Keek, ———. SEE Fisk & Keek

Keller, J. M.: 131

Kempland, ———: 206

Kenedy, ———. SEE King & Kenedy

Kentucky: Frank G. Brown from, 6; Colonel Groom from, 8; Colonel Groom in, 14, 62; purchase of cattle in, 36, 48 n, 60, 88, 301; Leon W. Moore from, 70; Senator Beck from, 119

Kidd, W. B.: care of Francklyn cattle by, 88, 95, 137

Index

Kimball, H.: and inventory of Francklyn ranch, 193

Kimberlin Cattle Company: and Greer County Notice, 123

King & Kenedy: sale of cattle of, 159, 162

Kingsmill, Andrew: 218, 275, 276; and Frederic Foster, 181, 225–226, 227–228, 245, 351; and purchase of Francklyn land notes, 203–204, 210, 211, 225, 226; as representative for Lord Rosebery, 203, 210; and Russell Benedict, 205–206, 208; at bondholders' meeting, 207; and Francklyn foreclosure suit, 208, 225; and Godden Son & Holme, 208; and sale of Fry's bonds, 209; and syndicate deed, 211; as manager of British Linen Bank, 226; and sale of Dixon Creek Pasture, 351; trip of, to Texas, 351–352; and T. D. Hobart, 352, 356, 360; M. K. Brown as nephew of, 359

——, Henry: as alternate trustee, 209; and Francklyn foreclosure sale, 244, 245, 275; related to M. K. Brown, 359

——, Texas: founding of, 352; M. K. Brown in, 366

Kiowa, Kansas: 264, 293; Russell Benedict at, 218, 220

Kiowa Indians: 109; Francklyn cattle on land of, 105; lease of land of, 107, 111, 114, 115, 116, 124; and James Haworth, 110; state of, 110; and George Fox, 113; and Indian schools, 119; agents for, 122

Klein, Mrs.: boarding house of, 132

Knight, Captain John: and Francklyn ranch, 93–94, 99

Kuper, Colonel W. S.: as surveyor and tank builder, 51–52

Kruse, ———: and death of George Tyng, 354 n

Labalanica (Indian): and Indian land lease, 114

land: surveying of, 18–20, 25; price of, 271, 281, 300, 307, 320, 321, 342, 344, 346; value of, 295, 367; sales of, 335–336; terms of sale of, 346

land, public. See school lands

land agents: activities of, 335; and White Deer Lands, 346

Landers, ———: 214

Land Office, Texas: 25; organization of, 19; filing claims with, 28; and Greer County lands, 124–125; sale of lands by, 258–259; lease of land by, 261; and George Tyng, 278–279; and surveying of White Deer Lands, 337

land speculators. See speculators, land

Lane, ———: 312

Langermann (clerk): and Francklyn survey dispute, 29

Las Vegas, New Mexico: mail route to, 57 n

Lawrence, Kansas: Indian school at, 119

laws, Texas: enforcement of, 13; effect of, on cattle sales, 163; and alien ownership of land, 172; and Francklyn Company, 179; and trespassers, 328

lawsuits: against Francklyn Company, 174–175, 183, 185–186, 190, 192, 203, 204, 208, 209, 223, 224–232, 268

Leach, ———: 14, 57; and Francklyn survey dispute, 39

Leake, ———. See Wellborn, Leake and Henry

Leary, Dan: as possible agent for White Deer Lands, 339

lease laws: in Texas Legislature, 256; nature of, 261

leasing: of White Deer Lands, 306–310, 315–319, 319–320, 323, 327, 329, 330, 331, 332, 334, 357–358; George Tyng on, 313

Leaven, Earl of: at bondholders' meeting, 207

Leavenworth, Kansas: 105, 112; Henry C. Young in prison at, 135

Lee, W. M. D.: digging of wells by, 253

LeFors, Perry: 49, 92–93, 196; as foreman of White Deer Lands, 73, 183; hiring of, 180; as manager for White Deer Lands, 195, 218; and Colonel Groom, 202; as settler on White Deer Lands, 300; and organization of Gray County, 347, 348, 349

Legislature, Kansas: and quarantine law, 157

—, Texas: and railroads, 4–5; and Texas Land Company, 5; and school lands, 19; and boundary conflicts, 20; and Greer County dispute, 102; and controversy over cattle trails, 156; on immigration, 216–217; passage of lease laws by, 256; sale of public lands by, 258–259; and cattle industry, 260–261; and White Deer Lands, 273–274

Lexington, Kentucky: Colonel Groom in, 9, 62, 171; purchase of cattle in, 36, 60, 71, 88

Liberal, Kansas: 273, 294

Lindell Hotel, St. Louis: 130

line camps: nature of, 46 n

Linen. SEE Kingsmill, Andrew; Rosebery, Lord

Lipscomb County: 273, 294

Liverpool, England: George Tyng in, 280

Livestock Commission, St. Louis: and Henry C. Young, 134

Live Stock Journal: 196

Lofan (White Deer employee): 243

London, Bank of. SEE Bank of London

—, England: Charles G. Francklyn from, 6; Russell Benedict's visit to, 204–212, 218; White Deer accounts in, 275; Andrew Kingsmill from, 351; T. D. Hobart in, 360–361, 363

Lone Wolf (Indian): and Indian land lease, 114, 116; Groom's meeting with, 115

Loring, Commissioner of Agriculture: 121–122; and quarantine line, 122

Lovell (Francklyn employee): 94; Harry Groom's problems with, 92–93

Lovetts, Henry: as settler on White Deer Lands, 300

Loving, George B.: 340

Lofing, J. C.: as collector for Northwest Cattlemen's Association, 145

Low, Judge Henry: 64, 67

Loyd, M. B.: 86, 147

Lubbock, Treasurer: and Greer County land, 125

Luckett, R.: and inventory of Francklyn ranch, 193

LX headquarters: mail route to, 57 n

Lytle, Captain John T.: 165; and Colonel Groom, 157, 186. SEE ALSO Stephens and Lytle

Mabry, Major Seth: 61, 157

Maddox, S. S.: Francklyn cattle handled by, 94

mail service: need for, 57; George Tyng on, 294

Mangum, Oklahoma: 294

"Manifest Destiny": in Southwest, 4

Marcy, Captain R. B.: and Greer County conflict, 102, 103

Market Harborough, England: Gordon Cunard from, 226

Matador Company: 305; establishment of ranch by, 13; lease of White Deer Lands by, 300, 308, 309, 311, 315, 316, 324, 332, 337

Mathews & Reynolds: 69

McClelland, ———: Francklyn ranch's conflict with, 49–50

McClelland Brothers: as possible agents for White Deer Lands, 338

McClelland Creek: 42, 45, 348; land on, 82

McCord & Nave: 131

McCormick, Judge A. P.: and Francklyn foreclosure suit, 231

McCoy (Kansun): 157

McGee, T. T.: 264

McGibbin (rancher): and Indian lease, 117

McKenzie, Murdo: 305; of Matador Company, 315, 316, 332

McKisker, Acting Indian Agent: 111

McMullen County: 133

Medical Board of the Panhandle: 264

Melish, ———: and Greer County conflict, 103

Memphis, Texas: 294

Meredith (Francklyn employee): 188

Merrill, ———: 98

mesquite grass: 71

Mexican War: and Texas Revolution, 4

Mexico: George Tyng in, 241, 326

Mexico City: George Tyng in, 241

Index

Miami, Texas: 252, 294, 296, 297, 302, 338; George Tyng in, 240, 347; and Purcell Company, 269 n, 288; establishment of, 288; mismanagement of, 289, 298; emigration from, 295; development of, 348; H. B. Hendricks from, 361

Miller, ———: on brands, 76

—, Judge James: and cattle trails, 121

—, Thomas S.: and Russell Benedict, 178, 179, 180, 215; and investigation of Francklyn ranch, 179, 180; and George Tyng, 201–202; and Francklyn foreclosure suit, 228, 230, 232; and Sanborn-Tyng conference, 242

Miller & Shepherd: 178

millet: raising of, 49

Milwaukee, Wisconsin: and J. R. Busk, 280

mineral leases: of White Deer Corporation, 366

mines: Charles G. Francklyn's interests in, 6–7, 65, 67, 79, 205

Missouri, Department of: 112

Missouri Pacific Railroad: and White Deer Lands, 343

Mississippi River: settlement along, 4; migration west of, 213–214

Mittenhall, ———: 278

Mobeetie, Texas: 16, 170, 237, 293, 294, 297; Colonel Groom in, 10, 13, 33, 181, 201, 202; road to, 14; freight from, 18, 34; Frank Brown in, 36; Colonel Kuper in, 52; mail route for, 57; Francklyn ranch deals with firms in, 74; Ferdinand Van Zandt in, 86; Harry Groom in, 98; Henry C. Young in, 128–129, 131, 133, 134; movement of southern cattle through, 160, 164, 166; Russell Benedict in, 178, 179, 180, 216, 217, 218, 220, 222; George Tyng in, 183, 202; establishment of, 292; bank in, 294

Mobeetie News: on the Grooms, 188

Mobeetie road: tank built near, 54

money, scarcity of: 163, 169, 310–311, 330; effect of, on White Deer Lands, 316–317, 318

money controversy. SEE gold-silver controversy

Montana: quarantine law in, 161; and Texas cattle prices, 257; cattle industry in, 258, 263; shipment of cattle to, 317–318

Montgomery, ———. SEE Quinlin & Montgomery

Moody, F.: sale of cattle by, 33; on brands, 76

Moore, Leon W.: 70

—, William C.: 57 n

Morris, Larry: 149

Morrow, S. W.: and Temple Houston, 173; investigation of Francklyn Company by, 173–174

mortgages: on Francklyn cattle, 179, 180

Mortimer Land Company: Colonel Groom as manager of, 301, 312; lease of White Deer Lands by, 313

mules, White Deer: 89, 142; pink eye among, 51; purchase of, 73; sale of, 240

Munson, ———. SEE Gunter & Munson

Munson T. Case Company. SEE Case Company, Munson T.

Muscatine Company: sale of cattle to, 33

mustang: nature of, 45 n–46 n

Natchitoches, Louisiana: 103

National Cattle & Horse Association: 156

Navajo Mountain: 110

Nave, ———. SEE McCord & Nave

Nelson, ———. SEE Bugbee and Nelson

nesters. SEE settlers

Neutral Strip, Indian Territory: conflict over land in, 102; problems in, 104–105; effect of, on settlement, 272–273

New Jersey: Francklyn Company chartered in, 6

New Mexico: retreat of Indians to, 13; quarantine law of, 160, 161; cattle industry in, 258, 314

Newport, Rhode Island: 278

News, Dallas: on weather, 350

News, Mobeetie: on the Grooms, 188

newspaper: for Pampa, 359

Newton, Kansas: S. R. Peters from, 122

New York: 118; Samuel Thorne from, 5; Francklyn Company from, 6; Charles

Francklyn from, 6; Alexander & Green in, 21; Swenson of, 173; Ferdinand Van Zandt in, 179; Colonel Groom in, 186, 189; Russell Benedict in, 201, 349; Frederic Foster in, 172, 235; George Tyng in, 255, 291, 317; mail service from, 294; Andrew Kingsmill in, 351

New York, Bank of: 141

New York & Texas Land Company: 219, 279; organization of, 4–5; land acquired by, 5, 6; and railroads, 5; sale of land by, to Francklyn Company, 6, 7–8, 20, 178–179; and surveying of Francklyn ranch, 14, 19, 21–24, 25–28; and Francklyn survey dispute, 21–24, 25, 28; and purchase of Harrold & Ikard cattle, 63; Francklyn Company debt to, 89, 99, 164, 166, 227; W. D. Searles as vice president of, 164; and Frederic Foster, 181; Francklyn land notes with, 185, 203; sale of land by, 320; T. D. Hobart with, 353; and title of White Deer Lands, 361, 362

New York Times: on Francklyn Company bonds, 146

Nichols (railroad official): 303

Nicholson, Gutherie: possible lease of White Deer Land to, 332

Niedringhaus, F. G.: establishment of ranch by, 13; possible cattle losses of, 307–308; lease of White Deer Lands to, 315–316; visit of brother of, 316

—, Heinrich: visit of, to Panhandle, 316

—, William F.: visit of brother of, 316

Niedringhaus Brothers: leasing of White Deer Lands by, 308

Northwest Cattlemen's Association: collection of dues for, 145

Northwest Live Stock Journal, Cheyenne: on Francklyn Company, 197–198

Northwest Texas. SEE Texas, West

O-Bar ranch: range problems of, 241

O Bar O Ranch: and Greer County Notice, 123

oats: raising of, 49

Ochiltree County: 273, 294

Ogalalla, Nebraska: Francklyn cattle in, 169

Ogden, Utah: George Tyng dies near, 177

oil: discovery of, on White Deer Lands, 364; production of, 367, 368

Oklahoma: Indian Territory in, 13; movement of settlers out of, 124. SEE ALSO Indian Territory

Olathe, Kansas: Colonel Groom in, 110

Oldham County: organization of, 13; Cape Willingham as sheriff of, 93; digging of wells in, 253; Tascosa in, 292

Omaha, Nebraska: George Tyng in, 318

Omohundro, Phil: 279

Otter Creek: 108, 113

Owens (settler): on White Deer Lands, 300

Palo Duro Canyon: 298; Colonel Goodnight's cattle in, 13; fence posts from, 33; well to be drilled in, 54

Palestine, Texas: New York & Texas Land Company offices in, 5; railroad meeting at, 5; Colonel Groom in, 20; Alfred B. Thatcher in, 21, 26; Major Evans in, 27

Pampa, Texas: 272 n, 309, 316; naming of, 253 n; establishment of, 299, 303, 305, 337, 349; George Tyng in, 299, 319, 354 n; farming near, 285; Matador Company at, 300; bank for, 302; plan for, 303; and Santa Fe Railway, 305; improvements at, 311; Henry Taylor at, 312, 326; White Deer Lands office in, 337; as proposed county seat for Gray County, 347–348, 349, 351; surveying of, 349; financing of, 351; Andrew Kingsmill in, 352; newspaper for, 359; T. D. Hobart in, 359. SEE ALSO Glasgow, Texas

Panhandle: 196

Panhandle, Texas (town): 252, 294, 296, 297, 298, 331, 337, 339; railroads at, 32; discrimination in, 41–42; well drilled at, 252, 253; celebration at, 264; and Purcell Company, 269 n, 288; mismanagement of, 289, 291, 298; Judge J. C. Paul's support of, 291; development of, 291; first bank in, 291, 294; Russell Benedict on, 299; Heinrich Niedringhaus in, 316; George Tyng in, 319

Index

Panhandle, the Texas: Francklyn Company land in, 6, 67; organization of counties in, 13, 19, 264; Capitol Syndicate moves cattle into, 13; sale of cattle in, 33; well-drilling machine in, 54; absence of banks in, 74; Red River heads in, 102; and Neutral Strip, 104; opposition to southern cattle in, 161; settlers in, 216–217, 265, 293, 322, 335, 355; scarcity of water in, 249; economic prospects of, 292; fencing in, 293; railroads through, 294; emigration from, 295; land situation in, 295; weather in, 299

Panhandle Bank: 326

Panhandle Cattle Company: creation of, 89–90; effects of, on Francklyn Company, 94

Panhandle Herald: on organization of counties, 264; on townsite companies, 291; on Gray County, 348

Panhandle Stock Association: 257; and movement of southern cattle into north, 161, 165

Panic of 1873: effect of, on Colonel Groom, 8–9

Panic of 1875: 101

Park National Bank, Kansas City: 99

Parker, Quanah: 111; and lease of Indian lands, 108–109; and Colonel Groom, 110; in Washington, D.C., 118; in employ of Francklyn ranch, 118; in Hardeman County, 294

Paton, John: 227, 239; and appointment of trustees, 209; on J. R. Busk, 276

—, Texas: 272, 279; railroad at, 288, 290, 296; development of, 289. SEE ALSO White Deer, Texas

Paul, Judge J. C.: as officer of Southern Kansas Railroad, 291; bank established by, 291; to George Tyng, 291; as representative of Tyler Tap Lands, 309; as agent for White Deer Lands, 309, 313, 326; as possible buyer of Dixon Creek Pasture, 343

Paxton, W. M.: 169

Payne, ———: on brands, 76

peaches: grown in Wheeler County, 272

Pease River: 81, 168

Pecos River: 166, 298

Pecos Valley extension (railroad): and Santa Fe Railroad, 298

Peeler, ———: 182

Penn, ———. SEE Cochran & Penn

Permanent School Fund: and public lands, 262

Peters, J.: to T. D. Hobart, 354 n

—, S. R.: on Kansas quarantine law, 122

Phelps, W. W.: as possible agent for White Deer Lands, 339

Pickwick Hotel: Russell Benedict at, 214

Pierce, J. F.: as boss of Greer County range, 73, 90; and Colonel Groom, 90–91

—, John: and movement of southern cattle into north, 165

pink eye: 51, 198

Plains, Great: nature of, 3, 298; attraction of, 3–4, 213–214; investment of British capital in, 59–60; effect of, on Russell Benedict, 214–217, 223; economic foundations of, 247; cultures on, 247–249; Spanish invasion of, 248; cattle industry on, 248–249; water on, 293; changes in, 355, 356. SEE ALSO Panhandle, the Texas; Texas, West

Plains Indians. SEE Indians, Plains

pleuropneumonia: in cattle industry, 261

plums: grown on White Deer, 272

politics: in West Texas, 12; and boundary conflicts, 19–20; and land sales, 335–336; and White Dear Lands, 350

Polly, E. E.: 264

ponds. SEE tanks, earthen

pools. SEE tanks, earthen

Pope, General John: on encroachment on Indian Territory, 105

Popham, ———. SEE Harrison & Popham

Portales, New Mexico: Russell Benedict goes to, 302

Porter, J. W.: and purchase of Harrold & Ikard cattle, 62, 63, 64, 65, 66, 67, 68, 69

Potter County: 244, 294; mail route to, 57 n; digging of wells in, 253; value of land in, 281; organization of, 293

Prairie Cattle Company: 15; Henry Cres-

well of, 14; sale of cattle to, 33; and cattle thefts, 90
Prairie Dog Town River: as name for South Fork of Red River, 103
Price, H.: 115; as commissioner of Indian affairs, 102; and Greer County conflict, 104, 105; and lease of Indian lands, 105, 110
Primrose Plateau, the: 212
Purcell Company: building of towns by, 269 n, 288; purchase of Tyler Tap Lands by, 288–289, 295; George Tyng on, 288–289; and Southern Kansas Railway, 288; and Atchison, Topeka and Santa Fe Railroad, 289; Frederic Foster on, 290; policy of, 298

Quahadas Indians: and Indian land lease, 116
quail: on Francklyn ranch, 16
Quanah, Texas: development of, 294
quarantine law, Kansas: Groom's support of, 121–124; extent of, 122; results of, 124, 163; and controversy over cattle trails, 155–156; terms of, 157, 159–160
—, U.S.: in Congress, 121, 156
quarantine laws: passage of, 161
quarantine line, Kansas: imposing of, 105
Quarter Circle Hearts: 13
Quinlin, Judge: 157
Quinlin & Montgomery: 157
Quitaque Ranch: sale of, 84, 308

Rachel, ———: and movement of southern cattle into north, 165
raccoons: on Francklyn ranch, 15
railroads: development of, 4–5, 31, 306; and public lands, 4–5, 216; consolidation of, 5; Charles Francklyn's interests in, 7; and White Deer Lands, 16, 255, 265, 266, 289, 290, 294, 296, 355; routes of, 32, 273, 296, 298, 299; and cattle industry, 263, 267; effect of, on settlement, 270, 287; in Northwest Texas, 292; George Tyng on, 294
Railway and Corporation Law Journal: on foreign corporations holding real estate in Texas, 239

Randall County: 294; Red River heads in, 102; organization of, 293
range, free: use of, by cattle industry, 13, 31, 267
Rath, Charles: 51, 151
Rath & Hamburg: 74
Rayland, ———: and movement of southern cattle into north, 165
razoopers: 289, 290
Red Deer Creek: 45, 253; hay made on, 50; fire near, 55; dam on, 250
Red River: 57; Colonel Goodnight's cattle on, 13; high water on, 149, 168; settlement along, 257; Palo Duro Canyon of, 298
Red River, North Fork of: 14, 108, 113; as boundary of Texas, 102, 103; Colonel Groom meets Indians at, 115; Indian land lease on, 117; cattle trail along, 121; railroad along, 296
Red River, Salt Fork of: 164; Colonel Groom at, 98, 113
Red River, South Fork of: Francklyn ranch drained by, 45; as boundary of Texas, 102
Reed, Captain James: on inspection of Harrold & Ikard holdings, 70
refrigeration: and cattle industry, 258, 261
reservations, Indian: placing of Indians on, 248
reservoirs. SEE tanks, earthen
Revolution, Texas: and Mexican War, 4
Reynolds, ———. SEE Mathews & Reynolds
Reynolds Creek: hay made on, 50
Richards, ———. SEE Sacra & Richards
Rio Grande: as boundary of Texas, 12
Ripley, A.: to Frank Brown, 54; to Harry Groom, 55–56
—, E. R.: as president of Santa Fe Railroad, 298
Roberts, Governor O. M.: and Greer County conflict, 102–104
Roberts County: 273, 294; White Deer Lands in, 6, 44, 227, 241, 298; organization of, 293; need for towns in, 296; and organization of Gray County, 347; production of oil and gas in, 364, 367

Index

Robinson, ———: payment to, 153
— (railroad official): 219
Robinson & West: as lawyers for Francklyn Company, 21; and Francklyn survey conflict, 28, 38
Robinson Bros. & Co.: 74, 77, 113, 140; drafts drawn on, 150
Rocking Chair ranch: 51
Rock Island Railroad: 273, 294
Rockwell, ———: 42
Roosevelt, Theodore: 212, 335
Rose, Henry R.: 64
Rosebery, Lord: and Charles Francklyn, 7, 120, 153–154; investment of, in White Deer Lands, 8, 181, 351, 352; and Ferdinand Van Zandt, 52 n, 86, 146, 167, 171; in British cabinet, 157; Andrew Kingsmill as representative of, 203, 210; commercial interests of, 205 n; possible sale of bonds by, 206; and Frederic Foster, 208; and purchase of land notes, 210; and syndicate deed, 211; wealth of, 222; and Francklyn foreclosure sale, 225, 244
Rosebud Indian Agency: Harrolds' land near, 165–166
Roswell, New Mexico: railroad to, 298–299
Rothschild family: and Lord Rosebery, 7, 222
Rowe, Alfred: 51; and movement of southern cattle into north, 166
Rowe & Co.: 33–34
rye: raising of, 49

Sacra & Richards: 51
sage: 71
St. Louis, Missouri: 130, 316, 317, 332; Francklyn ranch deals with firms in, 74; Hunter & Evans of, 108; Henry C. Young in, 133, 134; conventions in, 148, 153, 161, 318; Colonel Groom in, 158; Hughes and Simpson office in, 165; Russell Benedict in, 217, 218; George Tyng in, 307
St. Louis & Pacific Railroad: Francklyn's interests in, 7; effects of arrival of, 16
St. Louis & San Francisco Railroad: 294; through White Deer Lands, 296; and Southern Kansas Railroad, 296, 298
St. Paul's Cathedral: 212
"Saint's Roost." See Clarendon, Texas
Salesbury (Saulsbury), Texas: 294
Salt Fork Camp: 86
San Antonio, Texas: 26, 93; Colonel Groom in, 21, 165; horses purchased in, 73; Henry C. Young from, 129; George Tyng in, 313; cattlemen's convention in, 330
San Antonio Department: Northwest Texas as part of, 19
Sanborn, H. B.: White Deer dispute with, 240, 241; and George Tyng, 242; and digging of wells, 253. See also Glidden & Sanborn
San Domingo, West Indies: Francklyn's mines in, 6–7; Charles Francklyn in, 68
San Francisco, California: Ferdinand Van Zandt in, 146
San Juancito, Honduras: George Tyng in, 280, 307
Santa Fe Railroad. See Atchison, Topeka and Santa Fe Railroad
Santa Fe Town Company. See Purcell Company
Saulsbury, Texas: 294
Sayer, Governor: on cattle prices, 160
Schneider, ———: and sale of White Deer cattle, 240
—, Alex: band of, 264 n, 266
school lands: state control of, 4; and railroads, 4–5; speculation in, 5; in White Deer Lands, 19, 28, 38, 48, 82, 83, 135 n, 196, 296; settlers on, 19, 262–263, 296; sale and lease of, 28, 83, 256, 320, 333, 343–344; and the Grooms, 82, 135 n, 221, 312; Russell Benedict's investigation of, 178; Texas' policy on, 216–217; Glidden & Sanborn on, 240, 241–242; price of, 258–259; and Permanent School Fund, 262; and cattle industry, 262–263
schools, Indian: 110
screwworms: problems with, 77, 81, 141, 168–169
Searles, W. D.: letter from, to Charles Francklyn, 164
Selden (Francklyn employee): 49

settlers: in Indian Territory, 112, 281, 314; in Greer County, 112, 147; on White Deer Pastures, 48, 199–200, 215, 269, 270, 295, 300, 302, 367; attitude of cattlemen toward, 216; in Texas Panhandle, 216–217, 263, 264, 265, 287, 291, 293, 322, 335, 355; on school lands, 19, 262–263, 296; and railroads, 270, 287, 291; prosperity of, 321
Seward County, Kansas: 273
Shattuck, W. B.: 147
Shattuck and Hoffman: 147
Shaw, M. W.: and Francklyn forgery, 132, 133, 134
Sheedy herd: 169
Shepard, Seth: 215; and Francklyn foreclosure suit, 228
Shepherd, ———: 169. SEE ALSO Miller & Shepherd
silver controversy. SEE gold-silver controversy
Simpson, ———: and scarcity of grass, 257. SEE ALSO Hughes and Simpson
—, Judge: and cattle trails, 121, 122
—, James B.: 153
Simpson & Hughes: SEE Hughes and Simpson
Sloan & Fox: and Indian land lease, 108. SEE ALSO Fox, George
Smith, ———: 216
— (railroad official): 219
—, Colonel C. R.: 162
—, Colonel J. Peter: 69
—, John R.: claim of, against Francklyn Company, 205
—, M. K.: 181
—, William Jarrel: and liquidation of White Deer Corporation, 366
Snyder, ———. SEE Wood & Snyder
—, Andrew: 157
Somerville, David: of Matador Company, 300, 305
—, W. F.: to Frank Brown, 146–147
South, the: economic conditions of, 59–60
Southampton, England: Ferdinand Van Zandt to, 219

Southern Hotel, St. Louis: Russell Benedict at, 218
Southern Kansas Railroad: 218, 299, 302, 303; progress of, 200, 294; and White Deer Lands, 245, 267, 268, 269; water problems of, 252; settlement along, 255, 270, 291; in Hemphill County, 264; and Purcell Company, 269 n, 288; and Atchison, Topeka and Santa Fe Railroad, 290; Judge J. C. Paul as officer of, 291; and townsite development, 295; and St. Louis & San Francisco Railroad, 296, 298
Southern Pacific Railroad: 298
South Texas. SEE Texas, South
Spanish: invasion of Plains by, 248
Spanish-American War: effects of, in West, 299
Spanish Road, Great: 103
speculators, land: 32; and White Deer Land, 265; projects of, 287
Spiller, E. B.: and surveying of Francklyn ranch, 14, 29; political defeat of, 20; and Francklyn forgery, 128, 129, 131
Spring Creek: 44, 49, 183, 186, 250; dam on, 325
Spurs, the: establishment of ranch by, 13
squatters: on White Deer Lands, 255
squaw men: and Indian land lease, 114
Standard Cattle Company: contract of, with Francklyn Company, 174
staples: for fencing of ranch, 34
state land. SEE school land
Starkweather (railroad official): 302, 303
Stephens, John Henry: 157, 160, 165; sale of cattle by, 159, 162; to Frank Brown, 162; and sale of Francklyn cattle, 163–164, 167; and controversy over grass, 350. SEE ALSO Stephens and Lytle
Stephens and Lytle: 178; sale of Francklyn cattle by, 158, 160, 162, 165, 167, 168, 169; on cattle prices, 162–163; letter from, to Charles Francklyn, 169. SEE ALSO Lytle, Captain John T.; Stephens, J. Henry
Stevens, Acting Commissioner of Indian Affairs: 115, 118

Index 397

Stickney, ———: 204; and Francklyn foreclosure suit, 228, 230–231

Stimson, ———: 113

Strahorn, Robert: 70, 170

Strahorn & Co., R.: 74, 79; Francklyn cattle handled by, 86, 87, 94

Straughan, S. S.: 264

streams, underground: tapping of, 251

Street, J. O. B.: political victory of, 20; and Francklyn survey conflict, 39, 54

Suggs, Colonel: and Indian land lease, 109, 116; and Colonel Groom, 116–117; and Harrold & Ikard, 117; and action against George Fox, 117; in Washington, D.C., 122

Suggs, Cal: in Washington, D.C., 120; and Indian lease, 120

Suggs Brothers: 69

Sully, Alfred: 54; and Francklyn foreclosure sale, 232; sale of White Deer cattle to, 233–234, 237, 239–240, 267; and Clarendon Land & Cattle Company, 234; lease of White Deer Lands by, 234, 245; need of grass by, 236–237

Sully contract: controversy about, 234–238, 239–240; George Tyng on, 235–236

Sun Boy (Indian): and Indian land lease, 114

Surgeon, Dr. Newton: 221

surveying: of White Deer Lands, 18, 19, 20–30, 255, 268, 290, 323; Francklyn ranch disputes about, 18–20, 38–39; practices of, 25; pay for, 52; benefits of, 267; of Pampa, 349

Sutton, Texas: railroads near, 296; need for town at, 296, 297

Swain, Comptroller: and Greer County land, 125

Swan Land & Cattle Company: 169

Swenson, ———: ranch of, in Jones County, 173

Swenson & Jones: 173

Swisher, ———: 113

syndicate deed: nature of, 209, 210, 211

Sweetwater, Texas: railroad at, 296

Taber, H. A. W.: 171

Tallahone Creek: 44–45; tank built near, 51, 52, 54

tanks, earthen: building of, 46, 50, 51, 52, 128, 249; cost of, 47; on White Deer Lands, 128, 323, 333, 345

Tarrant County: 71 n

Tascosa, Texas: 293; road to, 14, 54; mail route to, 57 n; movement of southern cattle to, 164; establishment of, 292; development of, 294

taxes: in Greer County, 201–202; on White Deer Lands, 363–364, 364–365

Taylor, ———. SEE Goodnight and Taylor; Head, Taylor & Co.

Taylor, Henry W.: and Sutton contract controversy, 234, 235; letter to, from George Tyng, 236; driving of cattle from White Deer Lands by, 237; as White Deer representative, 312, 326

telegraph: development of, 31

Teller, H. M.: as Secretary of the Interior, 101–102; and Indian land leases, 101–102, 107, 110; and removal of intruders from Indian lands, 107; from E. B. Harrold, 107; and P. B. Hunt, 117, 118, 119; visit of Colonel Groom to, 119

Tepee Creek: 110

Teutonic: T. D. Hobart travels on, 360

Texans: Harry Groom on, 36; Russell Benedict's impression of, 215

Texarkana, Texas: sale of cattle in, 62

Texas: settlement of, 4; control of public land by, 4; Colonel Groom's opinion of, 10–12; inhabitants of, 12, 216–217; boundaries of, 12, 102; importance of cattle industry in, 13; economy of, 13; survey practices in, 18–20, 25; visit of Charles Francklyn to, 86; and Greer County dispute, 102, 104, 113; Senator Coke from, 121; Russell Benedict's trips to, 175–179, 195–196, 214–215, 218–223, 299–305; comparison of, with Kansas, 216; foreign corporations holding real estate in, 239; weather in, 350; Andrew Kingsmill in, 351–352

Texas, Northwest. SEE Texas, West

—, South: cattle from, driven north, 105

—, West: railroad building in 4–5,

294; New York & Texas Land Company in, 6; politics in, 12; topography of, 12–13; climate in, 12–13, 31–32; laws in, 13; hunting of buffalo in, 13; Colonel Groom's opinion of, 14–16, 16–17; boundary disputes in, 18–20; settlers in, 287, 292; first bank in, 291; mail service in, 294

Texas Banking & Insurance Company: 132

Texas fever: quarantine against, 95; preventative actions against, 105; on Francklyn ranch, 122, 145, 160–161; on Western Plains, 161

Texas Investment Company: 70

Texas Land Company. SEE New York & Texas Land Company

Texas Live Stock Journal, The: on scarcity of grass, 257–259

Thatcher, Alfred B.: and Francklyn survey dispute, 21–26, 27; to Ward, 21–26

Thorne, Samuel: as vice president of New York & Texas Land Company, 7; and Francklyn survey dispute, 20–21, 27, 28, 29, 63, 67

Thut, Henry: as settler on White Deer Lands, 300

Tidball, ———: 69

timber: on Francklyn ranch, 15

Timber Creek: 44

Timms City, Texas: 294

title: to White Deer Lands, 181, 192, 217, 268, 361–363

Topeka, Kansas: 133, 156, 269, 290; Colonel Groom in, 157; Russell Benedict at, 218, 221; George Tyng in, 270, 307

topography: in West Texas, 12–13

Towers (rancher): 34

Town Company. SEE Purcell Company

townsite companies: activities of, 288–291

townsites: and railroads, 271, 295, 305; establishment of, 287–288, 289, 295

Traders National Bank, Fort Worth: 149

trail drives: end of, 263–264; number of cattle on, 264

trails, cattle: through Greer County, 105; controversy over, 121, 155, 165, 166; and Kansas quarantine laws, 155–156

transportation: and White Deer Lands, 18, 34–35, 268; in West Texas, 31, 248; and cattle industry, 261, 263, 267

travel: problem of, on Francklyn ranch, 18

treaties, Indian: U.S. obligations under, 102

trespassers: on White Deer Lands, 255; and Texas law, 328

Trinidad, Colorado: 305, 331; George Tyng in, 299

Trinidad Advertiser: article on Francklyn Company in, 197–198

Trujillo, Texas: mail route to, 57 n

Tufts, General: on incroachment onto Indian lands, 105

Tulsa, Oklahoma: Atlantic Railroad at, 16

Turkey Creek: 163

turkeys, wild: on Francklyn ranch, 15, 16

Turkey Tracks: 74; J. M. Coburn of, 14

Turner, Avery: and Southern Kansas Railroad, 253

Tyler Tap Lands: purchase of, by Purcell Company, 288–289, 295; and White Deer Lands, 288–289, 296

Tyng, George: 244; investigation of Francklyn ranch by, 175, 176, 177, 178, 179, 182–183, 188, 193–194; as manager of White Deer ranch, 176, 182, 183, 184–185, 194, 196, 198–199, 217, 254–255, 307, 326, 327, 355, 356; and Frederic Foster, 176, 227–228, 244–245, 275, 276, 336, 350, 354; enthusiasm of, for White Deer Lands, 176, 222, 319, 322, 351, 364; and Russell Benedict, 176, 177, 186, 221, 222–223, 227–228, 231, 244–245, 275, 299, 301, 336, 347–349, 350, 351; background of, 176–177, 231; character of, 176–177, 275, 354, 356; death of, 177, 354 n; and the Grooms, 180, 183, 184, 186–187, 187–188, 188–189, 191, 194, 198, 201, 203; hiring of Perry LeFors by, 180; and Charles Francklyn, 184; collection of White Deer cattle by, 193, 200–201; description of White Deer Lands by, 193–194, 340; and W. S. Frazer, 195, 255; and program for

Index

White Deer Lands, 199–200, 217–218, 267, 273, 276–277, 287, 323, 333, 336, 343, 344–347, 349, 350; and T. S. Miller, 201–202; and British bondholders, 207–208, 350, 354; on value of White Deer Lands, 215, 217; and Francklyn foreclosure suit, 223, 226, 227, 228, 229, 230, 231, 232, 241, 268; and Gordon Cunard's suit, 229; and Sanborn range-cattle dispute, 240, 241, 242; sale of horses by, 240; in Victoria, 241, 242, 255, 278, 279, 280, 307, 313, 319, 324, 329, 331, 336, 341; in Mexico, 241, 326; and J. R. Busk, 254, 278, 280–281; and A. A. Holland, 255, 325; on scarcity of grass, 257; on plight of cattle industry, 263; on Purcell Company, 269 n, 288–289; on Neutral Strip, 272–273; and General Land Office, 278–279; in Central America, 280, 307; on farming at White Deer, 284–286, 293, 324; on mail service, 294; on railroad building, 294; on land situation, 295, 341; on towns on White Deer Lands, 296; and establishment of Pampa, 303; problems of, 306 325; in South America, 307; and leasing of White Deer Lands, 307, 313, 315, 319, 329; on gold-silver controversy, 316–317; on improvements on White Deer Lands, 317, 345; at cattlemen's convention, 332; on water supply for White Deer Lands, 333; and use of land agents, 335 n; and organization of Gray County, 347–348, 351; future plans of, 350; resignation of, 350–351; and sale of Dixon Creek Pasture, 351; public farewell of, 353–354; and T. D. Hobart, 357, 359–360

—communications from: to Frederic de P. Foster, 182–183, 184–185, 186–187, 190–191, 193, 195, 196, 202, 235–236, 236–237, 237–238, 240–241, 242–243, 249–250, 251–252, 253, 254, 256–257, 263, 265, 270, 272–273, 277–278, 278–279, 279–280, 281, 282, 288–290, 292–294, 298, 299, 307–308, 308–309, 310–311, 314, 315–316, 317–318, 320–321, 324, 325, 327, 329–330, 331–332, 333–334, 336–337, 341, 342–343, 344–345, 345–347, 347–348, 350–351; to Russell Benedict, 183, 186, 188–189, 193–194, 194–195, 198, 201, 202, 243–244, 244, 308, 313–314, 318–319, 324–325, 328–329, 336, 341; to Ferdinand Van Zandt, 198–199; to Henry Taylor, 236

—communications to: from Frederic de P. Foster, 189–190; from Avery Turner, 253; from J. C. Paul, 291; from W. S. Decker, 291–292

—, Stephen H.: 177

Underwood Clark & Co.: and Francklyn forgery, 130
Union Company: 65
Union Stock Yards: 169
United States: acquisition of land by, 4; settlement of, 4; economic conditions of, 59–60
United States government: and Indians, 102; and Greer County dispute, 104; removal of settlers from Greer County by, 112, 147
Utah: Francklyn's mines in, 6; George Tyng's death in, 354 n

Van Beuren, ———: and the Grooms, 301
Van Pelt, William F.: as treasurer of Francklyn Company, 6, 74; on Wheeler County lease, 87; letter to, from George Cranmer, 111, 137; and payment to Harrold, 141–142; and Harry Groom, 142, 150–151; and Ferdinand Van Zandt, 146, 167
Van Zandt, Ferdinand: 52, 69, 78, 214; account of, 52 n; as representative of Lord Rosebery, 52 n, 86, 146, 167, 171; and Charles Francklyn, 66, 68; visit of, in Texas, 86, 181; to Frank Brown, 86; Frank Brown's dissatisfaction with, 94; and William Van Pelt, 146, 167; and investigation of Francklyn ranch, 170–171, 176, 177, 178, 179; from George Tyng, 198–199; as trustee, 206, 209; trip of, to England, 219; and purchase of Francklyn land notes, 225; and Francklyn foreclosure sale, 239, 245, 275; and sale of land, 276
—, Major K. M.: 149
Vermont: Ira H. Evans from, 5
Vernon, Texas: 149, 171, 293; George Cranmer in, 111; George Tyng in, 201;

development of, 293–294
Victoria, Texas: George Tyng in, 175, 176, 177, 188, 241, 242, 255, 278, 279, 280, 307, 313, 319, 324, 329, 331, 336, 341
Vinewood Estate: 8
V-V range: 241

Waco, Texas: 226; search for horses in, 73; Gordon Cunard's suit in, 229, 230
wagons, freight: use of, 18
Waggoner, Daniel: and Indian land lease, 108, 116, 117, 120; Colonel Groom meets with, 116–117; sale of cattle by, 162
Waggoner Brothers: lease of White Deer Lands by, 319, 332
Wakefield (Francklyn employee): putting up of hay by, 49–50
Walsh (land commissioner): and Francklyn survey dispute, 28, 38
Wapella, Illinois: Harrold & Ikard from, 66, 107
Ward (of Alexander & Green): and Francklyn survey dispute, 21–26, 28
War, Secretary of: and intruders in Indian Territory, 107
Warren, Sam: and Francklyn survey dispute, 29
Washburn, Texas: 294; railroads at, 32; digging of well at, 253
Washington, D.C.: 110, 118; Indian delegation in, 111, 116, 120; Quanah Parker in, 118; Cal Suggs in, 120; Colonel Groom in, 121; Frank Brown in, 156
Washita Indian Agency: 77
Washita River: 103
Washita River, Little: 339
water: on White Deer Lands, 15, 43, 50, 255, 272, 310, 312, 322, 323, 325, 329–330, 331, 332, 333, 334, 336, 345; securing of, 50, 80, 356; hauling of, 51; on the Plains, 247, 249, 280, 293; need of railroads for, 252–253; for new towns, 289; property rights in, 328
Watkins, J. B.: 153
weather: in West Texas, 12–13, 31–32; effect of, on White Deer Lands, 36, 50,
81–82, 136, 137, 140–141, 143, 158, 197, 198, 217, 235, 240, 243, 255, 281, 284, 299, 306, 309, 325, 350; effect of, on cattle industry, 72, 263
Welch (railroad official): 219, 220
Welder, John: and George Fox, 113
Wellborn, Leake and Henry: 27
Wellesly & Co.: 153
Wellington, Kansas: 298
Wellington *Globe Democrat:* 298
well-drilling machine: introduction of, in Panhandle, 54
wells: drilling of, 50, 52–54, 55, 199, 251, 256, 280; on White Deer Lands, 250–251, 253, 254, 255, 256, 288, 296, 297, 300, 303, 310, 312, 323, 344, 345, 352; depth of, 251; cost of, 251, 256, 331
Werner, Henry. SEE Young, Henry C.
West, ———. SEE Hancock & West; Robinson & West
—, (lawyer): and Colonel Groom, 21
—, Thomas F.: and Henry C. Young, 130
—, the: economic conditions of, 59–60
Western Kansas Cattle Growers Association: and movement of southern cattle into north, 161
Western Mortgage & Investment Company: and Francklyn foreclosure suit, 231
West Indies: Charles Francklyn's mines in, 6–7
Westminster Abbey: 212
West Texas. SEE Texas, West
wheat: raising of, on White Deer Lands, 49, 282, 283–284, 285–286, 324; nature of farming of, 284–285; around Vernon, 293–294
Wheeler, Texas: 57
Wheeler County: 24, 26; organization of, 13; election in, 20; Francklyn ranch in, 44, 67, 68; lease of land in, 63, 67, 68, 85, 87; peaches grown in, 272; Mobeetie in, 292; railroads through, 342
White (of Land Company): 219
White Deer, Texas: 272 n; naming of, 279; farming near, 285; M. K. Brown in, 366. SEE ALSO Paton, Texas.

Index

White Deer Corporation: formation of, 365; and Bureau of Internal Revenue, 365; sale of land by, 365–366; liquidation of, 365–367; mineral leases of, 366. SEE ALSO Francklyn Land & Cattle Company; White Deer Lands

White Deer Creek: 14–15, 45; railroad route along, 32; cattle grazing on, 42; description of, 44; hay made on, 50; tank built near, 54; fire near, 55; and Neutral Strip, 273; as source of water, 322

White Deer farm: reasons for, 293, 298; location of, 295–296; A. A. Holland in charge of, 326

White Deer Estates. SEE White Deer Lands

White Deer Lands: 212; selling of land by, 199–200, 215, 246, 268, 269, 273, 276, 281, 287, 298, 303, 319, 320, 321, 323, 338, 342, 344–345, 345–346, 352, 357, 358; reorganization of, 212, 274–275; economic situation of, 244–245, 306, 318, 320–321, 326, 333; lease of lands by, 252, 255–256, 257–258, 300, 306–310, 311, 315–319, 319–320, 323, 324, 326, 327, 329, 330, 331, 332, 337; records of, 272, 275; and politics, 273–274, 350; and Tyler Tap Lands, 288–289, 296; and general land situation, 295; and gold-silver controversy, 316–317, 318–319; Russell Benedict as trustee of, 363; Williston Benedict as trustee of, 363–364; taxes paid by, 363–364, 364–365. SEE ALSO Francklyn Land & Cattle Company; Francklyn ranch; White Deer ranch

White Deer ranch: George Tyng's enthusiasm about, 176, 193–194, 222, 319–320, 322, 340–343, 351, 364; George Tyng as manager of, 179, 184–185, 194, 196, 199–200, 217, 254–255, 307, 323, 326, 327, 333, 336, 343, 355; value of land of, 180, 192, 214, 215, 216, 222, 265, 272, 280, 281, 292, 300, 340–341; land title of, 181, 192, 215, 217, 230–231, 268, 361–362, 363; Perry LeFors as foreman of, 183; tools and machinery on, 192; appearance of, 193–194, 203, 266, 340–343; employees of, 194, 202, 244; program for, 199–200, 217–218, 222–223, 267, 268, 269, 273, 323, 333, 336, 343, 349, 357; bondholders' lien on, 200; cattle on, 201, 224, 263, 267; Russell Benedict's enthusiasm for, 215, 222; and settlers, 215, 265, 270, 295, 296, 300, 302, 336, 367; effect of weather on, 217, 235, 240, 243, 255, 281, 284, 299, 306, 309, 325, 350; and railroads, 219, 255, 265, 266, 268, 269, 270, 289, 290, 294, 296, 342–343, 355; sale of cattle on, 233–234, 237, 239–240, 267; outside cattle on, 240–241, 242–243, 244, 312–313, 317, 327–329, 333, 337; water on, 249–250, 273, 310, 312, 322, 323, 325, 329–330, 331, 332, 333, 334, 345; wells on, 250–251, 253, 254, 255, 280, 288, 296, 297, 300, 305, 310, 312, 323, 345, 352; surveying of, 255, 265, 268, 290, 323, 337; farming on, 255, 268, 271–272, 281, 282–284, 284–286, 293, 312, 324, 325, 326, 340, 368; trespassers on, 255; conditions of, 255, 265, 280; and land speculators, 265; and transportation, 268; establishment of towns on, 270, 295–296; advertising of, 271–272, 313, 317, 339; improvements on, 276–277, 317, 345; visit of J. R. Busk to, 277; topography of, 284; investigation of, 299–305; fires on, 310, 312, 317; special problems at, 310–311; windmills on, 312, 323, 345; proposal to stock, with cattle, 316; fences on, 317, 323, 330, 345; tanks on, 323, 333, 345; subdivision of, 329–330; and professional land agents, 335 n, 337, 346; office for the sale of, 337; T. D. Hobart as manager of, 352–353, 356, 357, 363; M. K. Brown as joint manager of, 363; C. P. Buckler as joint manager of, 363; discovery of oil and gas on, 364, 367, 368; C. P. Buckler bids on lands of, 366; purchase of, by M. K. Brown, 366–367. SEE ALSO cattle, Francklyn; cattle, White Deer; Francklyn Land & Cattle Company; Francklyn ranch; White Deer Lands

White Horse Tank: George Tyng at, 183

White Wolf (Indian): and Indian land lease, 114

Whittock, ———: 205

Wichita, Kansas: Francklyn cattle in, 88, 93–94, 95, 136–137

Wichita County: 71 n

Wichita Falls, Texas: 73, 112, 113, 140, 149, 161; Francklyn ranch deals with firms in, 74; cattle at, 95, 162, 165; Francklyn cattle marketed at, 98; search for horses at, 98; Colonel Groom in, 107, 138; cattlemen meet in, 117; value of land near, 281

Wichita Indian Agency: 111

Wichita Indians: and Indian schools, 119

Wight, E. D.: possible lease of White Deer Lands by, 331

Wilbarger County: 70, 71 n; Harrold in, 293; growing of wheat in, 293–294

wild life: on Francklyn ranch, 15–16

Willard, ———: 157

Williams, ———. SEE Barton & Williams

Williams, ———: as Lord Rosebery's lawyer, 206; at bondholders' meeting, 207. SEE ALSO Williams, Deacon & Co.

Williams, Deacon & Co.: 211; ownership of Francklyn bonds by, 8, 181 n; Francklyn Company payment to, 99, 153; and Frederic Foster, 180–181, 208, 245; and purchase of Francklyn land notes, 203–204, 210, 225, 226; and bondholders' meeting, 207, 208; and Gordon Cunard, 208; and Francklyn foreclosure suit, 225, 244; and gold-silver controversy, 317. SEE ALSO Deacon, ———; Williams, ———

Willingham, Cape B.: as possible boss of Greer County range, 91, 93; and sale of Dixon Creek Pasture, 352

Willis, Judge Frank: on value of Francklyn ranch, 16

Wilson, ———: and Francklyn forgery, 130

Winchester, Kentucky: Colonel Groom in, 8, 14

windmills: on White Deer Lands, 50, 199, 250, 254, 255, 312, 323, 345; influence of, on Great Plains, 256, 356

Winnebago, Dakota Territory: movement of settlers out of, 124

wire, barbed. SEE barbed wire

Wisconsin: Munson T. Case Company of, 39

Wise County: 71 n

Wisner, ———: 156

Wittingham, Canon: 212

Wolf Creek: Russell Benedict on, 220

wolves, grey: on Francklyn ranch, 15

Wood, ———: 169

Wood & Snyder: 74; sale of cattle by, 33

Woodward, Orlando: and Indian schools, 119

Woodward, Thomas: 114; letter from, to Colonel Groom, 116; and Indian land lease, 115, 116, 119

W O Ranch: and Greer County Notice, 123

World War I: effect of, on White Deer Lands, 364

Worsham, ———: sale of cattle by, 162

Wright, R. M.: to Harry Groom, 129

Wright & Beverley: 74; on transportation problem, 37–38

Wright & Co., R. M.: and Francklyn forgery, 127, 128, 129–130, 131, 132, 133, 134, 135; Francklyn Company bills with, 151

Wynne, Jesse: 177 n, 354 n; as settler on White Deer Lands, 300

Wyoming: quarantine law in, 161; cattle industry in, 258, 263, 317–318

Yeager, A. A. SEE Young, Henry C.

Y Cross Y Ranch: and Greer County Notice, 123

Young, Henry C.: forgery of Francklyn Company drafts by, 126–135, 136; description of, 131, 132; to Harry Groom, 135

Young District: 25

Yokum, Dave: 150